Surprised by Sin

Surprised by Sin
The Reader in *Paradise Lost*
Second Edition

Stanley Fish

Harvard University Press

Cambridge, Massachusetts

This book has been digitally reprinted. The content
remains identical to that of previous printings.

First Harvard University Press paperback edition, 1998

Published by arrangement with Macmillan Press Ltd.

Library of Congress Cataloging-in-Publication Data

Fish, Stanley Eugene.
  Surprised by sin : the reader in Paradise Lost / Stanley Fish.—
2nd ed.
      p.   cm.
  Includes bibliographical references and index.
      ISBN 0-674-85747-X
1. Milton, John, 1608–1674. Paradise lost.   2. Christianity and
literature—-England—History—17th century.   3. Authors and
readers—England—History—17th century.   4. Christian poetry,
English—History and criticism.   5. Epic poetry, English—
History and criticism.   6. Fall of man in literature.   7. Reader-
response criticism.   8. Sin in literature.   I. Title.
PR3562.F5   1998
821´.4—dc21   97-38854

TO

MY STUDENTS

AT THE UNIVERSITY

OF CALIFORNIA

BERKELEY

1962–5

Contents

Acknowledgements

My primary debt is to my fellow Miltonists, especially to those whose views I engage in the Preface to the Second Edition. The community of Milton scholars has sustained me in more ways than I can enumerate since I wandered into it as a wide-eyed novice in the early sixties. The vitality of the work produced in sixteenth- and seventeenth-century studies is a continuing source of inspiration and aspiration. In writing the new preface, I have been encouraged and helped by a roster of generous friends who have commented on successive drafts: David Aers, Lana Cable, Jonathan Goldberg, Linda Gregerson, Marshall Grossman, Al Labriola, Michael Lieb, Jason Rosenblatt and Victoria Silver. I also owe much to the expert assistance of Lisa Haarlander, Sarah Pickard and Ben Saunders.

Preface to the
Second Edition

Soon after *Surprised by Sin* was published in 1967 I
received several letters from fellow Miltonists who offered
both generous praise and the information that each of them
had been about to write a book or essay making essentially
the same argument. I had no trouble believing it if only
because I knew and admired the quality of my
correspondents (Joan Webber was one of them), and later I
believed it for another reason when I came to understand
that what I had done was going to be done by somebody
sooner or later. I just happened to be lucky enough to have
done it sooner. When a worker in a discipline manages to
'advance the conversation', the step he or she has taken will
almost immediately be seen by his or her peers as inevitable.
This is because what is experienced as an advance will be a
function of the prevailing conditions in the discipline; an
advance is merely the realization of a need or desideratum
already specified, although not always explicitly, by the
shape of those conditions.

In the context of Milton criticism what was needed was
a way of breaking out of the impasse created by two
interpretive traditions. In one tradition, stretching from
Addison to C. S. Lewis and Douglas Bush, the moral of
Paradise Lost is 'dazzlingly simple':[1] disobedience of God is
the source of all evil and the content of all error; obedience
to God brings happiness and the righteous life. In the other
tradition, strongly announced by Blake's declaration that
Milton was 'of the Devil's party without knowing it'[2] and

Shelley's judgment that 'Nothing can exceed the energy
and magnificence of the character of Satan'[3] and continued
in our century by A. J. A. Waldock and William Empson
among others, disobedience of God is a positive act that
rescues mankind from an unvarying routine of mindless
genuflection and makes possible the glorious and
distinctively human search for self-knowledge and
knowledge of the Truth. For one party God and his only
begotten son are the obvious co-heroes of the epic; for the
other, the poem's true energy resides in the figures of Satan
and the Eve who 'Bold deed . . . has presum'd' (IX. 921),
figures whose actions would seem to exemplify Milton's
declared preference in his *Areopagitica* for a virtue that is
active rather than 'fugitive and cloister'd'.[4]

   Firmly ensconced in their respective camps, the
participants in this critical quarrel accused one another of
various heresies and congealed orthodoxies, each side
claiming that the other was not really reading the poem but
skewing it to fit a preconceived thesis. At stake, according to
one observer writing in 1960, was nothing less than the
'coherence and psychological plausibility' of the poem.[5] By
shifting the field where coherence was to be found from the
words on the page to the experience they provoked, I was
able to reconcile the two camps under the aegis of a single
thesis: *Paradise Lost* is a poem about how its readers came
to be the way they are; its method, 'not so much a teaching
as an intangling'[6] is to provoke in its readers wayward,
fallen responses which are then corrected by one of several
authoritative voices (the narrator, God, Raphael, Michael,
the Son). In this way, I argued, the reader is brought to a
better understanding of his sinful nature and is encouraged
to participate in his own reformation. The advantage of this
thesis, at least with respect to what was then called the
'Milton Controversy,' is that it achieved the full

enfranchisement of all combatants; everyone is partly right and everyone's perspective is necessary to the poem's larger strategy.

It is pleasant to report that this refocusing of the questions asked of the poem was almost immediately influential and continues to be so. The chief details of the historical record are generously noted by William Kerrigan in *The Sacred Complex*:

> In many readers the figure of Satan generates a tension between . . . two poles: his mythopoeic grandeur at the opening of the work opposes his discursive condemnation by the narrator and the heavenly characters. Stanley Fish's solution to this classic dilemma in *Surprised by Sin*, widely adopted now, has an elegance at once literary and psychological.
>
> In claiming that the tension was deliberate, Fish healed an old division in Milton studies. Provided that our sense of his splendor be corrected repeatedly by the normative declarations of discursive judgment, we may permit the romantic *and* the theological Satan to evolve in us. We are obeying intentional meaning, fulfilling the strategy of the poet, even when our feelings about the mythopoeic Satan contradicts this judgment. The psychological elegance of Fish's argument is that the pious reader can entertain potentially rebellious attitudes knowing that, as a sign of his fallenness, these attitudes already confirm the doctrinal argument of the poem and therefore have a piety all their own.[7]

Like any critic worth his salt, Kerrigan offers his praise preliminary to a reservation that flowers into a deep criticism. The point of entry is already prepared for when he observes (correctly) that in my reading we readers 'are obeying intentional meaning'; for, as he immediately goes on to say, by attributing the poem's every effect to an overarching authorial intention, I posit a closed system of

control in which an authoritative centre merely allows, and
is always reigning in, meanings and gestures that seem —
but only for a fleeting and self-delusive moment — to be in
opposition to it. Kerrigan's complaint is that in my *Paradise
Lost* real opposition is impossible, or to put it into the
vocabulary of some recent theory, difference is always and
already subordinate to the order of the same and is finally
illusory. What I am always discovering, he says, is 'a
duplication of discursive meaning,' and 'the overall effect of
[Fish's] reading is to promulgate a tyrannical notion of
aesthetic unity at the expense of introducing, without overt
recognition, a new and unheard-of-flaw in the poem: the
alarming idea that its mythopoesis is not generative but
repetitive' (99).

Kerrigan identifies what is probably the main criticism
directed at *Surprised by Sin*: it describes and attempts to
extend into the life of its readers a stifling authoritarianism.
In John Rumrich's words, the book's relentlessly reductive
argument substitutes for the voice heard in Milton's 'most
complex splendidly varied, and sublime composition' 'a
knuckle-rapping peremptory prig . . . who already knows
the truth of things, humiliates and berates his charges for
their errors and requires conformity to his authoritative
understanding.'[8] Those who write in this vein often assume
that it is my ambition to be the third in an unholy trinity:
God surrounds and circumscribes the motions of his
creatures; Milton wants to surround and circumscribe the
motions of his readers; and Fish tries to surround and
circumscribe the motions of all those who study and teach
the work of Milton. As Bill Readings declares in 1985: 'Fish
seeks to play God to the reader, saying, "you may not be
clever enough to understand all my points, but you must
recognize that I am right." He thus allows himself the same
process of accommodation to mere mortals that he

describes God as practising.[9] None dare blow the whistle on Fish's grandiose assertions,' Readings observes wonderingly, even though, 'In fact, Fish cannot authorise his reading over anyone else's.' (140, 139)

In fact, this was an inaccurate judgment in 1985 and continues to be so in 1997. In a book length expansion of his 1990 article, Rumrich reports ruefully that 'Fish's seminal study . . . is still basic to our contemporary understanding of Milton's works,'[10] and compares its influence to that of a triumphant paradigm as Thomas Kuhn might describe it: 'Fish inaugurated a period in Milton criticism analogous to what Kuhn describes as "normal science," a condition in which practitioners labor to extend and deepen a working paradigm rather than rehash fundamental issues that it resolved' (2). Rumrich supports this (for him) unhappy observation by noting how many award winning books, ostensibly committed to methodologies and perspectives quite different from mine (books by Georgia Christopher, William Kerrigan, Marshall Grossman, James Turner, Christopher Kendrick), nevertheless accept 'Fish's basic position as a premise' (7). No one,' he says, 'has successfully refuted Fish's main argument, not on its own terms' (3), and he resolves to be that one, unaware apparently of the (Kuhnian) irony involved in trying to dislodge or 'uninvent' something by conducting a book length argument on its terms.

Do not mistake me. I am not saying that because my reading of *Paradise Lost* hovers over or underwrites operations in the field that it is either true or helpfully productive. The institutional fact of its prominence (attested to by casual but gratifying statements found in student guides written by Thomas Corns (1994), David Loewenstein (1993) and Margarita Stocker (1988)) cannot be translated into any fact about the value of its analyses.

That value must be demonstrated (if it can be) in the context of the needs and goals of Milton criticism, not in the context of its sociology. Those needs and goals chiefly include explanation and understanding and it is to the explanatory power or poverty of *Surprised by Sin* that I shall turn in a moment.

But first one more consideration of a theoretical kind. Much of Readings' objection to *Surprised by Sin* is inseparable from his objection to reader response criticism of which he takes the book to be a prime instance. He characterizes the practice of reader response criticism 'as being a desperate striving for the reconstruction of the act of first reading,'[11] an immediacy, he contends, that I never recover and one that is available only as a secondary construct of 'the very theory that mediates it.' This would be a telling point had I not already made it myself (there's that God-like move again) first in 'Interpreting the Variorum' (1976), and then in *Is There a Text in This Class?* (1980) when I acknowledged the mistake of thinking that my 'method' was recovering an experience rather than producing one. I realized that instead of saying to readers 'this is the way you have always read even if you were unaware of it,' I was saying and had always been saying 'read it this way — within the assumption that the poem's method is to involve you in its plot by confronting you with interpretive crises — and see if this way of reading makes better sense of the poem than the way of reading (and there always has to be one) within which you were proceeding before.' In short, I abandoned the posture of a scientist bent on describing facts to which he made no positive contribution and embraced the role of agent-of-change, resting my case on the decision of my peers as to whether or not the change I urged was beneficial. (One form of the verdict was given by teachers who told me, and continue to tell me, that *Surprised by Sin* made it possible for them to teach *Paradise Lost* to modern students.)

If *Readings* (with more than a little help from me) mistakes the metacritical nature of my claim about the poem, Rumrich mistakes its substantive content when he criticizes me for burdening Milton with an 'anticarnal bias' that is at odds with the strong monism he expresses both in *Paradise Lost* and in *The Christian Doctrine*.[12] Rumrich is in part led to this mischaracterization of my position by the frequent opposition in *Surprised by Sin* of the carnal to the spiritual. But as I deploy it, this opposition does not line up either with a body/spirit distinction or a body/mind distinction; rather the appropriate distinction is between two internal orientations: on the one hand toward the forms of created nature; on the other toward the primacy and grandeur of the creator. The exemplar of the first orientation is Mammon who is described when we first meet him as 'the least erected Spirit that fell/ From heav'n, for ev'n in heav'n his looks and thoughts/ Were always downward bent, admiring more/ The riches of Heav'n's pavement, troden Gold/ Than aught divine or holy else enjoy'd/ In vision beatific' (I. 679–83). Mammon is faulted not for admiring Heaven's riches but for admiring them in and of themselves and not as signs of the power ('divine or holy else') that made them. In his eyes they are riches that just happened to be in Heaven rather than *Heaven's* riches. It is their 'lustre' (II. 271) not their source that impresses him, and that is why he is so pleased to find that same lustre in the 'gems and gold' of Hell's soil. 'What can Heav'n show more?' (273), he asks, making it as plain as could be that 'show' names the limit of his perception even as it names his desire.

When Milton allows Mammon thus to undercut himself, it is not to make an ascetic point. He is rejecting not gems and gold but the impoverished vision which, in a kind of negative transubstantiation, impoverishes *them*. Seen (and given life) by another vision, gems and gold would not be mere show and surface glitter; rather they would 'show' something in the sense of pointing to it, emblematizing it, embodying it; and the something they would thus show would bathe them in its glory. This is the vision that is oriented from the beginning toward the origin of value and sees everything in its light, a perceptual habit that Raphael urges when, in response to Adam's question about the apparent inefficiency of the planetary movements, he says, 'And for the Heav'n's wide Circuit, let it speak/ The Maker's high magnificence, who built/ So spacious, and his Line strecht out so far;/ That Man may know he dwells not in his own' (VIII. 100–3). Or in other words, since man did not make the solar system (an echo here of the *Book of Job*) he cannot hope to comprehend it, to contain it within his mind. His safest (because it cannot go wrong) course is to understand it as declaring — speaking — some pre-assumed property of the Maker.

Raphael's lesson extends beyond the present example to a general instruction for reading the world: whatever you encounter, either in nature or in the society of men, read it — see it — as a manifestation of godly power and beneficence. To proceed in the other direction and look for meaning in the phenomena themselves, as if they were their own cause and the independent determinants of their own value, is to mistake that which has been created for the creator, and the name of that mistake is idolatry. Idolatry, worship of the secondary, is what Mammon practices when he can find nothing higher than the lustre of gold and gems. Eve engages in an almost comic (yet tragic) form of idolatry when she bows down to a tree as if to 'the power/ That dwelt within' (IX. 835-6), attributing to it effects of illumination no merely natural process could produce. Adam, in his turn, commits idolatry when he can imagine nothing worse than losing Eve ('to lose thee were to lose my self,' IX. 959), drawing from the Son an instant and devastatingly concise rebuke, 'Was she thy God?' (X. 145); that is, don't you remember that there is only one proper object of worship and it isn't Eve (or gold, or a tree)?

It is Satan (appropriately enough) who alerts us to what always lies behind idolatry when he declares himself and his fellows 'self-begot, self-rais'd/ By our own quick'ning power' (V. 860–1). Worship of the secondary is at bottom self-worship because it accepts as full and complete — as godly — the limited perspective of the worshipper. As Linda Gregerson explains it, 'to rest content in worldly understanding is to make an idol of human insufficiency.'[13] Satan concludes that he and the other rebels created themselves because, 'We know no time when we were not as now' (V. 859). The reasoning is, 'I don't see anything but what I see; therefore there couldn't be anything else to see or to know, no prior creation to which I was not a witness.' Mammon looks around and says, 'all I can see in Heaven is metallic glitter; that must be all of it.' Eve's worship of the tree follows upon the deification of her own experience which she calls her 'Best guide' (IX. 808). Adam finds his best guide in Eve 'in whom excell'd/ Whatever can to sight or thought be form'd' (IX. 897–8), and dismisses (by failing to consider) the possibility of something that cannot be formed to his sight or thought but is nevertheless worth his fealty. As the verse says, he submits 'to what seem'd remediless' (IX. 919); that is, he submits, gives himself over to, the limitations of the horizon he presently commands.

If idolatry is always simultaneously worship of the secondary and self-worship, it is also a pollution of the thing or creature (or self) that is worshipped. When

Mammon admires the 'riches of Heav'n's pavement' to the exclusion of any vision of 'aught divine,' he does no favour to the object of his misplaced affection. Rather, by detaching the pavement from its position in Heaven's order and claiming for it an independent value, he takes all value from it and reduces it to the mere surface that captivates him. When Eve makes the tree the vehicle of her sin first by eating from it and then by adoring it, she turns what she calls the 'Cure of all' (IX. 776) into the death of all (she 'knew not eating death') and transforms the pledge of her obedience into the 'root of all our woe' (IX. 645). And when Adam chooses 'to incur/ Divine displeasure for her sake' (IX. 992–3), he does not, despite Eve's belief to the contrary, ennoble her; he (quite literally) degrades her by setting her up as a rival to God, thus doing to her again what she has already done to herself by affecting Godhead. In each instance, the idolatrous agent does to the thing idolized what Satan does to the serpent he 'enters' (IX. 188) and the tree he uses only 'For prospect' (IV. 200), 'perverts best things/ To worst abuse, or to thir meanest use' (IV. 203–4).

It should be clear that this is the opposite of the dualism of which Rumrich accuses me; for in every case the evil inheres not in the material or the bodily but in the intention of the perverter who puts it to a mean or malign use. Although the sin of idolatry envelops its object, that object remains innocent of the corruption it nevertheless suffers. Nor could it be otherwise given the rigorous logic of monism as it is laid out in Chapter 7 of *Christian Doctrine*. Rejecting the thesis that God created the world out of pre-existing matter (because matter would then be a joint first-cause with God), Milton declares that matter 'originated from God at some point in time' and that since all things are made of matter, 'all things came from God.'[14] It follows that if matter proceeds from God it cannot be evil or unworthy

— 'this original matter was not an evil thing, nor to be thought of as worthless' (308) — and indeed not only does matter issue 'from God in an incorruptible state' (309), but even after 'the fall it is still incorruptible, so far as its essence is concerned' (309). This strong statement provokes the obvious strong question. Where does evil come from? ('But the same problem, or an even greater one, still remains. How can anything sinful have come . . . from God?' (309).) The answer, as we have already seen, is that evil comes from free agents — angels or men — who for whatever reasons (and what those reasons might be and how they could arise are points I shall take up shortly), incorporate matter (gold, trees, Eve) into a project whose purpose, always frustrated, is to break away from God and establish an alternate kingdom and realm of values: 'it is not the matter nor the form which sins. When matter or form has gone out from God and become the property of another, what is there to prevent its being infected and polluted[?]' (309).

The centrality to Milton's thought of monism cannot be overestimated. Not only does it generate an account of evil, it dictates (*a*) an epistemology (all things are truly known in their relation to God), (*b*) a definition of heroism (a hero is someone loyal to God no matter what form, including inaction, that loyalty might take), (*c*) a morality (in any situation of choice the moral choice will always be the one that maintains fidelity to the Creator), (*d*) an erotics (love for the world and its creatures cannot be separated from, or opposed to, love of God), (*e*) a politics (act in any crisis so as to align yourself with the will of God), (*f*) a prescription for happiness ('That thou art happy, owe to God;/ That thou continu'st such, owe . . . / . . . to thy obedience,' v. 520–2), (*g*) an aesthetics (words and images are truly beautiful only when they either praise God's goodness or signify a submission to his will), and above all (*h*) a theory of value (since everything proceeds from God, everything is intrinsically valuable and nothing is to be rejected as if it were, in and of itself, the bearer of evil and error; this includes snakes, apples, trees, minerals, wine, women, and song).

It is this last that would seem to authorize the expansiveness and liberality Rumrich and others want to find in Milton. No narrow minded, Puritan prig, no 'censorious preacher'[15] busily adding to the list of 'thou shalt nots', the poet is in fact someone who celebrates the enormous fecundity of the multiform creation to which Adam is introduced in the garden of Eden: 'He brought thee into this delicious Grove/ This Garden, planted with the Trees of God,/ Delectable both to behold and taste;/ And freely all thir pleasant fruit for food/ Gave thee, all sorts are here that all th' Earth yields,/ Variety without end' (VII. 537–42a). But 'variety without end' is one of those Miltonic phrases, seemingly straightforward and even bland, that turns out to have a sting in its tail. The trigger is the word 'end' with whose several meanings Milton repeatedly plays in *Paradise Lost*. Here the relevant meanings are first 'limit' or 'cessation' and second 'purpose' or 'goal'. If one stops with the first meaning 'variety without end' reads simply as 'more than you could ever see, more choices than you could ever make, there's no *end* to the stuff.' But suddenly, in the very next half-line, an end in the sense of limit is imposed and brings with it an end in the sense of purpose: 'but of the Tree/ Which tasted works knowledge of Good and Evil/ Thou may'st not; in the day thou eat'st thou di'st' (542b–4).

Although the interdiction of one item in an inventory that still offers more than they could ever consume might seem a small matter, it changes everything because it puts at the centre of their experience a nodal point that orders every part of it. When this one tree is given a meaning in excess of its mere physical presence — it is 'a test of fidelity' placed here, says Milton in the *Christian Doctrine*, so that 'man's obedience might be thereby manifested' — the physical presence of everything that has not been prohibited acquires a meaning (an 'end') also; for if the unfallen pair are to refrain from eating of this one tree as a test of their allegiance to its creator, they are to be mindful of that same creator when partaking of the trees that remain available to them. If they abstain in a spirit of loyalty and reverence, they should eat in the same spirit. Although the prohibition literally applies only to a single fruit, its effects ripple outward finally touching all of creation. It is just like what happens when Wallace Stevens' jar is placed in Tennessee. The wilderness surrounds it — configures itself in relation to it — and is no longer wild. Here in book VII the 'variety without end' surrounds — is configured by — the prohibition, and is no longer variety in the sense of profusion without direction or constraint.

Paradise Lost is full of moments like this, moments in which the affirmation of variety is immediately countered by the imposition of unity and the insistence on an underlying sameness. These moments mime the logic of monism. God may, as *Christian Doctrine* tells us, allow his 'substantial virtue' to 'disperse' and 'propagate,' but only in what form and in what ways 'he wills'(308); however far from his centre the effects of his virtue may be scattered, they are always tethered to the origin whose imprint they bear. Indeed this is the sole business of apparent heterogeneity, of the 'various forms' (V. 473) that fill the world — to testify to a common source and to speak its glory. Whether it be the planets which are 'regular' (governed by rule) 'when most irregular they seem' (V.

623–4) or the elements whose 'ceaseless change' serves to 'Vary to our great Maker still new praise' (v. 183–4), the song has one and only one purpose: 'to extol/ Him first, him last, him midst, and without end' (v. 165), where the phrase 'without end' is to be understood not as profusion, but as an endless iteration of the same. Perhaps the most concise presentation of this reassertion of oneness in the face of apparent multiplicity is line 630 of book VII where Adam learns that his future (and his obligation) is to 'multiply a race of worshippers.' For the moment it takes to read it 'multiply' opens up on a vista of ever new possibilities, but then with the phrase 'race of worshipers' the new possibilities are revealed to be no more (or less) than variations on the same old theme, a theme that is *obligatory*. (The open palm followed by the closed fist, by the fist that has *always* been closed.)

What all of this means is that monism, the notion that gives coherence to Milton's thought and provides some of its most attractive features, is also the source of the resistance and dissatisfaction felt by so many readers. While monism redeems the world and generously gives value to everything, it doesn't let anything have its *own* value. Indeed either claiming or finding independent value are the ways of pride and idolatry. These are paths of danger only for free agents who are free not in any absolute sense, but in the sense permitted in a monistic universe. They are free to affirm the truth or to deny it, and by denying it to lose it and themselves. Freedom in a monistic universe is both a gift because not all creatures have it and a burden because not all creatures are subject to its risks. The free agent is one who has the capacity to make the right choice and therefore also the capacity to make the wrong one, as opposed to natural objects which do not wake up in the morning with the possibility of altering the conditions of their existence.

If happiness is being allied to the source of all virtue, then rocks and stones and trees are always happy (unless perverted by a man or angel), but involuntarily so. The happiness of free agents is also a property of their created existence, but they must will its persistence. They can also will its loss by deciding ('Oh event perverse') to 'break union' (V. 612).

But here's the rub. The loss that results will accrue to them and not to the God from whom they try to break away. Breaking union as a positive gesture — as a gesture whose effect is to inaugurate a new and separate mode of being in the spirit of Coriolanus' 'There is a world elsewhere' — is not a possible form of action in a monistic universe because there is literally nowhere to go. God is on all sides; you are surrounded by him even when you think either to contemplate him (As Herbert puts it in 'Providence', 'who hath praise enough? nay who hath any?') or to oppose — stand opposite to — him. You can't get away in two senses: you can't escape him, and you can't subtract yourself from him, you can't leave him less than he was before. The free agent who forsakes his freedom by choosing wrongly, by choosing an unavailable state of independence, merely returns to the state of chaos ('The Womb of nature,' II. 911), also part of God and the storehouse of 'materials' with which he can if he chooses 'create more Worlds' (II. 916). The point is made as forcefully as one might wish (or deplore) when the angels celebrate the act of creation:

. . . the proud attempt
Of Spirits apostate, and thir Counsels vain
Thou has repell'd, while impiously they thought
Thee to diminish, and from thee withdraw
The number of thy worshippers. Who seeks
To lessen thee, against his purpose serves
To manifest the more thy might.

(VII. 609–15)

Against his (the apostate's) purpose because there is only one purpose and it will be served no matter what the intentions or actions of other agents. 'Who can impair thee?' (VII. 608), 'who can make thee less?' God's choristers ask rhetorically, and the answer is obvious: No one, nothing.

(ii) 'ON OTHER SURETY NONE'

All of which brings us back to the question Milton raises in *Christian Doctrine*: if all things are of God, and if matter is both good and incorruptible in its essence, and if that incorruptibility remains so long as free agents do not break the connection that sustains it, why and how should any of them come to rebel or even think that they could? This is Adam's question to Raphael — 'can wee want obedience then/ To him or possibly his love desert/ Who form'd us[?]' (V. 514–16) — and it is answered first by Raphael's pointing out that while their state is instituted by God, its maintenance depends on them as free agents (V. 520–3), and second by the story of the first rebel, offered by the sociable angel as a cautionary tale ('let it profit thee to have heard/ By terrible Example the reward/ Of disobedience,' VI. 909–11). *Paradise Lost*, as everyone knows, opens *in medias res*, and it is only in Book V that we get the beginning of the story; in fact we get the beginning of story itself, for if there had been no first fall, no first breaking of union, there would have been no story, no plot, since plot and story depend on agents who are either not where they should be or not where they want to be. In Heaven, and for a while in Paradise, everyone is in his or her proper place (the place ordained by God), doing the right thing (exemplifying and attesting to God's goodness and glory), and perfectly happy (since happiness is defined as union with the highest and worthiest). Another (negative) way to put this is that in Heaven and in pre-lapsarian Paradise nothing happens, if we think of a 'happening' as something that alters basic conditions and sets in motion energies that either lead to the establishment of a new order or become reabsorbed into an old one. So the question, 'where did evil come from?' might be rephrased as 'how did anything ever happen?'

It is (literally) tempting to equate that question with the question posed by the epic voice at I. 28, 'what cause?' In that form the question assumes a psychology in which motives (causes) come from the outside: the agent's understanding of the world and his or her place in it is challenged by something (a new phenomenon, an anomalous outcome) and as a result he or she begins to act differently. But this view of causality and of change from a previous state of equilibrium turns out to be the wrong one, although for reasons I hope to make clear it is a view that remains powerfully attractive. We find out that it is wrong when Satan's story provides no answer to the question of cause, and instead piles mystery upon mystery. The first mystery is the identity of the agent who somehow changes and in changing brings evil into the world. We never see him, but see only what he has become, '*Satan*, so call him now, his former name/ Is heard no more in Heav'n' (V. 658–9). His former name is heard no more not because it is anathema to pronounce it (as might be the case in some blood feud when the patriarch says, 'never mention his name again in this house') but because *he* no longer exists. (As Regina Schwartz observes, this is true of all the fallen angels: 'Having lost their positive identity, they have lost their names.'[16]) At the very beginning of what promises to be an explanation of how the whole thing got started the agent whose act we hope to understand disappears. To be sure, we know something about him, but what we know only deepens the puzzle. Along with the other angels he has heard the Father's pronouncement — 'This day I have

begot whom I declare/ My only Son' (V. 603–4) — and it is
clear that before this moment he was in a particularly
favoured position:

> ...he of the first,
> If not the first Arch-Angel, great in Power,
> In favor and preëminence, yet fraught
> With envy against the Son of God.
>
> (659–662)

'yet' is the hinge word here, and what it means is
'nevertheless' or 'despite' or 'who would have thought it?'
It works exactly like 'Favor'd of Heav'n so highly'
(describing Adam and Eve) works in Book 1.1.30, to
emphasize the *absence* of an intelligible connection between
the agent's situation and his or her response to it: it's the
last thing you would have expected from the last person.
One moment there is the now obliterated (his-name-is-
heard-no-more) angel, and the next there is Satan, a new
being who is fraught with envy. That is to say, he is *full of*
envy; envy, the desire to be somewhere and/or someone else,
is what constitutes and animates him, and it is also what
determines his perception: 'fraught/ With envy against the
Son of God . . . / . . . could not bear/ Through pride that
sight, and thought himself impair'd./ Deep malice thence
conceiving and disdain' (661–2, 664–6).

The awkwardness of the syntax in these lines is
significant. Had Milton written 'could not bear/ That sight
through pride' the verse would have given 'that sight' an
independent status as something with its own perspicuous
features which are then — that is, subsequently — distorted
by Satan's prideful lens. But in the sequence as we have it
the 'sight' quite literally comes into view 'through' — under
the aegis of — Satan's pride, and the point is (again quite
literally) brought home to us when the verse insists that
before reaching 'that sight' we must go through the words

'through pride'. The effect is to alert us to the nature of Satan's 'mistake' which is not one he could have avoided by getting closer to the object (in the manner of an experimental scientist) or by acquiring more information about it; rather he could have seen 'that sight' (the exaltation of the Son) more clearly only if the lens through which he was looking was not made of envy or pride, but of something else, say, for example, faith and obedience. These alternative perspectives are not produced by events; it is the other way around: pride and obedience name the positions perceiving agents already occupy, and it is within those positions that the shape of events emerges, and it will emerge differently depending on the point of perspectival origin. The fact that Satan sees 'through pride' does not mean that he should have seen directly or without mediation, but that he should have seen through something else. 'Seeing through' is not a condition to be shunned; it is the condition of all agents who are partial and situated, and that includes angels as well as men. You have to see through something, just as you have to be fraught with (informed by) something, and the only questions are, through what shall you see and with what shall you be fraught?

But how do you make the choice if the facts do not precede that choice but are its results? How are you to know what is good and right? This is also Catherine Belsey's question — 'What . . . are the grounds of true knowledge?'[17] — which she answers by implying that in this poem there are none. (In a sense, but not her sense, this is true.) If Satan makes a wrong choice, she reasons, we only know it because the narrative turns out badly for him. In the scene where he debates with Abdiel the wisdom and rightness of rebellion neither he nor his opponent makes a point the other cannot dispute and each argues from what seems to be the relevant, but different, features of his experience. In the end, Belsey observes, the difference between the two parties and their respective positions is political and rhetorical, a matter of who seems the more plausible to the larger number of hearers: 'Satan succeeds in persuading one group: God retains the allegiance of the rest.' But given the equal plausibility of the cases they put, why should we be persuaded by one rather than the other? 'How are we to be sure that we recognize the truth?' (78).

The answer is (1) we (readers and/or characters) can't be sure; that's not the kind of world this is; and (2) the fact that we can't be sure is not a flaw in the poem's epistemology but a necessary condition of the drama of choice. If recognizing the truth meant simply attending to evidence that was self-declaring, the choosing intelligence would have nothing to do except assent to the undeniable. In the world Milton creates, however, such evidence (for which Satan searches endlessly in *Paradise Regained*) is unavailable to limited agents who make their choices not on the basis of indisputable facts but on the basis of prior dispositions — prior convictions as to how the universe is disposed — in relation to which the facts, now experienced as indisputable, emerge. When God 'retains the allegiance' of Abdiel and his fellow loyalists, it is not because events and actions unambiguously attest to his goodness (as Empson and others remind us, he sends his servants on unnecessary errands, commands them to actions they cannot perform, and stage manages situations in order to provide a showcase for his only begotten Son), but because they begin with the assumption of his goodness and then reason about events in the light of that prior assumption. And the same holds on the other side: when Satan decides to 'dislodge' his legions (v. 669) and take them to the North, it is not because the sight he sees compels that response, but because 'that sight' is itself seen through a lens, a conviction, that configures and precedes it. In both cases the sequence reverses the order of empirical investigation: first the conclusion (God is good or God is a tyrant) and then the proof which is presented as validating it, but is in fact produced by it. The anointing of the Son by God does not cause Satan's envy and pride; they are what is inside him and they determine for him what 'that sight' obviously signifies.

But this is only to push our original question (where does evil come from?) back further. How, given that he like the rest of the angels was created good, did pride and envy get inside him? The answer is given (by not being given) in V. I. 665:

...could not bear
Through pride that sight, and thought himself impair'd.
                                                   (664b–665)

The second half of the line — 'and thought himself impair'd' — reads first as what it surely is, an account of Satan's psychology. He saw the Son's exaltation and took it as a slight, as an affront to his honour, as a diminishing of his own status: he thought himself impaired, made less. But the phrase will bear another reading in which impairment is not simply what he thinks about but what he suffers as the result of so thinking. That is, by thinking of the honour done to the Son as something that made him less (as opposed to Abdiel who later in the book thinks of the same honour as returning to him and his fellows) he becomes less, becomes the diminished creature whom we know as Satan. In short he thought in a certain way when other ways were available and by so thinking he thought himself into a state of impairment ('thought himself impair'd'); he made himself less — a being made of envy and pride rather than of trust and faith — by his thoughts.

But the puzzle returns in another (really the same) form. Why does he think *that* way? The question arises naturally, but it cannot be answered without pointing to some cause or prompting external to Satan's mental and moral processes. In the psychology Milton imagines for his characters, however, promptings always well up from *within*, whether they be good ('those free and unimposed expressions which from a sincere heart unbidden come into the outward gesture'[18]) or bad ("Though ye take from a covetous man all his treasures, he has yet one jewell left, ye cannot bereave him of his covetousnesse'[19]). The only appropriate answer to the question 'why does Satan think himself into a state of impairment?' is tautological and unhelpful. Satan thinks that way (in a manner that impairs him even as he worries about being impaired) because he is capable of doing so, although the fact that he *can* think that way doesn't mean that he *must* think that way; it is a possible not a determined direction of thought. That is what free will means: a will poised between alternative conceptions (and therefore between alternative programmes for action) the choice of which is entirely within its power as opposed to being dictated by the pressures of external circumstance. As Adam puts it, the free agent is 'Secure from outward force; within himself/ The danger lies, yet lies within his power:/ Against his will he can receive no harm' (IX. 348–50). The formulation is precise and is designed to ward off two mistakes; the mistake of enthralling the will to forces outside it, and the mistake of turning the internal vulnerability of the will into a form of determinism, as Christopher Ricks does when he asks 'if they could fall, were they not already in some sense fallen?'[20] The danger within is also a danger within the agent's control, and the space of control (or of its loss) is precisely the space of free will.

If there can be no answer to the question, 'why does Satan think as he does?', then there can be no answer to the question, 'why does Satan fall?' for any answer will compromise the freedom of will he here exercises. In Dennis Danielson's words, 'a free choice is not, independently of the choice itself, sufficiently caused one way or the other. Therefore . . . there is finally no answer to the question *why*.'[21] At the point where we most want an explanation, we find only a mystery whose (non)shape is perfectly (un)represented in the spontaneous and unmotivated (*'yet* fraught with envy') emergence of a new being who has literally conceived himself without any outside aid: 'Deep malice thence conceiving and disdain.' (The fact that this conceiving occurs at line 666 speaks for itself and for the extraordinary care with which Milton structures almost every detail of the epic.) There is then a truth to Satan's claim to have been 'self-begot,' although not in the sense he makes it. What he means is that his first creation (out of primordial material or out of nothing) was self engineered by his 'own quick'ning power' (V. 861), a conclusion he draws (absurdly) from the fact that he doesn't remember being created by anybody else. But the second creation from the 'his-name-is-heard-no-more' angel to the present apostate is indeed his responsibility; it is a feat entirely self-accomplished by a will with the capacity either to maintain the state of original creation or to alter it for no other reason than that it is free to.

John Rogers in *The Matter of Revolution*[22] ties this moment to Milton's praise in *Defensio Populi* of the Puritan leaders as 'their own ancestors', *'ex se natos'*(128). But I would remark the difference rather than the similarity. Whereas Satan is claiming to be the origin of himself in an (impossible) absolute way, the Puritan leaders are nurturing the seed of virtue planted in them by God. (Like Adam and Eve as described by Marshall Grossman, they seek to 'author a life history conformable to that which God desires.'²³) They are their own ancestors only in the sense that they look inward to that seed (which they cultivate) rather than outward to the accidental marks of courtly or class honour. (Milton makes the same point in *An Apology* when the members of Parliament are found to be virtuous *despite* the advantages of birth, education, and family.) The self-fashioning of which Milton approves and of which he considers himself an example, is rooted in a recognition of dependence of exactly the kind Satan here flatly rejects in a moment of bad self-fashioning. The only thing that links the two kinds of self-fashioning is a will that is free in the sense that it cannot be forced by circumstances external to it.

But if the exercise of a free will is an internal event undetermined by circumstances, its effects are not so narrowly confined. Even though the operation of the will is independent of the world ('Vertue could see to do what vertue would/ By her own radiant light, though Sun and Moon/ Were in the flat Sea sunk' [*Comus*, 372–4]), the world is not independent of it and will change — at least for the willing agent — depending on the direction freely, but momentously, taken. When Satan decides in his freedom to break union he alters more than his relationship to the sustaining power of the universe; he alters the universe and creates a new one populated by persons, events, possibilities, aspirations and facts that come into being (for him) simultaneously with his self-transformation. At the moment he thinks himself impaired he also, necessarily and at a stroke, thinks into existence a cast of supporting characters: a Father who would play favourites with his children and elevate an undeserving youth over a loyal and long serving elder son; a younger son who would accept this undeserved honour and assume powers he hasn't earned; and an army of servile foot soldiers who continue to warble hallelujahs before a corrupt throne even as a gross injustice is done. And to think these is also to think the world in which they move and have their being, a world where merit can always be trumped by dynastic politics, where earned privileges and responsibilities can be lost in an instant, where you never know who's going to be created or ruined next and you had better grab what you can while there is still time.

This, then, is the world — fully elaborated and equipped with an ontology (things create themselves), an epistemology (seeing is believing), an ethics (when you don't get what you want, take it by force), a politics (might makes right), an aesthetics ('what can Heav'n show more?') — that springs full blown from Satan's brain (the moment is replayed in the allegory of the birth of Sin) in the instant when he thinks himself impaired. Moreover, once he generates this world, he has no choice (he has already made it) but to live in it, to see what it allows him to see, to draw conclusions based on its assumed outlines, to read the present and project possible futures by its lights. He has made his bed and now he must lie in it. What you freely will is what you get, and what he gets by choosing to read his situation (and the situation of everyone and everything else) in a certain way is a succession of experiences structured by that first choice. If he begins by conceiving of God as a paternal tyrant whose reign is an accident of time and power, that conception will structure his understanding of everything that happens subsequently.

When, for example, he and his followers endure a day of pain and humiliation in the battle, all he can see is a 'doubtful fight' (VI. 423), one so evenly contested that it might go on forever. Satan's language suggests a doubt generated by the events of the day; but the doubt (general, not specific) precedes the day and structures its events for those who act within its shadow. It is a doubt not about the fight but about God who is preconceived by Satan and his followers as a wizard of Oz-like pretender issuing mysterious pronouncements behind a curtain that need only be drawn to reveal the absence of true authority. If it is this diminished figure you face then it makes perfect sense to ask as Satan now does, 'And if one day, why not Eternal days?' (424). Why not, indeed, if outcomes are entirely contingent as they would be in a universe not presided over by an all-powerful creator and sovereign. Doubt about the sovereignty of God is what has brought them to this place, and the same doubt — by now the very basis of their being — prevents them from drawing any conclusions other than the one that already informs their every action, including the action of drawing conclusions.

In their eyes the fight will always be doubtful, even when what might be thought evidence to the contrary mounts up as it does on the battle's third day with the arrival of the Son and his terrible chariot. No evidence is sufficient to change their minds, a fact Raphael reports and finds literally incredible:

This saw his hapless Foes, but stood obdur'd,
And to rebellious fight rallied thir Powers
Insensate, hope conceiving from despair.
In heav'nly Spirits could such perverseness dwell?
But to convince the proud what Signs avail,
Or Wonders move th' obdúrate to relent?

(VI. 785–90).

They see the chariot and its terrors but do not read their fate in its appearance. The reason is given in 787: 'hope conceiving from despair'. Just as Satan conceives slight and dishonour out of a sight that might easily have been seen (as it is by Abdiel) to point elsewhere, so the devils conceive hope out of a sight that in Raphael's eyes leaves no room for it. In both cases the conceiving does not follow from the visibilia but configures them; the movement is from inner to outer and that is why nothing that enters the rebels' sphere of vision could alter it. Whatever the world presents to them will bear the significance they have stipulated in advance of its emergence. Raphael makes the point again with even more force: 'They hard'nd more by what might most reclaim,/ Grieving to see his Glory, at the sight/ Took envy, and aspiring to his highth,/ Stood reimbattl'd fierce, by force or fraud/ Weening to prosper, and at length prevail/ Against God and *Messiah*' (791–6). In short, they see 'the sight' *through* pride, envy, malice and disdain. This is nothing new; it is Satan's initial gesture, now collectively (re)performed as it will always be no matter what the external stimulus.

So much Raphael sees, but what he doesn't see is that his position is no different, at least with respect to the issue raised by Belsey, the issue of grounds. The answer to his question — 'But to convince the proud what Signs avail?' — is 'no signs' because signs by themselves do not avail, do not do the job of specifying what they are signs of, but acquire meaning in the light of a presupposed significance they cannot generate. But if this is true for Satan and his host it is no less true for Raphael to whom the same question might be put with only a slight difference — 'To convince the *godly* what Signs avail?' — and the answer would also be the same: no signs. (The Jesus of *Paradise Regained* makes exactly this point at IV. 489–91 when he refuses the signs Satan marshals and would interpret for him.) Like his opposite number, the loyal angel is grasped by a conviction (that God is, in fact, God and not some well-armed tyrant) within which any and all 'sights' are received and seen to bear an obvious significance. He cannot conceive how anyone could miss that significance and he can only regard the action of the rebels as a form of insanity, an obdurateness that is 'insensate'. 'They hardn'd more by what might most reclaim.' Raphael here speaks as if the category of sights that would reclaim is the same for everyone; but in fact he reports only on the reasoning he would engage in were he they, that is, were they he and not themselves. Just as no sign in and of itself avails, no sight in and of itself reclaims. Hardened in advance, thoroughly bound to a point of view that structures their very perception, the rebels see everything (not upon reflection, but immediately) as a confirmation and extension of that point of view. Hardened (fixed, anchored) in another direction, Raphael sees the same things (not really the same) as a confirmation and extension of the point of view he cannot see past because it is what he sees *with*. Both the disloyalty (or as they would put it, heroic opposition) of one party and the loyalty (or servility) of the other are antecedent to, and constitutive of, the particulars each testifies to so confidently. The 'grounds of knowledge' in *Paradise Lost* are not external, but interpretive; what you know flows from a prior orientation and rests on no other bottom, no substratum of brute empirical fact or rational truth to which everyone, no matter what his situation or history, will naturally assent.

This is in fact a lesson that Raphael has himself given (although he now seems to have forgotten it) just before he narrates the battle:

> Myself and all th'Angelic Host that stand
> In sight of God enthron'd, our happy state
> Hold, as you yours, while our obedience holds;
> On other surety none.

(v. 535–8a)

'On other surety none' means not only that their happy state depends on their obedience, but that obedience rests on nothing but itself. The world doesn't compel it as it would if its details sent unambiguous messages to all agents, and indeed the direction of dependence is the other way around: the presence or absence of obedience in the agent determines for him the details of the world he lives in. (Satan sees himself embarking on a brave new adventure; Abdiel responds, 'I see thy fall/ Determin'd' (v. 878–9)). Moreover, because obedience rests on itself and is not dictated by an authority external to its performance, it is only by that performance that the authority to which it pledges fealty is maintained in place. 'On other surety none.'

This does not mean that the existence of God depends on whether or not free agents obey him; only that his existence *for them* as a presence in their daily lives, as a reality they have always and already taken into account, as a ground for decision and action, depends on their obedience, on an act of belief that does not follow from evidence, but generates it. At the beginning of Book X, God says that man falls by 'believing lies/ Against his Maker' (42–3). The opposite of believing lies is not suspending belief and allowing the perspicuous truth about the Maker to impress itself on you; the opposite of believing lies is believing truths, with the emphasis on the believing as an exercise of the will that keeps the truth about the Maker alive for the believer. That truth, which once in place anchors all subsequent thought, is itself a product of thought, of conceiving.

It is because Milton regards the act of conceiving as so strongly constitutive that he reserves his greatest scorn in the polemical pamphlets for those whose arguments presuppose a God who has been *mis*conceived, that is, thought of and thought up in a form that is abhorrent. Responding to the claim that the permission to divorce granted under the Old Law has been withdrawn under the New, he asks indignantly, 'Can we conceave without vile thoughts, that the majesty and holines of God could endure so many ages to gratifie a stubborn people in the practice of a foul polluting sin[?].'[24] The vile thought would be of a God who is duplicitous, and it is because the argument against divorce requires such a God that it must be rejected. By the same reasoning the thesis that God has two wills, one revealed and calling us universally to Grace, and the other secret and predestining some of us to damnation, must also be rejected, for '[o]therwise we should have to pretend that God was insincere, and said one thing but kept another hidden in his heart.'[25] Even worse we would have to conceive of a God who would 'order us to do right, but decree that we shall do wrong! . . . Could anything be imagined more absurd than such a theory?' (177). That is, is there anything more absurd than imagining, thinking, conceiving such a God? Is that the kind of God you want to believe in? Is the world that would follow from the conceiving of such a God one you would want to live in? Wouldn't it be better, Milton advises, to conceive of God as predestining to reprobation only those whom he foresees choosing reprobate ways? Only 'imagine ["cogitate"] that you hear God voicing his predestination in these terms' and 'you will dispose of countless controversies' (179). Indeed you will do more than that. You will provide yourself with an account of justice, a basis for ethical action, and a bulwark against the slings and arrows of outrageous fortune. You will walk through the world with new eyes, seeing in it everywhere evidence of the God whose nature you have thus conceived. And it is only by the strength of your conceiving — it must be reaffirmed at every moment – that this evidence, and the hope it gives you, will appear: 'On other surety none.'

(iii) THE TEXTUALITY OF TRUTH

That is why at some moments in *Paradise Lost* characters who confront one another seem to be living in different worlds. In fact they are, for they are firmly embedded in whatever world their first conceivings have called up. When Michael comes upon Satan on the first day of battle he addresses him as 'Author of evil, unknown till thy revolt' (VI. 262) — note how 'unknown' refers both to the abstraction 'evil' and to the being who is not the same as the comrade Michael used to know — and predicts his imminent defeat. Satan responds by pointing out first that a day of fighting has seen no rebel decisively vanquished, and second, that Michael has mischaracterized the entire situation by failing to understand the heroic nature of what he and his legions are doing: 'The strife which thou call'st evil . . . wee style/ The strife of Glory' (VI. 289–90), the strife, that is, of those who against enormous odds nevertheless persist in their efforts to free themselves from the despotic rule of a tyrant. Satan's point is a version of the one I have made before: just as you have to be fraught with something (envy or adoration) and have to see 'through' something (pride or faith) so must you style — draw the lines and lineaments of the world — in some way or other. Styling or characterizing or interpreting is the necessary activity of all agents who are not God, not just of agents who have rejected him. If the devils style, and inhabit, the 'strife of Glory', then Michael and his friends style, and inhabit, the strife of obedience. Each party has no difficulty assimilating events to its story. No matter what happens each finds confirmation of the basic assumptions within which it experiences and structures life. Do the rebels find themselves afflicted for the first time with pain? It merely gives them something to 'contemn' (VI. 432) and therefore something that further proves their valour. Do the loyalists find themselves in the ridiculous posture of rolling around on the ground under the assault of the newly invented canons? It only serves to illustrate the many ways in which one can stand firm: 'none on thir feet might stand,/ Though standing else as Rocks' (VI. 592–3). Neither side will be impressed by the words or deeds of the other, nor will it yield its point of view to the force of independent facts because there are none; there are only the facts that come along with a certain styling.

Everything I have said in the preceding paragraph is at once a confirmation of and a challenge to Belsey's vigorous argument for what she calls 'the textuality of truth' (*John Milton*, p. 41). By that phrase she means that although truth is asserted to be independent of any representation of it, it is only in assertions and representations that the truth comes to us. Every signifier in the poem 'is a signifier whose signified is another text' (41). Although '*Paradise Lost* claims to inscribe the ways of God' (40), all it ever gives us, or could give us, are the inscribings, the stylings (whether Michael's or Satan's), not the 'ways' which are always displaced 'by the signifying process' (41). Whatever the truth about God may be, what we have, even in his 'first person' speeches, is 'the materiality of the signifier, . . . the creativity of language itself' (41). 'What is realized . . . in the verbal and metrical patterns of *Paradise Lost*, is . . . not the presence of God but the triumphant presence of the signifier.' (43).

In these terms I cheerfully stipulate to the textuality of truth (both in *Paradise Lost* and elsewhere), and I agree too with William Kolbrener when he insists that in Milton's epistemology 'language is itself the limit of truth' and 'mediations' the 'limits of knowledge.'[26] Where I disagree is with the further conclusions drawn from these observations, either that the competing textual truths are indifferently authorized so that, in Michael Lieb's words, '*Paradise Lost* encodes within its own fabric a discourse of conflict and indeterminacy that refuses to provide for the imposition of a "final" interpretation'[27], or that in opposition to the workings of his own poem (and of language in general) Milton seeks to impose a 'despotism' of Truth by identifying it with only one of the voices whose energies the verse lets loose.[28] The first line of thought testifies to the hold liberal humanism continues to have on Miltonists and on academics in general. The idea is that despite aspects of his theology and ethics that seem unyielding and ungenerous, Milton is really a good hearted celebrator of difference, and a proto-postmodernist to boot. Accordingly he is not doing anything so crude as urging one perspective at the expense of others; rather, as Lucy Newlyn puts it, he foregrounds the conflict of competing texts and moralities so that we can hold them 'in tension.'[29] In that way the reader 'becomes aware of the coexistence of moral opposites, perceives the implication that a choice might be made, and comes to the conclusion that not making it is a subtler kind of truth' (86). (Here Milton becomes indistinguishable from Richard Rorty.) Belsey is less generous and tends to see Milton as trying to reign in the power of signification even as he generates more and more evidence of it, but on the main point she is with Newlyn, Lieb and Kolbrener and finds the poem 'celebrating the possibilities released by an encounter with a process of production that cannot be arrested' (105).

What these critics do, in their slightly different ways, is confuse an epistemological limitation — partial beings, even angels, have only mediated access to the truths they affirm — with a moral imperative either to affirm no truth and be ever poised between alternatives or to affirm all versions of the truth and thus be faithful to a universe of proliferating fecundity. To say that textuality or mediation is an inescapable ingredient of human (and angelic) knowledge is not to deny the singleness of truth, but to specify the conditions under which it must be chosen, conditions that always fall short of what would be the case if the shape of truth were self-evident and indisputable.

The point I am trying to make is one Belsey slides off when she equates Milton's declaration in the *Areopagitica* that Truth 'may have more shapes than one' with the thesis that truth is 'plural' (78). The context of the very phrase she relies on disallows her reading of it. Here is the next sentence: 'What else is all that rank of things indifferent, wherein Truth may be on this side, or on the other, without being unlike herself[?].'[30] That is, Truth always remains what she is, single and unvarying, but the form in which she appears in the world may not always be the same and it would be a mistake (it would be idolatry) to identify her narrowly with a particular list of dos and donts even if the source of the list is the Ten Commandments: '. . . he who eats or eats not, regards a day or regards it not, may doe either to the Lord' (563). Not that this licenses any action whatsoever; it is not the obligation to act rightly that is indifferent (this is the other mistake; relativism rather than formalism) but the vehicle through which this obligation is exercised, so that something that on one occasion is being 'done to the Lord' may on another occasion be done in a spirit of pride and envy. The difficulty is in telling one from the other, but it is a difficulty that will never be removed (short of 'beatific vision'), and it sets the terms for the arduous labour of apprehending Truth on the basis of evidence — the 'evidence of things not seen' — that must be affirmed by an act of the will because the world will never proffer it unambiguously. The imperative is clear and single: follow Truth, worship the Lord; it is the possible paths to its fulfilment that are plural, but the pluralism is sharply limited in that not all paths are paths to truth and at moments of crisis you will have to choose some and disdain others.

Choice then is what is required (*pace* Newlyn) and the requirement is not to be avoided either by gracefully throwing up one's hand in the face of multiplicity, or by complaining that choice is exclusionary (of course it is; that's its job). There is (literally) a world of difference between acknowledging difference — acknowledging the competing claims of various moralities and the unavailability of an algorithm for deciding between them — and celebrating difference either in the liberal humanist spirit of Rumrich and Newlyn or the postmodern/feminist spirit of Belsey. Milton certainly acknowledges difference as a condition of our interpretive work (and of work in general), but what he enjoins is the affirmation of unity even if that affirmation is supported only by the internal strength of the affirmer and not by the confirmation of independent evidence.

Once this point is grasped, it allows us to give a new answer to an old question: if it is Milton's conviction that the world is everywhere informed by the same sustaining spirit and everywhere displays the same constant truth, why are so many moments in the poem marked by a radical openness, and why at almost every juncture are important interpretive choices at once demanded and rendered radically indeterminate? John Rogers is only the latest to answer that question by finding in Milton's thought and in *Paradise Lost* a tension between two incompatible discourses, one marked by a valuing of individual freedom and self-directed growth, the other by an ethic of obedience to an authoritative God: 'the epic has inscribed in its theodicy two strands of agential philosophy that can be reconciled only with considerable hermeneutic finesse.'[31] But finesse is required only if you assume that you cannot without contradiction attribute ultimate agency to God and yet give men and women room and time enough to work out their own fates. The apparent contradiction dissolves if men and women are seen as doing their work in the interpretive space God has marked out for them as both a gift and an obligation when he says, 'Do this and you shall remain happy.' Adam and Eve are left to determine in each instance what doing this (obeying the will of God) requires. Within the provisonality that marks their experience (but not the structure of the universe) they make decisions and hazard their faith, a faith that is never confirmed in unambiguous terms by the creator who requires it.

What Milton does, in effect, is join the ontology of monism — there is only one thing real — with the epistemology of antinomianism — the real is only known perspectivally, according to the lights of individual believers. The doctrine of the inner light marks out the area of interpretive labour; the doctrine of the single Truth names the goal of that labour, but withholds explicit directions for attaining it. The resulting life of strenuous indeterminacy is the condition of all creatures (men, angels, fallen, unfallen) who are not only free to interpret God's commands but unable to do anything except interpret them. When Adam and Eve exit paradise and are described as at once 'solitary' and guided by providence, this is neither a contradiction nor the announcement of a new state in which, as Rogers puts it, divine intervention has given way to 'a world of human choice' (170). Adam and Eve are at this moment in the same *epistemological* position they were always in (although they are now less equipped to perform); they live under the aegis of a providence that is ultimately all encompassing but they are enjoined to work out their relationship to that same providence in halting, uncertain steps. From the vantage point of eternity all is settled and in place, but in the temporal crucible of creaturely life one experiences only provisionality and the continual hazarding of being. (On other surety none.)

That is what both sides in the heavenly battle are doing — hazarding their being, first by conceiving of their situation in relation to a figure who is either the one true deity or an opportunistic tyrant, and then by acting on, and within, their different conceptions. Each lives out a story it has in large part authored and each deepens its chosen story-line by assimilating to it the 'evidence' of whatever happens. Belsey is right, then, to say of *Paradise Lost* that it is 'two texts in one' (60), but her characterization of those texts is off the mark:

> . . . an absolutist poem, which struggles to justify the ways of an authoritarian God, and a humanist narrative, which recounts how human beings become free subjects, knowing the difference between good and evil in a world of choice.
>
> (60)

There is no 'absolutist poem'; if there were, interpretations both inside it (like Satan's) and outside it (like Belsey's) would be impossible. There is instead a poem that offers to already free subjects a choice between believing in (styling) a universe presided over by a generative and omniscient deity or a universe presided over by chance, indeterminacy, opportunistic self-creation and the accidents of time. Nor is the God of *Paradise Lost* absolutist in the sense Belsey intends. His claim (or the claim made by and for him in the poem) is to be absolute in the sense that he is in fact God the Creator and not merely a feudal lord with a big throne and superior weaponry; but he is a God who relaxes his absolute control and gives over to some of his creations both the responsibility for maintaining their connection to him and the possibility of severing it, a possibility with disastrous consequences to be sure, but consequences that follow necessarily if he is really God, which is exactly the question he leaves angels and men free to decide. And finally, both narratives are, roughly speaking, 'humanist' in that decisions freely made by limited creatures are at their centre. Being a free subject is not, as Belsey would have it, a result of the Fall; being a free subject is what makes the Fall possible and also makes possible its non-occurrence, although that second possibility is not realized, a fact that does not tell against the freedom of either Satan or the pre-lapsarian couple, but emphasizes its reality and therefore the reality of the consequences that being free entails. It is a question of whether freedom is total (as Satan declares it to be when he says, 'The mind is its own place, and in itself/ Can make a Heav'n of Hell, a Hell of Heav'n,' I. 254–5) or whether freedom is exercised in a world with a bottom line; if the latter is the case, as at least one of the poem's competing moralities insists, then acting as if the former were the case will get you into the unhappy situation Satan finds himself in, the situation of having made a bad choice that he must live with through all of eternity.

Now in this last sentence, I have tipped my hand and let you know (what you already knew) which story line I buy into. No apology, because one of the things guaranteed by the textuality of truth is that you will not be able to refrain from reading and writing some text or other. The condition of keeping all options (interpretive and others) open and settling on none is not available to temporal beings, whether it goes under the name of the 'willing suspension of disbelief' or 'indeterminacy' or 'undecidability.' If Satan and Adam and Eve build their worlds by assimilating its details to a prior understanding (not deduced but assumed) of the way things basically are (who, if anyone, is God, what, if anything, free will means, and so on), so do readers. Every time a reader sees a moment in the poem in this way rather than that way he or she is deciding (or re-deciding) what story to be a part of, and in *Paradise Lost*, this means deciding whether or not there is a story in the first place. As Steven Knapp observes, 'Every detail in the account of Adam and Eve's experience . . . is transformed if one supposes that the narrative provides a causal explanation of their Fall, instead of merely describing options between which they are genuinely free to choose.'[32]

Consider as an example an apparently small moment in Book II. Satan has just thrown himself into the 'wild Abyss' (II. 910) and begun his journey to the solar system and to the new home of his chosen prey when he hits a deep air pocket, a 'vast vacuity':

> . . . all unawares
> Flutt'ring his pennons vain plumb down he drops
> Ten thousand fadom deep, and to this hour
> Down had been falling, had not by ill chance
> The strong rebuff of some tumultuous cloud
> Instinct with Fire and Nitre hurried him
> As many miles aloft.

$$(\text{II. } 932–8)$$

The account of this little mini-adventure is more extended than its place in the story deserves and one might wonder why Milton includes it. The answer is he includes it in order to give readers the opportunity to make more of it than they should by connecting it strongly to the poem's central (and foreknown) event. It is open (and inviting) to a reader to think, well, if he hadn't been propelled upward by that tumultuous cloud, he would have never got to Eden, and he would have never tempted them, and they would never have eaten the apple, and everything would be still all right; in short, if he were still falling ('to this hour') they would not have fallen, and we would not ourselves be fallen now. A reader who falls in with this line of reasoning will have done more than make an inference from one point in the poem to another: he or she will have imagined (conceived) the universe as one in which the outcome of events turns on accidents — good or ill chance — rather than on the exercise of moral choice and moral choice *alone*.

I emphasize 'alone' because a reader who strays down this interpretive path might still assume that Adam and Eve have a choice, but think that the choice has been compromised or at least made more difficult by the circumstances surrounding it, circumstances like the malign presence in the garden of the world's first and best rhetorician disguised as a snake, the unhappy fact of the morning quarrel and the subsequent separation at just the wrong moment, the inadequacy of Eve's rational powers in the face of Satan's formidable logic, and so on. Putting any of these into a causal relationship to the Fall, however attenuated, will have the effect of altering the moral structure of Milton's fable and turning it from the story of 'man's disobedience' and its fruit to any of the other stories that have proved so attractive to so many readers — the story of free choice overwhelmed, the story of a freedom that was always compromised and already lost because weaknesses internal to their own psychologies (they can make mistakes, they can misconstrue meanings, they don't know what death is) made them incapable of maintaining it, the story of a freedom that could only be realized when the energies within them were released by an act of rebellion (this is the story Satan tells Eve and the one Belsey and others now tell us).

These stories are attractive because they either shift the

responsibility for the Fall to God (who could have seen to it that Satan was falling still, or kept him from escaping Hell in the first place, or provided Eden with a better security system, or made them more capable of seeing through talking snakes) or make the Fall into an heroic and virtuous act in relation to which God is either an accomplice or an irrelevancy. Moreover the inherent attractiveness of these stories to readers (and characters; see Adam's soliloquy at X. 720 in which every evasion of the poem's flinty moral is rehearsed well in advance of modern criticism) in whose interests it is to believe them is abetted by the innumerable opportunities the poem provides to construct them. The 'ill chance' of Satan's not continuing to fall at II. 935 is only one of those opportunities; they pop up whenever a detail emerges (Uriel's failure to see through Satan's tinsely disguise, Adam's decision to tell Eve to 'go' after he's just given knock down reasons why she should not) that can draw to itself some portion of the responsibility that properly belongs to Adam and Eve if they are in fact 'Sufficient to have stood' (III. 99); they pop up *whenever anything happens.*

I put it that way so as to underscore the difficulty, if not the impossibility, of what is required if the poem is to be read correctly, that is, not read at all. What is required is that you not move from the centre, from the single axis linking man's will and God's command, a command in relation to which anything and everything else is beside the point — the presence or absence of Satan, the couple together or the couple separated, Eden as a fortress or Eden as a place you can enter 'At one slight bound' (IV. 181), talking snakes, hallucinogenic apples, whatever. What is required is that you resist story, not just the story of God-as-cause or the story of the Fall-as-fortunate, but any story, any movement outward from a focus that would only be obscured by any elaboration of it. Of course, elaborating, and therefore losing, the focus is what every reader is tempted to do, a temptation whose appeal has its source in the very event — the falling of creatures away from God — we strive (the striving is our unavoidable error) to understand. I said earlier that the beginning of story is coincident with Satan's fall, with his simultaneous invention of himself 'fraught with envy' and of the narrative in which he is the central figure, a worthy being whose merit has been misrecognized and injured by a bad father. Before this story emerges in the instant of his self-conception, there was no narrative, no 'let's see what happens next' since what happened next was exactly what had always happened before (although it happened with pleasant variation). Now, after V. 659–66, there is story, and the possibility of more than one (ever the same) outcome; there are two, which suggests still another meaning to the key half-line 'and thought himself impair'd': he thought himself into the state of there being two rather than one, his story as well as (and as a rival to) God's non (because endlessly repetitive) story.

A second (or third or fourth) story, a story that exchanges God's *uni*verse for a world of chance and surprise, is always the vehicle of idolatry because it gives over to contingency the responsibility for determining meaning and thereby makes a deity (a controlling principle) of empirical circumstance. If you are either living out or reading a second story (a 'real' story in the terms established by Aristotelian aesthetics), you are always revising your sense of what is crucial and recalculating your choices. You ask questions like, what are the odds of success (measured by the accumulation of wealth or power) if I do this rather than that? or, what are the resources available to me (followers, money, arms) and are they sufficient to my desires and ambitions? or, do I risk more by acting or by falling back and waiting? These and related questions (the list would be very long, and one can find much of it in Machiavelli's *The Prince*) seek guidance in the momentary confluence of forces and events, and those who ask them must be continuously alert to changes in fortune lest they hazard an action (or an interpretation) based on false or out-of-date information. That is what I call plot-thinking; but in another kind of thinking, which we can call faith-thinking, the information you need is always available (to the will) and always the same — obedience to God is the primary obligation — and the only question you ask is how that obligation is to be discharged given the present shape of things. Joan Bennett puts the question precisely: ' . . . [I]n the flux of events, in the midst of history, what am I to do?'33 The person who asks this question is not waiting for the flux of events to provide an answer; rather he or she is trying to figure out (and it may not be easy; there is real difficulty here) how to insert a pre-given answer — I am to do the will of God — into this particular flux. In plot-thinking, the flux controls meaning and obligations are always changing; in faith-thinking meaning and obligation, always the same, control (give form to) the flux and tame its apparent heterogeneity. Plot-thinking — the possibility of surprise and radical newness — is what gives difference life; God's plot makes difference a variation on the order of the same.

(iv) THE POLITICS OF BEING AND POLITICAL CRITICISM

The distinction between plot-thinking and faith-thinking is the key to understanding another of the vexed issues in Milton studies, the question of Milton's politics. It is a question, first, of what name to give it (liberal,

revolutionary, republican, apocalyptic, egalitarian, radical),
and, second, of whether or not Milton really has a politics,
given his insistence on the primacy of conscience and the
inner light over external guides or pressures. This second is
a false question because it assumes incorrectly that an
emphasis on interiority, on the 'paradise within', is
antithetical to political action, whereas in fact the contrast
should be between two kinds of politics. The first I would
call the 'politics of short joy' (plot-thinking by another
name) after a moment in Book XI when Adam has once
again been corrected for an interpretive mistake, this time
for the mistake of thinking that the marriage rites between
the sons of Seth and the daughters of Cain portend 'hope/
Of peaceful days' (XI. 599-600). No, says Michael; this is
the union of inventive men 'unmindful of thir Maker' (611)
with a 'female Troop' that appears 'fair' but is 'empty of all
good' (613-16). All that will come of it finally is a deluge
sent by God. 'O pity and shame,' cries Adam who is
described as 'of short joy bereft' (629, 628). The joy is short
because it has been generalized from a particular set of facts
as if facts could by themselves deliver not only their own
meaning but the larger and more permanent meaning of
which they are the temporal instantiation. Mammon-like,
Adam allows the 'show' of happiness to stand in for the real
thing; he lacks the inner equilibrium, immune to the appeal
of surfaces, with which Jesus declares to Satan, 'I discern
thee other than thou seem'st' (*Paradise Regained*, I. 348).
Michael's rebuke is precise, 'Judge not what is best/ By
pleasure, though to Nature seeming meet' (603-4). That is,
don't go from appearances to general conclusions; if you
take that route, every new appearance will yield a new
conclusion; if you look to specific fact situations for future
guidance (if you plot-think), every shift in the configuration
of facts (empirically observed as independent items waiting

to be aggregated) will turn you in a different direction, and you will careen wildly from hope to despair to cynicism as Adam does for almost all of Book XI until he learns how to read, and therefore to be in, the world in another way.

What he learns is the politics of long joy (faith-thinking by another name), the politics that begins with the general conclusion — with a conviction of what the world is basically like and therefore what meanings it will always display — and then sees whatever emerges as an extension and confirmation of that conclusion. In the politics of long joy the meaning of things and events is foreknown (meanings are never new); what is not known is the specific and often surprising form this unvarying meaning will take. It is in the space. between the meanings phenomena must surely have and the meanings they at first appear to have that the work, at once interpretive and political, is done. The theorist of the politics of long joy is Augustine who offers this recipe for dealing with passages in scripture that seem at first glance to point the wrong moral or even to approve immoral activities: subject them to 'diligent scrutiny until an interpretation contributing to the reign of charity is produced.'34 If this is a way of reading God's book it is also a way of reading the book of the world: when events (like the Restoration) seem to belie God's goodness or impugn his justice, subject them to diligent scrutiny until you can see in them evidence of what they superficially deny.

Because the politics of long joy refuses to derive general conclusions from bundles of particulars, it is determinedly anti-empiricist. This does not mean, however, that those who practice it turn away from the empirical world; only that when they interact with the world they do so not in its own terms (as if it had or could have its own terms), but in the terms mandated by a prior orientation. That is why the

Jesus of *Paradise Regained* typically responds to Satan's temptations by disputing his characterization of the situation. 'You say that I have a choice between permitting you to return or denying you access, but that formulation assigns the power to me, whereas it is my conviction that the power belongs to God. It follows that to perform in either of the ways you suggest would be to slight, or at least appear to slight, God's prerogatives. Therefore "I bid not or forbid" (I. 495)'. Although this looks like a decision not to act, it is in fact a decision to act as knowledge of God's power and majesty dictates. Satan, like many of the poem's critics, never sees this and spends the entire four books attempting to provoke Jesus to 'do something' ('what dost thou in this world?'), not understanding that by rejecting *his* politics — the politics of empirical urgency; you must do this *now* or the opportunity will pass forever — the Son enacts a politics of his own. The heart of that politics is an already-in-place pledge of allegiance that refuses to be unsettled by fluctuations in the external world, but instead orders those fluctuations and makes them signify in a pre-chosen direction.

> Ashraf Rushdy makes the point concisely:
> Jesus' act of descent into himself is the most rigorously political act of all . . . On the other hand, the Satan who is diffused in time and space represents the most reactionary of all politics . . . we may say that Satan's world is ephemeral because its proponent has run out of time, while Jesus' world is integral because Jesus is in himself collected.[35]

It is the 'collected self' — the self whose will is resolutely focused, as Jesus's is when he says, 'me hung'ring . . . to do my Father's will' (II. 259) — that can act with confidence, not confidence in the outcome — outcomes are always unpredictable — but confidence in the integrity of its desire. Before you can do right, you must first be right; you must have your eye on the proper object, even if its lineaments are only dimly (through a glass darkly) seen. Centered on an interior disposition, the politics of long joy might also be called the politics of being, the politics which at the moment of choice does not calculate the odds of success or failure, but looks only to a master imperative that has been written on the fleshly tables of the heart. It is the politics of being that Milton practices when he says of the *Areopagitica* that it 'will be a certaine testimony, if not a Trophey.'[36] For the tract to be a trophy, it would have to succeed in its stated aim of persuading the Parliament to revoke its licensing act. That may or may not happen (it didn't), but either way the act of writing will have been efficacious as a testimony to the author's readiness to hazard himself, whatever the likelihood of victory or the degree of risk. Milton practices the politics of being again in 1659 when he speaks what he knows may well be (they were) 'the last words of our expiring libertie.'[37] Here the realization that what he is doing may be of no immediate effect is overwhelming, but nevertheless

> Thus much I should perhaps have said though I was sure I should have spoken only to trees and stones; and had none to cry to, but with the Prophet, *'O earth, earth, earth!'* to tell the very soil itself, what its perverse inhabitants are deaf to.
>
> (462–3)

It cannot be too much emphasized that the politics of being — the politics of long joy — is not quietism. Its relative indifference to outcomes is not an unconcern with the way things go in the world, but a recognition that the turns of fortune and history are not in man's control and that all one can be responsible for is the firmness of one's resolve. Milton certainly wanted the Parliament to revoke the licensing act, and he hoped (against hope) that the English people would recover themselves and not choose a captain back to Egypt, and he did all that he could to bring these things about even though he knew that results were the work of God and could be neither predicted nor engineered. In writing these tracts, he is exactly in the position he imagines for the warring angels, committed to action but aware that effects are not in his power: 'each on himself reli'd/ As only in his arm the moment lay/ Of victory' (VI. 238–40). That is, each acts as if the fate of the world is in his hands, while knowing full well that it isn't.

This is action politics-of-being style, action rooted in a determination of the will which because it did not arise from circumstances will not be shaken when circumstances disappoint hopes and expectations. Rumrich gets it precisely wrong when he says that if Abdiel's expectation of victory in his single combat with Satan had been disappointed, 'God would by rights have some explaining to do.'[38] In fact it can be argued that Abdiel's expectation *is* disappointed since, after reeling from the loyalist's 'noble stroke' (VI. 189), Satan gets up none the worse for wear and leaps back into the fray. But whatever one makes of Satan's quick recovery and even if the encounter had gone badly for Abdiel and it was he who had been hurled 'ten paces' back (VI. 193), he would not have asked God for an explanation any more than he asks for one when, after flying all night to warn his fellows, he arrives only to find 'Already known what he for news had thought/ To have reported' (VI. 19–21). Abdiel had reason to believe that his warning was needed just as he had reason to believe that in a physical contest with Satan he should be the victor since he had won 'in debate of Truth' (VI. 122); but his faith and commitment do not depend on the world's responsiveness to his reasoning, and we can assume that if he had been (in some physical sense) bested by Satan in combat he would have received this unexpected turn of events with the same equanimity he displays in the face of his already-warned-before-he-gets-there peers: 'gladly then he mixt' (VI. 21). The verse makes my point nicely by allowing 'gladly' to attach itself to 'reported' and 'mix't' indifferently; it doesn't care because he doesn't care; the fact that he flew all night for nothing doesn't bother him at all. And of course from his perspective (one he doesn't have to reach for but just lives) it wasn't for nothing since the value of what he did was not a function of its efficacy (it was not a trophy), but of its intention (it was a testimony). At this moment, when he loses the spotlight he never sought anyway, Abdiel dramatizes (in a most undramatic fashion) the poised relationship between the politics of being and outcomes in the world, for he is at once, and without contradiction, heavily invested in, yet unperturbed by, what happens. (Beings with less than angelic powers of concentration might require a bit of time to recover the unperturbed state after something momentarily upsets it; so the Lady in *Comus* who reports herself 'startled' but not astounded (209) by her loss first of her brothers and then of the solace of light.)

I have introduced the politics of being as if it were a new topic, but in fact it is a variation on the single theme this preface has been elaborating (monism is not only my subject, but a structural principle of my analysis). The politics of being is what follows from monism: if God is the essence of all things and there is no space he does not already occupy, the only arena in which a free agent can act effectively — act so as to make a difference, either good or bad — is the internal arena of the will. The politics of being is the politics of *first conceiving*, the initial decision to see the world this way rather than that and thereby either think yourself obedient or think yourself impaired. The politics of being is the politics of *styling*, of affirming the real with no support except for the support provided by the strength of your affirmation ('On other surety none'). The politics of being is the politics of *faith-thinking* which refuses the lure of plot-thinking, the lure of allowing the accidents of time and history to determine meanings and define obligations. And not only does the politics of being reach out to draw into itself every issue the poem raises, it reaches out to pass judgment on the varieties of criticism that vie for the right to say what the poem means. If the politics of being is really what Milton is urging and enacting in *Paradise Lost*, certain critical questions will be to the point and others beside it. Curiously enough (some might say paradoxically) among the questions rendered beside the point by the politics of being are questions of politics as they are usually posed in political criticism.

By 'political criticism' I mean criticism that thematizes politics because it believes that politics (rather than theology or aesthetics or gender or language) is what *Paradise Lost* is about. This belief has methodological consequences to which we shall turn in a moment, but first I should acknowledge that in recent years political criticism has meant something else (some would say something more) than thematizing politics; it means regarding both the poem and the act of describing it as political interventions in the life of a society: Milton intervenes in seventeenth-century society by writing this poem rather than another and by writing it this way (that is, in blank verse, in a mode thought to be exhausted, as part of a publishing economy by which he is appropriated); we intervene in twentieth-century society by writing about *Paradise Lost* (rather than about Native American literature or State Department memos) and by choosing to write about it in one way rather than some other (as an aesthetic object or a 'classic' rather than as an event in the production of bourgeois culture). The assumption is that each act, whether the supposedly primary one of literary creation or the supposedly secondary one of literary interpretation, is at base political, and the conclusion is that if we want to get at what either means we have to ask self-consciously political questions rather than merely literary questions. (Indeed, the assumption that there could be a merely literary question is rejected by this kind of political criticism which sees it as an idealizing strategy employed by the guardians of the status quo.)

I find this second (its proponents would say deeper) version of political criticism both incoherent and unprofitable. My reasons are given at length in *Professional Correctness*39 but they boil down to saying (1) that political criticism of the interventionary kind, of the kind that seeks actively to alter material conditions in the world, cannot possibly succeed if it remains criticism — if its questions and answers will be recognized as appropriate by those who have been trained in the discipline — and that (2) if it does succeed it will either be an accidental success (Bill Clinton just happened to pick up your book on the way to Martha's Vineyard) or a success that follows from having abandoned criticism for politics pure and (not so) simple. Criticism that really is criticism cannot succeed politically because there are no regular routes by which its productions reach the ears and eyes of legislators, governors, CEOs, newspaper editors, and so on. Criticism that succeeds politically or has a realistic chance of doing so will not really be criticism because it will have exchanged one imperative — how can I give the best account of this poem? — for another — what account can I give of this poem that will best further the cause of welfare reform, or term limits, or environmental regulation? The easy riposte is that if enough critics ask the second question and reject the first as hopelessly naive, literary criticism will be what they do. My easy reply is that while they might continue to call what they do literary criticism, the answers they give to their preferred question will not illuminate the literary object but make it disappear in a description that looks right past its distinctive form.

These are provocative and controversial assertions that require more than a paragraph and probably more than a book to defend. I present them here only to indicate, however briefly, why in my view political criticism of the more ambitious kind is not a contender for the prize of saying what *Paradise Lost* really means. That leaves political criticism that thematizes politics and recommends (this is the methodological consequence I promised earlier) that if we want to find out what is going on in *Paradise Lost*, we should begin by steeping ourselves in the records of parliamentary debates, royal proclamations, the literature of popular protest, diplomatic communiques, and so on. That kind of criticism, however, will fall afoul of the politics of being (I am aware of the possibility of saying 'so much the worse for the politics of being') which will condemn it as an instance of the mistake it refuses to make, the mistake of thinking that you can get to the truth of a project by attending to the bits and pieces it makes use of. The politics of being tells us that you don't go to historical records to find out what Milton is up to; you already know (by some process of thought that cannot be charted or formalized) what he is up to because you know what kind of person he is (as Abdiel already knows what kind of person God is), and then you quarry historical records for further evidence of what you already know.

The two methods and the differences between them are

the great subject of *Paradise Regained*, a poem occupied at its centre by a being perfectly settled in himself, and at its margins by someone busily trying to determine the identity of that settled being by mining the trails and entrails of empirical evidence. In the course of his frantic fact-mongering Satan is sometimes an historian, sometimes a politician, and always an experimental scientist. He dutifully records every moment of the Son's life ('. . . seldom have I ceas'd to eye/ Thy infancy, thy childhood and thy youth,/ Thy manhood,' IV. 507–9), he offers means to achieve what he understands as the political goal of establishing a kingdom ('Great acts require great means of enterprise,' II. 412) and he subjects the Son to a series of tests (or, as he sometimes calls them, 'tastings') designed to reveal the deep truth that will make certain sense of surface phenomena like the dove that descended on his head ('what e'er it meant,' I. 83). Satan thinks that if he gathers enough data, it will eliminate his uncertainty as to the nature of his adversary. What he doesn't see (if he did he wouldn't be Satan) but repeatedly demonstrates is that if you begin with uncertainty — without an already in place sense of what the truth is and where evidence of it might be found — every new piece of information will be the vehicle (and extension) of that uncertainty which is only increased by the efforts to remove it. That is why even though Satan has turned a 'nearer view/ And narrower Scrutiny' (IV. 514–15) on the Son, even though he has 'collected' and continued to collect his 'best conjectures' (IV. 524) — note how Baconian the language is here — even though he has dogged the Son's 'footsteps' (IV. 522) and devised ingenious devices to 'try' and 'sift' him (532), 'Son of God to me is yet in doubt' (501). At the desperate end he is no closer to knowing what that phrase means than he is to knowing the meaning of the descending dove, and he never will be so long as he relies upon his 'collections' to deliver a truth that cannot be forced to show itself by mousetrap-like devices, a truth that does not arise from evidence, but, once affirmed, makes evidence of everything (as it does for Mary and the Apostles who achieve certainty on the basis of the same evidence Satan finds eternally inadequate).

The conclusion is one you will have seen coming: historical/political criticism commits the Satanic fallacy of thinking that basic interpretive questions can be settled by finding the right (self-interpreting) materials. The result is the spectacle to be observed in some corners of Milton studies: hitherto unexamined documents and stores of information are brandished aloft and declared to be the key to understanding what Milton is about; for a while critics flock to this new site of knowledge until news of an even more glittering archival discovery sends the seekers of material truth (or the truth of materials) scurrying in another direction. The scene is busy and full of movement (and publications), but its randomness and openness to surprise is finally (at least to me) dispiriting (pun intended) in just the way Satan's never-ending search for the perfect 'method' (IV. 540) is dispiriting; it goes everywhere and nowhere. I reject this kind of political criticism (as practiced, for example, by Michael Wilding and David Norbrook) because Milton rejects it, because in its positivism it gets the relationship between particulars and generals backwards.

There is another kind of historical/political criticism that begins not with a naive faith in its materials but with a thesis about them and then organizes bodies of information in ways guided by that thesis. When historical/political criticism is practiced in this manner, I have no *methodological* objection to it since the readings it yields are grounded in a coherent procedure and do not emerge as haphazard observations, randomly tied to discretely noted facts. What I might object to in this more self-aware form of historicism, in which the readings and the organization of the historical materials emerge together, is the thesis that links them. My objection would be, simply, that the thesis is wrong. That is my objection to John Rogers' *The Matter of Revolution*. Rogers links Milton to what he calls 'the vitalist movement' — a mid-century interval in which a doctrine of animist materialism, of matter instinct with life and motion, moves, in a manner befitting the concept, from medical science to philosophy to theology to politics. The argument is that because vitalism posits a matter that is either self-generating or self-sustaining once the higher power that impregnates it has withdrawn, it is compatible with, and a source of, an emerging liberalism in which 'the abstract principles of moral choice, independent action, and free association' (13) displace the interventionary eruptions into history 'of an arbitrary and unrestricted God' (6). *Paradise Lost* is read by Rogers both as a record of this passage from one political/moral vision to another and as an instance of the struggle of the new to free itself from the shadow and shackles of the old. Milton's best instincts, says Rogers, find expression in those places where 'a natural realm almost secular in its autonomy' (154) is offered as a political ideal. But unfortunately the voice of 'Milton the theologian' is too often heard, and in the final books 'a disappointing orthodox faith' with the 'arbitrary determinations of a capricious God' (160) at its centre 'nearly overwhelms the poem's attempt to engender a discourse of liberal individualism' (160).

Anyone who has got this far will know that I can only read this as a learned and lively (vital) version of Satan's 'we style it the strife of glory'. Rogers styles it the strife and emergence of liberalism, but the intent and effect is the same: to substitute for a radical dependence on the one source of being a radical assertion of self-creation. Moreover, their strategies are complementary. Satan characterizes God as capricious and arbitrary so that the obligation to obey him can be declared to have no basis. Rogers imagines God (in Wordsworthian fashion) as the great vitalist spirit that rolls through all things so that he can conclude that in the later books Milton is worshipping the wrong God, where by wrong he means a God hostile to the emergence of 'autonomous, independent agents' (160) as required by Jürgen Habermas. (Not my idea of an alternative deity.)

I need hardly say that in my view this gets everything backward. 'Capricious' is hardly the word for a contractarian God who cedes to his creations the responsibility for keeping faith with him and hews himself to a prior specification of rewards and punishment (although ultimately he manages to avoid if not evade the strict severity of his own letter). Liberal individualism can hardly be the goal of the Milton who consistently defined liberty as the right kind of bondage, as the capacity to 'approve the best, and follow [adhere to] what I approve' (VIII. 611). The assertion of a God who is really God is not at odds with human choice and its incredibly rich history in 'the Race of time' (XII. 554); rather, it is his absolute power that at once makes available the space of human choice and renders it meaningful by providing it with a centre.

In making these points, I am in danger of writing this preface all over again, but I shall resist the temptation. Suffice it to say that while Rogers has the right idea of how to bring literary and historical materials together, the direction in which he proceeds seems to me wrong because he begins (and wants to end) with the wrong picture of what Milton is about. (He wants to make Milton into a seventeenth-century John Rawls.) When a critic both knows what responsible historical criticism is and deploys it in the service of a thesis I agree with, my gratitude for his or her historical labours extends to the interpretive work that history is made to do. Thus I always pay close attention to what Joan Bennett or Georgia Christopher have to tell me because their Milton is in large outline my Milton, a man '[u]tterly committed to building a holy society,'[40] who finds both the resources and justification for his efforts not in worldly goods and aims, but in the internal strength of a faith that is itself an 'incipient history'[41] and a powerful politics. Since this is the thesis I already believe, I am more than open to Bennett's and Christopher's elaboration or refinement of it, and I take myself to be extending their project (not necessarily in a way they would approve) in my unfolding of the politics of being.

You will probably have noticed that in the course of defending *Surprised by Sin*, I have repeated the gesture that most infuriated some of its readers. I have turned objectors into devils and replied to their points by hitting them over the head with mine. Thus a criticism that puts its faith in empirical research is condemned because it flies in the face of the politics of being (as if the politics of being were an established fact and not a disputable thesis), which is also to condemn it for reversing the priority of first conceptions over the realm of experience, which is also to condemn it for surrendering to plot-thinking, which is also to condemn it for being idolatrous in that it looks for meaning and value in all the wrong places. The circularity of this is obvious but it is not one for which I apologize since circularity, of a deep not meretricious kind, is what I attribute to Milton's *universe* where, as I say in the first appendix to *Surprised by Sin*, all virtues are one virtue — acknowledgement of and obedience to God — and all errors one error — falling away from the worship of God to the worship of secondary forms. Literary criticism does not stand outside this vast circularity and it should be no surprise that my judgment on what critics say is inseparable from, and follows predictably from, my judgment of what Milton is (always) saying. This does not mean that my arguments are invulnerable to objections, only that objections to a detail here and there and not to an entire structure of thought will have been anticipated by that structure and discounted in advance. Only objections as massive (and some would say suffocating) as the structure itself will cause it to tremble, and I am sure you will forgive me if I confess myself unable to think of any.

What I can think of is a way of characterizing my reading of the poem that finds a place (of sorts) for what it seems to exclude or sell short, the force of difference. If, as I assert, so much effort is spent by God, by Milton, and by me clamping down on energies seeking to break free, does not that suggest something about the reality of those energies and the defensiveness of those efforts? Does not the very vigour with which the task of vigilance is performed tell us there must be something to be vigilant against? Well, yes and no. The energies (of both characters and readers) are real, but rather than giving the lie to the authority of God, they are testimony to his generosity, to the freedom he accords creatures who can then return to him, if they choose, the 'bad recompense' (IX. 994–5) of their disobedience. The fact that those who seek to escape God's sphere (to impair him) are repeatedly reclaimed and brought back within it (they never really left) does not mean that the act of containment is either illegitimate or unsuccessful; it means only that the structure of the poem and the structure of the universe is such that all free creatures — angels, men, women, readers — have many more ways to go wrong than go right, and that when they do go wrong, the safety net of a fortunate universe, presided over by a God who can bring good out of evil, will always be there to catch them whether they welcome it or not.

NOTES

1 C. S. Lewis, *A Preface to Paradise Lost* (London: Oxford University Press, 1942), p. 70.
2 William Blake, 'The Marriage of Heaven & Hell,' in *Blake's Complete Writings*, ed. Geoffrey Keynes (London: Oxford University Press, 1972), p. 150.
3 Joseph Anthony Wittreich, Jr, *The Romantics on Milton* (London: Case Western Reserve University, 1970), p. 537.
4 John Milton: *Areopagitica*, in *The Complete Prose Works of John Milton*, vol. II, ed. Ernest Sirluck (New Haven: Yale University Press, 1959), p. 515.
5 Bernard Bergonzi in *The Living Milton*, ed. Frank Kermode (London: Routledge, 1960), p. 174.
6 *Complete Prose Works*, II, ed. Ernest Sirluck, p. 642.
7 William Kerrigan, *The Sacred Complex* (Cambridge, Mass: Harvard University Press, 1983), pp. 98-9.
8 John Rumrich, 'Uninventing Milton', *Modern Philology* 87, no. 3 (1990), p. 259.
9 Bill Readings, 'On the New Forcers of Conscience: Milton's Critics', *Oxford Literary Review* 7, nos. 1 and 2 (1985): p. 140.
10 John Rumrich, *Milton Unbound* (Cambridge: Cambridge University Press, 1996), p. 4.
11 Readings, 'New Forcers,' p. 142.
12 Rumrich, 'Uninventing Milton,' p. 255-7.
13 Linda Gregerson, *The Reformation of the Subject* (Cambridge: Cambridge University Press, 1995), p. 247.
14 Milton, *The Christian Doctrine*, trans. John Carey, *Complete Prose Works of John Milton*, VI, 1973, p. 307. For a careful and detailed study of monism and materialism in the seventeenth century see Stephen M. Fallon, *Milton Among the Philosophers*

(Ithica and London: Cornell University Press, 1991).

15 Rumrich, 'Uninventing Milton,' p. 259.

16 Regina Schwartz, *Remembering and Repeating* (Cambridge: Cambridge University Press, 1988), p. 19.

17 Catherine Belsey, *John Milton: Language, Gender, Power* (Oxford: Oxford University Press, 1988), p. 79.

18 Milton, *Apology* in *Complete Prose Works*, I, ed. Don M. Wolfe, p. 941.

19 Milton, *Areopagitica* in *Complete Prose Works*, II, p. 527.

20 Christopher Ricks, *Milton's Grand Style* (Oxford: Oxford University Press, 1964), p. 99.

21 Dennis Danielson, *Milton's Good God* (Cambridge: Cambridge University Press, 1982), p. 146. Steven Knapp offers a powerful objection to this account of free will when he asks 'if the agent, in the moment of decision, is causally disconnected from his/her prior mental states, then what exactly makes the self that performs the act identical to the self that already existed before the decision occurred' (*Literary Interest*, Cambridge, Mass.: Harvard University Press, 1993, pp. 19-20). That is, in what sense can a discontinuous self — one unaffected by past experiences — be said to *be* a self? George Herbert worries over the same problem from the other direction. It is his project to *un*weave or *un*build his life so that its fragmentary condition will offer no resistance to God's will. What blocks him is the inescapably temporal nature of his self-understanding. Both Herbert and Milton wish to escape from continuity for opposite reasons. One wants to be wholly taken over, the other to be wholly free. Knapp's analysis suggests that both states are impossible (something Herbert at least knows) and that Milton's libertarian account of the fall is rationally incoherent. As he observes, the only way out of this dilemma is to declare that the thesis of a will disconnected from its own history is in the poem a point of doctrine not to be inquired into, a position he correctly attributes to me.

22 John Rogers, *The Matter of Revolution* (Ithaca: Cornell University Press, 1996).

23 Marshall Grossman, *Authors to Themselves* (Cambridge: Cambridge University Press, 1987), p. 8.

24 Milton, *Doctrine and Discipline of Divorce* in *Complete Prose*

Works, II, p. 316.

25 Milton, *Christian Doctrine* in *Complete Prose Works*, VI, p. 177.

26 William Kolbrener, *Milton's Warring Angels: A Study of Critical Engagements* (Cambridge: Cambridge University Press, 1997), pp. 145, 157.

27 Michael Lieb, 'Two of Far Nobler Shape: Reading the Paradisal Text,' in *Literary Milton: Text, Pretext, Context*, eds. Diana Benet and Michael Lieb (Pittsburgh: Duquesne University Press, 1994), p. 132.

28 Belsey, *Milton*, p. 84.

29 Lucy Newlyn, *Paradise Lost and the Romantic Reader* (Oxford: Oxford University Press, 1993), p. 66.

30 Milton, *Complete Prose Works*, II, p. 563.

31 Rogers, *The Matter of Revolution*, p. 157.

32 Knapp, *Literary Interest*, p. 16.

33 Joan Bennett, *Reviving Liberty* (Cambridge, Mass.: Harvard University Press, 1989), p. 162.

34 Augustine, *On Christian Doctrine*, ed. and trans. D. W. Robertson, Jr (New York and Indianapolis: Bobs Merrill, 1958), p. 93.

35 Ashraf Rushdy, *The Empty Garden* (Pittsburgh: University of Pittsburgh Press, 1992), p. 268.

36 Milton, *Complete Prose Works*, II, p. 487.

37 Milton, *The Ready and Easy Way.* in *Complete Prose Works*, VII, ed. Robert W. Akers, pp. 462-3. See the discussion of this and other passages in Kol-brener, *Milton's Warring Angels*, op. cit. pp. 28–49. Kol-brener articulates a position close to mine when he speaks of 'Milton's indifference to *mere* politics' (39) and notes that Milton 'elaborates a political program . . . while manifesting a profound distrust of politics' (35).

38 Rumrich, 'Uninventing Milton,' p. 263.

39 Stanley Fish, *Professional Correctness* (Oxford and New York: Oxford University Press, 1995).

40 Bennett, *Reviving Liberty*, p. 185.

41 Georgia Christopher, *Milton and the Science of the Saints* (Princeton, N.J.: Princeton University Press, 1982), p. 29.

Preface

There are currently two strains in criticism of *Paradise Lost*, one concerned with providing a complete reading of the poem (in so far as that is possible), the other emphasizing a single aspect of it, or a single tradition in the light of which the whole can be better understood. Somewhat uneasily this book attempts to participate in both strains. My subject is Milton's reader, and my thesis, simply, that the uniqueness of the poem's theme — man's first disobedience and the fruit thereof — results in the reader's being simultaneously a participant in the action and a critic of his own performance. I believe Milton's intention to differ little from that of so many devotional writers, 'to discover to us our miserable and wretched estate through corruption of nature' and to 'shew how a man may come to a holy reformation and so happily recover himself'. (Richard Bernard, *The Isle of Man*.) In the course of the poem, I shall argue, the reader

(1) is confronted with evidence of his corruption and becomes aware of his inability to respond adequately to spiritual conceptions, and

(2) is asked to refine his perceptions so that his understanding will be once more proportionable to truth the object of it.

The following chapters, then, will explore two patterns — the reader's humiliation and his education — and they will make the point that the success of the second depends on the quality of his response to the first. Whenever possible, the crises of the reading experience will be related to the crisis at the centre of the narrative, the fall of Adam and Eve.

My debts and obligations are many. I owe much to the

Miltonists whose opinions are recorded in the text. They are the best of Milton's readers. I have been most influenced (as far as I am aware) by the work of Joseph Summers and A. J. A. Waldock, although it can be fairly said that everyone who has written on the poem since 1940 has improved my understanding of it. I have benefited greatly from the advice and counsel of George A. Starr and A. E. Dyson. I have learned much from Mr. Starr's excellent study, *Defoe and Spiritual Autobiography* (Princeton, 1965), which I would cite to support the tenability of my general position. Mr. Dyson provided encouragement, moral and material, when it was most needed. At different times I have profited from the cogent criticisms of Paul Alpers, John Coolidge, Norman Rabkin, Christopher Ricks, and Wayne Shumaker. Gilbert Robinson and Laurence Jacobs, my research assistants, know how much of their labours have been incorporated here.

The students to whom this book is dedicated have contributed materially to it. I have made use of the insights and suggestions of Edward Pechter, Gilbert Robinson, Roger Swearingen and Beatrice Weisner. Others are no doubt represented, but unacknowledged. No measure of the debt to my wife is possible: for in addition to the laborious tasks of typing, editing, and proof-reading, she has borne the burden of the crises of confidence suffered daily by the author.

The writing of this book was made possible by two grants-in-aid; one in the form of a Humanities Research Professorship awarded by the University of California at Berkeley, and the other a fellowship from the American Council of Learned Societies.

Portions of Chapters 1, 2, and 4 have appeared in *The Critical Quarterly* and *The Southern Review* (Australia). I am grateful for permission to reprint.

All citations to the poems of Milton are to *John Milton: Complete Poems and Major Prose*, ed. Merritt Y. Hughes (New York, 1957).

S. E. F.

London
September 1966

1 Not so much a Teaching as an Intangling[1]

> The right thing in speaking really is that we should be satisfied not to annoy our hearers, without trying to delight them: we ought in fairness to fight our case with no help beyond the bare facts: nothing, therefore, should matter except the proof of those facts. Still, as has been said, other things affect the result considerably, owing to the defects of our hearers.   ARISTOTLE, *Rhetoric*

(i) THE DEFECTS OF OUR HEARERS

I would like to suggest something about *Paradise Lost* that is not new except for the literalness with which the point will be made : (1) the poem's centre of reference is its reader who is also its subject; (2) Milton's purpose is to educate the reader to an awareness of his position and responsibilities as a fallen man, and to a sense of the distance which separates him from the innocence once his; (3) Milton's method is to re-create in the mind of the reader (which is, finally, the poem's scene) the drama of the Fall, to make him fall again exactly as Adam did and with Adam's troubled clarity, that is to say, 'not deceived'. In a limited sense few would deny the truth of my first two statements ; Milton's concern with the ethical imperatives of political and social behaviour would hardly allow him to write an epic which did not attempt to give his audience a basis for moral action ; but I do not think the third has been accepted in the way that I intend it.

[1] This chapter incorporates, with some additions, two articles published in the Summer and Autumn issues of *The Critical Quarterly* (1965).

A. J. A. Waldock, one of many sensitive readers who have
confronted the poem since 1940, writes : '*Paradise Lost* is an
epic poem of singularly hard and definite outline, expressing
itself (or so at least would be our first impressions) with
unmistakable clarity and point.'[1] In the course of his book
Waldock expands the reservation indicated by his parenthesis into a reading which predicates a disparity between
Milton's intention and his performance :

> In a sense Milton's central theme denied him the full expression
> of his deepest interests. It was likely, then, that as his really deep
> interests could not find outlet in his poem in the right way they
> might find outlet in the wrong way. And to a certain extent they
> do; they find vents and safety-valves often in inopportune places.
> Adam cannot give Milton much scope to express what he really
> feels about life; but Satan is there, Satan gives him scope. And
> the result is that the balance is somewhat disturbed; pressures are

[1] *Paradise Lost and its Critics* (Cambridge, 1947), p. 15. I consider
Waldock's book to be the most forthright statement of an anti-Miltonism
that can be found in the criticism of Leavis and Eliot, and, more recently, of
Empson, R. J. Zwi Werblowsky, H. R. Swardson and John Peter. Bernard
Bergonzi concludes his analysis of Waldock by saying, 'no attempt has been
made to defend the poem in the same detailed and specific manner in which it
has been attacked' (*The Living Milton*, ed. Frank Kermode, London, 1960,
p. 171). This essay is such an attempt. Bergonzi goes on to assert that 'a
successful answer to Waldock would have to show that narrative structure of
Paradise Lost does possess the kind of coherence and psychological plausibility
that we have come to expect from the novel. Again there can be no doubt that
it does not' (p. 174). I shall argue that the coherence and psychological
plausibility of the poem are to be found in the relationship between its effects
and the mind of its reader. To some extent my reading has been anticipated
by Joseph Summers in his brilliant study, *The Muse's Method* (Harvard, 1962).
See especially pp. 30–31: 'Milton anticipated ... the technique of the
"guilty reader".... The readers as well as the characters have been involved
in the evil and have been forced to recognize and to judge their involvement.'
See also Anne Ferry's *Milton's Epic Voice: The Narrator in Paradise Lost*
(Harvard, 1963), pp. 44–66: 'We are meant to remember that the events of
the poem have already occurred ... and that it is because of what happens in
the poem, because we and all men were corrupted by the Fall, that we stand

set up that are at times disquieting, that seem to threaten more than once, indeed, the equilibrium of the poem.[1]

The 'unconscious meaning' portion of Waldock's thesis is, I think, as wrong as his description of the reading experience as 'disquieting' is right. If we transfer the emphasis from Milton's interests and intentions which are available to us only from a distance, to our responses which are available directly, the disparity between intention and execution becomes a disparity between reader expectation and reading experience; and the resulting 'pressures' can be seen as part of an intelligible pattern. In this way we are led to consider our own experience as a part of the poem's subject.

By 'hard and definite outline' I take Waldock to mean the sense of continuity and direction evoked by the simultaneous introduction of the epic tradition and Christian myth. The 'definiteness' of a genre classification leads the reader to expect a series of formal stimuli — martial encounters, complex similes, an epic voice — to which his response is more or less automatic; the hardness of the Christian myth predetermines his sympathies; the union of the two allows the assumption of a comfortable reading experience in which conveniently labelled protagonists act out rather

in need of a guide to correct our reading of it. The narrative voice is our guide' (p. 47). Finally I refer the reader to Douglas Knight's excellent article, 'The Dramatic Center of *Paradise Lost*', *South Atlantic Quarterly* (1964), pp. 44–59, which reached me only after this manuscript was substantially completed. Mr. Knight argues, as I do, for the analytic nature of the reading experience. Our emphases are different (he focuses mainly on the similes) but our general conclusions accord perfectly: 'The poem's material and structure fuse as they put pressure on the reader to assess and estimate the place where he is to stand; Adam and Eve can almost be said to dramatize for him a mode of action which is his own if he reads the poem properly. For *Paradise Lost* is a work of art whose full achievement is one of mediation and interactivity among three things: a way of reading the poem, an estimate of it as a whole work, and a reader's proper conduct of his life' (pp. 56–57).

[1] *Paradise Lost and its Critics*, p. 24.

simple roles in a succession of familiar situations. The reader is prepared to hiss the devil off the stage and applaud the pronouncements of a partisan and somewhat human deity who is not unlike Tasso's 'il Padre eterno'. But of course this is not the case; no sensitive reading of *Paradise Lost* tallies with these expectations, and it is my contention that Milton ostentatiously calls them up in order to provide his reader with the shock of their disappointment. This is not to say merely that Milton communicates a part of his meaning by a calculated departure from convention; every poet does that; but that Milton consciously wants to worry his reader, to force him to doubt the correctness of his responses, and to bring him to the realization that his inability to read the poem with any confidence in his own perception is its focus.

Milton's programme of reader harassment begins in the opening lines; the reader, however, may not be aware of it until line 84 when Satan speaks for the first time. The speech is a powerful one, moving smoothly from the *exclamatio* of 'But O how fall'n' (84) to the regret and apparent logic of 'till then who knew / The force of those dire Arms' (93–94), the determination of 'courage never to submit or yield' (108) and the grand defiance of 'Irreconcilable to our grand Foe, / Who now triumphs, and in th' excess of joy / Sole reigning holds the Tyranny of Heav'n' (122–124). This is our first view of Satan and the impression given, reinforced by a succession of speeches in Book 1, is described by Waldock: 'fortitude in adversity, enormous endurance, a certain splendid recklessness, remarkable powers of rising to an occasion, extraordinary qualities of leadership (shown not least in his salutary taunts)'.[1] But in each case Milton follows the voice of Satan with a comment which complicates, and according to some, falsifies, our reaction to it:

[1] Ibid., p. 77.

So spake th' Apostate Angel, though in pain,
Vaunting aloud, but rackt with deep despair.

(125–6)

Waldock's indignation at this authorial intrusion is in-
structive :

> If one observes what is happening one sees that there is hardly a
> great speech of Satan's that Milton is not at pains to correct, to
> damp down and neutralize. He will put some glorious thing in
> Satan's mouth, then, anxious about the effect of it, will pull us
> gently by the sleeve, saying (for this is what it amounts to): 'Do
> not be carried away by this fellow: he *sounds* splendid, but take my
> word for it. . . .' Has there been much despair in what we have
> just been listening to? The speech would almost seem to be in-
> compatible with that. To accept Milton's comment here . . . as
> if it had a validity equal to that of the speech itself is surely very
> naïve critical procedure . . . in any work of imaginative literature
> at all it is the demonstration, by the very nature of the case, that
> has the higher validity; an allegation can possess no comparable
> authority. Of course they should agree; but if they do not then
> the demonstration must carry the day.   (pp. 77–78)

There are several assumptions here :

(1) There is a disparity between our response to the
speech and the epic voice's evaluation of it.
(2) Ideally, there should be no disparity.
(3) Milton's intention is to correct *his* error.
(4) He wants us to discount the effect of the speech
through a kind of mathematical cancellation.
(5) The question of relative authority is purely an
aesthetic one. That is, the reader is obliged to hearken
to the most dramatically persuasive of any conflicting
voices.

Of these I can assent only to the first. The comment of the
epic voice unsettles the reader, who sees in it at least a partial
challenge to his own assessment of the speech. The implica-

tion is that there is more (or less) here than has met the ear ; and since the only ear available is the reader's, the further implication is that he has failed in some way to evaluate properly what he has heard. One must begin by admitting with Waldock the impressiveness of the speech, if only as a *performance* that commands attention as would any forensic *tour de force* ; and attention on that level involves a corresponding inattention on others. It is not enough to analyse, as Lewis and others have, the speciousness of Satan's rhetoric. It is the nature of sophistry to lull the reasoning process ; logic is a safeguard against a rhetorical effect only after the effect has been noted. The deep distrust, even fear, of verbal manipulation in the seventeenth century is a recognition of the fact that there is no adequate defence against eloquence at the moment of impact. (The appeal of rhetoric was traditionally associated with the weakness of the fallen intellect — the defect of our hearers ; its fine phrases flatter the desires of the cupidinous self and perpetuate the disorder which has reigned in the soul since the Fall.)[1] In other words one can analyse the process of deception

[1] The tradition begins with Plato's opposition of rhetoric to dialectic. Socrates' interlocutors *discover* the truth for themselves, when, in response to his searching questions, they are led to examine their opinions and, perhaps, to refute them. The rhetorician, on the other hand, creates a situation in which his auditors have no choice but to accept the beliefs he urges on them. In *The Testimony of the President, Professors, Tutors, and Hebrew Instructor of Harvard College in Cambridge, Against the Reverend Mr. George Whitefield, And his Conduct* (Boston, 1744), Whitefield is censured because of 'his power to raise the People to any Degree of Warmth he pleases, whereby they stand ready to receive almost any Doctrine he is pleased to broach ...' (p. 13). The danger lies in the weakness of the fallen intellect which is more likely to be swayed by appearances than by the naked presentation of the truth. In recognition of this danger, the Puritan preacher first sets out the points of doctrine in the form of a Ramist 'proof' before turning in the 'uses' to the figures of exhortation. 'For a minister to lure men to an emotional reception of the creed before their imaginations had conceived it, before their intellects were convinced of it and their wills had deliberately chosen to live by it, was

fully as immoral as openly to persuade them to wrong doing' (Perry Miller, *The New England Mind: The Seventeenth Century*, Beacon Press Edition, Boston, 1961, p. 308). A similar distrust of rhetoric manifests itself in the writings of the Baconian empiricists. Figurative language is said to be useless for the description of experiments or the formulation of conclusions, and rhetorical appeals are disdained because they dull intellects which should be alertly analytic. Bacon protests against the delivery (presentation) of knowledge 'in such form as may be best believed, and not as may be best examined' and advises instead 'the method of the mathematiques' (*Selected Writings*, ed. H. G. Dick, New York, 1955, p. 304). To Hobbes geometry is 'the only science that it has pleased God hitherto to bestow on mankind', a science which, as Aristotle said, no one uses fine language in teaching (*Leviathan*, ed. H. W. Schneider, New York, 1958, p. 41). Sprat believes that eloquence, 'this vicious volubility of *Tongue*' should be 'banish'd out of all *civil Societies*' because the ornaments of speaking 'are in open defiance against *Reason*' and hold too much correspondence with the passions, giving the mind 'a motion too changeable, and bewitching, to consist with *right practice*' (*The History of the Royal Society of London*, 1667, p. 111). (In Chapter 3 I shall have occasion to examine the philosophical-linguistic objections to rhetoric at greater length.) Complementing the fear of rhetoric is a faith in the safeguards provided by the use of analytical method. Where one short-circuits the rational and panders to the emotions, the other speaks directly to the reason. Where one compels assent without allowing due deliberation, the other encourages the auditor or reader to examine the progress of a composition at every point, whether it be a poem, a sermon, or the report of an experiment. 'Now my plan', announces Bacon, 'is to proceed regularly and gradually from one axiom to another.' However complex the experiment, he proposes to 'subjoin a clear account of the manner in which I made it; that men knowing exactly how each point was made out, may see whether there be any error connected with it' (*Preface to the Great Instauration*, in *The English Philosophers From Bacon to Mill*, ed. E. A. Burtt, New York, 1939, p. 21). Puritan preachers dispose their texts with the same care so that their auditors can receive the discourse according to the manner of its composition. The focus is always on the mind, which must be led, step by step, and with a consciousness of an answering obligation, to a clear understanding of conceptual content. (Again we see the similarity to Platonic dialectic.) In writing *Paradise Lost*, then, Milton is able to draw upon a tradition of didacticism which finds its expression in a distrust of the affective and an insistence on the intellectual involvement of the listener-pupil; in addition he could rely on his readers to associate logic and the capacity for logical reasoning with the godly instinct in man, and the passions, to which rhetoric appeals, with his carnal instincts.

only after it is successful. The reader who is stopped short by Milton's rebuke (for so it is) will, perhaps, retrace his steps and note more carefully the inconsistency of a Tyranny that involves an excess of joy, the perversity of 'study of revenge, immortal hate' (a line that had slipped past him sandwiched respectably between will and courage), the sophistry of the transfer of power from the 'Potent Victor' of 95 to the 'Fate' of 116, and the irony, in the larger picture, of 'that were *low* indeed' and 'in *foresight* much advanc't'. The fit reader Milton has in mind would go further and recognize in Satan's finest moment — 'And courage never to submit or yield' — an almost literal translation of *Georgic* IV. 84, 'usque adeo obnixi non cedere'. Virgil's 'praise' is for his bees whose heroic posturing is presented in terms that are at least ambiguous :

> ipsi per medias acies insignibus alis
> ingentes animos angusto in pectore versant,
> usque adeo obnixi non cedere, dum gravis aut hos
> aut hos versa fuga victor dare terga subegit.
> hi motus animorum atque haec certamina tanta
> pulveris exigui iactu compressa quiescunt.
>
> (82–87)[1]

If we apply these verses to Satan, the line in question mocks him and in the unique time scheme of *Paradise Lost* looks

[1] As Davis Harding points out (*The Club of Hercules*, Urbana, Ill., 1962, pp. 103–8), this passage is also the basis of the bee simile at line 768. The reader who catches the allusion here at line 108 will carry it with him to the end of the book and to the simile. One should also note the parallel between the epic voice's comment at 126 and Virgil's comment on Aeneas' first speech (as Milton's early editors noted it): 'Talia voce refert, curisque ingentibus aeger/spem voltu simulat, premit altum corde dolorem'. But as is always the case in such comparisons, Satan suffers by it, since his deception is self-deception and involves an attempt to deny (to himself) the reality of an authority greater than his, while Aeneas' deception is, in context, an evidence of his faith in the promise of a higher authority. The hope he feigns is only partially a pretence; if it were all pretence, he would not bother.

both backward (the Victor has already driven the rebel host to flight) and forward (in terms of the reading experience, the event is yet to come). I believe that all this and more is there, but that the complexities of the passage will be apparent only when the reader has been led to them by the necessity of accounting for the distance between his initial response and the *obiter dictum* of the epic voice. When he is so led, the reader is made aware that Milton is correcting not a mistake of composition, but the weakness all men evince in the face of eloquence. The error is his, not Milton's; and when Waldock invokes some unidentified critical principle ('they should agree') he objects to an effect Milton anticipates and desires.

But this is more than a stylistic trick to ensure the perception of irony. For, as Waldock points out, this first epic interjection introduces a pattern that is operative throughout. In Books I and II these 'correctives' are particularly numerous and, if the word can be used here, tactless. Waldock falsifies his experience of the poem, I think, when he characterizes Milton's countermands as gentle; we are not warned ('Do not be carried away by this fellow'), but accused, taunted by an imperious voice which says with no consideration of our feelings, 'I know that you *have been* carried away by what you have just heard; you should not have been; you have made a mistake, just as I knew you would'; and we resent this rebuke, not, as Waldock suggests, because our aesthetic sense balks at a clumsy attempt to neutralize an unintentional effect, but because a failing has been exposed in a context that forces us to acknowledge it. We are angry at the epic voice, not for fudging, but for being right, for insisting that we become our own critics. There is little in the human situation more humiliating, in both senses of the word, than the public acceptance of a deserved rebuke.

Not that the reader falls and becomes one of Satan's party. His involvement in the speech does not *directly* compromise his position in a God-centred universe, since his response (somewhat unconscious) is to a performance rather than to a point of view that he might be led to adopt as his own. As Michael Krouse notes, 'the readers for whom Milton wrote . . . were prepared for a Devil equipped with what appear on the surface to be the best of arguments'. (*Milton's Samson and the Christian Tradition*, p. 102). As a Christian who has been taught every day to steel himself against diabolical wiles, the reader is more than prepared to admit the justness of the epic voice's *judgment* on Satan. It is the phrase 'vaunting aloud' that troubles, since it seems to deny even the academic admiration one might have for Satan's art as apart from his morality and to suggest that such admiration can never really be detached from the possibility of involvement (if only passive) in that morality. The sneer in 'vaunting' is aimed equally at the performance and anyone who lingers to appreciate it. (Satan himself delivers the final judgment on this and on all his speeches at IV. 83 : 'Whom I seduc'd / With other promises and other *vaunts*'.) The danger is not so much that Satan's argument will persuade (one does not accord the father of lies an impartial hearing), but that its intricacy will engage the reader's attention and lead him into an error of omission. That is to say, in the attempt to follow and analyse Satan's soliloquy, the larger contexts in which it exists will be forgotten. The immediate experience of the poetry will not be qualified by the perspective of the poem's doctrinal assumptions. Arnold Stein writes, 'the formal perspective does not force itself upon Satan's speech, does not label and editorialize the impressive wilfulness out of existence ; but rather sets up a dramatic conflict between the local context of the immediate utterance and the larger context of which

the formal perspective is expression. This conflict marks
... the tormented relationship between the external boast
and the internal despair.'¹ Stein's comment is valuable, but
it ignores the way the reader is drawn into the poem, not as
an observer who coolly notes the interaction of patterns
(this is the mode of Jonsonian comedy and masque), but as a
participant whose mind is the *locus* of that interaction.

¹ *Answerable Style: Essays on Paradise Lost* (Minneapolis, 1953), p. 124.
Frank Kermode's analysis in *The Living Milton* (p. 106) supports my position:
'He uses the epic poet's privilege of intervening in his own voice, and he does
this to regulate the reader's reaction; but some of the effects he gets from this
device are far more complicated than is sometimes supposed. The corrective
comments inserted after Satan has been making out a good case for himself
are not to be lightly attributed to a crude didacticism; naturally they are
meant to keep the reader on the right track, but they also allow Milton to
preserve the energy of the myth. While we are hearing Satan we are not
hearing the comment; for the benefit of a fallen audience the moral correction
is then applied, but its force is calculatedly lower; and the long-established
custom of claiming that one understands Satan better than Milton did is
strong testimony to the tact with which it is done.' Anne Ferry (*Milton's
Epic Voice*) is closer to Stein: 'The speech is meant to belie the inner experience and the comment to point out the power of the contradiction.
Satan's words do not sound despairing precisely because the division within
him is so serious. Only the inspired narrator can penetrate the appearance to
discover the reality' (p. 120). Mrs. Ferry's discussion of this pattern focuses
on her conception of the narrator as a divided being: 'These didactic comments
remind us of the narrator's presence and his special vision in order that we
may accept his moral interpretation of the story.... They are not *opposed*
to the action of the poem, but are part of the total pattern of that action, not
checks upon our immediate responses to drama, but a means of expressing the
speaker's double point of view, his fallen knowledge and his inspired vision'
(p. 56). It seems to me that the didactic comments *are* checks upon our
immediate responses; nor do I believe it an oversimplification 'to make the
speaker' a judge 'who lectures us like a prig just when we are most involved
in the story'. I agree whole-heartedly, however, with Mrs. Ferry's arranging of
interpretative hierarchies: 'So that when we find complexity in our response
to the behavior or speech of a character and to the statement of the narrator
which interprets it, we must judge the character by the interpretation, not
the interpretation by the character's words or acts' (p. 16). I would add (and
this is the heart of my thesis) that we must judge ourselves in the same way.

Milton insists on this since his concern with the reader is necessarily more direct than it might be in any other poem ; and to grant the reader the status of the slightly arrogant perceiver-of-ironies Stein invents would be to deny him the full *benefit* (I use the word deliberately, confident that Milton would approve) of the reading experience. Stein's 'dramatic conflict' is there, as are his various perspectives, but they are actualized, that is translated into felt meaning, only through the more pervasive drama (between reader and poem) I hope to describe.

A Christian failure need not be dramatic ; if the reader loses himself in the workings of the speech even for a moment, he places himself in a compromising position. He has taken his eye from its proper object — the glory of God, and the state of his own soul — and is at least in danger. Sin is a matter of degrees. To think 'how fine this all sounds, even though it is Satan's', is to be but a few steps from thinking, 'how fine this all sounds' — and no conscious qualification. One begins by simultaneously admitting the effectiveness of Satan's rhetoric and discounting it because it *is* Satan's, but at some point a reader trained to analyse as he reads will allow admiration for a technical skill to push aside the imperative of Christian watchfulness. To be sure, this is not sin. But from a disinterested appreciation of technique one moves easily to a grudging admiration for the technician and then to a guarded sympathy and finally, perhaps, to assent. In this case, the failure (if we can call it that) involves the momentary relaxation of a vigilance that must indeed be eternal. Richard Baxter (*The Saints Everlasting Rest, c.* 1650) warns : 'Not only the open profane, the swearer, the drunkard, and the enemies of godliness, will prove hurtful companions to us, though these indeed are chiefly to be avoided : but too frequent society with persons merely civil and moral, whose conversation is empty and

unedifying, may much divert our thoughts from heaven.'
In Book IX, Eve is 'yet sinless' when she talks with Satan
and follows him to the forbidden tree; but Milton indicates
the danger and its vehicle at line 550:

> Into the heart of Eve his words made way,
> Though at the voice much marvelling.

Eve (innocently) surrenders her mind to wonderment
('much marvelling') at the technical problem of the seeming-
serpent's voice ('What may this mean? Language of Man
pronounc't / By Tongue of Brute') and forgets Adam's
injunction to 'strictest watch' (363). There is at least one
assertion of Satan's that Eve should challenge, since it contradicts something she herself has said earlier. The proper
response to Satan's salutatory 'Fairest resemblance of thy
Maker fair' (538) has been given, in effect, by Eve when she
recognizes Adam's superior 'fairness' at IV. 490 ('I . . . see /
How beauty is excell'd by manly grace / And wisdom, which
alone is truly fair'). Her failure to give that response again is
hardly fatal, but it does involve a deviation (innocent but
dangerous) from the strictness of her watch. Of course to
rebuke the serpent for an excess in courtesy might seem
rude; tact, however, is a social virtue and one which Milton's
heroes are rarely guilty of. Eve is correct when she declares
that the talking serpent's voice 'claims attention due' (566),
but attention *due* should not mean *complete* attention. Satan
is the arch-conjurer here, calling his audience's attention to
one hand (the mechanics of his articulation), doing his real
work with the other ('Into the heart of Eve his words made
way'). In Book I, Milton is the conjurer: by naming Satan
he disarms us, and allows us to feel secure in the identification of an enemy who traditionally succeeds through
disguise (serpent, cherub). But as William Haller notes, in
The Rise of Puritanism, nothing is more indicative of a

graceless state than a sense of security: 'Thus we live in
danger, our greatest danger being that we should feel no
danger, and our safety lying in the very dread of feeling
safe'. (New York/London, 1957, p. 156). Protected from one
error (the possibility of listening sympathetically to a
disguised enemy) we fall easily into another (spiritual
inattentiveness) and fail to read Satan's speech with the
critical acumen it demands. In the opening lines of Book x,
Milton comments brusquely on Adam's and Eve's fall :

> For still they knew, and ought to have still remember'd. (12)

Paradise Lost is full of little moments of forgetfulness — for
Satan, for Adam and Eve, and, most important, for the
reader. At 1. 125–6, the epic voice enters to point out to us
the first of these moments and to say in effect, '"For still you
knew and ought to have still remembered," remembered
who you are (Paradise has already been lost), where you are
("So spake th'Apostate Angel")', and what the issues are
(salvation, justification). In this poem the isolation of an
immediate poetic effect involves a surrender to that effect,
and is a prelude to error, and possibly to sin. Milton challenges his reader in order to protect him from a mistake he
must make before the challenge can be discerned. If this
seems circular and even unfair, it is also, as I shall argue
later, necessary and inevitable.

   The result of such encounters is the adoption of a new
way of reading. After 1. 125–6 the reader proceeds determined not to be caught out again ; but invariably he is. If
Satanic pronouncements are now met with a certain caution,
if there is a new willingness to search for complexities and
ironies beneath simple surfaces, this mental armour is never
quite strong enough to resist the insidious attack of verbal
power ; and always the irritatingly omniscient epic voice is
there to point out a deception even as it succeeds. As the
poem proceeds and this little drama is repeated, the reader's

only gain is an awareness of what is happening to him; he understands that his responses are being controlled and mocked by the same authority, and realizes that while his efforts to extricate himself from this sequence are futile, that very futility becomes a way to self-knowledge. *Control* is the important concept here, for my claim is not merely that this pattern is in the poem (it would be difficult to find one that is not), but that Milton (*a*) consciously put it there and (*b*) expected his reader to notice it. Belial's speech in Book II is a case in point. It is the only speech that merits an introductory warning:

> On th'other side up rose
> *Belial*, in act more graceful and humane;
> A fairer person lost not Heav'n; he seem'd
> For dignity compos'd and high exploit:
> But all was false and hollow; though his Tongue
> Dropt Manna, and could make the worse appear
> The better reason to perplex and dash
> Maturest Counsels: for his thoughts were low;
> To vice industrious, but to Nobler deeds
> Timorous and slothful: yet he pleas'd the ear,
> And with persuasive accent thus began.
>
> (II. 108–18)

The intensity of the warning indicates the extent of the danger: Belial's apparent solidity, which is visible, must be contrasted to his hollowness, which is not, the manna of his tongue to the lowness of mind it obscures; and the 'yet' in 'yet he pleas'd the ear', more than a final admonition before the reader is to be left to his own resources, is an admission of wonder by the epic voice itself (*yet* he pleased . . .) and one of the early cracks in its façade of omniscience. Belial's appeal is a skilful union of logical machinery ('*First*, what Revenge?') and rhetorical insinuation. The easy roll of his periods literally cuts through the contortions of Moloch's

bluster, and the series of *traductiones* around the word
'worse' is an indirect comment on the 'what can be worse'
of the 'Sceptr'd King's' desperation. The ploys are effective,
and since in the attempt to measure the relative merits of
the two devils we forget that their entire counsel is baseless,
the return of the epic voice yields one more slight shock at
this new evidence of our susceptibility. Again we are led to
forget what we know ; again we take our eye from the object
(the centrality of God) ; again we are returned to it with an
abruptness that is (designedly) disconcerting :

> Thus *Belial* with words cloth'd in reason's garb
> Counsell'd ignoble ease, and peaceful sloth,
> Not Peace:

> (226–8)

Waldock complains, 'Belial's words are not only "cloath'd
in reason's garb" : they *are* reasonable.'[1] Belial's words are
not reasonable, although a single uncritical reading will yield
the appearance of reason rather than the reality of his
ignoble ease. Again the flaw in the speech is to be located
precisely at its strongest point. Belial cries at line 146 : 'for
who would lose, / Though full of pain, this intellectual being,
/ Those thoughts that wander through Eternity, / To perish
rather, swallow'd up and lost / In the wide womb of un-
created night.' In other words, do we wish to give up our
nature, our sense of identity? The rhetorical question
evokes an emphatic 'no' from the assembled devils and the
reader. Yet at line 215 Belial offers his final argument, the
possibility of adapting to their now noxious environment :
'Our purer essence then will overcome / Thir noxious
vapor, or enur'd not feel, / Or chang'd at length, and to the

---

[1] *Paradise Lost and its Critics*, p. 79. Cf. John Peter, *A Critique of Paradise
Lost* (London, 1960), p. 44: 'the comments [of the epic voice] seem simply
biased. . . . His premises are correct and he deduces from them a perfectly
feasible plan.'

place conform'd / In temper and in nature, will receive / Familiar the fierce heat, and void of pain.' If this is less spectacular than the question posed at 146, it is still a direct answer to that question. *Belial* is willing to lose 'this intellectual being'. The choice is not, as he suggests, between annihilation and continued existence, but between different kinds of annihilation — Moloch's suicidal thrust at the Almighty or his own gradual surrender of identity, no less suicidal, much less honest. This will be obvious on a second reading. My intention is not to refute Waldock, but to suggest that while his reaction to the epic voice ('they *are* reasonable') is the correct one, Milton expects his reader to go beyond it, to see in the explicitness of the before and after warnings a comment on his own evaluation of the speech.

Satan and his host need not speak in order to betray us to ourselves. When Satan and Beelzebub move from the lake of fire to dry land, 'if it were Land that ever burn'd', their actions become their rhetoric. Milton's introductory stage direction (or is it a marginal note) 'nor ever thence / Had ris'n or heav'd his head, but that the will / And high permission of all-ruling Heaven' (I. 210–12) parallels the warning against Belial; and again the experience of the verse leads us (literally) to lose sight of the warning. If Belial's words seem reasonable, Satan's act certainly seems autonomous. He *rears* himself 'from off the Pool', and the sense of directed force communicated by the verb is channelled into an image that suggests the rocket thrust of modern propellants : 'on each hand the flames / Driv'n backward slope their pointing spires.' Do the flames move upward ('pointing') or downward ('backward')? The answer is both ; and the impression is one of great movement, Satan's movement. He steers 'incumbent' and while his cumbrousness is introduced to impress us with the strain his unusual weight places on 'the dusky air', we are finally impressed by his ability to manage that weight; Satan rather than the air is the hero of these lines. The 'force' that 'transports a Hill / Torn from *Pelorus*' is not identified, but since the 'Archfiend' is the nearest available agent, it is attached to him, as is the entire image. Carried forward by the sequence that began at 'Forthwith upright he rears' (a second reading will emphasize the irony in 'upright'), the reader accepts 'Both glorying to have scap't the *Stygian* flood' (239) as an accurate summary of the scene presented to him. Not that Satan and Beelzebub are consciously granted the status of self-sufficient agents; rather, the question of self-sufficiency does not seem at this point to be relevant to the reading experience. But of course it is the central question, or at least it was at 210 when the epic voice introduced the action; and is again as that same voice returns us to it — in stages: 'Both glorying to have scap't the *Stygian* flood / As Gods, and by thir own recover'd strength, / Not by the sufferance of Supernal Power' (239–41). First, the words 'As Gods' recall 'the high permission of all-ruling Heaven' and indicate the blasphemy of 'glorying'. To the reader, 'As Gods' is less a continuation of line 239 than a qualification of the line's literal assertion that protects him (a half-second too late) against accepting it as true. 'By thir own recover'd strength' changes as we read it, from an extension of the momentarily neutral 'scap't the *Stygian* flood' to the ironic complement of 'nor ever thence / Had ris'n . . .'. 'Not by the sufferance of Supernal Power' is a flat statement that disdains irony for the simple declarative of truth; the passage is suddenly and firmly placed in the larger perspective which the reader again enjoys after a defection to Satan's. Milton's point here is one he will make again and again; all acts are performed in God's service; what is left to any agent is a choice between service freely rendered and service exacted against his will. Satan continually deludes himself by supposing that he can act apart from God, and in this passage we come to understand that delusion by (momentarily) sharing it. The lesson will be repeated on a larger scale when the contrition Adam and Eve evidence at the close of the tenth book is attributed by the poet to 'Prevenient Grace descending' (xi. 3) and by God himself to the result of 'My motions in him' (xi. 91). Thomas Greene observes that 'it is a little anti-climactic for the reader after following tremulously the fallen couple's gropings toward redemption . . . to hear from the Father's lips that he has decreed it — that all of this tenderly human scene, this triumph of conjugal affection and tentative moral searching, occurred only by divine fiat',[1] while John Peter thinks God's claim 'downright unfair'.[2] By encouraging the reader to follow the 'fallen couple's gropings' and by refraining all the while from direct references to grace or to heavenly powers, Milton allows the illusion of independent action on the human level; and when the reader has (predictably) acquiesced in the illusion, if only by failing to struggle against it, he then reminds him of the truth he ought to have remembered, but *somehow*, in the isolating persuasiveness of a seemingly self-contained experience, forgot.[3] (Life lived

[1] *The Descent from Heaven: A Study in Epic Continuity* (New Haven, 1963), p. 407.

[2] *A Critique of Paradise Lost*, p. 145.

[3] Cf. *The Pilgrim's Progress*, ed. J. B. Wharey, rev. R. Sharrock (Oxford, 1960), p. 134. 'He asked them then, If they had not of them Shepherds *a note of direction for the way*? They answered; Yes. But did you, said he, when you was at a stand, pluck out and read your note? They answered, No. He asked them why? They said they forgot. He asked moreover, If the Shepherds did not bid them beware of the *Flatterer*? They answered, Yes: But we did not imagine, said they, that this fine-speaking man had been he . . . So they . . . went softly along in the right way, Singing. *Come hither, you that walk along the way;/See how the Pilgrims fare, that go a stray!/They catched are in an intangling Net,/'Cause they good Counsel lightly did forget:/. . . Let this your caution be.*'

or viewed on the human level alone is itself a rhetorical deception.)

These are almost laboratory experiments, tests insulated by rigid controls, obviously didactic. The pattern that unites them is reminiscent of Spenser's technique in *The Faerie Queene*, I. ix. There the approach to Despair's cave is pointedly detailed and the detail is calculated to repel; the man himself is more terrible than the Blatant Beast or the dragon of I. xii, for his ugliness is something we recognize. Spenser's test of his reader is less stringent than Milton's; he makes his warning the experience of this description rather than an abstract statement of disapproval. It is, of course, not enough. Despair's adaptation of Christian rhetoric (guilt, grace) is masterful and the Redcross Knight (along with the reader) allows the impression of one set of appearances (the old man's ugliness) to be effaced by another (the Circean lure of his rhetoric): 'Sleepe after toyle, port after stormie seas, / Ease after warre, death after life does greatly please' (40). Spenser eases us along by making it impossible to assign stanza 42 to either the knight or Despair. At that point the syntactical ambiguity is telling; the dialogue is over, and we have joined them both in a three-part unanimity that leads inexorably to the decision of 51 :

> At last, resolv'd to worke his finall smart
> He lifted up his hand that backe again did start.

Una's exhortation and accusation—'Come, come away, fraile, feeble, fleshly wight' (53)—is for us as well as her St. George, and we need the reminder that she brings to us from a context *outside* the experience of the poem: 'In heavenly mercies has thou not a part?' Without this *deus ex machina* we could not escape; without Milton's 'snubs' we could not be jolted out of a perspective that is after all *ours*. The lesson in both poems is that the only defence against verbal manipulation (or appearances) is a commitment that stands above the evidence of things that are seen, and the method of both poems is to lead us beyond our perspective by making us feel its inadequacies and the necessity of accepting something which baldly contradicts it. The result is instruction, and instruction is possible only because the reader is asked to observe, analyse, and *place* his experience, that is, to think about it.

In the divorce tracts Milton reveals the source of this poetic technique when he analyses the teaching of Christ, 'not so much a teaching, as an intangling'.[1] Christ is found 'not so much interpreting the Law with his words, as referring his owne words to be interpreted by the Law'.[2] Those who would understand him must themselves decipher the obscurities of his sayings, 'for Christ gives no full comments or continu'd discourses . . . scattering the heavenly grain of his doctrin like pearle heer and there, which requires a skilfull and laborious gatherer.'[3] In order better to instruct his disciples, who 'yet retain'd the infection of loving old licentious customs', he does not scruple to mislead them, temporarily: 'But why did not Christ seeing their error informe them? for good cause; it was his profest method not to teach them all things at all times, but each thing in due place and season . . . the Disciples took it [one of his gnomic utterances] in a manifest wrong sense, yet our Saviour did not there informe them better. . . . Yet did he not omitt to sow within them the seeds of sufficient determining, agen the time that his promis'd spirit should bring all things to their memory.'[4] 'Due season' means when they are ready for it, and they will be ready for it when the seeds he has sown obliquely have brought them to the point where a more direct revelation of the truth will be efficacious; until then

---

[1] *Complete Prose Works of John Milton*, vol. ii, ed. Ernest Sirluck (New Haven, 1959), p. 642.   [2] Ibid., p. 301.   [3] Ibid., p. 338.   [4] Ibid., pp. 678–9.

they are allowed to linger in error or at least in partial ignorance. Recently H. R. MacCallum has shown how Michael uses just this strategy of indirection and misdirection to lead Adam from the sickness of despair to faith and spiritual health.[1] Michael's strategy in Book xi is Milton's strategy in the entire poem, whereby his reader becomes his pupil, taught according to his present capacities in the hope that he can be educated, in tract of time, to enlarge them. By first 'intangling' us in the folds of Satan's rhetoric, and then 'informing us better' in 'due season', Milton forces us to acknowledge the *personal* relevance of the Arch-fiend's existence ; and, in the process, he validates dramatically one of western man's most durable commonplaces, the equation of the rhetorical appeal (representative of the world of appearances) with the weakness of the 'natural man', that is, with the 'defects of our hearers'.

(ii) YET NEVER SAW

The wariness these encounters with demonic attraction make us feel is part of a larger pattern in which we are taught the hardest of all lessons, distrust of our own abilities and perceptions. This distrust extends to all the conventional ways of knowing that might enable a reader to locate himself in the world of any poem. The questions we ask of our reading experience are in large part the questions we ask of our day-to-day experience. Where are we, what are the physical components of our surroundings, what time is it? And while the hard and clear outline of *Paradise Lost* suggests

[1] 'Milton and Sacred History: Books XI and XII of *Paradise Lost*', in *Essays in English Literature from the Renaissance to the Victorian Age, Presented to A. S. P. Woodhouse*, ed. Millar MacLure and F. W. Watt (Toronto, 1964), pp. 149–68.

that the answers to these questions are readily available to us, immediate contexts repeatedly tell us that they are not. Consider, for example, the case of Satan's spear. I have seen responsible critics affirm, casually, that Satan's spear is as large as the mast of a ship; the poem of course affirms nothing of the kind, but more important, it deliberately encourages such an affirmation, at least temporarily :

> His spear, to equal which the tallest Pine
> Hewn on *Norwegian* Hills to be the Mast
> Of some great Ammiral, were but a wand.
>
> (1. 292–4)

Throughout *Paradise Lost*, Milton relies on the operation of three truths so obvious that many critics fail to take them into account : (1) the reading experience takes place in time, that is, we necessarily read one word after another ; (2) the childish habit of moving the eyes along a page and back again is never really abandoned although in maturity the movement is more mental than physical, and defies measurement ; therefore the line as a unit is a resting place even when rhyme is absent ; (3) a mind asked to order a succession of rapidly given bits of detail (mental or physical) seizes on the simplest scheme of organization which offers itself. In this simile, the first line supplies that scheme in the overt comparison between the spear and the tallest pine, and the impression given is one of equality. This is not necessarily so, since logically the following lines could assert any number of things about the relationship between the two objects ; but because they are objects, offering the mind the convenience of focal points that are concrete, and because they are linked in the reading sequence by an abstract term of relationship (equal), the reader is encouraged to take from the line an image, however faint and wavering, of the two side by side. As he proceeds that image will be re-

inforced, since Milton demands that he attach to it the information given in 293 and the first half of 294; that is, in
order to maintain the control over the text that a long syntactical unit tends to diminish, the reader will accept 'hewn
on *Norwegian* hills' as an adjunct of the tallest pine in a very
real way. By providing a scene or background (*memoria*) the
phrase allows him to strengthen his hold on what now
promises to be an increasingly complex statement of relationships. And in the construction of that background the pine
frees itself from the hypothetical blur of the first line; it is
now real, and through an unavoidable process of association
the spear which stood in an undefined relationship to an
undefined pine is seen (and I mean the word literally) in
a kind of apposition to a conveniently visual pine. (This all
happens very quickly in the mind of the reader who does not
have time to analyse the cerebral adjustments forced upon
him by the simile.) In short, the equation (in size) of the two
objects, in 292 only a possibility, is posited by the reader in
292–4 because it simplifies his task; and this movement
towards simplification will be encouraged, for Milton's fit
reader, by the obvious reference in 'to be the Mast / Of
some great Ammiral' to the staff of the Cyclops Polyphemus, identified in the *Aeneid* as a lopped pine[1] and
likened in the *Odyssey* to 'the mast of some black ship of
twenty oars'.[2]

The construction of the image and the formulation of the
relationship between its components are blocked by the
second half of line 294, 'were but a wand'. This does

---

[1] iii. 659. Harding insists that 'if this passage does not conjure up a mental
picture of Polyphemus on the mountaintop, steadying his footsteps with a
lopped pine . . . it has not communicated its full meaning to us' (*The Club of
Hercules*, p. 63). In my reading a 'full meaning' of the passage involves the
recognition of the inadequacy of the mental picture so conjured up.

[2] The translation is E. V. Rieu's in the Penguin Classic Edition (Baltimore,
1946), p. 148.

several things, and I must resort to the mechanical aid of enumeration :

(1) In the confusion that follows this rupture of the reading sequence, the reader loses his hold on the visual focal points, and is unable to associate firmly the wand with either of them. The result is the momentary diminution of Satan's spear as well as the pine, although a second, and more wary reading, will correct this; but corrected, the impression remains (in line 295 a miniature Satan supports himself on a wand-like spear) and in the larger perspective, this aspect of the simile is one of many instances in the poem where Milton's praise of Satan is qualified even as it is bestowed.

(2) The simile illustrates Milton's solution of an apparently insoluble problem. How does a poet provide for his audience a perspective that is beyond the field of its perception? To put the case in terms of *Paradise Lost*, the simile as it functions in other poems will not do here. A simile, especially an epic simile, is an attempt to place persons and/or things, perceived in *a* time and *a* space, in the larger perspective from which their significance must finally be determined. This is possible because the components of the simile have a point of contact — their existence in the larger perspective — which allows the poem to yoke them together without identifying them. Often, part of the statement a simile makes concerns the relationship between the components and the larger perspective in addition to the more obvious relationship between the components themselves; poets suggest this perspective with words like smaller and greater. Thus a trapped hero is at once like and unlike a trapped wolf, and the difference involves their respective positions in a hierarchy that includes more than the physical comparison. A complex and 'tight' simile then can be an almost scientific description of a bit of the world in which for 'the immediate relations of the crude

data of experience' are substituted 'more refined logical entities, such as relations between relations, or classes of relations, or classes of classes of relations'.[1] In Milton's poem, however, the components of a simile often do not have a point of contact that makes their comparison possible in a meaningful (relatable or comprehensible) way. A man exists and a wolf exists and if categories are enlarged sufficiently it can be said without distortion that they exist on a comparable level ; a man exists and Satan (or God) exists, but any statement that considers their respective existences from a human perspective, however inclusive, is necessarily reductive, and is liable to falsify rather than clarify ; and of course the human perspective is the only one available. To return to Book 1, had Milton asserted the identity of Satan's spear and the tallest pine, he would not only have sacrificed the awe that attends incomprehensibility ; he would also have lied, since clearly the *personae* of his extra-terrestrial drama are not confined within the limitations of our time and space. On the other hand, had he said that the spear is larger than one can imagine, he would have sacrificed the concreteness so necessary to the formulation of an effective image. What he does instead is grant the reader the convenience of concreteness (indeed fill his mind with it) and then tell him that what he sees is not what is there ('there' is never located). The result is almost a feat of prestidigitation : for the rhetorical negation of the scene so painstakingly constructed does not erase it ; we are relieved of the necessity of believing the image true, but permitted to retain the solidity it offers our straining imaginations.

[1] A. N. Whitehead in *The Limits of Language*, ed. Walker Gibson (New York, 1962), pp. 13–14. In classical theory, metaphor is the figure of speech whose operation bears the closest resemblance to the operations of dialectic and logic. Aristotle defines it in the *Poetics* as 'a transference either from genus to species or from species to genus, or from species to species'.

Paradoxically, our awareness of the inadequacy of what is described and what we can apprehend provides, if only negatively, a sense of what cannot be described and what we cannot apprehend. Thus Milton is able to suggest a reality beyond this one by forcing us to feel, dramatically, its unavailability.

(3) Finally, the experience of reading the simile tells us a great deal about ourselves. How large is Satan's spear? The answer is, we don't know, although it is important that for a moment we think we do. Of course, one can construct, as James Whaler does, a statement of relative magnitudes (Spear is to pine as pine is to wand)[1] but while this may be logical, it is not encouraged by the logic of the reading experience which says to us : If one were to compare Satan's spear with the tallest pine the comparison would be inadequate. I submit that any attempt either to search out masts of Norwegian ships or to determine the mean length of wands is irrelevant.

Another instance may make the case clearer. In Book III, Satan lands on the Sun :

> There lands the Fiend, a spot like which perhaps
> Astronomer in the Sun's lucent Orb
> Through his glaz'd optic Tube yet never saw.
>
> (588–90)

Again in the first line two focal points (spot and fiend) are offered the reader who sets them side by side in his mind ; again the detail of the next one and one half lines is attached to the image, and a scene is formed, strengthening the implied equality of spot and fiend ; indeed the physicality of the impression is so persuasive that the reader is led to join the astronomer and looks with him through a reassuringly specific telescope ('glaz'd optic Tube') to see —

[1] 'The Miltonic Simile', *PMLA*, xlvi (1931), 1064.

nothing at all ('yet never saw'). In both similes the reader is encouraged to assume that his perceptions extend to the object the poet would present, only to be informed that he is in error ; and both similes are constructed in such a way that the error must be made before it can be acknowledged by a surprised reader. (The parallel to the rhetorical drama between demonic attraction and authorial rebuke should be obvious.) For, however many times the simile is re-read, the 'yet never saw' is unexpected. The mind cannot perform two operations at the same time, and one can either cling to the imminence of the disclaimer and repeat, silently, ' "yet never saw" is coming, "yet never saw" is coming', or yield to the demands of the image and attend to its construction ; and since the choice is really no choice at all — after each reading the negative is only a memory and cannot compete with the immediacy of the sensory evocation — the tail-like half line always surprises.

Of course Milton wants the reader to pull himself up and re-read, for this provides a controlled framework within which he is able to realize the extent and implication of his difficulty, much like the framework provided by the before and after warnings surrounding Belial's speech. The implication is personal ; the similes and many other effects say to the reader : 'I know that you rely upon your senses for your apprehension of reality, but they are unreliable and hopelessly limited.' Significantly, Galileo is introduced in both similes ; the Tuscan artist's glass represents the furthest extension of human perception, and that is not enough. The entire pattern, of which the instances I analyse here are the smallest part, is, among other things, a preparation for the moment in Book viii when Adam responds to Raphael's astronomical dissertation : 'To whom thus Adam clear'd of doubt'. Reader reaction is involuntary : cleared of doubt? by that impossibly tortuous and equivocal description of two all too probable universes?[1] By this point, however, we are able to place our reaction, since Adam's experience here parallels ours in so many places (and a large part of the poem's meaning is communicated by our awareness of the relationship between Adam and ourselves). He *is* cleared of doubt, not because he now knows how the universe is constructed, but because he knows that he cannot know; what clears him of doubt is the certainty of self-doubt, and as with us this certainty is the result of a superior's willingness to grant him, momentarily, the security of his perspective. Milton's lesson is one that twentieth-century science is just now beginning to learn:

> Finally, I come to what it seems to me may well be from the long-range point of view the most revolutionary of the insights to be derived from our recent experiences in physics, more revolutionary than the insights afforded by the discoveries of Galileo and Newton, or of Darwin. This is the insight that it is impossible to transcend the human reference point. . . . The new insight comes from a realization that the structure of nature may

[1] Milton clearly anticipates this reaction when he describes the dialogue in the 'argument'; 'Adam inquires concerning celestial Motions, is *doubtfully* answer'd' (emphasis mine). See also v. 261–6: 'As when by night the Glass/of *Galileo*, less assur'd, observes/Imagin'd Lands and Regions in the Moon: /Or Pilot from amidst the *Cyclades/Delos* or *Samos* first appearing kens/A cloudy spot.' It should be noted that in all these passages certain details form a consistent pattern: Galileo, the moon, spots (representing an unclear vision), etc. The pattern is fulfilled in Raphael's disquisition on the possible arrangement of the heavens. See Greene's excellent reading of Raphael's descent (*The Descent from Heaven*, p. 387): 'The fallen reader's imperfect reason must strain to make out relations as the pilot strains with his physical eyes, as Galileo strains with his telescope, as the fowls gaze with mistaken recognition on the angel, as Adam and Eve will fail to strain and so blur our vision.' See also Northrop Frye, *The Return of Eden* (Toronto, 1965), p. 58: 'Galileo thus appears to symbolize, for Milton, the gaze outward on physical nature, as opposed to the concentration inward on human nature, the speculative reason that searches for new places, rather than the moral reason that tries to create a new state of mind.'

eventually be such that our processes of thought do not correspond to it sufficiently to permit us to think about it at all.[1]

In *Paradise Lost*, our sense of time proves as illusory as
our sense of space and physicality. Jackson Cope quotes with
approval Sigfried Giedion and Joseph Frank, who find in
modern literature a new way of thinking about time :

> The flow of time which has its literary reflection in the
> Aristotelian development of an action having beginning, middle
> and end is . . . frozen into the labyrinthine planes of a spatial
> block which . . . can only be perceived by travelling both
> temporally and physically from point to point, but whose form
> has neither beginning, middle, end nor center, and must be
> effectively conceived as a simultaneity of multiple views.[2]

And Mrs. Isabel MacCaffrey identifies the 'simultaneity of
multiple views' with the eternal moment of God, a moment,
she argues, that Milton makes ours :

> The long view of time as illusory, telescoped into a single vision,
> had been often adopted in fancy by Christian writers. . . . Writing of
> Heaven and the little heaven of Paradise, Milton by a powerful
> releasing act of the imagination transposed the intuitive single
> glance of God into the poem's mythical structure. Our vision of
> history becomes for the time being that of the Creator 'whose
> eye Views all things at one view' (ii. 189–90); like him, we are
> stationed on a 'prospect high Wherin past, present, future he
> beholds.'   (iii. 77–78)[3]

The experience of every reader, I think, affirms the truth
of these statements ; Milton does convince us that the world
of his poem is a static one which 'slights chronology in favor
of a folded structure which continually returns upon itself,
or a spiral that circles about a single center'.[4] The question I

[1] P. W. Bridgman, quoted in *The Limits of Language*, p. 21.
[2] *The Metaphoric Structure of Paradise Lost* (Baltimore, 1962), pp. 14–15.
[3] *Paradise Lost as 'Myth'* (Cambridge, Mass., 1959), p. 53.
[4] Ibid., p. 45.

would ask is how does he so convince us? His insistence on simultaneity is easily documented. How many times do we see Christ ascend, after the war in Heaven, after the passion, after Harrowing Hell, after giving Satan his death wound, after the creation, after the final conflagration, at the day of final judgment? How many times do our first parents fall, and how many times are they accorded grace? The answer to all these questions is, 'many times' or is it all the time (at each point of time) or perhaps at one, and the same, time. My difficulty with the preceding sentence is a part of my point: I cannot let go of the word 'time' and the idea of sequence; timelessness (I am forced to resort to a question-begging negative) is an interesting concept, but we are all of us trapped in the necessity of experiencing in time, and the attempt even to conceive of a state where words like day and evening measure space rather than duration is a difficult one; Chaucer's Troilus, among others, is defeated by it. Mrs. MacCaffrey asserts that 'spatial imagining' is part of Milton's 'mental climate' and the researches of Walter Ong, among others, support her; but if Milton has implanted the eternal moment 'into the poem's mythical structure', how does the reader, who, in Cope's words, must travel 'temporally and physically from point to point', root it out? Obviously many readers do not; witness the critics who are troubled by contradictory or 'impossible' sequences and inartistic repetitions. Again the reactions of these anti-Miltonists are the surest guide to the poet's method; for it is only by encouraging and then 'breaking' conventional responses and expectations that Milton can point his reader beyond them. To return to Waldock, part of the poem's apparently 'hard and definite' outline is the easy chronology it seems to offer; but the pressures of innumerable local contexts demand adjustments that give the lie to the illusion of sequence and reveal in still another way the inability of the reader to consider this poem as he would any other.

In the opening lines of Book 1, chronology and sequence are suggested at once in what is almost a plot line: man disobeys, eats fruit, suffers woe and awaits rescue. It is a very old and simple story, one that promises a comfortable correlation of plot station and emotional response: horror and fear at the act, sorrow at the result, joy at the happy ending, the whole bound up in the certain knowledge of cause and effect. As Milton crowds more history into his invocation the reader, who likes to know what time it is, will attempt to locate each detail on the continuum of his story line. The inspiration of the shepherd, Moses, is easily placed between the Fall and the restoration; at this point many readers will feel the first twinge of complication, for Moses is a type of Christ who as the second Adam restores the first by persevering when he could not; as one begins to construct statements of relationship between the three, the clarity of lines 1–3 fades. Of course there is nothing to force the construction of such statements, and Milton thoughtfully provides in the very next line the sequence-establishing phrase, 'In the Beginning'. Reassured both by the ordering power of 'beginning' and by the allusion to Genesis(which is, after all, the original of all once-upon-a-times), the reader proceeds with the invocation, noting, no doubt, all the riches unearthed by generations of critical exegesis, but still firmly in control of chronology; and that sense of control is reinforced by the two-word introduction to the story proper: 'Say first', for with the first we automatically posit a second and then a third, and in sum, a neat row of causal statements leading all the way to an end already known.

The security of sequence, however, is soon taken away. I have for some time conducted a private poll with a single question: 'What is your reaction when the second half of line 54 — "for *now* the thought" — tells you that you are *now* with Satan, in Hell?' The unanimous reply is, 'surprise', and an involuntary question: how did I come to be here? Upon re-reading, the descent to Hell is again easy and again unchartable. At line 26 the time scheme is still manageable: there is (*a*) poem time, the *now* in which the reader sits in his chair and listens, with Milton, to the muse, and (*b*) the named point in the past when the story ('our Grand Parents . . . so highly to fall off') and our understanding of it ('say first what cause') is assumed to begin. At 33, the 'first' is set back to the act of Satan, now suggested but not firmly identified as the 'cause' of 27, and a third time (*c*) is introduced, further from (*a*) than (*b*), yet still manageable; but Satan's act also has its antecedent: 'what time his Pride / Had cast him out from Heav'n' (36–37); by this point, 'what time' is both an assertion and a question as the reader struggles to maintain an awkward, backward-moving perspective. There is now a time (*d*) and after (that is, before) that an (*e*) 'aspiring . . . He trusted to have equall'd the most High' (38, 40). Time (*f*) breaks the pattern, returning to (*d*) and providing, in the extended description of 44–53, a respite from sudden shifts. To summarize: the reader has been asked repeatedly to readjust his idea of 'in the beginning' while holding in suspension two plot lines (Adam's and Eve's and Satan's) that are eventually, he knows, to be connected. The effort strains the mind to its capacity, and the relief offered by the vivid and easy picture of Satan falling is more than welcome.[1] It is at this time, when the

---

[1] The technique is reminiscent of Virgil's 'historical present', which is used to bring the action of the epic before the reader's eyes. Recently Helen Gardner has reached conclusions similar to those offered here concerning the operation of time and space in the poem. See her *A Reading of Paradise Lost* (Oxford, 1965), pp. 39–51: 'Milton's poem must move in time, yet he continually suggests that the time of the poem is an illusion' (39); 'Milton, as he plays us into his poem, is using our human measurement to convey vastness sensuously' (40); 'He continually satisfies and then defeats our powers of

reader's attention has relaxed, that Milton slips by him the
'now' of 54 and the present tense of 'torments', the first
present in the passage. The effect is to alert the reader both
to his location (Hell) and to his inability to retrace the
journey that brought him there. Re-reading leads him only
to repeat the mental operations the passage demands, and
while the arrival in Hell is anticipated, it is always a surprise.
The technique is of course the technique of the spot and
spear similes, and of the clash between involuntary response
and authorial rebuke, and again Milton's intention is to
strip from us another of the natural aids we bring to the
task of reading. The passage itself tells us this in lines 50–51,
although the message may pass unnoted at first : 'Nine times
the Space that measures Day and Night'. Does space measure
day and night? Are day and night space? The line raises
these questions, and the half-line that follows answers them,
not 'to mortal men' who think in terms of duration and
sequence, not to us. In this poem we must, we will, learn a
new time.

The learning process is slow at first ; the reader does not
necessarily draw the inferences I do from this early passage ;
but again it is the frequency of such instances that makes my
case. In Book II, when the fallen Angels disperse, some of
them explore 'on bold adventure' their new home. One of
the landmarks they pass is 'Lethe the River of Oblivion',
and Milton pauses to describe its part in God's future plans :
'At certain revolutions all the damn'd / . . . They ferry over
this *Lethean* Sound / Both to and fro, thir sorrow to
augment, / And wish and struggle, as they pass to reach /
The tempting stream, with one small drop to lose / In sweet
forgetfulness all pain and woe, / All in one moment and so

visualization' (41). See also Roy Daniells, *Milton, Mannerism and Baroque*
(Toronto, 1963), p. 98; W. B. C. Watkins, *An Anatomy of Milton's Verse*
(Baton Rouge, 1955), p. 44; Anne Ferry, *Milton's Epic Voice*, pp. 46–47.

near the brink; / But Fate withstands' (597–8, 604–10). At 614 the poet continues with 'Thus roving on / In confus'd march forlorn', and only the phrase 'advent'rous bands' in 615 tells the reader that the poet has returned to the fallen angels. The mistake is a natural one : 'forlorn' describes perfectly the state of the damned, as does 'Confus'd march' their movements 'to and fro': indeed a second reflection suggests no mistake at all ; the fallen angels *are* the damned, and one drop of Lethe *would* allow them to lose their woe in the oblivion Moloch would welcome. Fate *does* withstand. What Milton has done by allowing this momentary confusion is to point to the identity of these damned and all damned. As they fly past Lethe the fallen angels are all those who will become them ; they do not stand for their successors (the word defeats me), they *state* them. In *Paradise Lost*, history and the historical sense are denied and the reader is forced to see events he necessarily perceives in sequence as time-identities. Milton cannot recreate the eternal moment, but by encouraging and then blocking the construction of sequential relationships he can lead the reader to accept the necessity of, and perhaps even apprehend, negatively, a time that is ultimately unavailable to him because of his limitations.

This translation of felt ambiguities, confusions, and tautologies into a conviction of timelessness in the narrative is assured partially by the uniqueness of Milton's 'fable'. 'For the Renaissance', notes Mrs. MacCaffrey, 'all myths are reflections, distorted or mutilated though they may be, of the one true myth.'[1] For Milton all history is a replay of the history he is telling, all rebellions one rebellion, all falls one fall, all heroism the heroism of Christ. And his readers who share this Christian view of history will be prepared to make the connection that exists potentially in

[1] *Paradise Lost as 'Myth'*, p. 14.

the detail of the narrative. The similes are particularly
relevant here. The first of these compares Satan to Leviathan,
but the comparison, to the informed reader, is a tautology ;
Satan *is* Leviathan and the simile presents two aspects of one,
rather than the juxtaposition of two, components. This
implies that Satan is, at the moment of the simile, already
deceiving 'The Pilot of some small night-founder'd Skiff' ;
and if the reader has attended to the lesson of his recent
encounter with the epic voice he recognizes himself as that
pilot, moored during the speech of I. 84–126 by the side of
Leviathan. The contests between Satan and Adam,
Leviathan and the pilot, rhetoric and the reader — the
simile compresses them, and all deceptions, into a single
instant, forever recurring. The celebrated falling-leaves
simile moves from angel-form to leaves to sedge to Busiris
and his Memphian Chivalry, or in typological terms
(Pharaoh and Herod are the most common types of Satan)
from fallen angels to fallen angels. The compression here
is so complex that it defies analysis : the fallen angels as they
lie on the burning lake (the Red Sea) are already *pursuing* the
Sojourners of Goshen (Adam and Eve, the Israelites, the
reader) who are for the moment *standing* on the safe shore
(Paradise, the reader's chair). In Book XII. 191, Pharoah
becomes the River-Dragon or Leviathan (Isaiah xxvii. 1),
pointing to the ultimate unity of the Leviathan and falling
leaves similes themselves. As similes they are uninformative ;
how numberless are the falling angels? they are as numberless
as Pharaoh's host, that is, as fallen angels, and Pharaoh's host
encompasses all the damned who have been, are, and will be,
all the damned who will fly longingly above Lethe. As
vehicles of perception, however, they tell us a great deal,
about the cosmos as it is in a reality we necessarily distort,
about the ultimate subjectivity of sequential time, about
ourselves.

There are many such instances in the early books and together they create a sensitivity to the difficulties of writing and reading this particular poem. When Milton's epic voice remarks that pagan fablers err in relating the story of Mulciber's ejection from Heaven (I. 747), he does not mean to say that the story is not true, but that it is a distorted version of the story he is telling, and that any attempt to apprehend the nature of the angels' fall by comparing it to the fall of Mulciber or of Hesiod's giants involves another distortion that cannot be allowed if *Paradise Lost* is to be read correctly. On the other hand the attempt is hazarded (the reader cannot help it), the distortion is acknowledged along with the unavailability of the correct reading, and Milton's point is made despite, or rather because of, the intractability of his material. When Satan's flight from the judgment of God's scales (IV. 1015) is presented in a line that paraphrases the last line of the *Aeneid*, the first impulse is to translate the allusion into a comparison that might begin, 'Satan is like Turnus in that . . .'; but of course, the relationship as it exists in a reality beyond that formed by our sense of literary history, is quite the opposite. Turnus's defiance of the fates and his inevitable defeat are significant and comprehensible only in the light of what Satan did in a past that our time signatures cannot name and is about to do in a present (poem time) that is increasingly difficult to identify. Whatever the allusion adds to the richness of the poem's texture or to Milton's case for superiority in the epic genre, it is also one more assault on the confidence of a reader who is met at every turn with demands his intellect cannot even consider.

(iii) THE GOOD TEMPTATION

Most poets write for an audience assumed fit. Why is the fitness of Milton's audience a concern of the poem itself? One answer to this question has been given in the preceding pages : only by forcing upon his reader an awareness of his limited perspective can Milton provide even a negative intuition of what another would be like; it is a brilliant solution to the impossible demands of his subject, enabling him to avoid the falsification of anthropomorphism and the ineffectiveness of abstraction. Another answer follows from this one : the reader who fails repeatedly before the pressures of the poem soon realizes that his difficulty proves its major assertions — the fact of the Fall, and his own (that is Adam's) responsibility for it, and the subsequent woes of the human situation. The reasoning is circular, but the circularity is appropriate to the uniqueness of the poem's subject matter ; for while in most poems effects are achieved through the manipulation of reader response, this poet is telling the story that *created* and still creates the responses of its reader and of all readers. The reader who falls before the lures of Satanic rhetoric displays again the weakness of Adam, and his inability to avoid repeating that fall throughout indicates the extent to which Adam's lapse has made the reassertion of right reason impossible. Rhetoric is thus simultaneously the sign of the reader's infirmity and the means by which he is brought first to self-knowledge, and then to contrition, and finally, perhaps, to grace and everlasting bliss.

St. Paul articulates the dilemma of fallen man when he cries, 'For the good that I would I do not : but the evil which I would not, that I do' (Romans vii. 19). The true horror of the Fall is to be found here, in the loss of that happy state in which man's faculties worked in perfect

harmony, allowing him accurately to assess his responsibilities and to meet them. Fallen man is hopelessly corrupt
and his corruption resists even the grace freely offered to
him through the intercession of Jesus Christ. Man's soul
becomes the scene of a battle between the carnality of the
first Adam (the old, unregenerate, man) and the righteousness of the second (the new, regenerate, man); and in the
seventeenth century the image of an intestine warfare that is
simultaneously the sign of the Fall and an indication of the
possibility of redemption is to be seen everywhere :

> There is in Man, by reason of his general *Corruption*, such a
> distemper wrought, as that there is not onely *crookednesse* in, but
> *dissension* also, and fighting betweene his parts: And, though the
> Light of our *Reason* be by Man's Fall much dimmed and decayed;
> yet the remainders thereof are so adverse to our unruly *Appetite*,
> as that it laboureth against us.
>
> <div align="right">(Edward Reynolds, <i>A Treatise of the Passions and
Faculties of the Soul of Man</i>, London, 1640)</div>

> Reason therefore may rightly discern the thing which is good,
> and yet the will of man not incline itself thereunto, as often the
> prejudice of sensible experience doth oversway.
>
> <div align="right">(Hooker, <i>Ecclesiastical Polity</i>, i, vii. 6)</div>

> Our erected wit maketh us know what perfection is, and yet our
> infected will keepeth us from reaching unto it.
>
> <div align="right">(Sidney, <i>Apology</i>)</div>

Milton transforms this commonplace into a poetic technique ;
he leads us to feel again and again the conflict between the
poem's assumed morality and our responses, and to locate
the seat of that conflict in our fallen nature and not in any
failure in composition. In short, the reader's difficulty is
the result of the act that is the poem's subject. The reading
experience becomes the felt measure of man's loss and since
Milton always supplies a corrective to the reader's errors
and distortions, what other critics have seen as the 'dis-

quieting' aspect of that experience can be placed in a context that makes sense of it.

When, in the second part of *Pilgrim's Progress*, Christiana wonders why she and her companion Mercy were not fore-warned of the danger lurking 'so near the Kings Palace' or, better still, provided with a 'Conductor', Reliever answers : 'Had my Lord granted you a Conductor, you would not neither, so have bewailed that oversight of yours in not asking for one, as now you have occasion to do. So all things work for good, and tend to make you more wary' ;[1] and Mercy adds, 'by this neglect, we have an occasion ministred unto us to behold our own imperfections'.[2] With the same compassionate and deliberate neglect, Milton makes the whole of *Paradise Lost* just such an occasion, the poet's version of what the theologian calls a 'good temptation' :

> A good temptation is that whereby God tempts even the righteous for the purpose of proving them, not as though he were ignorant of the disposition of their hearts, but for the purpose of exercising or manifesting their faith or patience ... or of lessening their self confidence, and reproving their weakness, that ... they themselves may become wiser by experience.[3]

[1] p. 196.
[2] Loc. cit.
[3] *The Works of John Milton*, ed. F. A. Patterson *et al.* (New York, 1933), xv. 87–89. Cf. David Pareus, quoted in Arnold Williams's *The Common Expositor* (Chapel Hill, 1948), p. 113: 'God is said to try man not that he may discover what he does not know (he knows even our inmost thoughts), but that we may discover our weakness, which *we* do not know' (emphasis mine). In his 'Apology for his Book' Bunyan defends a method similar to Milton's: 'You see the ways the Fisher-man doth take / To catch the Fish; what Engins doth he make? /. ... Yet Fish there be, that neither Hook, nor Line, / Nor Snare nor Net, nor Engine can make thine; / They must be grop'd for, and be tickled too, / Or they will not be catcht, what e're you do' (p. 3); 'This Book will make a Travailer of thee, / If by its Counsel thou wilt ruled be; / It will direct thee to the Holy Land, / If thou wilt its Directions understand; / Yea, it will make the sloathful active be; / The Blind also, delightful things to see' (pp. 6–7).

The temptation is good because by means of it the secret corruption within is exposed, and consequently we are better able to resist the blandishments of less benevolent tempters. In the struggle against sin, no weapon is more effective than a knowledge of the areas likely to be under attack :

> Thou must be carefull and diligent to finde out the subtilty, devices, and sleights of the devill, by which he doth assault thee very cunningly; for he hath a neere conjecture unto what sinnes thou art most inclined . . . and accordingly he fits his temptations.
>
> (*A Garden of Spirituall Flowers*, 1638, p. 285)

> There is secret corruption within, which will never be found out but by searching . . . the benefit is great which waysoever things turn. If upon examination we find that we have not grace in truth, then the mistake is discovered, and the danger prevented. If we find that we have grace, we may take the comfort of it.
>
> (Thomas Watson, *Christian Soldier; Or, Heaven Taken By Storm*, 1669, p. 52)

> I feelingly know the weakness of my own heart, and I am not ignorant of the Devil's malice and subtilty, and how he will make the fiercest assaults where I am weakest.
>
> (John Corbet, *Self-Imployment in Secret*, 1681, pp. 41–42)

The deceitfulness of man's heart is such, writes Daniel Dyke, that we should welcome 'fit occasions' of trial which 'give a vent to corruption'; for 'many are inwardly full of corruption ; but they shew it not, onely for want of occasion' (*The Mystery of Selfe-Deceiving*, 1615, p. 329). It is our duty, insists John Shower, to 'bring [our] Hearts and Ways to a Trial, but 'most . . . are unwilling [because] they are stupidly secure and see not the necessity of this duty' (*Serious Reflections On Time And Eternity*, Glasgow, 1828, 1st ed., 1689, p. 175). Milton compels this duty by fitting temptations to our inclinations and then confronting us immediately with the evidence of our fallibility. And in the

process, he fosters the intense self-consciousness which is the
goal of spiritual self-examination :

> When on the Sudden, and by Incogitancy I have spoken a Word,
> which upon Second Thoughts is doubtful to me, though I had
> not such doubt in the speaking of it, I have been much perplexed
> about it, and have engaged myself to a greater watchfulness.
>
> (Corbet, op. cit., p. 32)

> And when upon this inquiry, we find we have contracted any
> sullages or pollutions, then we must cleanse them from that filth,
> and *take heed to them*, that is, keep a continual watch over them,
> and be still upon our guard, that we be not surpriz'd by any new
> Temptation.
>
> (Edmund Arwaker, *Thoughts well Employ'd*,
1697, p. 21)

Note the similarity between the sequence of mental actions
described by Corbet — mistake, correction, instruction —
and my description of the reader's experience in Books i
and ii.

The long-range result of this technique is the creation
of a 'split reader', one who is continually responding to two
distinct sets of stimuli — the experience of individual poetic
moments and the ever present pressure of the Christian
doctrine — and who attaches these responses to warring
forces within him, and is thus simultaneously the location
and the observer of their struggle. This division in the reader
is nowhere more apparent or more central to Milton's
intention than in Book ix when Adam chooses to disobey.
Waldock raised a very real question (which he then answered too quickly) when he argued that at its most crucial
point, 'the poem asks from us, at one and the same time, two
incompatible responses ... that Adam did right, and ...
that he did wrong. The dilemma is as critical as that, and
there is no way of escape'.[1] Almost immediately Paul

---

[1] *Paradise Lost and its Critics*, p. 56. See also Peter, *Critique*, pp. 130–1.

Turner replied by pointing out that the poet does not want us to escape: 'What would happen if . . . the reader did *not* feel inside himself a strong, almost overwhelming impulse to do what Adam did. What sort of significance . . . would remain?'[1] The ambivalence of the response is meaningful because the reader is able to identify its components with different parts of his being: one part, faithful to what he has been taught to believe (his 'erected wit') and responsive to the unmistakable sentiments of the poem's official voice, recoils in the presence of what he *knows* to be wrong; but another part, subversive and unbidden (his 'infected will') surprises and overcomes him and Adam is secretly applauded. It would be a mistake to deny either of these impulses; they must be accepted and noted because the self must be accepted before it can be transformed. The value of the experience depends on the reader's willingness to participate in it fully while at the same time standing apart from it. He must pass judgment on it, at least on that portion of it which is a reflection of his weakness. So that if we retain Waldock's formula, a description of the total response would be, Adam is wrong, no, he's right, but, then, of course he is wrong, and so am I. This last is not so much a product of the scene itself as of the moral conditioning the poem has exposed us to and of the self-consciousness it encourages. In effect the reader imposes this final certainty on the ambiguity of the poetic moment (this is the way of escape), but, in doing so, he does not deny its richness; indeed he adds to it by *ordering* it, by providing another perspective which gives the ambiguity meaning and renders it edifying; *he* now supplies the correcting perspective supplied earlier by the epic voice. Moreover, the uneasiness he feels at his own reaction to the fact of sin is a sign that he is not yet lost. The saint is known not by the absence of sin, but by his hatred of it:

1 'Woman and the Fall of Man', *English Studies*, xxix (1948), 16.

First, before hee come to doe the sinne, he hath no purpose to doe
it, but his purpose and desire is to doe the will of God, contrary to
that sinne. Secondly, in the act of doing of the sinne, his heart
riseth against it, yet by the force of temptation, and by the mighty
violence of the flesh hee is haled on and pulled to do wickednesse.
Thirdly, after hee hath sinned, he is sore displeased with himself
for it and truly repenteth.[1]

In the pattern I discern in the poem, the reader is continually surprised by sin and in shame, 'sore displeased with
himself,' his heart 'riseth against it'.

One might ask at this point, why read a poem that treats
its reader so badly? Why continue to suffer an experience
that is unpleasant? The answer is simply that for the
seventeenth-century Puritan and indeed for any Christian
in what we might call the Augustinian tradition, the kind of
discomfort I have been describing would be paradoxically a
source of comfort and the unpleasantness a source of pleasure.
Milton did not write for the atheist, but for the 'cold'
Christian (neither saint nor apostate) who cannot help but
allow the press of ordinary life to 'divert his thoughts from
Heav'n'. In the same way, the sense of sin so necessary to a
properly disposed Christian soul, is blunted rather than
reinforced by the familiar recitation of scriptural commonplaces in sermons. One may hear every day of the depravity
of natural man and of the inefficacy of unaided human
efforts, but, inevitably, the incantational repetition of a

---

[1] *A Garden of Spirituall Flowers* (1638), p. 212. See also John Preston, *Sins
Overthrow or A Godly and Learned Treatise of Mortification* (London, 1633),
p. 60: 'But there is great difference betwixt the slacknesse of the Saints, and
the wicked backsliding: the godly [61] they may slacke, but it is for a time;
he is cold and remisse in the duties of holinesse, but it lasts not, it vanisheth
away: on the other side, the wicked lye and continue in Apostacy unto the
end; in these it is naturall, but unto the other it is but the instigation of the
divell working by some lust upon one of the faculties.' These are of course
commonplace statements, and examples could be multiplied *ad infinitum*.

truth lessens its immediate and personal force, and the sinner becomes complacent in a verbal and abstract contrition. *Paradise Lost* is immediate and forceful in the communication of these unflattering truths, again following the example of Christ who administers to the Pharisees 'not by the middling temper . . . but by the other extreme of *antidote* . . . a sharp & corrosive sentence against a foul and putrid licence ; not to eate into the flesh, but into the sore'.[1] In the manner of the Old Law, the poem is designed to 'call forth and develop our natural depravity; . . . that it might impress us with a slavish fear . . . that it might be a schoolmaster to bring us to the righteousness of Christ'.[2] And since perpetual vexation and self-doubt are signs that the spirit of the Lord is at work, the reader welcomes an experience he knows to be salutary to his spiritual health ; a 'good temptation' Milton points out 'is therefore rather to be desired'.[3] 'They whose hearts are pierced by the Ministry of the word, they are carryed with love and respect to the Ministers of it' (Thomas Hooker).

It should be noted, in addition, that the reading offered here is a partial one. I have isolated this pattern in order to make a precise and rather narrow point about the way the poem works on one level. In Milton's larger scheme the conviction that man can do nothing is accompanied by the conviction that Christ has taken it upon himself to do it all. As Joseph Summers writes, in another context, 'The essential "act" is that the individual should abandon the pretence that he *can* act in any way pertaining to salvation : he must experience the full realization that salvation belongs to God, that nothing he can do either by faith or works can help. The doctrine is moreover, "comforting", for "all things" are "more ours by being his" ' (*George Herbert*, p. 61). We are

---

[1] *Complete Prose Works*, ii. 668.   [2] *The Works of John Milton*, xvi. 131.
[3] See note 3, p. 40.

told this at the first — 'till one greater Man / Restore us
and regain the blissfull Seat' — but in the course of our
struggles with Books I and II, we *forget*, as Milton intends us
to, so that we can be reminded dramatically by the glorious
sacrifice of Book III. Milton impresses us with the negativity
and despair of one aspect of Christian doctrine so that he
can send us joyfully to the promise of another.

We shall learn Milton's lessons only if we enter the poem
on his terms. The fifth inference I drew from Waldock's
criticism of the intrusive epic voice was that for him the
question of relative authority is a purely aesthetic one.
'Milton's allegations clash with his demonstrations . . . in
any work of imaginative literature at all it is the demonstration . . . that has the higher validity : an allegation can
possess no comparable authority.' In his brilliantly perverse
Milton's God William Empson asserts 'all the characters are
on trial in any civilized narrative'[1] and Waldock would, I
think, include the epic voice in this statement. The insistence
on the superiority of showing as opposed to telling is, as
Wayne Booth has shown, a modern one, and particularly
unfortunate in this case since it ignores the historical reality
of the genre.[2] When Homer calls Achilles wrathful, do we
search the narrative for proof he is not ; is Odysseus' craft
on trial or do we accept it because we accept the authority
of the epic voice ? Do we attempt to make a case for Aeneas'
*im*piety ? There is an obvious retort to all this : the authority
of epic voices in other epics is accepted because their com-

[1] *Milton's God* (Norfolk, 1961), p. 94.
[2] *The Rhetoric of Fiction* (Chicago, 1961), p. 4. '. . . even Homer writes
scarcely a page without some kind of direct clarification of motives, of expectations, and of the relative importance of events. And though the gods
themselves are often unreliable, Homer — the Homer we know — is not.
What he tells us usually goes deeper and is more accurate than anything we are
likely to learn about real people and events.'

ments either confirm or anticipate the reading experience; Milton invites us to put his epic voice on trial by allowing the reading experience to contradict it. (Waldock: 'Of course they should agree.') I agree that the reader cannot help but notice the clash of authorities; his familiarity with the genre would lead him to look to the epic voice for guidance and clarification. But I do not think that any fit reader would resolve the problem, as Waldock does, and decide immediately and happily for the poem (and for himself) and against the prescience of its narrator. Milton assumes a predisposition in favour of the epic voice rather than a modern eagerness to put that voice on trial; he expects his reader to worry about the clash, to place it in a context that would resolve a troublesome contradiction and allow him to reunite with an authority who is a natural ally against the difficulties of the poem.

There is at least a Virgilian precedent: in the fourth book of the *Aeneid*, a great deal of Virgil's meaning is communicated through the felt contrast between the persuasiveness of Dido's appeal to Aeneas and the quiet firmness of his rejection of her. So successful is the poet that at least one of his editors becomes angry with him: 'To an appeal which would move a stone Aeneas replies with the cold and formal rhetoric of an attorney ... Aeneas is left "stammering and preparing to say many things" — a hero who had, one would think, lost his character for ever. But Virgil seems unmoved by his own genius, and begins the next paragraph quite placidly 'at pius Aeneas ...' ! How the man who wrote the lines placed in Dido's mouth could immediately afterwards speak of "the good Aeneas etc." is one of the puzzles of literature'.[1] Not so puzzling when one realizes that the scene is designed to dramatize for the reader exactly what the

[1] From the introduction of T. E. Page's edition of the *Aeneid*, 2 vols. (London, 1894), pp. xviii–xix.

adjective *pius* means. The reader is allowed to feel the pull
Dido exerts on him and then to hear the reply of Aeneas,
Iovis monitis inmota (331). With Page, many readers will for
a moment hesitate to accept this action as a truly virtuous
one, until the narrator steps in authoritatively with his
'placid' 'at pius Aeneas'. In the following lines the reality of
Dido's claim on our attention is acknowledged, but sub-
ordinated to a higher claim :

> at pius Aeneas, quamquam lenire dolentem
> solando cupit et dictis avertere curas,
> multa gemens magnoque animum labefactus amore,
> iussa tamen divom exsequitur, classemque revisit.

(393–6)

The dramatic and moral tensions of the moment are exhibited in the syntax ; the main clause is a simple declarative,
cold, absolute, and, one could say, insensitive to complexity,
'the good Aeneas followed the orders of the Gods and
returned to the fleet' ; but contained within the main clause
and literally surrounded by it are all the considerations
Aeneas must reject along with Dido, her sorrow, his own
inclinations, the fact of love : 'although he desires to assuage
her sorrows and turn aside her grief with his words, sighing
much, his soul shaken by his mighty love'.[1] The firmness
and precision of the narrator's comment guides the reader
and leads him to a clearer conception of Aeneas' heroism,
which is here measured by the effort of will it requires to
leave Dido, and the reader, in turn, must measure himself
against the hero's response.

Indeed, the experience of the scene redefines heroism
completely, as does our experience of Satan in the first six
books of *Paradise Lost*. Satan's initial attractiveness owes as

[1] Again there is a Christian analogue in *The Pilgrim's Progress* when
Christian stops his ears against the cries of his family 'and ran on crying, Life,
Life, Eternal Life'. See edition quoted above, p. 10.

much to a traditional idea of what is heroic as it does to our weakness before the rhetorical lure. He exemplifies a form of heroism most of us find easy to admire because it is visible and flamboyant (the epic voice also admires : the 'though in pain' of 'So spake th' Apostate Angel, though in pain' is a recognition of the steadfastness that can belong even to perversity ; the devil is always given his due).[1] Because his courage is never denied (instead Milton insists on it) while his virtue and goodness are (in the 'allegations' of the epic voice), the reader is led to revise his idea of what a true hero is. If this poem does anything to its readers, it forces them to make finer and finer discriminations. Perhaps the most important aspect of the process I have been describing — the creation of a reader who is fit because he knows and understands his limitations — begins here at 1. 125 when Milton's authorial corrective casts the first stone at the ideal of martial valour and points us towards the meaningful acceptance of something better.

To summarize : *Paradise Lost* is a dialectical experience which has the advantage traditionally claimed for dialectic of involving the respondent in his own edification. On one level at least the poem has the form of a Platonic dialogue, with the epic voice taking the role of Socrates, and the reader in the position of a Phaedrus or a Cratylus, continually forced to acknowledge his errors, and in this way moving toward a confirmation in the Truth :

> The genius of *elenchos* . . . is that whatever eventuates in the course of cross-examination is not the examiner's importation, but the respondent's own contribution and finding. If there are summations and conclusions, they are the respondent's. He has not

[1] Patrick Hume in his notes to the poem (1795) suggests still another possible reading for this couplet: 'Though in torment, making vain boastings' (10). That is, even while he is racked with pain, Satan cannot resist an occasion for hearing his own voice. Presumably, he would find something better to do.

been shown; he has himself made a discovery. . . . Dialectic is the true rhetorical and persuasive art, because it permits a man to convict himself of error, and, on the other hand, to confirm himself in the truth. He is *self* persuaded.[1]

If the demands Milton makes on his readers seem excessive, they flow from a sense of his responsibility to them (his is 'the office of a pulpit, to inbreed . . . the seeds of virtue . . . and set the affections in right tune')[2] and correspond to what they asked of themselves in their daily ('yea, hourly') exercises of self-examination. 'Self-examination', explains Watson in *The Christian Soldier*, 'is the setting up a court in conscience, and keeping a register there, that by strict scrutiny a man may know how things stand between God and his own soul' (p. 47). This court is in session always, considering the innumerable ways and byways of the human heart whose falseness, asserts Dyke, 'so often deceiving us, must make us to be very strict and severe in examining':

> Let us never therefore let reckonings runne on, but every day let us make all even. Let us chastise ourselves every morning, examine ourselves every evening, even in the still silence of the night, as wee lye waking in our beds.
>
> (*The Mystery of Selfe-Deceiving*, p. 355)

Inevitably, the practice of self-examination becomes formalised. Dyke devotes hundreds of pages to a Ramist analysis of the varieties of self-deception, urging eternal vigilance and

---

[1] Robert Cushman, *Therapeia* (Chapel Hill, 1958), p. 230.

[2] Milton's didacticism is no more radical than Sidney's for whom poetry is a branch of learning, sharing with other arts a great purpose 'to lead and draw us to as high a perfection as our degenerate souls, made worse by their clay lodgings, can be capable of', and accomplishing that end to better effect: 'The poet . . . doth draw the mind more effectually than any other art doth.' (Again the familiar emphasis on the exercise of the reader's mind.)

meditation as antidotes to all of them. Diarists commit their daily 'audits' to paper in a systematic fashion, answering set questions designed to organize for them the spiritual history of the day :

> Observe, what sin 'tis you are most unwilling to part with. . . . Which you have formerly been most apt to plead for, to extenuate or excuse, and hide.
>   Which an awaken'd Conscience hath most plainly told you of . . .
>   Which the Temperament of your body doth most incline to . . .
>   Observe . . . what *Passion* was most predominant in each *Period* of Time. Consider further what dangerous *Temptations* you have met with : how you have fallen by 'em or been inabled to resist. Consider withal the *Time* and the *Means* whereby God hath at any time . . . awaken'd, convinc't and humbled you.
>   (John Shower, *Serious Reflections*, pp. 179–81)

By the last quarter of the century 'the duty of Self-Observation' has acquired the status of a science and an apparatus that is the counterpart of the analytical method developed in connection with the new empiricism; 'For this considerate thinking on our ways, separates and discriminates things that are confusedly huddled together, . . . gathers and collects those that are scattered and dispersed, . . . traces and finds out truth, examines likelihoods and appearances, and discovers and explores pretences that are feigned and varnished' (Arwaker, *Thoughts well Employ'd*, p. 22). This might be a summary of the claims Bacon makes for his method were it not for the inclusiveness of the final sentence : 'This is it that preordains what is to be done, revolves what is already acted, governs the Affections, restrains excess, and betters and improves our lives in all respects' (22–23).

The habit of *self*-analysis is only one aspect of an age of analysis. Ramists teach that a discourse, written or oral, is built up of a series of axiomatic sentences, arranged in a descending order from the most general to the most special ; and that, since composition or genesis involves the accretion of discrete units of thought, analysis is able to break down the finished product into the same units and so verify the correctness of the procedure. The Puritan preacher anatomizes doctrine in the same way, beginning with the text and dividing it and sub-dividing it until nothing remains to be explained. His auditors, in turn, co-operate with him by carefully noting each sub-division and reflecting on its application :

> When the Word of God is preached before thee . . . be attentive . . . observe these directions . . . marke the Text, observe the division ; marke how every point is handled : quote the places of Scripture which he alledgeth for his Doctrines proofe, fold downe a leafe in your Bible from whence the place is recited, that so at your leisure after your returne from the Church, you may examine it : apply that which is spoken to thy self ; and endeavour to be bettered by it. Continue in thy attentive hearing without wearinesse, from the beginning unto the end of the sermon.[1]

Literary texts are also 'opened' by the rules of method. Schoolboys were taught to cull out figures of speech, parse grammar, and resolve orations and poems into 'matter' or doctrine.[2] The value of much of this analysis is questionable, but its effect on those who are encouraged to practise it is undeniable. Commenting on Dudley Fenner's analysis of St. Paul's *Epistle to Philemon*, an example of the 'complete Ramist technique of reading', Sister Miriam Joseph observes that,

---

[1] *A Garden of Spirituall Flowers*, pp. 116–7.

[2] See Walter J. Ong, S.J., *Ramus, Method, and the Decay of Dialogue* (Cambridge, Mass., 1958), pp. 263–7.

If it makes us somewhat dizzy to follow Fenner through these analytical gymnastics, we must remember that such exercise, like parsing in grammar or noting rhetorical features such as loose and periodic sentences, parallel structure, balance and rhythm, establishes habits of subconscious observation and appreciation which contribute greatly to mature reading even when rapid and preoccupied with content. A habit of logical analysis subconsciously associates itself with one's reading even more deeply than a grammatical or rhetorical analysis, for it is more closely related to the thought itself.[1]

And Ong makes a similar point when he remarks on the pervasiveness of analysis in the schools :

Although it often meant mere naming of the 'ornaments' of tropes and figures, such rhetorical analysis, particularly when abetted by dialectical analysis, demanded that the pupil get into the text, struggle with it, and, in general, involve himself in the linguistic situation.[2]

We have then two analytical traditions, one concerned with the inner life and encouraging introspection, the other concerned with objects and artifacts and encouraging a sense of responsibility to 'the linguistic situation'. And as a poem whose subject is man's disobedience and the 'fruit thereof', a poem which tells the story of how its readers came to be what they *now* are, *Paradise Lost* is uniquely fitted to draw forth a response rooted in both traditions.

[1] *Rhetoric in Shakespeare's Time*, (New York, 1947), p. 353.
[2] Op. cit., p. 285. See also Harding, *The Club of Hercules*, p. 10: 'The poets of the period would not have written in such a highly figurative manner unless they knew they could count on an audience capable of responding to it. . . . Whatever else we may say about Milton's "fit audience, though few" there can be no doubt that it was unusually well equipped to understand his uses of classical literature and had, furthermore, developed a background of reading and listening habits which guaranteed a closer and more intelligent inspection of *Paradise Lost* than most modern readers are qualified to give it.'

The possibility of such a response, and of a reader who becomes the detachedly involved observer of his own mental processes, is attested to by the commentary of Jonathan Richardson, the elder (*Explanatory Notes and Remarks on Milton's Paradise Lost*, 1734). Repeatedly Richardson pays tribute to the subtlety of Milton's method and acknowledges the special claim the poem has on his Christian attention. The reading experience, he insists, must. be a consciously analytical one. The business of poetry is to 'awaken' (clv), and Milton is praised because his style rouses the reader from drowsiness into attention, and makes him like it; 'There is Something in Every Man's whereby he is Known, as by his Voice, Face, Gait, &c. in *Milton* there is a certain Vigour, whether *Versing or Prosing*, which will Awaken Attention be She never so Drowsy, and then Persuade her to be Thankful though She was Disturb'd.' Richardson's description of the poem's demands accords perfectly with my own :

> a Reader of *Milton* must be Always upon Duty; he is Surrounded with Sense, it rises in every Line, every Word is to the Purpose ... he Expresses himself So Concisely, Employs Words So Sparingly, that whoever will Possess His Ideas must Dig for them, and Oftentimes pretty far below the Surface. If This is call'd Obscurity let it be remembered 'tis Such a One as is Complaisant to the Reader, not Mistrusting his Ability ... if a Good Writer is not Understood 'tis because his Reader is Unacquainted with, or Incapable of the Subject, or will not Submit to do the Duty of a Reader, which is to Attend Carefully to what he Reads.
>
> (cxliv–cxlv)

The fit reader, then, will regard the difficulty of the poem as a compliment to his own powers, and his reward will be commensurate with the effort: the poem is not only a vehicle for sublime ideas, it is an instrument by which the reader's mind can be educated to receive them :

and all These Sublime Ideas are Convey'd to Us in the most Effectual and Engaging Manner: the Mind of the Reader is Tempered, and Prepar'd, by Pleasure, 'tis Drawn, and Allured, 'tis Awaken'd and Invigorated to receive Such Impressions as the Poet intended to give it: it Opens the Fountains of Knowledge, Piety and Virtue, and pours Along Full Streams of Peace, Comfort and Joy to Such as can Penetrate the true Sense of the Writer, and Obediently Listen to his Songs (clx).

And the reader who does listen obediently will have participated in something more than a literary experience, since this poem is concerned with his very salvation :

what does the War of *Troy*, or the Original of the *Roman* Name, say it was That of *Britain*, Concern You and Me? the Original of Things, the First Happy, but Precarious Condition of Mankind, his Deviation from Rectitude, his Lost State, his Restoration to the Favour of God by Repentance, and Imputed Righteousness. . . . These Concern Us All Equally, and Equally with our First Parents, whose Story, and That of the Whole Church of God, this Poem sets before us. . . . Whereas Whoever Profits, as he May, by This Poem will, as *Adam* in the Garden, Enjoy the Pleasures of Sense to the Utmost, with Temperance, and Purity of Heart, the Truest and Fullest Enjoyment of them; and will Moreover perceive his Happiness is Establish'd upon a Better Foundation than That of his Own Impeccability, and Thus possess a Paradise Within Far more Happy than that of *Eden*.
(clxi–ii).

In short, for the Christian reader *Paradise Lost* is a means of confirming him in his faith, and Richardson goes so far as to suggest a comparison with Scripture, 'the Best of Books . . . said to be *Profitable for Doctrine, for Reproof, for Correction, for Instruction in Righteousness*' (clviii).

Doctrine, reproof, correction, instruction. Milton could not have wished for higher praise, and he should not be judged by a lesser standard.

2 The Milk of the Pure Word

the man that is truly regenerate and renewed
hee doth best relish the Word when it is alone
without any mixture, and therefore he cals it
the *sincere milke*; that is, the pure Word.

JOHN PRESTON, *Sins Overthrow*

(i) THE FORMAL DEFENCE

Now had th' Almighty Father from above,
From the pure Empyrean where he sits
High Thron'd above all highth, bent down his eye,
His own works and their works at once to view:
About him all the Sanctities of Heaven
Stood thick as Stars, and from his sight receiv'd
Beatitude past utterance; on his right
The radiant image of his Glory sat,
His only Son; On Earth he first beheld
Our two first Parents, yet the only two
Of mankind, in the happy Garden plac't,
Reaping immortal fruits of joy and love,
Uninterrupted joy, unrivall'd love
In blissful solitude; he then survey'd
Hell and the Gulf between, and *Satan* there
Coasting the wall of Heav'n on this side Night
In the dun Air sublime, and ready now
To stoop with wearied wings, and willing feet
On the bare outside of this World, that seem'd
Firm land imbosom'd without Firmament,
Uncertain which, in Ocean or in Air.
Him God beholding from his prospect high,
Wherein past, present, future he beholds,
Thus to his only Son foreseeing spake:
Only-begotten Son, seest thou what rage
Transports our adversary, whom no bounds

Prescrib'd, no bars of Hell, nor all the chains
Heapt on him there, nor yet the main Abyss
Wide interrupt, can hold; so bent he seems
On desperate revenge, that shall redound
Upon his own rebellious head. And now
Through all restraint broke loose he wings his way
Not far off Heav'n, in the Precincts of light,
Directly towards the new-created World,
And Man there plac't, with purpose to assay
If him by force he can destroy, or worse,
By some false guile pervert; and shall pervert;
For Man will heark'n to his glozing lies,
And easily transgress the sole Command,
Sole Pledge of his obedience: So will fall
Hee and his faithless Progeny: whose fault?
Whose but his own? ingrate, he had of mee
All he could have; I made him just and right,
Sufficient to have stood, though free to fall.
Such I created all th' Ethereal Powers
And Spirits, both them who stood and them who fail'd;
Freely they stood who stood, and fell who fell.
Not free, what proof could they have giv'n sincere
Of true allegiance, constant Faith or Love,
Where only what they needs must do, appear'd,
Not what they would? what praise could they receive?
What pleasure I, from such obedience paid,
When Will and Reason (Reason also is choice)
Useless and vain, of freedom both despoil'd,
Made passive both, had serv'd necessity,
Not mee? They therefore as to right belong'd,
So were created, nor can justly accuse
Thir maker, or thir making, or thir Fate;
As if Predestination over-rul'd
Thir will, dispos'd by absolute Decree
Or high foreknowledge; they themselves decreed
Thir own revolt, not I: if I foreknew,
Foreknowledge had no influence on their fault,
Which had no less prov'd certain unforeknown.

So without least impulse or shadow of Fate,
Or aught by me immutably foreseen,
They trespass, Authors to themselves in all
Both what they judge and what they choose; for so
I form'd them free, and free they must remain,
Till they enthrall themselves: I else must change
Thir nature, and revoke the high Decree
Unchangeable, Eternal, which ordain'd
Thir freedom: they themselves ordain'd thir fall.
The first sort by thir own suggestion fell,
Self-tempted, self-deprav'd: Man falls deceiv'd
By th' other first: Man therefore shall find grace,
The other none: in Mercy and Justice both,
Through Heav'n and Earth, so shall my glory excel,
But Mercy first and last shall brightest shine.

(III. 56–134)

In recent years, several critics have asserted that the stylistic characteristics of the voice of Milton's God are answerable to the idea of deity demanded by the poem and by seventeenth-century theology. Arnold Stein notes that God's 'language and cadence are as unsensuous as if Milton were writing a model for the Royal Society and attempting to speak purely to the understanding', and offers as a defence the observation that 'Poetry is human and metaphorical, and the Father's speeches are intended to express divine Justice as if directly: to seem without seeming: to create the illusion of no illusion'.[1] Jackson Cope makes more explicit Stein's coupling of the human and the metaphorical: 'This eye of God does not see things metaphorically, but in their essential natures.... God in his own voice can never speak metaphorically.'[2] Thomas

---

[1] *Answerable Style*, p. 128.
[2] *The Metaphoric Structure of Paradise Lost*, p. 168. Actually Cope goes on to argue that God does indeed use metaphoric language, but he is using the word 'metaphoric' in a sense that makes his inclusion here not much of a distortion.

Kranidas insists on the decorum of the presentation : 'The purity of his image of God requires the kind of rhetorical isolation, the dialectic and schematic movement of language, which strikes the reader as barer than mere simplicity.'[1] And Irene Samuel points to the obvious contrast between diabolic and heavenly rhetoric : 'The flat statement of fact, past, present, and future, the calm analysis and judgment of deeds and principles — these naturally strike the ear that has heard Satan's ringing utterances as cold and impersonal. They should.'[2] There is general agreement here as to Milton's intention : he is trying to communicate philosophical and moral distinctions through stylistic (rhetorical) signatures. The question criticism asks quite properly is, does he succeed? Stein abstains, 'I pass the problem of trying to judge them [God's speeches]'[3] while J. B. Broadbent replies in the negative :

> The least successful contrast is between the Father's rhetoric in Book III and Satan's . . . This is not enough to mark the vast gap that the poem supposes to exist between the minds of God and Satan. The fault seems to lie in rhetoric itself. For all its elaborations as a system, it is not a flexible enough instrument for the dramatic function of distinguishing between characters.[4]

In other words, while the distinction exists in the abstract, that is in the system, it is not *felt* strongly enough by the reader and is therefore finally not made. This would be a telling argument were the two styles attached to a merely

[1] *The Fierce Equation: A Study of Milton's Decorum* (The Hague, 1965), p. 135.
[2] 'The Dialogue in Heaven: A Reconsideration of *Paradise Lost*, III, 1–417', in *Milton: Modern Essays in Criticism*, ed. Arthur Barker (New York, 1965), p. 235.
[3] *Answerable Style*, p. 128.
[4] *Some Graver Subject. An Essay on Paradise Lost* (London, 1960), pp. 150–1.

literary theory of decorum, but as Kingsley Widmer reminds us, 'the entire Miltonic view, and thus much of Protestant Christian mythology is involved in the stylistic antithesis between Heaven and Hell'.[1] Rhetoric is the verbal equivalent of the fleshly lures that seek to enthral us and divert our thoughts from Heaven, the reflection of our own cupidinous desires, while logic comes from God and speaks to that part of us which retains his image. Through rhetoric man continues in the error of the Fall, through logic he can at least attempt a return to the clarity Adam lost. Stephen Hawes advises early in the sixteenth century, 'Who wyll take payne to folowe the trace / In this wretched worlde of trouthe and ryghtwysenes / In heven he shall have dwellynge place / . . . So by logyke is good perceyveraunce / To devyde the good and the evyll a sondre' (*Pastime of Pleasure*: ll. 624–7, 631–2). In the seventeenth century this injunction is translated into a programme of scientific action and a theory of sermonry ; metaphorical and affective language are rejected in favour of the objective style of Baconian empiricism and the plain style of Puritan preaching. Stein, Kranidas, Miss Samuel and, to a lesser extent, Cope, defend God's speeches by isolating them as objects whose meaning is derived from an abstract system, inviting Broadbent's objection that they are deficient in poetical force. In the context of contemporary attitudes, however, the reader's response to a rhetorical pattern like this one would be emotional, even visceral, as well as intellectual. To the watchful Christian, the rhetorical appeal is something to be feared because it panders to a part of him he knows to be subversive, while the philosopher disdains it as a clouder of men's minds and an impediment to scientific investigation ; conversely, bareness and clarity or organization are not only

[1] 'The Iconography of Renunciation: The Miltonic Simile', *ELH*, xxv (1958), 269.

valued, but welcomed, with the kind of physical pleasure men in other ages reserve for beautiful (lyric) poems or beautiful women. In other words, the prevailing orthodoxies — linguistic, theological, scientific — make possible an affective response to a presentation *because* it is determinedly non-affective.

God's presentation is determinedly non-affective, although it certainly does not give that impression. His first speech is a fine example of logical method being applied to a universe of things. Cope might well be describing it when he speaks of 'the spatialized form of logic which reduced reality to a visual object, and supplanted dialogue by the monologue of the expositor pointing out the connections among parts'.[1] Walter Ong's characterization of Ramist–Puritan poetry is similarly apposite :

> When the Puritan mentality which is . . . the Ramist mentality, produces poetry, it is at first blatantly didactic, but shades gradually into reflective poetry which does not talk to anyone in particular but meditates on objects.[2]

To those who are accustomed to think Milton's God querulous or self-justifying, the suggestion that he does not talk to anyone in particular may seem curious. Technically, however, the tonal qualities usually ascribed to his voice are accidental, the result of what the reader reads *into* the speech rather than of what is there. The form of his discourse is determined by the nature of the thing he contemplates rather than by the desire to project a personality (*ethos*) or please a specific audience (*pathos*); its mode is exfoliation; that is, the speech does not build, it *unfolds* according to the rules of method.

Seventeenth-century method is based on a faith in

---

[1] *Metaphoric Structure*, pp. 33–34.
[2] *Ramus, Method, and the Decay of Dialogue*, pp. 287–8.

'natural order', the rather naïve assumption that the satis-
faction the mind feels at seeing things arranged one after
the other, from general to special or special to general,
corresponds to the arrangement of reality :

> Méthode est disposition par laquelle entre plusieurs choses la
> première de notice est disposée au premier lieu, la deuziesme au
> deuziesme, la troiziesme au troiziesme et...
>
> Méthode de nature est par laquelle ce qui est du tout et absolu-
> ment plus évident et plus notoire est préposé, ce qu'Aristote
> appelle au premier de la *Démonstration* ores plus notoire de nature,
> ores précédent de nature, d'autant que ce qui est naturellement
> plus évident doibt précéder en ordre et déclairation de doctrine
> comme sont les causes de leurs effectz et partant, aussi leurs
> symboles comme le général et universel du spécial et singulier.
> Et d'autant que chacune sera plus générale, tant plus précédera.
> Et le généralllissime sera le premier en rang et ordre car il est le
> premier de clairté et notice. Les subalternes suyvront car ilz sont
> prochains de clairté. Et d'iceux les plus notoires précéderont, les
> moins notoires suyvront. Et enfin les exemples qui sont spécialis-
> simes seront mis les derniers. Ceste méthode est singulière et
> unique ès doctrines bien instituées car en elle, singulière et
> unique, est procédé par choses antécédentes du tout et absolu-
> ment plus cleres et notoires pour esclarcir et illustrer les choses
> conséquentes obscures et incognues.[1]

We can see here that while the doctrine is non-affective, it
is nevertheless rhetorical or at least pedagogical, since the
emphasis is on the perceiving mind, and the end is to
produce visible patterns or groupings that the mind will
find easy to follow.[2] It is a rhetoric of the mind, leading from
and looking to a God who is all mind (Ramus remarks that

[1] Pierre de la Ramée, *Dialectique*, edition critique avec introduction,
notes et commentaires de Michel Dassonville (Genève, Librairie Droz, 1964),
pp. 144–5.
[2] This does not contradict my assertion that method attends to things since
Ramism equates the objects in the real world and the sets of mental items in
the mind. See Ong, *Ramus, Method*, passim.

God is the perfect logician) but it respects neither persons nor occasions. When Milton's God asks 'whose fault?' and answers 'Whose but his own? ingrate', the question is posed because the exposition of the thing or item under consideration (man's position in the universe) requires that it be answered ; and in the answer given, 'ingrate', is a term not of reproach, but of definition. That is to say, the names God imposes reflect the accuracy of his perception rather than his attitude toward the object named. Consider, in support of this statement, John Wilkins' account of the difference between man's knowledge and God's :

> His knowledge is most deep and intimate, reaching to the very essence of things, ours but slight and superficial. . . . He hath a perfect comprehension of all things that have been, that are or shall be, according to all the various relations, dependences, circumstances, belonging to each of them. So that this Attribute of his [knowledge] must be infinite and unbounded, both *extensive* with respect to the several kinds of objects which it comprehends; and likewise *intensive* as it sees every single object with a most perfect infallible view. He doth not only understand all particulars; but he knows every particular so exactly; as if he were wholly taken up and intent in his thought upon that alone.[1]

Wilkins' conception of deity is at base linguistic; the contrast between human and divine sight is grounded in the assumption that for both God and man the problem is the accurate description of a shared universe of fixed objects. The things of the world are the measure of God's knowledge as well as man's. God's superiority is, in a sense, merely optical, and one can assume that he speaks the language Wilkins triumphantly offers to the world in *An Essay Towards a Real Character and a Philosophical Language*, 1668, a language free of 'synonymous words', 'Equivocals', words of 'several significations', and of metaphors, those 'affected

[1] *On the Principles and Duties of Natural Religion* (1678), pp. 125–6.

ornaments' which prejudice the native simplicity of speech 'and contribute to the disguising of it with false appearances' (p. 18). God is the perfect name-giver whose word *is* the thing in all its aspects. In the ultimate philosophical sense his words are true. 'Ingrate' is not a judgment, but a scientific notation with the *emotional* value of an X or a Y; and later when God commands the 'Abyss' of unformed matter, 'Silence, ye troubl'd waves ... / ... your discord end' (VII. 216–17), 'troubl'd' and 'discord' are to be understood only in a physical sense, notwithstanding anything else we may read into them.

God's monologue, then, is the union of method — the self-generating exposition of what is — and a philosophically accurate vocabulary, admitting neither ambiguity or redundancy.[1] Rather than true, that is conversational, interrogatives, God's questions are a part of the machinery of method; 'whose fault?' is not the defensive exclamation of an angry parent disclaiming responsibility for the sins of his offspring, but a logically necessary inquiry if the fact (of the Fall) is to be placed in the context of *total* reality. If God's comprehension of things extends to 'all the various relations, dependences, circumstances, belonging to each of them', his *verbal* consideration of anything is correspondingly all-inclusive. For Bacon and those who follow him the application of an empiricist methodology will lead eventually to a complete description of the universe. Bacon envisions an army of committed methodologists who proceed in a business-like manner — 'one shall take charge of one thing, another of another' — to illuminate areas of a segmented whole. The end product will be a spatialized diagram of reality in which each object is presented in the

[1] The interpretation of the speech as an unfolding picture of reality in all its aspects was first suggested to me by Edward Pechter in a paper written for a seminar at the University of California, Berkeley.

context of all other objects and all relationships can be seen at a single glance. While man must work toward that goal slowly, 'gathering up limb by limb' the shattered body of Truth, God enjoys it now, in his eternal present, and any utterance of his says everything about anything. He will open with the fact ('will fall') and proceed to connect it to all other facts ('the monologue of the expositor pointing out the connections among parts'); he does this not to anticipate objections (the speech is a meditation, not an argument, directed if it is directed at all, to the Son who is a reflection of his Father), but because his vision 'Wherein past, present, future he beholds' sees each thing as it exists in the total picture of reality, and his report of any particular answers to that vision, extending to 'all the various relations, dependences, circumstances' — to everything.

For God to fix his eye on any one thing is to fix his eye on all things; reality is spread before him on a table, as it were, a finite complex of interconnections in which each fact implies and indeed contains all others. In his monologue God follows the network of relationships that lead out from the point of his 'momentary' concentration without ever abandoning that point. Satan regards his ascent from Hell as an assertion of self and a proof of his independence : 'whom no bounds / Prescrib'd, no bars of Hell ... can hold'; but in the larger view, which the reader is allowed to share with God, Satan's action, or pseudo-action, is (1) a sign of his dependence and service and hence of his eternally recurring defeat ('shall redound') and (2) part of another action ('so will fall') in which his role is ultimately secondary ('they themselves ordain'd thir fall'). That action in turn is imbedded in a configuration of particulars that radiate out from it, surround it, and define it; and God's questions ('whose fault', 'Not free, what proof', 'what praise could they receive') serve to bring that configuration into focus. The process is one of continuing clarification; that is, Satan 'Coasting the wall of Heav'n' is never abandoned as an object for comprehension; when God concludes (stops) at Book III, line 134, he does so because that object is now known (understood) in 'every particular', both intensively and extensively, and in God's 'most perfect infallible view' to know so completely one object is to know all objects. The effect is analogous to the operation of an expanding spotlight which at first illuminates a single point of reference and then widens to take in the panorama that finally determines its meaning. While the monologue touches on all actions and happenings — even Christ's offer of himself, soon to be made, is implied in the word 'mercy' — it is in no sense digressive, since it ends where it begins, with the *complete* identification (unfolding) of a single entity.

In the process, of course, other entities are identified, placed, unfolded, disposed, defined, displayed, known, understood:

> So will fall
> Hee and his faithless Progeny: whose fault?
> Whose but his own? ingrate, he had of mee
> All he could have; I made him just and right,
> Sufficient to have stood, though free to fall.
> Such I created all th' Ethereal Powers
> And Spirits, both them who stood and them who fail'd;
> Freely they stood who stood, and fell who fell.
> Not free, what proof could they have giv'n . . .
>
> (III. 5–103)

The thing (fact, item) under consideration here is the Fall. In accordance with the traditional order as exemplified in Milton's *Art of Logic, arranged after the method of Peter Ramus,* the first of the arguments or logical topics to be applied is cause: 'This first place of invention is the fount of all knowledge; and in fact if the cause of something can

be comprehended it is believed to be known.'¹ God asks
'whose fault?' (what cause?) and replies immediately,
'Whose but his own?'. (The mode of Ramist logic is *self-*
interrogation.) Before the answer can be said to be truly
comprehensive the agent must be more precisely identified.
Man has already been characterized as 'faithless'; like
'ingrate' the word is literal not metaphorical; *faithlessness*
is the essence of disobedience, and when Adam chooses it,
it becomes his essence. Ingratitude is one aspect of faithlessness–disobedience in the context God is establishing. 'He
had of mee / All he could have' circumscribes and delimits
this particular instance of ingratitude, but that statement
too must be divided or 'opened' before the situation is fully
'known'. 'Sufficient to have stood, but free to fall' defines
the 'all' God has given Adam, a will strong enough to make
steadfastness possible, and flexible enough to make it
meaningful. This definition is educed specifically in respect
to Adam; it is now extended to the *genus* of which he is a
species, that is to all free agents: 'Such I created all th'
Ethereal Powers / And Spirits, both them who stood and
them who fell'. The fact of God's having created these
agents leads naturally and necessarily to an exposition of
their place in his benevolent plan: 'Not free, what proof
could they have giv'n ... what praise could they receive
... What pleasure I from such obedience paid?' There
follows a proof or argument (in the Ramist sense) by nega-
tives: Adam is at fault because no one else is ('Not I'). The
unfolding of the discourse continues until nothing remains
to be clarified or disposed, and we end with God's mercy,
that attribute which shows him to be independent of his
own causal sequences while indicating his willingness to
extricate his creatures from them.

¹ *A Fuller Institution of the Art of Logic, arranged after the method, of*
Peter Ramus, trans. A. S. Gilbert, *The Works of John Milton*, xi. 31.

(ii) THE RHETORICAL DEFENCE

One might say at this point that the aesthetic objection remains unanswered:

> Theology's demand for ... clearness ... and Poetry's demand for a characterization of God that will support our love and reverence cannot, on Milton's terms, be reconciled.[1]

Of course, in 'Milton's terms', poetry's demands are illegitimate because they proceed from, and return to, the affections (art-truth is psychological and *self*-centred), and he would want his readers to resist them. Yet he would be aware also of his obligation to readers 'of soft and delicious temper who will not so much as look upon Truth herselfe, unlesse they see her elegantly drest', and as a teacher he would know that 'Truth ... ere she can come to the triall and inspection of the Understanding' must first 'passe through many little wards and limits of the several Affections and Desires', putting on 'such colours and attire as those Pathetick [appealing to the emotions] handmaids of the soul please to lead her in to their Queen'.[2] In this passage from *Reason of Church Government*, Milton joins those who echo Aristotle's reluctant concession to the 'defect of our hearers', admitting rhetoric into their systems in recognition of a basic human weakness. Ramus provides for the weakminded in his audience by allowing them the 'prudential' method, 'en laquelle les choses précédentes non pas du tout et absolument plus notoires, mais néantmoins plus convenables à celluy qu'il fault enseigner'.[3] Puritan preachers stress

---

[1] John Peter, *A Critique of Paradise Lost*, p. 18.
[2] *Complete Prose Works of John Milton*, ed. Don Wolfe (New Haven, 1953), i. 817, 818, 830.
[3] *Dialectique*, p. 150.

the importance of adding exhortation to the exposition of doctrine. Not surprisingly, the clearest statement is Bacon's :

> if the affections in themselves were pliant and obedient to reason, it were true there should be no great use of persuasions and insinuations to the will, more than of *naked proposition and proofs*; but in regard of the continual mutinies and seditions of the affections, . . . reason would become captive and servile, if Eloquence of Persuasion did not practise and win the Imagination.[1]

Ideally, the reader should respond to the 'naked proof' of God's word, but the fallen intellect being what it is, a more emotive stimulus is required. Somehow poetry's demands must be made to accord with theology's.

Milton secures a positive response to the figure of God by creating a psychological (emotional) need for the authority he represents. The experience of the first two books is unsettling ; the reader's confidence in his own powers is shaken, and other guides prove similarly unreliable. There is of course the epic voice, but his reliability is largely negative and hardly comforting, extending to what Satan is not, to what the human mind cannot do, to what cannot be trusted. The devils present themselves as authorities in the debate, but they are exposed one by one, and the reader can only feel further uneasiness at having surrendered even momentarily to their eloquence. At one point Beelzebub seems about to transfer to his 'Atlantean shoulders' the task of distinguishing the true from the false. He sweeps away the self-deceptions of the previous speakers with a single word — 'doubtless' — and goes on to recall to the fallen host and to the reader what they have forgotten in the exhilaration of debating : God is God. 'For he, be sure, / In highth or depth, still first and last will Reign' (ii. 323–4). Figuratively, and

[1] *Francis Bacon, Selected Writings*, ed. H. G. Dick (New York, 1955), pp. 310–11.

perhaps literally we nod in approval as he continues: war
with God is unthinkable and peace (he conjectures correctly)
will not be offered; let us, therefore, — and the reader
awaits expectantly for his conclusion — *attack man!* 'Seduce
them to our Party, that thir God / May prove thir foe'
(368–9). At once the promise of the angel's Atlantean
shoulders is seen as illusory (there is an analogue in the
foolishness of the pilot who places his anchor in the scaly
rind of Leviathan-serpent-Satan); more disturbing than
Beelzebub's treachery is our involuntary involvement in it;
for the success of his strategy depends on our willingness to
conspire against ourselves, and our response to the debate
indicates that such a conspiracy is all too possible. Of
course, Beelzebub does not escape the poem's irony. We
know that his final taunt — 'Advise if this be worth /
Attempting, or to sit in darkness here / Hatching vain
Empires' (376–8) — is directed as much at him as at his
fellow devils; any empire apart from God is vain, even one
secured through subversion. But this is cold comfort since
Beelzebub's ultimate defeat does not preclude his assault
on us, and his error in no way mitigates ours. To God and
those who know God, the devilish counsel and Beelzebub's
plan are equally absurd; to the devils Beelzebub offers a
rational solution to a difficult military problem; the reader
has the advantage (or is it the disadvantage) of both perspectives and therefore of a third whose complexity defies
literal transcription. When Satan struggles up to the seat
of Chaos, he describes his situation in words that apply to
us as well: 'Wand'ring this darksome Desert/ . . . Alone,
and without guide, half lost, I seek' (973, 975). Satan is
wholly and irretrievably lost; we are but partly lost, redeemed finally by the true promise of Jesus Christ and
guided in the poem by an inspired poet. At this point, however, the incarnation is far from our minds and the poet

seems to have joined with his characters to unsettle us. We do wander; we are alone, without a guide, facing the threat of Satan who approaches 'this frail world' : 'Thither full fraught with mischievous revenge, / Accurst, and in a cursed hour he hies'. And in the midst of our confusion we know at least that the cursed hour is now.

It is from this experience that we move toward our encounter with Milton's God; and the sense of imminent and inevitable danger we bring with us from Book II is only accentuated by the lines that precede him. While the invocation to light does many things, it proves neither a defence against the menacing shadow of Satan nor a clarification of the issues that have been obscured in Hell. If the soliloquy is finally the first stage in the progressive humanization of the epic voice, it is also a revelation of his fallibility. The tersely confident declaratives, so familiar in Books I and II, give way here to the provisionality of the suppliant ('that I may see'). The blind poet who wanders 'where the Muses haunt' and seeks guidance is suddenly with us rather than above us (it is the father who now bends down 'from above'), and however comforting this admission of fellowship may be in Book XII, it hardly answers to our present need. In context, that need is objectified in the precarious position of 'our two first Parents' who are discovered 'in the happy Garden plac't, / Reaping immortal fruits of joy and love' (III. 65–67). From God's prospect high this is a blighted pastoral, existing under the shadow of Satan's impending attack. The reader views simultaneously the happy garden and the enemy despoiler *now* touching down on the 'bare outside of this World'; he is the helpless observer who, by chance, commands the vantage point of an intersection and sees two vehicles about to collide.

As Satan descends, the epic voice's new status is indicated by the ambiguous placing of the word 'Uncertain' :

To stoop with wearied wings and willing feet
On the bare outside of this World, that seem'd
Firm land imbosom'd without Firmament,
Uncertain which, in Ocean or in Air.

(73–76)

'Uncertain' is, as Hughes notes, 'an impersonal and absolute construction', and it could apply either to Satan, stooping with wearied wings, or to the general state of knowledge concerning the bare outside of this world. The second reading, which will suggest itself because 'Uncertain' is so far from Satan, is a reflection on the observer–narrator who is unable to make out the scene he is supposedly describing ('which' is the question *he* asks). The inspired poet's vision, like ours, is limited, although it is a higher order of limitation. 'There is a vast difference', writes Wilkins, 'between the wisest of men, and such as are grossly ignorant and sottish. . . . And yet these things hold some proportion to one another being finite ; whereas betwixt Gods knowledg and mans, the distance is infinite.'[1] At this point the distance betwixt God and man is being defined dramatically, although the drama takes place in the reader's mind rather than in the poem's action : the threat Satan poses is now felt personally because it is directed at Adam and Eve, the natural objects of our affection and sympathy ; the epic voice fails to provide even the negative protection we have come to expect from him ; an authority vacuum exists just as an authority is most needed. Consequently, while God talks to no one in particular and is unconcerned with the effect his words may have, the occasion of his speech is rhetorical, even though the audience it is delivered to is technically not there.

If Empson's law — 'all the characters are on trial in any civilized narrative' — applies at all to Milton's God, its application is rhetorical. Rhetorical persuasion or demon-

[1] *Natural Religion*, pp. 126–7.

stration, Aristotle tells us, depends first 'on the personal
character of the speaker' (*Rhetoric*, 1356a) and second 'on
putting the audience into a certain frame of mind'. God's
personal character is established through his language
which is conspicuously biblical and assures conviction by
virtue of its references to scriptural passages every reader
knows. Aristotle's orator is advised to rely heavily on
sententia because 'if the maxims are sound, they display the
speaker as a man of sound moral charater' (*Rhetoric*, 1395b).
This is a principle of decorum which has a Christian parallel
in Augustine's advice to young preachers: 'For one who
wishes to speak wisely ... it is above all necessary to
remember the words of Scripture ... He shall give delight
with his proofs.'[1] The 'maxims' of the Bible are not merely
sound, they are true, or more properly Truth itself; they
persuade by being. Milton can rely on his readers to
recognize the propriety of the language God speaks and
therefore to acquiesce in his authority:

> Milton's divine persons are divine persons indeed, and talk in the
> language of God, that is in the language of Scripture. He is so very
> scrupulous and exact in this particular that perhaps there is not a
> single expression which may not be *justified* by the *authority* of
> holy Writ.[2]

James Sims lists eight biblical sources for lines 85–86 alone.[3]
   God's syntax also contributes to the 'proof' or demonstration of his character. Satan's fallacies are wrapped in
serpentine trains of false beginnings, faulty pronoun
references, missing verbs and verbal schemes which
sacrifice sense to sound ('Surer to prosper than prosperity /
Could have assur'd us'); it is a loose style, irresponsibly

---

[1] *On Christian Doctrine*, trans. D. W. Robertson (New York, 1958), p. 122.
[2] Thomas Newton's note to III. 344 in his variorum edition of *Paradise Lost*, 1749.
[3] *The Bible in Milton's Epics* (Florida, 1962), p. 262.

digressive, moving away steadily from logical coherence (despite the *appearance* of logic) and calling attention finally to the virtuosity of the speaker. In contrast, God practises a Stoic austerity; his syntax is close and sinewy, adhering to the ideal of brevity (*brevitas*) by 'employing only what is strictly necessary for making the matter clear';[1] the intrusion of personality is minimal, the figures of speech are unobtrusive and to the point, and one has little sense of a style apart from the thought. The speech is an example of the lucidly anonymous style Cicero recommends to anyone seeking to appear authoritative: 'The *exordium* ... should contain everything which contributes to dignity ... It should contain very little brilliance, vivacity, or finish of style, because these give rise to a suspicion of preparation and excessive ingenuity. As a result ... the speech loses conviction and the speaker, authority.'[2]

Evidence of an awareness of Milton's rhetorical skill is provided by Addison's instructions to the reader:

> The beauties ... which we are to look for in these speeches, are not of a poetical nature. ... The passions which they are design'd to raise, are a divine love and religious fear. The particular beauty of the speeches in the third book consists in *that shortness and perspicuity of stile.* ... He has presented all the abstruse doctrins ... with great energy of expression, and in a stronger and clearer light than I have met with in any other writer ... the *concise and clear* manner, in which he has treated them is very much to be admir'd. (*Spectator*, No. 315)

What Addison admires is the art that conceals art, the rhetoric that denies itself recognition. The effort required to secure this effect may have been great, but the impression

[1] George Kennedy, *The Art of Persuasion in Greece* (Princeton, 1963), p. 294.

[2] *De Inventione, De optimo genere oratorum Topica*, trans. H. M. Hubbell (Cambridge, Mass.), pp. 51, 53.

given is one of effortlessness. As we read, God is innocent of Milton's skill; his eloquence is not eloquence at all, but the natural persuasiveness that is inseparable from wisdom. The distinction between the truth and the form the truth takes in speech disappears, as it does in Stoic theory; 'The Stoic concept made unnecessary any distinction between a ... philosopher ... and a good orator ... for to the Stoics the thought of the speech *was* the speech and would produce its own natural and good expression. *Rem tene, verba sequentur*, "hold to the subject, the words will follow" was Cato's expression of it'.[1] (One can see here the similarity to Ramist method which also holds to the subject or object.) Augustine declares, 'in those places where ... eloquence is recognized by the learned such things are said that the words with which they are said seem not to have been sought by the speaker but to have been joined to the things spoken about as if spontaneously, like wisdom coming from her house (that is, from the breast of the wise man) followed by eloquence as if she were an inseparable servant who was not called.'[2] The Bible is not composed of tropes and figures which are merely the names rhetoricians give to the effects of its true eloquence. As critics, engaged in an analytic act, we can see how God's eloquence has been 'sought' by Milton, but as readers who are involved in an experience that has its own frame of reference, we accept it, unthinkingly, as an adjunct of the wisdom we have sought so long.

---

[1] Kennedy, *The Art of Persuasion*, 292–3.

[2] *On Christian Doctrine*, p. 124. Cf. the characterization of Christ by Satan in *Paradise Regained*, 'Thy actions to thy words accord, thy words / To thy large heart give utterance due, thy heart / Contains of good, wise, just, the perfect shape' (III. 8–10). In *Comus* the Lady imagines that eloquence will come to her because of or along with the cause she speaks for, 'the uncontrolled worth / Of this pure cause would kindle my rapt spirits / To such a flame of sacred vehemence, / That dumb things would be mov'd to sympathize' (793–5).

For of course the true force of God's speech as a rhetorical performance stems from its success in satisfying the needs of a specific audience, in 'putting the audience into a certain frame of mind'. In this case the orator's task is not so much to arouse passions as to assuage them by providing reassurance and clarification to counteract the fear and confusion his auditors feel when they come to him. The emotion Milton is reaching for here is *relief*, the physical sense of having exchanged the chaotic liveliness of Hell for the calm stasis of Heaven. Broadbent is finally unsympathetic to this part of the poem because he believes that divinity should be 'enclosed in an experiential context more immediate than Milton's'; yet his own words reveal, inadvertently, how immediate Milton's context is: 'There is a stolid honesty about this [Puritan pulpit rhetoric] that carries over into the Father's sermon — at least we know, what we don't usually from an Anglican pulpit, precisely what he is saying.'[1] The point is, we *need* to know what he is saying, and to know it precisely, that is, unambiguously. A distinction that Broadbent regards as theoretical and abstract is the basis, in the poem, of a response the reader gives to a dramatic moment. Pope is correct when he calls God a 'School-Divine'; the pedagogical stance (God does not assume it consciously) is just right, following as it does the multiple failures of pseudo-authorities in the earlier books; for a moment we are caught up in and share the confidence and detachment of the speaker, and returned to the unambiguous exactness of the opening line, 'Of Man's First Disobedience . . .':

> seest thou what rage
> Transports our adversary, whom no bounds
> Prescrib'd, no bars of Hell, nor all the chains

---

[1] *Some Graver Subject. An Essay on Paradise Lost*, pp. 146–7.

> Heapt on him there, nor yet the main Abyss
> Wide interrupt can hold; so bent he seems
> On desperate revenge, that shall redound
> Upon his own rebellious head.

(III. 80–86)

The visual image complements the tone : the Father points, assuredly, to a single spot in the vast panorama before him and proceeds to consider calmly events that have agitated and bewildered us ('thou' is the Son's pronoun, but we appropriate it). He sees what we see, but his reaction differs from ours and the difference is corrective. The rage that transports *our* adversary is, from the prospect high, an object of interest or amusement rather than fear. One can almost hear in the casualness of 'seest thou' the derisiveness of 'Nearly it now concerns us to be sure / Of our Omnipotence' (v. 721–2). Satan as threat has no reality in this place. When God says 'so bent he seems', Bentley demurs : 'Satan was already broke out of Hell, and more than *seem'd* to be bent on Revenge. 'Tis likely the Poet gave it, Wide interrupt *COULD* hold : so bent he *IS*' (*Paradise Lost*, 1732, p. 80). This emendation is unsatisfactory in two respects : (1) in God's eternal present there is no distinction of tenses, and (2) the qualifying 'seems' is proof of God's prescience. He sees beyond (or around) the ominous appearance of Satan descending on Adam and Eve 'In blissful solitude'; while Satan is confident in the evidence of things seen and the reader fears them, with 'seems' God dismisses them, almost contemptuously, and insists that all be interpreted, in this case quite literally, *sub specie aeternitatis*. This seems is the seems of certainty; it reflects the speaker's perfect confidence in the justness of his perception, in contrast to the 'seem'd' of line 74, the sign, as we have seen, of the uncertainty (Uncertain, which, in Ocean or in Air) of the narrator and the reader. Being reminded of our limitations is a familiar experience in Books I and II; here it is for the first time comforting since the imposition of the heavenly perspective brings with it the promise of Satan's eventual defeat.

The task of reassuring the reader is completed with the words 'shall redound'. The three syllables receive almost equal stress; the force of the phrase, however, resides in 'shall' which is at once a prediction and a command, indicating a union of absolute knowledge and absolute control.[1] The circularity implicit in 'redound' provides a visual image of that control: Satan hurls himself against the superstructure of a God-centred universe only to see his own efforts turned against him. The movement is mirrored in the verse; straining against limits, Satan breaks through barrier after barrier — bars, chains, Abyss — only to reach the verb 'hold'; technically negative ('nor . . . can hold'), it restrains him nevertheless (the force of 'nor' is not felt) so that with 'seems' and 'redound' he snaps back like a boomerang, although the illusion of freedom continues. We have seen this before; in Book I, Satan's summoning of the fallen angels is compared to Moses' calling up of the locusts, and for a moment the comparison seems inapposite, since Moses sends the locusts against Pharaoh who is anti-Christ and a type of Satan; but of course Satan does just that — raises the devils against himself (to 'redound Upon his own rebellious head') and against his will. In his final appearance on our stage, the archfiend is made to assume the shape he once adopted — so he thought — on his own initiative. Satan's powerlessness is revealed many times in *Paradise Lost*, but never so nakedly as here in Book III when God

[1] Not that God causes Satan's rebellion and the woes attendant on it; but he could if he wished prevent it or remit the punishment; all lies within his power. In the case of angels and men, however, he delegates responsibility to lesser agents.

declares 'that shall redound'. From this point, Satan ceases to be a problem for the reader.

The emphasis in the preceding paragraphs on the rhetorical propriety of God's first utterance is in no way meant to invalidate the earlier analysis of the lines as a demonstration of formalist perfection. The speech can be said to move on two fronts : as a self-contained organism, it unfolds according to its own inner logic ; as a performance, it inspires confidence and offers consolation. The God who tenders reassurance and guidance to a reader in need of both is still the logician whose existence supports the seventeenth-century ideal ; it is Milton's triumph to make the two figures one in terms of their effect, while maintaining the integrity of each. God is not a rhetorician, but he has a rhetorician's success. The formal proof of deity, rigorously non-rhetorical, becomes part of the rhetorical proof (in Stoic–Ramus theory the oratorical and philosophical ideals tend to merge). We flee our compromising involvement with the affective in Books i and ii and respond affectively to its antithesis in Book iii. Milton turns the intellectual–linguistic bias of his age into a dramatic reality and gives his readers an intuition of ultimate authority and absolute reliability. Theology's demands have become poetry's.

(iii) INGRATE

The defence, however, cannot rest without admitting that the difficulties Milton's God poses for most readers remain. Northrop Frye's lifelong experience with the poem is a case in point :

> When as a student I first read the speech in Book Three of *Paradise Lost* in which 'God the Father turns a school divine', I thought it was grotesquely bad. I have been teaching and

studying *Paradise Lost* for many years, and my visceral reaction
to that speech is still exactly the same. But I see much more
clearly than I did at first why Milton wanted such a speech at
such a point.

(*The Aims and Methods of Scholarship in Modern
Languages and Literatures*, ed. James Thorpe, p. 64)

Frye's 'visceral reaction' is what all readers (who are not
saints) feel to some extent — dismay, disappointment, and
a reluctant hostility. The argument of the preceding pages
holds, I think, through the phrase 'that shall redound'; but
the confidence we have in the voice that intones this prediction soon becomes the source of new anxieties and
discomforts. Milton has provided God with a dramatic
moment so rhetorically effective that it secures for him a
believing audience. This is fine when God is telling us what
we want to hear — Satan will be defeated and the threat he
represents in the poem dispelled — but our complacence
does not survive the inexorability of 'and shall pervert, /
For Man will heark'n to his glozing lies, / And easily
transgress the sole Command, / Sole pledge of his obedience'
(92–95). The force of 'shall redound' is transferred to 'shall
pervert' — the parallels extend beyond the repeated stress
on 'shall' to the number of syllables and the position in the
line — and having accepted the first 'shall', and with it the
authority of the speaker, we automatically accept the second
(which is vaguely threatening rather than reassuring), and
with it the accusation that follows. Where God had a willing
audience at line 85, he holds us captive from line 92 on.
(To dethrone him now would be only to add one more false
deity to the roll call of Book 1 and one more error of judgment
to a list already too long.)

The problem for the reader is compounded by the pace of
the presentation. The closeness of God's methodical logic
works against any effort to follow it. God dwells on a point

only for the length of time it takes to state it concisely (truly), and that time is insufficient for a merely human mind to assimilate the various parts of a complex argument (Boethius spends five books saying something God says in six lines). Given no opportunity to make the psychological and mental adjustments the speech finally requires, the reader is always off balance as he struggles to place statements that refuse to stand still for him ; his reactions lag behind his eye.

Contributing to his discomfort is the experience of over-hearing a legal brief in which he is the defendant and pronounced guilty. We have seen how God's speech exists simultaneously on two levels within a single space : it is an exhaustive and objective description of what is ; it is an oration delivered before auditors 'in a certain frame of mind'. For a few moments these two levels are perceived as one by the observer and draw from him an integrated response ; but this harmony is disturbed when the diagramming of reality is discovered to involve the stating of facts that cannot be heard with equanimity. In other words, at some point, the formal and rhetorical proofs of deity cease to be complementary ; the rhetorical proof fails as God does nothing to assure the good will of the jury ; instead the traditional oratorical situation is reversed since the speaker judges the audience. To be sure, the oratorical situation does not actually exist for the expositor, who is unaware of his fallen auditors. Milton employs a familiar stage technique : a soliloquy is spoken within earshot of a character for whom it was not meant, and the result is a series of complications that are more or less created by this accident of coincidence. In this case the complication is the creation in the reader's mind of attitudes and modes of thought that have nothing to do with the intentions (if the word can be used) of the speaker, but which affect him as an object of worship and make the experience of the poem even more disquieting and arduous than it has been heretofore.

At this point modern critics divide into two camps, one holding 'that God escapes the requirements of *decorum personae* by not being a person', the other insisting, with Waldock, that 'the human impression is what is important'.[1] These views can be reconciled if the unimpeachability of God's word is distinguished from the manner in which the reader receives it. The 'human impression' if it is there (and for most of us it will be) is what the reader must answer for; it is after all *his* impression. 'The very essence of Truth', Milton writes in *Of Reformation*, 'is plainnesse, and brightnes, the darknes and crookednesse is our own.'[2] In the poem, God's speech represents the essence of Truth, and the reader's response is a judgment on him (a reflection of his 'crookednesse'), not on the dispassionate voice of the Logos. What seems 'disagreeable' (the word is Peter's)[3] or distressing is the result of the fallen reader's inability to come to terms with what he knows to be true. According to John Preston, one of the signs 'whereby you may examine yourself whether you bee earthly minded or no', is the 'delight you have of the hearing of the pure Word'. The earthly minded man will be pleased with *'entising words*, such wordes doe rather feed the humour [flatter the self] than work upon the conscience of a man'; but 'if the heart be regenerate, then it will find sweetnesse in nothing but in heavenly things', and in the 'sincere milke of the word' even if the word 'crosseth his corruptions'.[4] The quality of the auditor's response measures his humility; if he can hear the

---

[1] Kranidas, *The Fierce Equation* (The Hague, 1965), p. 131; *Paradise Lost And Its Critics*, p. 102.

[2] *Complete Prose Works*, i. 566.　　[3] Peter, *Critique*, p. 11.

[4] *Sins Overthrow or A Godly and Learned Treatise of Mortification* (London, 1633), 98, 100, 103.

judgment of the word — 'They are corrupt, they have done abominable works, there is none that doeth good' (Psalm 14) — and answer with the psalmist 'cleanse me from my sin, For I acknowledge my transgressions' (Psalm 51), his motions are godly; but if he protests at the accusation ('ingrate !') and turns aside to the flattery of worldly counsel or to the evasions of his own reason, he betrays his iniquity and is deficient in contrition.

The idea that books (sacred or profane) read the reader is not a novel one. Replying to the charge that poets are 'corruptors of morals', Boccaccio replies, 'Rather, if the reader is prompted by a healthy mind, not a diseased one, they will prove actual stimulators to virtue, either subtle or poignant, as occasion requires.'[1] And Milton is even more explicit in *Areopagitica*, when he declares

> To the pure all things are pure, not only meats and drinks, but all kinde of knowledge whether of good or evill; the knowledge cannot defile, nor consequently the books, if the will and conscience be not defil'd. For books are as meats and viands are; some of good, some of evill substance; and yet God in that unapocryphall vision, said without exception, Rise *Peter*, kill and eat, leaving the choice to each mans discretion. Wholesome meats to a vitiated stomack differ little or nothing from unwholesome; and best books to a naughty mind are not unappliable to occasions of evill. Bad meats will scarce breed good nourishment in the healthiest concoction; but herein the difference is of bad books, that they to a discreet and judicious Reader serve in many respects to discover, to confute, to forewarn, and to illustrate.[2]

Books draw out what is in a man, and Scripture, the best of books, searches out a man's corruption and reveals it to him. In hurling the naked word at the reader, Milton is

[1] *Boccaccio On Poetry*, trans. and ed. C. G. Osgood (New York, 1965), p. 74. The passage is from the fourteenth book of the *Genealogia Deorum Gentilium*.

[2] *Complete Prose Works*, ii. 512–13.

performing the office of a minister, who should, Preston insists, 'be a Physician', and 'apply the pure Word of God unto the Consciences of men, and so to purge out the sicknesse of the soule before it grow incurable' (pp. 102–3). Critics of Milton's God complain of his harshness and wish that the poet had been able 'to suggest a loving God' or at least a God less 'obstinately there', rather than this 'invitation . . . to stare God full in the face';[1] but Milton would be derelict in his duty if he were inconsiderately kind and protected his reader from the full force of the Truth. Salvation, not comfort, is the issue :

> the part of a wise Physician is not to satisfie the humour of his Patient, for so he may encrease the disease, but to labour to cure him by ministring such Physicke unto him, as he knowes by experience the necessitie of the disease requireth : even so, to humour men in Preaching, is not the way to cure them, or to change the evill disposition of their nature, but rather a meanes to encrease their disease.
>
> (pp. 102–3)

The poet has his reader–pupil–patient's best interests at heart when he 'takes the risks' (the phrase is Waldock's and quite appropriate) of the 'direct, unshaded vision',[2] and provides an occasion for self-knowledge :

> Preach the pure Word, and nothing but the pure Word; and let men examine themselves whether they bee heavenly minded or no, by their tasting and relishing of the Word when it is Preached purely.
>
> (p. 103)

The division some see in the logical and rhetorical aspects of God's public personality is a reflection of the division in the fallen reader, between that part of him which recognizes the truth and that part of him which rises,

[1] Waldock, op. cit., p. 100.   [2] Ibid.

unbidden, against it, and resists its efforts to make him free. To God belongs the essence of the speech, the completeness, the logical perfection, the perfect accuracy of its perceptions ; all else is the reader's, the harshness, the sense of irritation, the querulousness. The monologue of the divine expositor 'pointing out the connections among parts' is dispassionate, and if we find it unsatisfactory the fault (quite literally) is ours. 'If our understanding have a film of ignorance over it, or be blear with gazing on other false glisterings ['entising words'] what is that to Truth.'[1] The emotional content of a word like 'ingrate' (if it is felt) is provided by the reader who receives it defensively, his pride resisting the just accusation, and confers on the speaker a tone compatible with his own reaction ; the recalcitrance of the sinner, not the vindictiveness of his God, is the source of the difficulty. The word leads a double life ; it leaps from the page to evoke a 'visceral' response and it falls into place as a perfect (accurate) definition of an object (you) in space ; only one life, however, is real, the other is an illusion projected by the reaction of a guilty reader. Equally illusory is God's vaunted defensiveness. He does not argue, he asserts, disposing a series of self-evident axioms in an objective order, 'not talking to anyone in particular but meditating on objects'. (Of course, God technically addresses the Son, but he is not in any sense, we feel, initiating a discussion, although he is, as we discover, creating a situation within which the poem's first truly heroic act will be performed.) The most provocative of God's propositions, 'they themselves decreed / Thir own revolt, not I', is merely a stage in the impersonal unfolding of the discourse, and it reflects no attitude on the speaker's part towards man or towards himself. A logical proof in the Ramist (non-syllogistic) manner proceeds by contraries. The positive

[1] *Complete Prose Works*, i. 566.

('Whose but his own?') is proved by eliminating alternative possibilities; 'indeed in the establishment of any true axiom', Bacon insists, 'the negative instance is the more forcible.'[1] The tendency to argue with God, like the sense of injury we feel at hearing his words, is *self*-revealing, a manifestation of the rebellion of the carnal reason in defiance of heavenly disposition; the flesh has not yet been mortified. This distinction — between the objective reality of the speech and the 'human impression', for which the fallen perspective, to the degree we are bound to it, is responsible — is not external to the reading experience. I make it as a reader in the confidence that Milton would have expected his contemporary reader, trained in analysis, committed to introspection, acutely aware of logical and rhetorical categories, to make it, consciously, while seeing in it evidence of his own intransigence.

The possibility of recovering an integrated response to God, of healing the split between the erected wit and the infected will, is represented by the poet, who joins in the heavenly songs of praise, and by the angelic audience :

> Thus while God spake, ambrosial fragrance fill'd
> All Heav'n, and in the blessed Spirits elect
> Sense of new joy ineffable diffus'd.

(135–7)

Waldock wonders ironically, 'And it is in response to such words as these [i.e., as God's] that the blessed spirits . . . feel new joy suffusing them' (*Paradise Lost and Its Critics*, p. 103). The angels' joy, signifying as it does a recognition of God's goodness and glory, is a rebuke to those of us who cannot share it whole-heartedly. If the poem is successful, the reader will finally be able to hear the Word joyfully, and join, with Milton, in the angelic hallelujahs.

---

[1] *Novum Organum*, I. xlvi, in *The English Philosophers from Bacon to Mill*, ed. E. A. Burtt (New York, 1939), p. 36.

(iv) CARNAL AND SPIRITUAL RESPONSES

The relationship between God and the reader is the obverse of the relationship between the reader and Satan, and together they establish the dominant patterns of the poem :

(1) *A morality of stylistics.* The poem embodies a Platonic aesthetic or anti-aesthetic in which the still clarity and white light of divine reality, represented (figured forth) in the atonal formality of God's abstract discourse, is preferred to the colour and chaotic liveliness of earthly motions, represented in Satan's 'grand style'.[1] This is the aesthetic Milton ascribes to elsewhere when he opposes the trappings of gold and robes and surplices (mere 'corporeal resemblances') to an 'inward holiness and beauty', and the simple directness of gospel truth to 'artful terms', the reflection of the artist's pride, 'swelling epithets thick laid / As varnish on a harlot's cheek.'[2] Reflected in this stylistic antithesis (which may be posed physically as well as verbally) are the contrasting appeals of the beauty of the created world and the heavenly (true) beauty of which all bodily forms are an expression.

(2) *Response as choice.* The reader's response to the two styles, and thus to what each of them represents, determines his spiritual status, measuring the extent to which in his soul the pride of life has been supplanted by love of Heaven.

---

[1] This is essentially Herbert's aesthetic. See 'The Forerunners' where the embellishments of language (the visible expression of the brain's 'sparkling notions') are opposed to the naked simplicity of 'thou art still my God': 'Let a bleak palenesse chalk the doore, / So all within be livelier than before.' See also Marvell's 'The Garden', where the red and white of carnal love are rejected for the cool rationality of green, and the mind transcends the physical world ('all that's made') to withdraw into a world of abstract forms.

[2] *Reason of Church Government, Complete Prose Works*, i. 828; *Paradise Regained*, iv. 343–4.

A delight in the fleshly (rhetorical) style indicates a preference for that which flatters the carnal self; in worshipping corporeal resemblances (of which rhetorical flourishes are the verbal extension) man worships the projected image of his own corrupted (darkened) understanding. Those who clothe the naked gospel do so to make it 'decent' *in their own eyes (Reason of Church Government)*; unable or unwilling to 'make themselves *heavenly* and *Spirituall*' they labour instead to 'make God earthly and fleshly' (*Of Reformation*). Spiritual apprehension, on the other hand, which is achieved only when the self acknowledges its own powerlessness and unworthiness, will incline to spiritual things.[1] Only the pure mind, Richardson remarks, is able to be touched with the beauties of Heaven:

> We have seen Hell; Now Heaven opens to our View; from Darkness Visible we are come to Inconceivable Light; from the Evil One, to the Supream Good, and the Divine Mediator; from Angels Ruin'd and Accurs'd to Those who hold their First State of Innocence and Happiness; the Pictures Here are of a very Different Nature from the former: Sensible things are more Describable than Intellectual; Every One can Conceive in some Measure the Torment of Raging Fire; None but Pure Minds, and Minds Capable Of, and Accustom'd To Contemplation Can be Touch'd Strongly with the Things of Heaven, a Christian Heaven; but He that Can may Find and possess Some Ideas of what he hopes for, where there is a *Fullness of Joy and Pleasure for Evermore.*
>
> (*Explanatory Notes and Remarks on Milton's Paradise Lost*, p. 99, note to III. 51)

[1] Cf. Plato, *Laws*, VII. 802c–d (trans. R. G. Bury, London, 1926): 'For if a man has been reared from childhood up to the age of steadiness and sense in the use of music that is sober and regulated, then he detests the opposite kind whenever he hears it, and calls it "vulgar"; whereas if he had been reared in the common honeyed kind of music, he declares the opposite of this to be cold and unpleasing.' Thus the 'uneducated' reader finds God's music 'cold and unpleasing', but responds to the 'honeyed kind' of Satan.

(3) *The unavoidability of choice.* Milton constructs his narrative in such a way as to make the avoidance of response, and therefore of choice and (possibly) self-betrayal, impossible. Waldock is quite right when he grumbles, 'With the best will in the world, we cannot avoid Milton's God or refuse to react to him' (p. 100). Neither, in the context of the Puritan habit of referring all experiences to the inner life, can one avoid acquiring the kind of self-knowledge regarded as particularly valuable. Of course this technique — learning by doing in a controlled situation — has already been discussed in connection with the spear–spot similes, and we see it employed here (and subsequently) on a larger scale.

(4) *The invitation to ascend.* Once the reader becomes aware of his situation with respect to the contraries of Heaven and Hell, and has located himself somewhere between the two, he is invited to ascend on the stylistic scale by 'purging his intellectual ray' to the point where his understanding is once more 'fit and proportionable to Truth the object and end of it', and his affections follow what his reason (the eye of the mind) approves.[1] Whether or not he makes the ascent depends on the strength of his will, which in turn depends on his appetite for true knowledge and illumination. As in dialectic, 'the final step *may* be the embracement of truth, but the decision rests with the

---

[1] The arc of the narrative describes a Platonic ascent, which culminates (for the reader who is able to move with it) in the simultaneous apprehension of the absolute form of the Good and the Beautiful, 'without shape or colour, intangible, visible only to reason, the soul's pilot' (*Phaedrus*, 247). In Christian terms, the movement imitates the return of the soul to God and pre-figures Christ's victory over death: 'The reader realizes that through the manipulation of scene, from the dark lake to the blinding throne, he has been led to mimetic enactment of precisely the promised resurrection into life which is the argument of the epic, an argument . . . never more explicit than just here at the close of the ascending action when it reaches the voice of God unfolding the plan of the *felix culpa*. We, not Adam, have climbed the *scala paradisa*' (Jackson Cope, op. cit., p. 108).

individual man', who may decline to ascend because the apex
coincides with the achieving of total humility, 'the full, and
absolute abnegation of all his wit, reason, will, desires,
strength, wisdome, righteousness, and all humane glory
and excellencies whatsoever, . . . that self-hood might be
totally annihilated, that he *might live, yet not he*, but *that Christ
might live in him*' (Gal. ii. 20).[1] The success of the reader's
education will be in direct proportion to his own efforts, but
at the least he will be aware, through his responses, of his
distance from the ideal. His models in the poem are Eve,
who, enamoured at first of her own image, turns in time
from that 'fair outside' to the superior fairness of Adam's
wisdom (IV. 491); and the narrator, who turns gladly from
the 'sight of vernal bloom' to the inner vision of 'things
invisible to mortal sight' (III. 40–55). If he is successful as a
guide, the narrator confers on us the gift of his blindness (to
earthly things) and persuades us to value it above the sight
he has lost and we acknowledge as unreliable.

At base, the 'responsive choice' is always between the
flattering and superficially dazzling constructs of the carnal
mind and the absolute simplicity (unity) of the divine
reality (the milk of the pure Word), and it is posed exactly
in those terms when we are asked to respond in Book IX
to the Fall itself. But our consideration of that crisis, which
is the reader's as well as Adam's and Eve's, must wait upon
the exploration of other matters.

[1] Cushman, *Therapeia*, p. 235; John Webster, *The Examination of
Academies* (1654), p. 16.

3 Man's Polluting Sin

My sin is ever before me.   PSALM li

(i) MORE CARNAL RESPONSES

When Bishop Joseph Hall sought a visual symbol for the
waywardness of sinful man, he found it in the image of a
woman with a 'loose lock erring wantonly over her shoulders'.[1] It was an apt choice: loose, erring, wantonly, do
double duty as indicators of spatial position and moral status.
The image is particularly effective because the abstraction
it seeks to figure forth is contained in the physical representation; the response of the auditor is made in terms of
the physical: he sees or *imag*ines a lock of hair moving
independently of an ordered configuration to which it
nominally belongs; the lock 'strays' from the 'path' assigned
to it; it is wayward. No translation is necessary; one need
not allegorize the icon to extract from it the abstraction;
comprehension is instantaneous, assured by the innumerable
associations of female hair with seduction, and by a habit of
mind which sees moral meaning in direction. Hall is hardly
original. Indeed the success of the presentation depends on
the familiarity of the tradition it calls upon. For students of
Paradise Lost, however, Hall's word-grouping is significant
because it finds an almost exact analogue in the description
of Eve. First impressions are unreliable, but their impact is
likely to be lasting. Why then does Milton introduce Eve in
a garment woven of adjectives traditionally associated with
the scarlet woman of so many sermons and moral harangues?

[1] Quoted by Douglas Bush in *English Literature in the Earlier Seventeenth
Century* (Oxford, 1945), p. 116.

Shee as a veil down to the slender waist
Her unadorned golden tresses wore
Dishevell'd, but in wanton ringlets wav'd
As the Vine curls her tendrils, which impli'd
Subjection, but requir'd with gentle sway,
And by her yielded, by him best receiv'd,
Yielded with coy submission, modest pride,
And sweet reluctant amorous delay.

(IV. 304–11)

Part of the answer has been given by Arnold Stein, Christopher Ricks and Anne Ferry, who explain that Milton uses words like 'loose' and 'wanton' to indicate linguistically the movement from innocence to experience and sin :

> Before the Fall, the word *error* argues, from its original meaning, for the order in irregularity, for the rightness in wandering — before the concept of error is introduced into man's world and comes to signify wrong wandering.[1]
> *Error* here is not exactly a pun, since it means only 'wandering' — but the 'only' is a different thing from an absolutely simple use of the word, since the evil meaning is consciously and ominously excluded. Rather than the meaning being simply 'wandering', it is 'wandering (not error)'. Certainly the word is a reminder of the Fall, in that it takes us back to a time when there were no infected words because there were no infected actions.[2]

This is brilliant criticism, although a sceptic might ask whether Stein and Ricks are not confusing their own subtlety with Milton's and creating a response no reader could be expected to deliver. Indeed Ricks himself approaches this section of his book with a certain tentativeness : 'is Milton reaching back to an earlier purity — which we are to

[1] Stein, *Answerable Style*, pp. 66–67.
[2] Ricks, *Milton's Grand Style* (Oxford, 1964), p. 110. See also Anne Ferry's *Milton's Epic Voice*, pp. 112–15.

contrast with what has happened to the word, and the world, since? Or is he simply being forgetful? The answer is likely to depend on one's general estimate of Milton.'[1] The answer, I believe, can be more firmly grounded in contemporary attitudes towards language as they are related to the traditional nostalgia for the linguistic purity of Paradise. An examination of the verbal texture of the poem against the background of the concerted effort during the century to evolve a truly scientific system of denotation reveals a pattern in the appearance of words like 'error' and shows them to be an important part of the interior drama Milton creates in the reader's mind.

From the beginning of the poem, the reader is aware that certain moral distinctions are being conveyed to him by an unconventional kind of word play. A number of words are placed so firmly and immediately in specific contexts that it becomes impossible to use them in any other way without calling attention to a deviation from the established meaning. Every reader knows them — woe, man, fruit, disobedience, loss, high, low, dark, light, and most obviously, fall. Before Satan speaks, the epic voice has already set up a system of relationships between physical–spatial concepts and moral ones. Our first parents are favoured of heaven *highly* and from this height, of favour or grace, they *fall* off (30). Satan, *aspiring*, wishes to set himself *above* the most High, that is above the greatest Good, and his reward is to be 'Hurled headlong flaming from th' Ethereal Sky / With hideous ruin and combustion *down*.' The directional preposition 'down' is withheld to the last so that the reader will associate exile from Heaven and all it stands for with the movement downward. When the epic voice surveys the scene in Hell, he cries 'O how unlike the place from whence they fell' (75)

[1] Op. cit., 111.

and we know that place means status or spiritual position ('the angels which kept not their first estate') and that their fall was a fact before they were moved one inch from the physical boundaries of Heaven.[1]

It is surprising and finally amusing, then, to hear Satan and Beelzebub betray themselves by employing this spatio-moral vocabulary with no sense of what it means in a God-centred universe. Within ten lines of his first words ('But O how *fall'n*') Satan is gauging God's power by the distance between Hell and Heaven: 'into what Pit thou seest / From what highth fall'n, so much the stronger prov'd'; but as always the apostate can think only in physical terms. God's strength is measured by what he has done to his enemies, by the length of his cast (he becomes a kind of heavenly discus thrower) and in the 'great consult' it is assumed that he could do no more. What we would think of as metaphorical (the might of his arm) is for them literal and limiting, a belief in the evidence of things seen, with a vengeance. And when Satan complains 'from what highth fall'n' he predicates a hierarchy that is political, and subject to the vicissitudes of war. He fears to sink lower (an impossibility, as we know), that is to a position in command of less territory or administrative authority: 'To bow and sue for grace ... / that were *low* indeed, / That were an ignominy and shame *beneath* / This *downfall*' (1. 111, 114–16). The breaking of union involves the danger of speaking nonsense, especially if the heavenly vocabulary or one reflecting heavenly values is retained. Once the fallen angels deny the centrality of God, they are committed to a moral and linguistic anarchy. All goals and objectives are equally arbitrary, and there is no justification at all for preferring one

[1] See the discussion of basic image patterns in Thomas Greene's *The Descent From Heaven: A Study In Epic Continuity* (New Haven, 1963), pp. 388–95.

position to another ; any situation can be designated the best
or the worst, words which now lose their meanings as do
'fall', 'low', and 'beneath' in their spiritual significations.[1]
Beelzebub, who is always more obvious than Satan is, sets
the seal to the literal demoralization of direction and distance when he offers a laughably empiricist explanation of
their present discomfort :

> we erewhile, astounded and amaz'd;
> No wonder, *fall'n* such a pernicious *highth*.
>
> (281–2)

Other words along with the concepts attached to them
suffer similar diminutions. Satan describes his new habita-
tion as 'void of light' but the following line and one half —
'Save what the glimmering of these livid flames / Casts pale
and dreadful' (182–3) — suggest that the problem, as he
sees it, could be solved by a virtuoso electrician. Most
readers are shocked and disgusted when Mammon quite
unconsciously reveals the extent of his spiritual blindness :

> As he our darkness, cannot we his Light
> Imitate when we please? This Desert soil
> Wants not her hidden lustre, Gems and Gold; . . .
> . . . and what can Heav'n show more?
>
> (ii. 269–71, 273)

But Mammon's question is only the logical end of Satan's
declaration of independence — 'The mind is its own place'
— and his plan for interior lighting, soon to be implemented
by Mulciber ('many a row / Of Starry Lamps and blazing
Cressets fed / With *Naphtha* and *Asphaltus* yielded light /
As from a sky'), has been anticipated by Satan's earlier
complaint. One wonders what Satan could possibly mean or

---

[1] Cf. Anne Ferry, *Milton's Epic Voice*, p. 138: 'Physical reality is totally
sundered from moral meanings, things can only arbitrarily be made to *stand
for* values.'

think he means by 'our own *loss* how repair' (188) or 'Th'
associates and co-partners of our *loss*' (265) or 'what more
lost in Hell' (270). Milton urges us in another place to
'repair the ruins of our first parents' but the repairing must
be preceded by some awareness of what the loss or ruin is,
and Satan clearly has no such awareness. In the end of
course Satan can decide that his loss (whatever he takes it to
be) has been repaired at any moment he likes ; and the awful
freedom of complete relativity is captured in the anti-
thetical alternatives of this couplet :

> What reinforcement we may gain from Hope,
> If not what resolution from despair.

(190–1)

It really doesn't matter, hope or despair (*despero*, without
hope), since the words signify nothing in the Satanic perspective.

The fallen angels are not altogether unaware of their
linguistic problem. Some words and phrases are too
obviously out of place if the pretence of a rational society is
to be kept up. God, for example is likely to be a difficult
word to utter. Quite soon the devils resort to circumlocutions
and diabolic euphemisms, and begin to fashion a new
language, one more consistent with the version of history
they now proceed to write. When Beelzebub salutes Satan
as the Prince who 'endanger'd Heav'n's perpetual King ; /
And put to proof his high Supremacy, / Whether upheld by
strength, or Chance or Fate,' Newton is moved to comment :

> The reader should remark here the propriety of the word
> *perpetual*. Beelzebub doth not say *eternal king*, for then he could
> not have boasted of *indangering* his kingdom; but he endeavours
> to detract as much as he can from God's everlasting dominion,
> and calls him only *perpetual king*, king from time immemorial or
> without interruption. . . . What Beelzebub means here is
> express'd more at large afterwards by Satan, ver. 637.

> — But he who reigns
> Monarch in Heav'n, till then as
>   one secure
> Sat on his throne, upheld by old
>   repute,
> Consent or custom, &c.[1]

One can take Newton's analysis further and note how
Beelzebub moves from the slight equivocation of 'perpetual'
to the comforting synecdoche of 'strength' and finally
arrives at the sophistry of 'Chance' or 'Fate'. (Satan has
provided the basis for this semantic prestidigitation by
insisting in his debate with Abdiel that he was self-begot by
'fatal course'.) There are many other places where the
reader should (and will) remark on the proprieties or
improprieties of diabolic diction. Satan thinks himself
grandly ironic when he reminds his grovelling and prostrate
legions of the titles they fought to preserve :[2]

> Princes, Potentates,
> Warriors, the Flow'r of Heav'n, once yours, now lost,
> If such astonishment as this can seize
> Eternal spirits; or have ye chos'n this place
> After the toil of Battle to repose
> Your wearied virtue, for the ease you find
> To slumber here, as in the Vales of Heav'n?
> Or in this abject posture have ye sworn
> To adore the Conqueror?

(315–23)

What Satan fails to realize is that physical posture has
nothing to do with virtue, a cast of mind now unavailable
to the rebels. The right to be styled 'Flow'r of Heav'n' is
theirs as long as they receive the title willingly from God.

[1] *Paradise Lost* (1749), I. 131.
[2] In Book v Satan taunts the gathered host: 'Thrones, Dominations,
Princedoms, Virtues, Powers, / If these magnific Titles yet remain / Not
merely titular' (772–4).

To fight for it is to lose it, and it is lost in the ambiguous syntax of Satan's taunt. For while 'now lost' refers primarily to the place Heaven, it also modifies 'Princes, Potentates...'. From the military point of view this speech succeeds in its objective — to 'rouse the rebels...with the bark of a sergeant-major' — but the reader is not limited to that point of view and he will recognize a transparent exercise in self-deception: God is a 'Conqueror' (323) who has won a victory that can be reversed if the devils are careful to grant him no further 'advantage' (327). Any admiration one might have for Satan's rhetoric as a piece of strategy is submerged in the terrible irony of 'Awake, arise, or be for ever fall'n' (330). What is meant to be the climactic moment in a nicely calculated call to action becomes in effect the most damning of self-revelations, no less damning because it is unconscious. Of course the fallen angels do awake and do arise, 'abasht', but Milton will not allow Satan even a small success. His forces are only half awake ('ere well awake'):

> Nor did they not perceive the evil plight
> In which they were, or the fierce pains not feel.

> (335–6)

The double negative is unexpected and for an instant the sense of the line remains unresolved. Do they or don't they perceive? Actually, they do and they don't and by forcing the hesitation Milton leads the reader to understand how the alternatives he hovers between are equally true. They do perceive the fire, the pain, the gloom, but they are blind to the moral meaning of their situation, that is to their evil plight. This is to be their punishment, to be always half awake and forever fallen, to rise at the command of a leader who has chosen his own mind as his place and their prison.

Innumerable instances of this kind of word play could be cited, and each of them contributes to the construction of a

morality of stylistics. 'Nor did they not perceive' is particularly nice since a defect in language is only the visible
phase of a problem in perception. The reader comes to know
the limitations of the Hellish mentality by remarking how
the fallen angels misuse or under-use words of whose larger
significance he is aware. The result is a gain in confidence as
well as in knowledge: in the early stages of the poem the
distinction between the Satanic and mortal perspectives is
sometimes blurred, but when 'fall' is taken to have no
meaning beyond the obviously physical, and 'loss' is a
political concept, and light the province of the interior
decorator, the reader is entitled to congratulate himself on
his superior understanding. In *Paradise Lost*, however, such
gains are only temporary and when Adam and Eve are
introduced in Book IV, Milton teaches us a new humility
through a habit of mind he has himself encouraged.

What we learn from Adam and Eve is that corruption is a
relative matter once one moves away from purity. The
fallen angels betray themselves when they fail to see that
physical configurations are to be interpreted morally; the
fallen reader betrays himself when he feels obliged to pass
moral judgment on every action or utterance. 'Wanton' and
'loose' and 'error' trouble us because we cannot help but
read into them moral implications that are not relevant
until the Fall has occurred. Milton warns us of what is to
come even before we see our first parents, although the
warning goes unrecognized and unheeded:

> the Fiend
> Saw undelighted all delight, all kind
> Of living Creatures new to sight and strange:
> Two of far nobler shape . . .
>
> (285–7)

Nobler than what or whom? Strange and new to whom?
The questions may seem unnecessary in view of the narrative

situation : the creatures are new to Satan, and among them Adam and Eve stand out 'erect and tall'. But in fact it is the reader in addition to Satan who is the stranger in Paradise, although he may not realize it until the description of Eve presents a problem he can solve only at his own expense :

> Shee as a veil down to the slender waist
> Her unadorned golden tresses wore
> Dishevell'd, but in wanton ringlets wav'd
> As the Vine curls her tendrils, which impli'd
> Subjection.

(304-8)

These lines move easily, lulling the reader into a complacency that renders him vulnerable to the shock of 'dishevell'd'. The tradition calls for an idealized Eve, and this expectation is answered in the veil image. Eve is seen at a distance, unapproachable, even modest. 'Golden tresses' is a cliché of romance epic, but it is made new by the qualifier 'unadorned'. The suggestion is that gold is not the nonpareil it is in other places (the golden age) since it could be further adorned. Milton need not reveal what that further adornment might be, since his effect is secured the moment the reader is aware of the possibility. The thought is complete at the end of line 305 and 'dishevell'd' is an unwelcome complication. The adjective modifies both the verb and its object : Eve wears disordered golden tresses, Eve wears her golden tresses in a disorderly fashion. In either position the word troubles. Is there, can there be, disorder in Paradise? The involuntary question would seem to be anticipated by the epic voice who immediately counters with a 'but'. This is not however a 'but' of clarification, as it should be or as we expect it to be ; instead still another complicating element is introduced in the word 'wanton'. A reading of 'not disorderly but lascivious' is hardly reassuring. To some extent the reader's difficulty is an accident of syntax since the following line absorbs 'dishevell'd' and 'wanton' into the vine simile ('As the Vine curls her tendrils'), the traditional analogy in nature for the proper relationship between husband and wife. Yet even this image is not presented straightforwardly. The curling of the vine, the epic voice tells us, implies 'Subjection'; but that word is somewhat of a surprise at the beginning of the line, since in conjunction with 'wanton', 'dishevell'd' and 'wav'd' the tendrils seem to imply invitation. (All of Eve, not merely her 'ringlets', seems to curl, even coil, in the manner, perhaps, of a serpent.) In retrospect, 'dishevell'd' is seen to mean 'not arranged in any symmetrical pattern' and 'wanton' to be standard seventeenth-century usage for 'unrestrained' (there are no restraints in Paradise). If Eve's tresses were plaited or bejewelled, she would be open to the suspicion of vanity; as it is, her 'sweet disorder', her 'wantonness' is innocent precisely because it is not 'too precise in every part'.

In short, the reader will declare Eve innocent of a sensuality whose only existence is in his mind; but it is a conscious effort, made necessary ultimately by his inability to delimit the connotations of a prelapsarian vocabulary and more immediately by Milton's deliberate evocation of the preachers' scarlet woman. To paraphrase Ricks, 'wanton' is read as 'unrestrained' (not lascivious), but of course 'lascivious' is suppressed at a price and Eve can never appear without recalling this scene and the uneasiness it arouses. The reader pays a heavier price than she does (Eve remains ignorant of her detractors), for he is forced to admit again and again that the evil he sees under everyone's bed is his own. Fallen man's involvement with the vocabulary of direction and spatial configuration is not unlike his bondage to the old law: in both cases the moral implications are largely negative, a network of thou-shalt-nots which have come into being because we cannot help but. The law 'was

added because of transgressions' and man's transgressions
have taken from him the freedom of moving about without
anxiety, tainting actions (and the names of actions) which are
innocent apart from the transgressing mind. The fact of the
law is an ever-present reminder of our peccability and in the
structure of *Paradise Lost* a small group of words serves a
similar function. Fall, wanton, light, dark, dishevelled, loose
are like litmus paper. They test acidity (sin) by taking on the
hue of the consciousness that appropriates them. On an
absolute scale, according to the norm established in Paradise,
Satan's demoralization of language is no more reprehensible and revealing than the over-moralization which makes
it necessary for the reader to exclude meanings that properly
are not there. The one advantage Milton grants us is the
advantage of self-awareness. Satan is immobilized and complacent in his confusion, moral and verbal; we are pro-
foundly uncomfortable in ours, and our discomfort like the
Law acts to 'evince our depravity' and brings us to contrition.

The relationship between the reader and the vocabulary
of Paradise is one aspect of his relationship with its inhabitants. Just as the fallen consciousness infects language, so
does it make the unfallen consciousness the mirror of itself.
'Of paradys', says Sir John Mandeville, 'ne can I not speken
propourly for I was not there.' Mandeville's statement is
true for every one of us, for as he himself adds, 'And yee
schull understande that no man that is mortell ne may not
approchen to that paradys.' The inaccessibility of Paradise
is more a question of psychology than geography. 'Assuredly
we bring not innocence into the world, we bring impurity
much rather' (*Areopagitica*). Fallen man's perceptual equipment, physical and moral, is his prison; any communication
from a world beyond the one he has made for himself
reaches him only after it has passed through the distortions

of his darkened glass, and this applies to man's prior state in Paradise as well as to the Heaven he has never known. We know God or unfallen man indirectly if at all, by attributing to them qualities which are in fact the negations of our limitations. God is all powerful, omnipresent, perfectly knowledgeable, timeless, infinite in extension (spaceless?); Adam knows intuitively, is in complete control of all his faculties, enjoys bliss and contentment (is not discontent) and is innocent (knows no evil). In the poem Milton gives the reader Paradise (innocence) by making him know how far he is from it. The apprehension is negative, but in poetry negatives can have a substantial reality if they are communicated in a way which gives them an emotive 'body'. The technique is simple and familiar: Adam and Eve are shown acting and speaking in situations which at first encourage the reader to see in them qualities he recognizes as fallen; almost immediately, however, something in the text reminds him of the distance separating the first man from all others (save one) and he is asked to make a mental adjustment — not them, but me — which becomes the felt measurement of that distance, and thus the reality of innocence, in the poem; and he is also asked to judge himself against that reality. (Again the sequence: mistake — correction — instruction.) As before, the reader must admit that his perceptions do not extend to the object the poet would present, and, in addition, he is forced to come to terms with his tendency to remake everything in his own sinful image.

Consider, for example, the embrace we witness at IV. 492:

> with eyes
> Of conjugal attraction unreprov'd,
> And meek surrendur, half imbracing lean'd
> On our first Father, half her swelling Breast
> Naked met his under the flowing gold
> Of her loose tresses hid; he in delight ...   (492–7)

Beginning with the verb 'lean'd' there is a steady progression of physically stimulating images. At the end of the line, 'lean'd' is only an indication of posture, a direction waiting for an object; the preposition 'on' is an extension of the directional force which now finds an object by making contact with 'our first Father'. What follows is almost cinematic in technique: the camera eye moves in from the full embrace to examine the detail of 'half her swelling Breast'; 'Naked' at the beginning of the next line is unnecessary as a piece of information, but as a delayed action adjective it attaches itself to the entire scene as well as to 'Breast'. The present-participles 'swelling' and 'flowing' continue to evoke the sense of movement and still-to-be-completed action suggested first in 'half-embracing'; and the adjective 'loose', recalling 'Dishevell'd' and 'wanton' (306), locates the sensuality of the scene in the seductiveness of Eve's tresses.

The response these lines draw from the reader, however, must be distinguished finally from what Adam and Eve feel as they embrace. The poem is quite explicit, in a negative way, about this: Eve's eyes draw a 'conjugal attraction' which is 'unreprov'd' and not passionate; these are 'kisses pure' (502) we are told *after* our own impressions have registered. A pure sexuality may seem a contradiction in terms, but only because it is unavailable to us in our present state; and here the psychological effects of our loss manifest themselves in an attempt to bring Adam and Eve down to our level. The reader will ignore 'unreprov'd', a weakly felt qualification, and warm to this demonstration of sinless love-making with a body and mind infected by sin. When the verse turns to describe *Adam's* response to Eve's swelling breast and loose tresses, there is a tendency (and classroom experiments bear this out) to read 'hee in de*sire*' where the poet writes 'hee in de*light*'. (In Book IX. 1013, where this scene is echoed, desire is unequivocally desire; the qualities the fallen reader *imposes* on Adam and Eve in Book IV have become theirs by right: 'Carnal desire inflaming, hee on *Eve* / Began to cast lascivious Eyes, she him / As wantonly repaid; in Lust they burn; / Till *Adam* thus 'gan *Eve* to dalliance move.') At this point, the distinction between innocence and experience has been blurred, at least in the reader's mind.

Quite deliberately, then, the description moves away from the realistic detail of the actual embrace toward a more generalized statement of its meaning — for them: 'hee in delight / Both of her Beauty and submissive Charms / Smil'd with superior Love, as *Jupiter* / On *Juno* smiles, when he impregns the Clouds / That shed May Flowers; and press'd her Matron lip / With kisses pure' (497–502). Raised to the level almost of ritual,[1] the kisses become the visible signs of their inner (spiritual) unity, and the reader is left to ponder the discrepancy between his response and the purity of the action. If the distinction seems difficult or abstruse, it is made easier (and inescapable) by the sudden introduction of a third perspective:

> With kisses pure: aside the Devil turn'd
> For envy, yet with jealous leer malign
> Ey'd them askance.   (502–4)

The effect of the devil's entrance (he has been there all along as our window on the scene, but we have forgotten him) is not unlike the effect of '*Then* was not guilty shame' (313). The reader is alerted to the contrast between the 'kisses pure' and the impurity of the voyeur's response and is forced to acknowledge whatever part of that response he shares. No reader, of course, is the devil, and few readers will actually leer, but the Satanic perspective is uncomfortably

---

[1] Harding suggests an allusion to *Georgics*, ii, where the impregnating of the earth is celebrated (*Club of Hercules*, p. 77).

recognizable as one we can at least understand, whereas we cannot understand innocence at all. Once again a controlled situation has been the occasion of self-knowledge, in accordance with the Puritan's obligation to 'know himself... without flattering himself in the slightest, without concealing from himself a single unpleasant fact about himself' (*The Puritans*, ed. Miller and Johnson, i. 284). The entire scene works on the principle we observed in connection with 'error' and 'wanton', taking us back 'to a time when there were no infected words because there were no infected actions'; and the technique is basic to Milton's method whereby the reader is both a participant in the action and a critic of his own performance.

(ii) LANGUAGE IN PARADISE

By using language to point up the distortion that results whenever fallen man attempts to make sense of the world around him, Milton passes judgment on the scientific and linguistic optimism of his own century. If the end of education is to repair the ruins of our first parents, many in the seventeenth century believed the end to be in sight, and took to constructing systems with which to describe reality and languages accurate enough to serve their systems. The history of this effort has been written many times and it is not my intention to write it again, but certain basic tendencies of thought must be noted if the relationship between the vocabulary of *Paradise Lost* and the larger philosophical movement of the age is to be clarified:

(1) Reality is assumed to consist of a finite and discoverable number of corpuscular units, species, clusters of which constitute genera which in turn are themselves the species of more general genera. Thus Milton in his *Art of Logic*: 'That is, a thing can be now genus, now species;

genus, if it is referred to the species subject to itself, species
if it is referred to its genus. ... Thus man is a subaltern
genus, or subaltern species ; a species if you refer to animal,
a genus if you refer to single men.'[1]

(2) The operation of scientific method is twofold: the
identification or isolation of each unit (thing, concept, item)
and the arranging of the units according to the hierarchy of
genera and species, that is according to the relationships (of
cause, effect, adjunct, opposite, etc.) which pertain between
them in the objective order of nature. Bacon collects and
arranges, Ramus invents and disposes. Of course there are
important differences between Baconian empiricism and
Ramus' common-sense rhetoro-logic, but in their concern
with 'things' ('resolutely entering on the true road, and
submitting my mind to *things*')[2] and their concentration on
the data of experience at the expense of abstraction (conscious in Bacon, unconscious in Ramus), and, most important, in their insistence on precision in naming, they
contribute to the attitude of mind I am describing. One may
cite here Plato, whose dialectic, while it should be distinguished from the methods of both Ramus and Bacon,
displays the same two-part structure: Dialectic 'discerns
clearly *one* Form everywhere extended throughout many,
where each one lies apart, and *many* Forms, different from
one another, embraced from without by one Form ; and again
one Form connected in a unity through many wholes, and
many Forms, entirely marked off apart.'[3]

---

[1] *The Works of John Milton*, xi. 241. Milton illustrates the nominalistic
basis of much of Ramist thought when he explains that genus is merely a
'symbol of the common essence' of the species: 'For genus does not properly
communicate essence to species (since in itself it is in truth nothing outside the
species) but merely signifies their essence' (p. 239).

[2] *Novum Organum*, I. cxiii.

[3] *Sophist*, 235c, in Francis M. Cornford's *Plato's Theory of Knowledge*
(New York, 1957), pp. 262–3. Cornford comments: 'The expert in Dialectic

(3) Since the first operation is basically a *labelling* procedure, it requires a language free of redundancy or ambiguity, i.e., a word-thing language. (In some of the more sophisticated methodologies a logical syntax accompanies the quantitative vocabulary.)

'The fancy that if we can only discover the original names of things', writes A. E. Taylor in an introduction to Plato's *Cratylus*, 'our discovery will throw a flood of light on the realities named, seems to recur periodically in the history of human thought. There are traces of it in Heraclitus and Herodotus; in the age of Pericles it was reinforced by the vogue of allegorical interpretations of Homer, which depended largely on fanciful etymologies.'[1] In the seventeenth century this fancy had a remarkable hold on both the popular and academic imaginations, although its limitations as a philosophic ideal had long ago been exposed by Plato. Asked to arbitrate between Hermogenes, who as a Heraclitean holds that names are arbitrarily imposed, and Cratylus who regards true naming as the foundation of all

will guide and control the course of philosophical discussion by his knowledge of how to "divide by kinds", not confusing one Form with another. He will discern clearly the hierarchy of Forms which constitutes reality, and make out its articulate structure, with which the texture of philosophic discourse must correspond, if it is to express truth. The method is that method of Collection and Division which was announced in the *Phaedrus*' (pp. 263–4). See also Hobbes, *Leviathan*, 1. 4: 'The manner how speech serves to the remembrance of the consequences of cause and effects consists in the imposing of *names* and the *connection* of them' (in the edition of Herbert W. Schneider, New York, 1958, p. 39). In this century one might compare the aims of the logical positivists: 'If grammatical syntax corresponded exactly to logical syntax pseudo-statements could not arise. If grammatical syntax differentiated not only the word-categories of nouns, adjectives, verbs, conjunctions etc., but within each of these categories made the further distinctions that are logically indispensable, then no pseudo-statements could be formed.' Rudolf Carnap's 'The Elimination of Metaphysics', in *Logical Positivism*, ed. A. J. Ayer (Glencoe, Ill., 1959), p. 68.

1 *Plato: The Man and His Work* (Meridian Books, New York, 1957), p. 77.

knowledge and discourse, Socrates takes a middle course, admitting with Hermogenes that there is no perfect correspondence between the names and the things they are taken to signify, joining Cratylus in wishing that there were:

> I quite agree with you that words should as far as possible resemble things ... for I believe that if we could always, or almost always, use likenesses which are perfectly appropriate, this would be the most perfect state of language; as the opposite is the most imperfect.[1]

Likenesses which are perfectly appropriate are an impossibility however since all likenesses are images or imitations and are at best approximate. Complete accuracy of perception exists only in the face-to-face confrontation of the perceiving mind and the ideal forms; and this kind of knowledge is intuitive rather than discursive or imitative, available only at the end of a 'long travail of thought'.[2] To place an undue reliance on representations, whether pictorial or verbal, is to confuse levels of reality, an error Plato warns against repeatedly:

> *Soc.* We will suppose ... that some God makes not only a representation such as a painter would make ..., but also creates an inward organization like yours ... and in a word copies all your qualities, and places them by you in another form; would you say that this was Cratylus and the image of Cratylus, or that there were two Cratyluses?
> *Crat.* I would say that there were two Cratyluses..
> *Soc.* Then you see, my friend, ... that images are very far from having qualities which are the exact counterpart of the realities which they represent?[3]

Socrates finally forces Cratylus to admit that the study of

[1] *The Dialogues of Plato*, trans. B. Jowett (Random House, 2 vols., New York, 1937), I. 224.
[2] The phrase is Taylor's, *Plato*, p. 231.   [3] *Dialogues*, i. 221.

things as they really are is to be preferred to the study of names and the dialogue ends somewhat inconclusively :

> Whether there is this eternal nature in things, or whether the truth is what Heracleitus and his followers and many others say, is a question hard to determine; and no man of sense will like to put himself or the education of his mind in the power of names: neither will he so far trust names as to be confident in any knowledge which condemns himself and other existences to an unhealthy state of unreality.[1]

Neither reduce the problem of philosophy to the knowledge of names nor accept the implications of a theory which makes one name as good or bad as another.

Socrates never denies the relevance of names to the philosophical inquiry ; the end of dialectic is the apprehension of the ideal forms, and while knowledge of the forms is finally intuitive rather than discursive, less a matter of 'knowing about' than possessing and being possessed by, the process *is* largely rational. In the *Phaedrus* dialectic is defined as the effort to 'divide into species according to natural articulations, avoiding the attempt to shatter the unity of a natural part as a clumsy butcher might do',[2] and in the *Sophist* the Stranger inquires rhetorically, 'Dividing according to kinds, not taking the same for a different one or a different one for the same — is not that the business of the science of dialectic?', and receives the expected answer, 'Yes'.[3] Clearly the business of 'collecting and dividing', as it is described elsewhere in the dialogues, demands a precise nomenclature, if only as a means of avoiding the clumsiness of a butcher or the mistaking of one form for another. Naming is therefore a preliminary step

---

[1] *Dialogues,* i. 229.
[2] *Plato's Phaedrus,* trans. W. C. Helmbold and W. G. Rabinowitz (New York, 1956), p. 55.
[3] In Cornford's *Plato's Theory of Knowledge,* p. 262.

which imparts some measure of control to the dialectical investigation. Names are necessary if the divisions made are to be free of overlappings and obvious inconsistencies. Presumably the apparatus and the names will be abandoned when the forms are finally discerned.

Like all other methods which aim at a mathematical description of a static reality, dialectic operates primarily to neutralize the distorting tendencies of the human mind which is notoriously sloppy when left to itself. Plato is aware that in view of the limitations of our perceptive equipment, neutralization is an impossible goal. At best we can attain a relative rigour. Yet unless we wish to give up the problem entirely, we must commit ourselves to dialectic and be prepared to accept the results as provisional, not final. The cardinal intellectual rule then is 'be as careful as possible without assuming that you can be as careful as necessary':

> Plato never assumes... that he can do the world's scientific thinking for it once for all... Plato was far too true to the Socratic conception of the insignificance of human knowledge by comparison with the vastness of the scientific problem.... But though the final 'rationalization' of things may be an unattainable goal, there is no reason why we should not try to get as near to the goal as we can. If we can not expel the element of 'brute fact' for which we can see no reason from science, we may try, and we ought to try, to reduce it to a minimum. We cannot completely 'mathematize' human knowledge, but the more we can mathematize it the better.[1]

In the seventeenth century some men believed that they could be as careful as necessary and completely mathematize human knowledge.

If the search for a perfect language can be extended as far back as Heraclitus and Herodotus, it exists also in another tradition, more religious than philosophical. Pressed to

---

[1] Taylor, *Plato*, pp. 294–5.

identify the source of the names he believes in, Cratylus replies, 'I believe ... the true account of the matter to be, that a power more than human gave things their first names.'[1] In the Judeo–Christian epistemology, the 'power more than human' is of course God who endowed Adam and Eve with an accurate language which was lost in the confusion of Babel or perhaps at the time of the Fall itself.[2] Speculation about this language is traditional. A primary goal was its identification. Hebrew was the most successful candidate, although other tongues are occasionally championed.[3] A subsidiary concern, naturally, is the construction or nature of the language, and in the seventeenth century this question takes on a new urgency. For there is a tendency, on the part of the reformers, to assume that the word-thing language, to which they are committed as philosophers, represents nothing less than a return to the linguistic purity of Paradise.

The scriptural basis of this position is Adam's naming of the animals at Genesis ii. 19 : 'And out of the ground the Lord God formed every beast of the field, and every fowl of the air, and brought them unto Adam to see what he would call them ; and whatsoever Adam called every living

[1] *Dialogues*, i. 227.

[2] In his *Academiarum Examen or The Examination of the Academies* (London, 1654), John Webster seems to suggest that Adam lost the Paradisical language when he fell: 'And therefore it is not without a deep and abstruse mystery that the *Seraphical Apostle* speaks that *he knew a man caught up into the third heaven, into Paradise, and heard ... ineffable words ...* for this was the *Paradisical* language ... which Adam understood while he was unfaln in Eden and lost after' (p. 27).

[3] At least one theorist, John Webb, proposed Chinese (see the account of his work in D. C. Allen's 'Some Theories of the Growth and Origin of Language in Milton's Age', *Philological Quarterly*, xxviii. 1949, 5–16) a language which answers in some ways to the theoretical demands. In *The Advancement of Learning*, Bacon notes 'that it is the use of China and the kingdoms of the high Levant to write in Characters Real, which express neither letters nor words in gross, but Things or Notions.' (*Selected Writings*, p. 300.)

creature, that was the name thereof.' This act is taken to be proof of Adam's superior knowledge, and the names he gives the animals are thought to be exact, corresponding in each case to the essence of the species. Adam's knowledge is infused into him directly by God, and the names he imposes, like God's, are accurate, intensively and extensively. There are several references to this event in *Paradise Lost*. Raphael alludes to it in passing in his account of the Creation : 'the rest [of the animals] are numberless, / And thou thir Natures know'st, and gav'st them Names' (vii. 492–3). Knowing and naming are one, an equation made explicitly when Adam recalls the same scene :

> I nam'd them, as they pass'd, and understood
> Thir Nature, with such knowledge God endu'd
> My sudden apprehension.
>
> (viii. 352–4)

(One should note that 'sudden apprehension' is still possible in Ramist theory. Even now, he implies, the mind assents immediately to any truth presented to it.)[1] Milton provides a prose gloss to this passage in *Tetrachordon* : '*Adam* who had the wisdom giv'n him to know all creatures, and to name them according to their properties, no doubt but had the gift to discern perfectly.'[2] These names, in Sylvester's words are 'Fit sense-full' :

> For, soon as ever he had framed thee,
> Into thy hands he put this monarchy;
> Made all the Creatures know thee for their Lord,

---

[1] For discussions of this aspect of Ramus' thought see P. Albert Duhamel, 'The Logic and Rhetoric of Peter Ramus', *Modern Philology*, xlvi (1949), 163–71 and 'Milton's Alleged Ramism', *PMLA*, lxvii (1952), 1035–53; also Walter J. Ong, S.J., *Ramus, Method, and the Decay of Dialogue*, passim.

[2] *Complete Prose Works of John Milton*, ed. Ernest Sirluck (New Haven, 1959), ii. 642.

And come before thee of their own accord:
And gave thee power (as Master) to impose
Fit sense-full Names.[1]

The manner in which this commonplace finds its way
into the works of the empiricist propagandists is well
illustrated by this excerpt from John Webster's *Academiarum
Examen*:

> Further, when I find the great and eternal being, speaking and
> conversing with *Adam*, I cannot but believe that the language
> which he uttered, was the living and serviceable word, and that it
> was infinitely high, deep, and glorious like himself, and that
> which was radically and essentially one with him, and preceded
> from him, and was indeed the language of the divine nature,
> and not extrinsecally adventitious unto him; and when I find
> *Adam* understanding this heavenly *Dialect* (which had been
> uttered in vain if he had not understood it) I cannot but believe
> that this was the language of nature infused into him in his
> Creation, and so innate and implantate in him, and not inventive
> or acquisitive, but merely dative from the father of light, *from
> whom every good and perfect gift doth come and descend.*
>
> (Jam i. 17)
>
> Again, when I find the Almighty presenting all the Creatures
> before Adam to see what he would call them, and whatsoever
> *Adam* called every living creature, *that is the name thereof*, I
> cannot but conceive that *Adam* did understand both their internal
> and external signatures, and that the imposition of their names
> was adequately agreeing with their natures: otherwise it could
> not univocally and truely be said to be their names, whereby he
> distinguished them; for names are but representations of notions,
> and if they do not exactly agree in all things, then there is a
> difference and disparity between them, and in that incongruity
> lies error and falsehood: and the notions also are but the images
> or *ideas* of things themselves reflected, in the mind, as the outward
> face in a looking-glasse, and therefore if they do not to an hair

[1] *The Complete Works of Joshua Sylvester*, ed. A. B. Grosart (2 vols.,
Edinburgh, 1880), i. 80–81.

correspond with, and be *Identical* one to the other, as punctually and truly as the impression in the wax agrees with the seal that instamped it, and as face answers face in a glass, then there is not absolute congruency between the notion and the thing, the intellect and the thing understood, and so it is no longer verity, but a lye and falsity. And therefore if Adam did not truly see into and understand their intrinsecall natures, then had his intellect false notions of them, and so he imposed lying names upon them, and then the text would be false too, which avers that what he called them was their names. Also Adam was in a deep sleep when Eve was framed of his bone, and yet when she was brought before him being awaked, he could tell that *she was bone of his bone, and flesh of his flesh,* and therefore *he called her woman, because she was taken out of man.* Nor if it be denied that he understood by his intrinsick and innate light, what she was, and from whence she was taken (which I hold altogether untrue) and that God by extrinsic information told Adam from whence she was taken, yet did he immediately give unto her an adequate name, suiting her original, which most significantly did manifest what was her nature, and from whence it came, and doubtless the name being exactly conformable, and configurate to the *Idea* in his mind, the very prolation, and sound of the word, contained in it the *vive* expression of the thing, and so in verity was nothing else but that pure language of nature, which he then spake, and understood, and afterwards so miserably lost and defaced.[1]

This is a perfect example of the easy union that was effected between the old theology and the new science. Adam's language is now precisely identified as a word-thing language with which he can comprehend the 'internal and

[1] pp. 29–30. See also Hobbes, *Leviathan,* i. 4, p. 37: 'The first author of *speech* was God himself, that instructed Adam how to name such creatures as he presented to his sight.' Ramus, too, attests to the pervasiveness of this commonplace: 'Before Adam lost the image of God, Ramus said, almost all of his judgments had been simply axiomatical; in his integrity he had been able to see and to pronounce sentence immediately, as when he named the animals' (Perry Miller in *The New England Mind: The Seventeenth Century* (Beacon Press Edition, Boston, 1961, p. 133).

external signatures' of all the creatures. (Significantly, Adam is here described in terms John Wilkins reserves for God.)[1] Webster defends his thesis by employing the Ramus method of arguing by contraries or absurdities : Adam's names must be perfectly congruent, the name with the notion with the thing, for if there were a disparity between them, the scriptures could be said to lie. In his enthusiasm, he sees meaning implicit in the very sound of the Edenic word, a notion Socrates plays with and seems to reject in the *Cratylus*.

Earlier attempts to reconstruct the language of Paradise had about them an archaeological flavour since they were usually tied to the search for the terrestrial Eden. Webster's impetus, on the other hand, is provided by the pervasive intellectual climate of the century, specifically by the movement in all disciplines toward what Sprat calls a 'Mathematicall plainness'. R. F. Jones, whose researches are indispensable for this period, argues that 'the remarkable development of mathematics in the seventeenth century, to which Descartes contributed much, and especially the improved mathematical symbols that were coming into use, exerted no small influence upon conceptions of what language should be . . . the movement toward clear definitions characteristic of this period drew much of its inspiration from mathematics.'[2] Jones cites the example of Seth Ward, professor of Astronomy at Oxford, who in 1654 declares his confidence in a universal mathematics : 'My first proposall was to find whether other things might not as well be designated by symbols and herein I was presently resolved that Symboles might be found for every *thing* and *notion*.'[3] Ward

[1] See Wilkins's *Principals and Duties of Natural Religion* (1678), pp. 125–7.
[2] *The Seventeenth Century, Studies in the History of English Thought and Literature from Bacon to Pope* (Stanford, 1951), pp. 150–1.
[3] Loc. cit.

goes on to make an explicit connection between his goal and the recovery of Adam's language : 'Such a language as this (where every word were a definition and contain'd the nature of the thing) might not unjustly be termed a naturall language, and would afford that which the *Cabalists* and the *Rosycrucians* have vainly sought for in the Hebrew, And in the names of things assigned by Adam.'[1] Note that Adam's mastery now includes not only the animals, but 'things', all things.

Behind these statements is the assumption that linguistic reform is the key to all the problems that beset fallen man, and again this is an extension of a traditional attitude. Complaints against mortality are likely to lament the Curse of the Confusion and to characterize fallen man's lot as 'a Babel'. The loss of the perfect language is more than anything else the sign of the Fall, since in Eden speech is the outward manifestation of the inner Paradise. Adam's speaking grace, Raphael notes, signifies his inner grace :

> for God on thee
> Abundantly his gifts hath also pour'd
> Inward and outward both, his image fair:
> Speaking or mute all comeliness and grace
> Attends thee, and each word, each motion forms.
>
> (VIII. 219–23)

The congruency between the word and the thing implies a congruency between the mind and the thing. Adam's mind is the ideal instrument, the clear glass :

> But our now-*knowledge* hath, for tedious train,
> A drooping life and over-racked brain,
> A face forlorn, a sad and sullen fashion,
> A restlesse toyl and Care's self-pining passion.

[1] Op. cit., 153.

Knowledge was then even the soule's soul for light,
The spirit's calm Port, and Lanthorn shining bright
To strait-stept feet: cleer knowledg; not confus'd:
Not sowr, but sweet: not gotten, but infus'd.[1]

This instant infusion of knowledge will be experienced
again when the soul finally joins Christ in the bliss of everlasting union. In this connection, Mrs. MacCaffrey cites a
sermon of Donne's: 'God shall create us all Doctors in a
minute ... no more preaching, no more reading of Scriptures, and that great School-Mistress, Experience, and
Observation shall be remov'd, no new thing to be done, and
in an instant, I shall know more, than they all could reveal
unto me.'[2] According to Donne, this awaits us in the life to
come, but for Ward, Webster, Sprat and others it is a goal
attainable on the earth, if not immediately, then within
several generations. In the early years of the century Bacon
holds out a promise to those who will join him in the task of
scientific inquiry :

> the true end ... of Knowledge is a restitution and reinvesting (in
> great part) of man to the sovereignity and power (for whensoever
> he shall be able to call the creatures by their true names he shall
> again command them) which he had in his first state of creation.
> And to speak plainly and clearly, it is a discovery of all operations
> and possibilities of operations from immortality (if it were possible)
> to the meanest mechanical practice.
>   (*The Philosophical Works of Francis Bacon*, ed.
>   Spedding, Ellis, and Heath (London, 1876), iii, 222)

His followers, who are legion, ignore the parenthetical
qualification ('if it were possible') and transform what may
have been only a figurative and hyperbolic statement of
purpose — the recovery of true names — into a programme
for action.

[1] *The Complete Works of Joshua Sylvester*, i. 102.
[2] *Paradise Lost as 'Myth'*, p. 36.

In 1668 John Wilkins published his *An Essay Towards a Real Character and a Philosophical Language*. This document, along with Sprat's *History of the Royal Society* (1667) and Cowley's ode to the same body indicate the extent to which a mathematically quantitative methodology had won the day. In contrast to the polemic stance Bacon takes in the *Preface to the Great Instauration*, Wilkins' tone in his 'Epistle Dedicatory' is easy and familiar. Obviously he is confident that the public will approve his stated purpose, 'namely the distinct expression of all things and notions that fall under discourse'. His readers are his colleagues, aware of their common problem and thoroughly conversant with the commonplaces which attend its consideration : 'He that knows how to estimate that judgement inflicted on Mankind, in the curse of the Confusion with all the unhappy consequences of it, may thereby judge, what great advantage and benefit there will be in a remedy against it.' Again in contrast to Bacon, Wilkins does not hesitate to take theology as his province :

> This design will likewise contribute much to the clearing of some of our Modern difficulties in Religion, by unmasking many wild errors, that shelter themselves under the disguise of affected phrases; which being Philosophically unfolded and rendered according to the genuine and natural importance of Words, will appear to be inconsistencies and contradictions.
>
> ('Epistle Dedicatory')

'Modern difficulties in Religion' is marvellously ingenuous when one recalls the Civil Wars ; yet the phrase is less surprising than the implied equation of religious and linguistic 'difficulties'. The idea that heresy and controversy are the by-products of metaphorical language is not a novel one ; but Wilkins' confidence in his ability to establish the truths of religion by fashioning a language free of affectation is new,[1] and perhaps, if one takes seriously the doctrine of original sin, blasphemous.

When Wilkins lists the deficiencies he intends to supply, he does so in the context made familiar by his predecessors. One begins by referring to Paradise:

> 'tis evident enough that the first Language
> was *con-created* with our first Parents, they
> immediately understanding the voice of God.[2]

The nostalgia in 'they immediately understanding the voice of God' is comparable to Aristotle's 'nobody uses fine language when teaching geometry';[3] the difference is that Aristotle's statement is an admission of defeat while Wilkins presses resolutely on: All languages, 'except the first, (of which we know nothing so certain as that it was not made by Human Art upon Experience) have been either taken up from that first, and derived by way of *Imitation*; or else in a long tract of time, have, upon several emergencies, admitted various and *casual alterations*.'[4] The 'various and casual alterations' can be subsumed under three headings:

(1) *Redundancy.* 'Synonymous words, which make Language tedious, and are generally *Superfluities*, since the end and use of speech is for humane utility and mutual converse.'[5]

(2) *Equivocals.* 'which are of several significations and therefore must needs render speech doubtful and obscure;

---

[1] Not that Wilkins was the first to suggest this. Jones cites Cave Beck, *The Universal Character* (1657), who believed that a universal character would be the means of 'propogating all sorts of Learning and true Religion' (*The Seventeenth Century*, p. 154). The 'newness' of the idea belongs to the age and not to any one individual proponent of it.

[2] *Real Character*, p. 2.

[3] Cf. Hobbes: 'In geometry, which is the only science that it has pleased God hitherto to bestow on mankind, men begin at settling the significations of their words, which settling of significations they call *definitions* and place them in the beginning of their reckoning' (*Leviathan*, i. 4, p. 41.)

[4] *Real Character*, p. 19.   [5] Ibid., p. 18.

and that argues a *deficiency*, or want of a sufficient number of words.'[1]

(3) *Metaphor.* 'may seem to contribute to the elegance and ornament of speech ; yet like other affected ornaments, they prejudice the native simplicity of it, and contribute to the disguising of it with false appearances.'[2]

The warning against metaphor is related to more general warnings against rhetoric as the instrument of the devil ; the 'false appearances' and the 'disguises' are his weapons, the efficacy of which flows from their correspondence to the 'natural' weakness of his victims. For the scientific philosophers, however, the devil is almost an anachronism, recalled in phrases like 'luxuriant swellings' only to be dismissed along with equivocals, redundancy, and figurative language. In a remarkable passage, Sprat combines echoes of the *Republic*, Saint Augustine, Bacon, and countless denunciations of pulpit enthusiasm in attributing all of man's ills to the ascendancy of tropes and figures :

> When I consider the means of *happy living*, and the causes of their *corruption*, I can hardly forbear recanting what I said before ; and concluding, that *eloquence* ought to be banish'd out of all *civil Societies*, as a thing fatal to Peace and good Manners. . . . They [the Ornaments of speaking] are in open defiance against *Reason* ; professing not to hold much correspondence with that ; but with its Slaves, *the Passions :* they give the mind a motion too changeable, and bewitching, to consist with *right practice.* Who can behold, without indignation, how many mists and uncer-

[1] Ibid., p. 17.

[2] Ibid., p. 18. Cf. Hobbes on the abuses of words: 'When men register their thoughts wrong by the inconstancy of the signification of their words, by which they register for their conception that which they never conceived . . . when they use words metaphorically — that is, in other senses than that they are ordained for — and thereby deceive others' (*Leviathan* i. 4, p. 38). Similar statements can of course be found in Bacon's works. Rudolf Carnap terms the meaningless words of metaphysical speculation 'metaphorical' ('The Elimination of Metaphysics', p. 71).

tainties, these specious *Tropes* and *Figures* have brought on our Knowledg? How many rewards, which are due to more profitable, and difficult arts, have been still snatch'd away by the easie vanity of *fine speaking*? For now I am warm'd with this just anger, I cannot with-hold myself, from betraying the shallowness of all these seeming mysteries; upon which, *we Writers*, and *Speakers*, look so bigg. And, in a few words, I dare say; that of all the Studies of men, nothing may be sooner obtained, than this vicious abundance of *Phrase*, this trick of *Metaphor*, this volubility of *Tongue* . . . and I think, it may be plac'd amongst those *general mischiefs*; such as the *dissension* of Christian Princes, the *want* of *practice* in Religion, and the like.[1]

Sprat qualifies his indictment with the usual concession to the importance of rhetoric as a defensive weapon, lest 'the *naked Innocence*' of virtue, would be on all occasions 'expos'd to the *armed malice* of the wicked', but for all practical purposes the devil has disappeared or has at least been disarmed by the corrective control of methodical plainness. While Sprat dare not mount a frontal attack on the doctrine of natural depravity ('The operations, and powers of the *mind* . . . will still be subject to the same errors'), he does effect a separation between the distorting potentiality of the fallen mind and the inevitable triumph of natural philosophy. The rigour of method will provide 'means and exercises for *direction*' and turn men from the vanity of 'being wholy imployd about the *productions* of their own *minds*' to a fruitful consideration of 'all the works of Nature that are without them'. By regarding the laws of method as absolute and God-given, Sprat and Wilkins and their fellows in the Royal Society manage first to isolate a variable — the defect of the species — and finally to eliminate it as a serious obstacle to clear and distinct knowledge. Since the senses are now directed and controlled by a system independent of the individual consciousness, they are rehabilitated, much as

[1] *The History of the Royal Society of London* (London, 1667), pp. 111-13.

Bacon insisted they could be in the *Advancement of Learning* :

> But here was their [the Academies] chief error; they charged the
> deceit upon the Senses; which in my judgement (notwithstanding
> all their cavillations) are very sufficient to certify and report truth,
> though not always immediately, yet by comparison, by help of
> instrument. . . . But they ought to have charged the deceit upon
> *the weakness of the intellectual powers, and upon the manner of*
> *collecting and concluding upon the reports of the senses* . . . for no
> man . . . can make a straight line or perfect circle by steadiness of
> hand, which may easily be done by help of a ruler or compass. [1]

By 1667, the senses take their place in a perfectly articulated
series of intellectual operations : the data of the physical
world are received by them, ordered by an intellect equipped
with the rule of method, and transcribed into a language
which admits only words that are things. What Miller says
of the Puritan–Ramist mentality will serve to characterize
the intellectual bias of a full half-century :

> Thus armed with a system that was competent to do all things
> required of it, the . . . intellect could ascertain objectively the
> individual entities, perceive their relations, clarify doubts, and
> finally set everything in its proper place in elegant order; thus
> equipped to end all the disputes which ever had been or ever
> would be . . . logicians were prepared to inaugurate a new era in
> intellectual history. [2]

The plain style associated with the scientific movement
is not the plain style Morris Croll has identified with anti-
Ciceronianism. The two share an ideal — mirror-like fidelity
to a reality. It is the realities that differ, at least in the early
stages of each movement when goals are unambiguously
stated. The anti-Ciceronians attempt in their style to
portray 'exactly those athletic movements of the mind by
which it arrives at a sense of reality and the true knowledge

---

[1] *Selected Writings*, ed. Dick, p. 290.
[2] *The New England Mind: The Seventeenth Century*, p. 153.

of itself'.[1] The emphasis is on the uniqueness of the individual mind's movement toward the truth and a value is placed on a style which is faithful to that movement. The objectivity is interior : 'its function is to express individual variances of experience in contrast with the general and communal ideas which the open design of the oratorical style is so well adapted to contain.'[2] In brief the style is the man and is most 'true' when it accurately reflects his individuality. On the other hand, the philosophy that yields the mathematical plainness of Sprat and Wilkins implicitly denies or skirts the concept of individuality. In Croll's terms, the scientific style is oratorical (members of the Royal Society would blanch at the accusation) because it concerns itself with 'general and communal ideas' and does not recognize the thinking mind as an active part of the cognitive process. The universal applicability of method makes all minds one mind, a common and passive machine harnessed and directed by a power independent of it ; and the machine, properly controlled, is assumed to be answerable to the reality it would record. In this way, the human factor is phased out and the epistemological gap between concepts in the mind and their objective existence in nature is bridged. There is no problem of the observer because the observer, except as a transparent medium, does not exist. While this effacing of the individual mind might encourage personal humility, its most important by-product is racial pride, that is to say, the idea of progress, the assumption that soon all the secrets of the universe will yield themselves up to the new methodology. Lip service is still paid to the inherent weakness of mortal faculties, but once that weakness has been isolated, it can be discounted, at least in practice, and finally ignored, even in theory ; except, perhaps, for an

[1] 'Attic Prose in the Seventeenth Century', *Studies in Philology*, xviii (1921), p. 95. [2] Ibid., p. 88.

occasional expression of conventional (and old-fashioned) piety.

Actually, as modern physicists are quick to admit, mathematical or neutral notations are no more objective, in a final sense, than are the 'reports from within' sent out to us by a lyric poet. The rigour of scientific statements is a relative rigour within a system of discourse adopted as a working hypothesis. Recently one theorist has suggested that true objectivity, as far as we can approximate it, demands that our observations take into account the fact of the observer's consciousness : 'A spoken or a written word was spoken or written by someone, and part of the recognition of the word as activity is a recognition of who it was that said it or wrote it. When I make a statement, even as coldly and impersonal a statement as a proposition of Euclid, it is I that am making the statement, and the fact that it is I that am making the statement is part of the picture of the activity. In the same way, when you quote a proposition of Euclid the fact that it is you who quote it is part of the picture which is not to be discarded.'[1] By discarding that part of the picture a scientist oversimplifies his problem, and a Christian forgets who he is. 'The insight that we can never get away from ourselves', P. W. Bridgman has said, 'is an insight which the human race through its long history has been deliberately, one is tempted to say wilfully, refusing to admit.'[2] One admission of this insight, indeed a basic admission of it, is the doctrine of original sin which places a permanent screen (dark glass) between the mind and the full and clear comprehension of what is. The entire scientific programme, of which we have been examining a small part, is from one point of view a *wilful* refusal to face up to that insight as it had been traditionally urged by orthodox

[1] P. W. Bridgman, 'The Way Things Are', in *The Limits of Language*, ed. Walker Gibson (New York, 1962), p. 42.

[2] 'The Way Things Are', p. 44.

Christianity. The heritage of the second half of the century is as much the Deist natural religion for a naturally good man as it is a curiosity like Wilkins' *Real Character*.

Sympathetic though he may be to the more limited aims of his contemporaries, especially as they relate to the distrust of rhetoric he everywhere evidences, Milton is unable to share their optimism, largely because it contains a latent impiety. It is this that D. C. Allen discerns when he explains Milton's reticence on the subject of the original tongue, despite the fact that he 'was quite aware of the general linguistic theories of his age' :[1]

> A scientific study of the Original Language ... is an unwarrented intrusion on the mysteries of theology. It is this sin against which both Raphael and Michael warn Adam, and one of which Milton himself would not be guilty.... His long experience with the rationalists who had attempted to establish the data of revelation by reason led him, I am sure, to the conclusion that exercises of this sort often produced results that were antithetical to revelation itself.[2]

A similar observation underlies P. Albert Duhamel's insistence that Milton could never have been a committed Ramist :

> ... the faith in the immediate intuitive perception of logical relations, which is the ultra-spiritual epistemology, implied throughout the Ramistic logics, [was] much more in keeping with the enthusiasm of the radical sects ... than with the rationalism of Milton.[3]

Leaving aside for the moment the question of his rationalism, one can say that for Milton 'the immediate intuitive perception of logical relations' is the hallmark of prelapsarian thought processes, as is the possession of a perfect language. Any claims to the contrary, whether they were made by the members of the Royal Society or by the enthusiasts, he

[1] 'Some Theories of the Growth and Origin of Language', p. 6.
[2] Ibid., pp. 6–7.   [3] 'Milton's Alleged Ramism', p. 1035.

would regard as a huge and dangerous self-deception, dangerous because it indicates a deficiency in humility. Humility is what he seeks to instil in his readers by exploding the promise of a terrestrial Paradise which they may have accepted in the name of a secular faith. Every time a reader is unable to limit his response to the literal signification of a word descriptive of Paradise or its inhabitants, he is in effect attesting to the speciousness of a programme that offers salvation in the guise of linguistic reform. If ambiguity and metaphor are the enemies because they are the basis of all distortion, then the enemies live within him, for it is beyond his power to withhold the metaphorical or ambiguous reading. Milton need not believe wholeheartedly in the ideal language in order to take advantage of his reader's belief in it. As long as the reader identifies Edenic perfection with a word–thing vocabulary, he must admit his distance from that perfection whenever he reads into the word more than is literally there, more than the thing. (It is Satan who scoffs in ambiguous words, ringing ingenious but frivolous changes on the terms of cannonry; while Adam and Eve pun etymologically, declining a word in its single significance and therefore not punning at all.)[1] The would-be rational man is hoisted with his own petard, and it is the self-consciousness of his attitude toward language which enables Milton to teach him humility by the careful patterning of a few words.

If we miss the lesson at first, Milton is there to point the moral. As Adam and Eve pass on, naked ('Nor those mysterious parts were then conceal'd'), the epic voice steps in with one of his periodic lectures:

---

[1] Thus Eve: 'small store will serve, where store, / All seasons, ripe for use hangs on the stalk; / Save what by frugal storing firmness gains' (v. 322–4). This resembles the arguments from etymology Milton discusses in the chapter *De Notatione* of his *Art of Logic* (i. xxiv).

> Then was not guilty shame: dishonest shame
> Of Nature's works, honor dishonorable,
> Sin-bred, how have ye troubl'd all mankind
> With shows instead, mere shows of seeming pure,
> And banisht from man's life his happiest life,
> Simplicity and spotless innocence.
> So pass'd they naked on, nor shunn'd the sight
> Of God or Angel for they thought no ill.
>
> (IV. 313–20)

The purpose of this is, as Davis Harding explains, to make us 'almost ashamed of any suspicions we may have momentarily entertained' (I would delete 'almost').[1] *Then* was not guilty shame, but now is. Adam and Eve are not troubled by their nakedness, but we are. Shame is described by Adam in his first awareness of sin, as 'the last of evils' (IX. 1079) especially difficult to bear because it sits there to '*reproach us as unclean*' (1098, emphasis mine). Shame is 'guilty' because it wells up in us involuntarily to testify to an inner corruption. 'Shame to Milton', writes Northrop Frye, 'is something deeper and more sinister in human emotion than simply the instinctive desire to cover the genital organs. It is rather a state of mind which is the state of the Fall itself: it might be described as the emotional response to the state of pride.'[2] This is the emotional response the reader gives to the description of Eve, and subsequently to the unfallen embrace, and repeatedly to the key words this chapter examines. If he does not immediately recognize his uneasiness at 'wanton' and 'dishevell'd' for what it is, he will certainly do so when Milton reminds him that 'nature's works' remain spotless and innocent unless they are perverted by the sin-bred mind of a guilty mankind. His own reaction to a guiltless word or a guiltless being is more of a

1 *The Club of Hercules*, p. 73.
2 *The Return of Eden*, (Toronto, 1965), p. 37.

reproach than anything the epic voice might say to him. The implication of the concluding half line, 'for they thought no ill', is inescapable: *they* thought no ill, but *we* do, and therein lies our shame and our guilt. Adam and Eve share neither until they fall in Book ix and at that moment 'wanton' receives its fallen meaning:

> hee on Eve
> Began to cast lascivious Eyes, she him
> As wantonly repaid: in Lust they burn.   (1014–16)

Wanton is defined here by the words that surround it, 'lascivious' (to which 'As wantonly' stands in a kind of apposition) and 'Lust'; and its appearance is a signal to the reader, telling him that he can now relax, since Adam and Eve speak his language at last. But by then he knows enough to wish that their vocabulary had remained pure.

(iii) IN WAND'RING MAZES LOST

I cannot emphasize too much the deliberateness of this pattern. The placing of 'wanton' and 'dishevell'd' and later of 'loose' (IV. 497) is too conspicuously awkward to be accidental. They are there to create problems or puzzles which the reader feels obliged to solve since he wishes, naturally, to retain a sense of control over the reading experience. Consider, as another example, the present participle 'wand'ring', noted by Mrs. MacCaffrey as a 'key word, summarizing the theme of the erring, bewildered human pilgrimage, and its extension into the prelapsarian world with the fallen angels'.[1] Its first appearances are significant only in retrospect: the fallen angels lose their heavenly names by rebelling and get 'them new names' by 'wand'ring

[1] *Paradise Lost as 'Myth'*, p. 188.

o'er the Earth, / Through God's high sufferance for the
trial of man, / By falsities and lies the greatest part / Of
Mankind they corrupted' (I. 365–8). There is a paradox
here that will be exploited in other contexts: wandering
signifies undirected movement, but the fallen angels wander
through God's high sufferance; even their aimlessness is not
their own. One cannot help but serve God. These are the
same devils who are the 'wand'ring Gods' of I. 481 and
who as the Sons of Belial 'wander forth ... flown with
insolence and wine' (501–2). 'The word *wander*', according
to Mrs. MacCaffrey, 'has almost always a pejorative, or
melancholy connotation in *Paradise Lost*',[1] but in these
early instances the word has a neutral connotation. It is an
empty counter, awaiting the meanings that will accrue to it.
When Belial asks 'who would lose ... / Those thoughts
that wander through Eternity' (II. 146, 148), 'wander' has
the force of promenade or stroll, and it is surely neither
pejorative nor melancholy. Some hint of what will finally
become of the word is contained in Beelzebub's 'who shall
tempt with wand'ring feet / The dark unbottom'd infinite
Abyss' (II. 404–5). By 'wand'ring' Satan means without
guide or aimlessly and the association of the verb with
'tempt' is ominous (although here tempt means 'try') since
we know that Eve will wander from Adam and together,
tempted, they will wander from God into the dark unbottom'd abyss of sin (in Book x Adam acknowledges his new
kinship to Satan — 'to Satan only like' — and cries 'O
Conscience, into what *Abyss* of fears / And horrors hast thou
driv'n me').

It is pleasant to cross-reference Milton's poem in this
way, finding echoes and anticipations, but this is a synthetic
operation performed after the fact and with the aid of a
concordance. If 'wand'ring' and words like it are to exist

[1] Loc. cit.

in a pattern that the reader will recognize and carry with
him, his attention must be called to them in a very specific
way. At II. 523 the devils exit from the 'great consult' and go

> . . . wand'ring, each his several way
> Pursues, as inclination or sad choice
> Leads him perplext, where he may likeliest find
> Truce to his restless thoughts.

Here the word is given in its 'innocent' or neutral meaning
as a descriptive of a physical movement ('each his several
way'); the potential moral signification does not occur to
the reader. But when the equally neutral 'inclination'
becomes 'sad choice' and the devils become 'perplext'
(confused, entangled) sojourners whose activity is the
manifestation of 'restless thoughts', 'wand'ring' is caught in
a backwater effect and takes on in retrospect the moral
connotations of these words (on the printed page, 'wand'-
ring', 'inclination', 'perplext', and 'restless' appear in a
vertical line). Within thirty-five lines 'wand'ring' recurs in a
context inescapably moral, as if Milton were confirming for
the reader its new meaning :

> and reason'd high
> Of Providence, Foreknowledge, Will, and Fate,
> Fixt Fate, Free will, Foreknowledge absolute,
> And found no end, in wand'ring mazes lost.
>
> (558–61)

Every reader remembers this last line, and the image is one
that expands to include other figures in other scenes. Both
the good and bad angels participate in an inconclusive battle
— 'Whence in perpetual fight they needs must last /
Endless and no solution will be found' (VI. 693–4, emphasis
mine) — ended only by the intervention of Christ. Adam
and Eve awake to sin and the fruitlessness of 'mutal
accusation' — 'And of thir vain contest appear'd *no end*'

(IX. 1189, emphasis mine) — until 'Prevenient Grace'
descends from Christ ('the Mercy-seat above') and softens
their hearts. Throughout the poem the reader struggles
with the concepts enumerated here — the oxymoron-like
juxtaposition of 'Fixt Fate' and 'Free Will' anticipates all
our difficulties with the pronouncements of God and all our
efforts to deny the Fall by making Adam and Eve the victims
of impulses beyond their control — and again only faith,
in Christ, can extricate us from these philosophical tangles.
In Book X Adam is able to 'find no way' (844) out of the
maze of his consciousness until Eve in imitation of Christ
offers herself as a redeemer. And in Book XII the depressing
cycle of an endlessly wand'ring humanity, powerless through
sin to keep to the straight and narrow, is broken only by the
entrance into history of Christ who shall 'bring back /
Through the world's wilderness long wander'd man / Safe
to eternal Paradise of rest.' Of course each Christian wanders
his personal wilderness from which he is brought back only
by Christ. The devils have no redeemer (Satan says he
would like to fly to Christ's protection in *Paradise Regained*,
IV. 215); and for them (although not *to* them) 'wand'ring'
always has the meaning it assumes for the first time at
II. 561, perplexed and hopelessly entangled, condemned to
meaningless movement without end and without rest, lost.
When Satan presents himself as a petitioner at the court of
Chaos and ancient Night, he unwittingly summarizes the
history and development of the word as it has so far been
seen in the poem:

> Wand'ring this darksome Desert, as my way
> Lies through your spacious Empire up to light,
> Alone, and without guide, half lost, I seek.

(973–5)

These lines anticipate the final appearance of 'wand'ring'

and will serve to contrast, for the last time, the wanderings of Satan and the wanderings of man.

   While the reader will surely remember these instances of 'wand'ring', he will not yet necessarily apply the word to his own situation or see in its repetition a pattern that is especially meaningful to him. There are still neutral occurrences, although it becomes increasingly difficult to accept 'wand'-ring' as a merely physical concept. Satan intends very little when he characterizes his journey as a 'wand'ring quest' (ii. 830) yet we are free and indeed obliged to compare his quest with Gawain's or Percival's and draw the obvious conclusion. Similarly Satan's hope 'To find who might direct his wand'ring flight to Paradise' (iii. 631) is literal enough until one realizes that in the true sense he can never be directed to Paradise and must wander like his successors in the Paradise of Fools (458). Uriel accepts his 'alone thus wand'ring' (667) innocently because his uprightness prevents him from considering any other possibility. We see through Satan and even beyond him to a level on which his feigned wandering is all too true, but our advantage is in reality a liability or a defect (it takes one to know one) and it is this that our involvement with the word will finally bring us to acknowledge.

   The extent to which these distinctions are made consciously will vary with the individual reader; but in Books iv, v, and vii the placing of 'wand'ring' is obviously and unmistakably provocative. In Paradise the four main streams are said to run 'diverse wand'ring many a famous realm' (iv. 234). Why 'wand'ring'? Even to a reader who has thought little about the word, its appearance here, in Paradise, is disconcerting and on Milton's part, tactless. Paradise is that place and time where roses are without thorns and fables are true ('If true, here only') and language is perfect, no redundancy, no equivocals, and above all no ambiguities. But ambiguity is the attribute most easily attached to 'wand'ring' on the basis of its previous occurrences. And if the reader somehow passes by the word without pausing to think about it, he is brought up short by the line Ricks and Stein seize on in their discussions of paradisical language :

> And now divided into four main Streams,
> Runs diverse, wand'ring many a famous Realm
> And Country whereof here needs no account,
> But rather to tell how, if Art could tell,
> How far from that Sapphire Fount the crisped Brooks,
> Rolling on Orient Pearl and sands of Gold,
> *With mazy error under pendant shades.*

(233–9)

Syntactically 'With mazy error' modifies 'Rolling', but if the force of 'wand'ring mazes lost' is at all as I have described it, the eye will involuntarily glance back to 'wand'-ring' (234), which functions much as 'Rolling' does in the earlier clause, and read 'wand'ring with mazy error'. Later, in Book VII, Milton will combine the same words in an even more ominous grouping, thereby indicating the deliberateness of their previous association in Book IV : in response to the command of God the waters of the earth hasten toward their appointed places 'With Serpent error wand'ring' (303). In both cases the reader is surprised to encounter complications where he least expects them. If there are any moments in the poem which should be free of evil or even of the suggestion of evil, surely they are when Paradise is put before our eyes and again when God performs his first and greatest mercy, creation. Mrs. MacCaffrey seems almost to attribute the 'sense of danger' we feel in the presence of innocence and Godhead, respectively, to a potential for evil in nature.[1] But Milton everywhere insists

[1] *Paradise Lost as 'Myth'*, p. 165.

that 'matter . . . proceeded incorruptible from God, and even since the fall it remains incorruptible.'[1] Again one must exclude (consciously) the tainted meaning, rejecting with it the idea of a guilty nature. The serpent too must be pronounced innocent. He is chosen to accompany 'error' only because his physical aspect (accidentally) resembles the movement being described, which is also innocent. Evil exists only in the fallen mind which makes a naturally good universe the reflection of its own corruption. This truth is not easily understood by those who are in bondage to a law that locates evil in actions and things — thou shalt not steal, thou shalt not covet thy neighbour's wife — but it is the covetous eye that transforms a woman or a jewel into an object of temptation and an apple into an idol; and in the sharply delineated structure of *Paradise Lost* one cannot evade responsibility for evil by foisting it off on a passive and guiltless universe. By confronting the reader with a vocabulary bearing the taint of sin in a situation that could not possibly harbour it, Milton leaves him no choice but to acknowledge himself as the source, and to lament.

A similar effect is achieved earlier in vii when 'wand'ring' is structured into a deliberately misleading verse paragraph :

> lest the like befall
> In Paradise to *Adam* or his Race,
> Charg'd not to touch the interdicted Tree,
> If they transgress, and slight that sole command,
> So easily obey'd amid the choice
> Of all tastes else to please thir appetite,
> Though wand'ring.   (44–50)

At first 'Though wand'ring' seems to refer directly to Adam and Eve : they should be able to resist the temptation of the interdicted tree despite a tendency to wander: *'though'* becomes 'even though'. The effect depends on the position-

[1] *The Works of John Milton*, xv. 23–25.

ing of the phrase; it springs out at the reader before he has time to place it. When he does go back he will attach 'wand'ring' to 'appetite', but as a second reading this is more problematical than the first. 'Wand'ring appetite' immediately translates itself into immoderation, excess, lust. Is there lust in Paradise? Do we glimpse here in Adam's and Eve's domestic habits a weakness which will lead to the fall? The answer to both questions is no and in the necessary third reading the thought is finally unravelled: the prohibition does not represent an appreciable gustatorial restraint since the number of trees in Paradise precludes satiation even if the inhabitants happen to be gourmets (being a gourmet in Paradise is no more reproachable than any other action). It is an unnecessary point, awkwardly made, and its only purpose is to seduce the reader into an interpretation he must give up (Adam will fall because he wanders or has a wandering appetite), and in the process remind him of a tendency to impose his own inadequacies, verbal and moral, on Adam and Eve, Paradise, and God. (It is *we* who must watch our appetites.) One can see from this that the over-moralization of a word can have consequences far beyond the resulting misreading. The technique, in which the reader is led by the inconsistencies (puzzles) of the 'surface materials' to a point which is not made directly in the text, is, as D. W. Robertson has taught us, basic to the method of Christian didacticism.[1] More specifically, it is an extension of the method Milton describes as Christ's — 'not so much a teaching, as an intangling' —[2] the allowing (or forcing) of an error so that it can be corrected in an experiential context (learning by doing) within which the pupil will have an opportunity to come to terms with his tendency to err. Because it suggests

[1] *A Preface to Chaucer* (Princeton, 1962), pp. 52–137.
[2] *Complete Prose Works*, ii. 642.

that there is something already wrong with Paradise, and therefore implies, at a remove, I admit, that the Fall is the fault of the situation and not of Adam and Eve, the reading of 'Wand'ring appetite' as 'lustful appetite' is attractive (seductive). We give it up reluctantly, and our reluctance indicates how much we need the poem's instruction. But more about that later.

After Book VII, the reader is ready at any time to deliver two definitions of 'wand'ring' — (1) movement that is not patterned or directed (2) straying from moral probity — and the self-consciousness of his attitude toward the word has created a third — irregular, but innocent. Moreover he feels obliged to define the word precisely each time it occurs. In his astronomical dissertation Raphael is careful to ascribe no superiority to regular motions. The stars may pursue a 'wand'ring course' (VIII. 126) or at least one that appears to wander and still be part of the praise the universe sends up to God. In fact, the Ptolemaic system is scorned as an attempt to 'save appearances' by making the heavens conform to *man's* sense of order. 'Wand'ring' seems less innocent when Adam agrees not to seek 'anxious cares ... with wand'ring thoughts and notions vain' (187), but even in this configuration 'wand'ring' means something like 'not as profitable as they could be' and 'vain' is almost a synonym for indifferent, or at the worst frivolous. All actions and thoughts are permitted in Paradise, although some are more advisable than others. The ascent that Raphael promises 'in tract of time' will perhaps be more rapid if Adam directs his thoughts to the goodness of heaven and leaves its maintenance to God. Still the worst to be said of 'wand'ring thoughts' is that they are unprofitable.[1]

As the Fall becomes imminent, the pressure (on the reader) to moralize spatial language increases. When Satan

[1] But later Adam will accuse Eve of 'wand'ring vanity' (X. 875).

leads Eve to the forbidden tree his movements trace out the morality of *his* action :

> Hee leading swiftly roll'd
> In tangles, and made intricate seem straight,
> To mischief swift. Hope elevates, and joy
> Bright'ns his Crest, as when a wand'ring Fire,
> Compact of unctuous vapor, which the Night
> Condenses, and the cold invirons round,
> Kindl'd through agitation to a Flame,
> Which oft, they say, some evil Spirit attends,
> Hovering and blazing with delusive Light,
> Misleads th' amaz'd Night-wanderer from his way.
>
> (ix. 631–40)

With 'tangles' and 'intricate' we return to the mazes of philosophical vanity. Suddenly directions are no longer innocent although Eve is innocent as she takes them since her will does not yet concur in Satan's mischief. Satan's wandering is evil, but Eve's is not. This distinction, between the intention of the 'wand'ring Fire' and the 'wanderer' who is misled by it, is a difficult one, since it requires the apportioning of a single word ; but it must be made (the possibility of not making it constitutes a temptation) lest the reader slip into the error of pre-dating the actual commission of sin and denying the spontaneousness of the Fall. (*At this point*, Eve is in Uriel's position, involved in an evil which cannot be imputed to her without distorting the facts.) The awaited metamorphosis of 'wand'ring' is effected by Adam and Eve themselves : Awaking to shame and uncleanliness, Adam turns on Eve to upbraid her in what the epic voice calls 'alter'd style' :

> Would thou hadst heark'n'd to my words, and stay'd
> With me, as I besought thee, when that strange
> Desire of wand'ring this unhappy Morn,
> I know not whence possess'd thee.   (1134–7)

The reader who has lived with the word for nine books will realize at once that Adam has slipped into the fallen habit of imputing evil to things and actions rather than persons. The desire of wandering *possesses* Eve in some mysterious fashion; even as he indicts her, Adam excuses her. Of course Adam's use of 'wand'ring' is the correct one, now : the straight and narrow way is no longer merely advisable, it is necessary since any deviation may lead to eternal woe. Adam is wrong, however, to apply the fallen meaning retroactively, and it is on this basis that Eve challenges him :

> What words have past thy Lips, Adam severe,
> Imput'st thou that to my default, or will
> Of wand'ring, as thou call'st it.
>
> (1144–6)

Eve's 'what words' should be taken literally ; she is questioning Adam's vocabulary as well as his accusation or identifying one with the other. Adam's 'alter'd style' is more 'strange' than her desire. 'Wand'ring as thou call'st it' is shorthand for, 'Is it now our lot to regard with anxiety the "various motions" that have before signified the joyous freedom of innocence?' What we see here is a new kind of naming, or, as Eve characterizes it, calling, one that contrasts unfavourably to Adam's naming of the animals ; the newly fallen consciousness becomes aware of itself just as the reader has been aware of himself all along, and for both recognition comes through language. From this point on Adam and Eve and the reader wander together in a fellowship either party would be happy to forgo.

For the fallen Adam and Eve, wandering seems at first to represent exile and hopelessness. Eve cries 'How shall I part, and whither wander down / Into a lower World' (xi. 282–3), and Adam echoes her fears when he despairs for Noah whom 'Famine and anguish will at last consume /

Wand'ring that wat'ry Desert' (xi. 778–9). But in Book xii, 'wand'ring' undergoes a final transformation and is absorbed into the Christian vision. The new meaning is first seen in the description of Abraham: 'Not wand'ring poor, but trusting all his wealth / With God, who call'd him, in a land unknown' (xii. 133–4). *Not* 'wand'ring poor' although he *is* wandering because Providence is directing him even if he himself is unsure of the direction. Later Abraham's seed will repeat his journey, wandering a wide wilderness, but accompanied by 'The clouded Ark of God . . . in Tents' (333). Wandering is now the movement of faith, the sign of one's willingness to go out at the command of God; and so it is for Adam and Eve when, enlightened by Michael, they descend from Paradise:

> The World was all before them where to choose
> Thir place of rest, and Providence thir guide:
> They hand in hand with wand'ring steps and slow,
> Through *Eden* took thir solitary way.

One is meant to recall, as I have already suggested, the wandering of Satan: 'Wand'ring this darksome Desert, as my way / Lies through your spacious Empire up to light, / Alone and without guide, half lost, I seek.' Certainly, however, the contrast is all. Satan wanders without hope of a place of rest, either temporary or final while man wanders but can choose to rest anywhere because his 'light' is with him as long as he believes in it; therefore he doesn't wander at all. Under Providence, through the medium of faith, the word is able to include all its meanings, even those which are literally contradictory, and is thus returned, after many permutations, to its original purity and innocence. Its ambiguity, like all other refractions of the divine unity, has been an illusion, *our* illusion. Despite anything we can do to it, language, proceeding incorruptible from God, remains incorruptible in its essence.

(iv) THE GUILTY READER AND THE
INNOCENCE OF NATURE

The accumulated arguments of this chapter have been anticipated in part by Joseph Summers who attributes to Milton an early use of Henry James' technique of the 'guilty reader' : 'The readers as well as the characters have been involved in the evil and have been forced to recognize and to judge their involvement.'[1] For the most part the reader's sense of guilt is bound up in the distinction he is repeatedly asked to make between Adam and Eve and himself. He is encouraged to compare his perceptions and reactions and linguistic habits with theirs (insofar as they can be compared) and to fashion from the comparisons a working definition of innocence. The experience is primarily a dialectical one and leaves little room for extended and considered self-recriminations. But from time to time, and in one instance for an entire book, the pace slows and the reader is invited to consider in a more leisurely fashion his relationship to the totality of God's universe. It is then that sin becomes the kind of burden it is for Bunyan's Christian :

> *I saw a Man cloathed with Raggs, standing in a certain place, with his face from his own House, a Book in his hand, and a great burden upon his Back.* I looked, and saw him open the Book, and Read therein; and as he read, he wept and trembled: and not being able longer to contain, he brake out with a lamentable cry; saying, *what shall I do ?*[2]

By reading in his book, Christian is given an insight into his situation that staggers him and takes from him forever

[1] *The Muse's Method*, p. 31.
[2] *The Pilgrim's Progress*, ed. J. B. Wharey, rev. Roger Sharrock (Oxford, 1960), p. 8.

the complacency he once shared with those who have not had his experience.

Complacency is most certainly not what Milton's reader feels, even after only one hundred lines of the first book; but there is a certain exhilaration in the mental calisthenics he is put through which works against the conviction of sin and the feeling of helplessness before the fact of sin that must precede any real contrition. The reader does not think to cry, 'What shall I do?', because he is always doing something — analysing, judging, comparing, recalling. The intuition that man is unworthy and can do nothing is not likely to be properly humbling if one has worked very hard to earn it. (It is physically and psychologically exhausting to read this poem.) What the reader must finally learn is that the analytical intellect, so important to the formulation of necessary distinctions, is itself an instrument of perversion and the child of corruption because it divides and contrasts and evaluates where there is in reality a single harmonious unity. The probing and discursive mind may be essential to the piecing together of the shining oneness of Truth, but at the end of the effort is the abandonment of self-consciousness and the surrender to a truth which is no longer perceived but participated in. Active seeking is a good only because of the stasis assumed as its goal. Overvalue the process and you deny the goal as something to be desired; indeed the lack of it becomes a virtue since it makes necessary the activity you judge to be virtuous. This is in fact what happens in some philosophies which place the highest premium on 'becoming', but it will not do for Christianity unless you are prepared to make the fortunate fall the virtuous fall. Watkins, among others, does not shrink from this final step:

> The challenge she [Eve] meets is fundamental to the human mind which to become civilized at all beyond a wild or vegetable

> state has had to break innumerable taboos, always risking failure to distinguish the one true prohibition among so many false.
>
> Granted the choice between unconscious good in mindless immortality, and a period of wisdom followed by death, Milton would choose the latter.[1]

Trial and error, however, is the way to distinguish the one true prohibition only when it is not known. The challenge Eve meets does not exist except as a result of her having invented it. The same confusion informs Watkins' second statement. By 'mindlessness' he means that since Adam and Eve know no other possibility they do not really know the good; but this is what we have (literally) fallen into, knowing good by evil. Adam and Eve do not know good, as we do, by separating it from evil. They are a part of Good, as they must be (everything proceeds incorruptible *de deo*), because there is no evil. Evil is not a thing; it is a state of being which exists only in and for the will that chooses it; it is the voluntary breaking away from God, a voluntary metamorphosis of the self from unity with God, and therefore with the good, into an isolated bit of evil. Choosing disunion creates the fractured vision Watkins calls consciousness; to say that Adam and Eve are unconsciously good is meaningless unless it is intended as praise. The reader must understand that mindlessness — a sense of well-being because the mind knows nothing else (no *better*, we might say mistakenly) — is virtuous, and that his inability to be mindless is his punishment. This insight awaits the reader in Book vii, the creation scene, when Milton gives him an opportunity to relax, and be at his ease, and lets him feel the horror of being able to do neither.

Watkins' phrase for the joyous movement of a universe informed (made pregnant) by God is 'the rhythm of plenitude'

[1] *An Anatomy of Milton's Verse* (Baton Rouge, 1955), pp. 132, 131.

and Adam and Eve are included in the picture he draws:

> Having already surrounded with rich imagery of generation the universe which Adam and Eve inhabit, he has only to gather them silently into the rhythm of plenitude, so that they seem, till eating the forbidden fruit, never self-conscious, . . . sharing in a general process of nature.[1]

(This is so good that I wonder how Watkins can later applaud the action that sets them apart from the 'general process of nature'.) The rhythm of plenitude, on display gloriously in Book VII, has been exhibited before in the 'various style' of the morning hymn. Their prayer is various, that is non-patterned, because prayer is a praise of God ; and in a universe that proceeds from God, the praise of any one part is the praise of all. There really are no parts, only multiple expressions of a single informing spirit. When the harmony is broken, at least from man's point of view, and he stands in relationship to God rather than in God, the easy and various expression of praise will be replaced by the rigidity of ritual, which, as C. S. Lewis explains, 'is a pattern imposed on the mere flux of our feelings by reason and will',[2] necessary because the reason and the will are themselves inadequate to the task. This formally distanced way of communicating with deity is introduced at the close of Book x when the epic voice echoes ritualistically Adam's design for praying :

> What better can we do, than to the place
> Repairing where he judg'd us, prostrate fall
> Before him reverent, and there confess
> Humbly our faults, and pardon beg, with tears
> Watering the ground, and with our sighs the Air
> Frequenting, sent from hearts contrite, in sign
> Of sorrow unfeign'd, and humiliation meek.
>
> (1086–92)

---

[1] *An Anatomy of Milton's Verse*, p. 69.
[2] *A Preface to Paradise Lost* (Oxford, 1942), p. 21.

> they forthwith to the place
> Repairing where he judg'd them prostrate fell
> Before him reverent, and both confess'd
> Humbly thir faults, and pardon begg'd, with tears
> Watering the ground, and with thir sighs the Air
> Frequenting, sent from hearts contrite, in sign
> Of sorrow unfeign'd, and humiliation meek.
>
> (1098–104)

The repetitions indicate stylistically that prayers will here-after be patterned, and not, as they had been in Eden, spontaneous. But now, in Book v, Adam and Eve can say anything that comes to mind because both the thing and the mind live in God and are worthy of praise. A key line in the prayer is 'Him first, him last, him midst, and without end' (165), or in other words, without distinction or hierarchical order. It does not matter where you begin to pray or where you begin to look for God. Significantly, the first of God's works to declare his goodness does not have a fixed position in the universe : 'Fairest of Stars, last in the train of Night, / If better thou belong not to the dawn' (166–7). Summers comments perceptively, 'The fact that the star may be conceived either as "last in the train of Night" or as first "pledge of day" is a matter for glory rather than doubt, as is also, perhaps, the thought of the identity of Hesperus, the holy Venus, and the unfallen Lucifer.'[1] It is a matter for glory also that terms like first and last are qualitatively neutral. Throughout the prayer our first parents employ with a fine indifference words and images we associate with an evil that does not yet exist. The sun 'climb'st' or 'fall'st' (' "Fall'st" occupies the strongest possible position as the final syllable of the line, the sentence, and the section')[2] and one motion is as much a vehicle for praise as the other.

[1] *The Muse's Method*, p. 80.   [2] Loc. cit.

The planets are '*wand'ring* Fires' (177), wandering not through God's sufferance, but as part of his easy order, whereby things are 'regular . . . when most irregular they seem' (623–4). 'Mists and Exhalations' (185) rising *or* falling 'still advance his praise' (191), as do the constituents of Chaos 'the eldest birth / Of Nature's Womb' (180–1) which (from the Satanic perspective) has presented so villainous an aspect in Book II. Later Raphael describes the movements of heavenly bodies as 'mazes intricate' (622), and thus baptizes another image which had appeared irredeemable in Hell. Obversely, usually positive images and symbols lose their preferred status. God is presented as he 'who out of Darkness call'd up Light' (179), but the praise is for the miracle, not its content; darkness out of light would be equally praiseworthy. Not that the line can be read without an awareness of the symbolic pattern which has operated in the poem from the first; but one must realize that for Adam and Eve no such pattern yet exists; they have no need of it. The prayer ends with a wish which seems to us fraught with moral implications : 'Hail universal Lord, be bounteous still / To give us only good; and if the night / Have gathered aught of evil or conceal'd, / Disperse it, as now light dispels the dark' (205–8). It is impossible to read this without substituting good for light and evil for dark, but Adam is merely reaching for an analogy in nature (he looks up and sees it happening; had it been evening the thought might have been reversed) and the fact that he hits upon the symbolism of fallen moral discourse is an accident. (Even in Book XII Adam uses the bringing of light out of darkness as an analogy for, rather than an instance of, bringing good out of evil : 'That all this good of evil shall produce, / And evil turn to good; more wonderful / Than that which by creation first brought forth / Light out of darkness !') Summers speaks of the 'ultimate implications of their

prayers'[1] which include 'the chief metaphysical theme of the
poem, the Fall',[2] But if the Fall is implied or foreshadowed
in the prayer it is no part of their intention, nor is it their
responsibility. Summers adds, 'a reading of the morning
hymn necessarily entails a consideration of much beyond
the hymn.' The necessity is ours and defines the difference
between us and Adam and Eve who need consider nothing
beyond their present bliss. There are no implications in
Paradise.

The reader's inability to simulate the mindlessness of
innocence by reading passively (without implications) is
especially noticeable in Book VII where there are no narrative
concerns to draw attention away from the operations of his
own consciousness. Adam and Eve are not yet created, and
have not been directly presented to us as characters since
v. 560. (Adam does comment on the war in Heaven and
asks Raphael to go on, but his remarks are little more than
offstage promptings and do little to return him to centre
stage.) Satan has been swept off the scene, ignominiously,
not even by name, one of a flock of timorous goats; in strict
sequential time he is safely battened away in Hell and
guarded by a heavenly patrol led by Raphael. Raphael too,
although he is nominally our narrator is 'completely forgotten during his narrative: mainly because this is the
familiar transition in the second chapter of Genesis, which
Milton follows almost word for word'.[3] The reader is alone
with God and with all the thoughts he has brought with him
from the experience of the poem.

God begins by asserting 'I am who fill / Infinitude'
(168-9). All creation flows from him, is him, and is therefore good. This includes chaos, 'the vast immeasurable
Abyss / Outrageous as a Sea, dark, wasteful, wild' (211-12).

[1] *The Muse's Method*, pp. 83, 80.   [2] Ibid., p. 84.
[3] Watkins, *An Anatomy of Milton's Verse*, p. 65.

Chaos is merely that part of God from which he has with-drawn his *active* goodness. 'Though I uncircumscribed my-self retire' — although I still fill infinitude I leave portions of myself without informing direction. Chaos is a storehouse of materials and is at worst morally neutral ('wasteful' means not yet used, or left over from previous creations). Its outrageousness and wildness and darkness are conditions of its relationship to the active presence of God; the dis-tinction to be made is between one kind of perfection — we might call it chaotic perfection — and another, the perfection of God's imposed order :

> Silence, ye troubl'd waves, and thou Deep, peace,
> Said then th' Omnific Word, your discord end.
>
> (216–17)

Chaos's discord is also God's. We are not to imagine a recalcitrantly independent matter resisting the constraint of an enemy power. Chaos *hears* God's voice and obeys it willingly (the adverb may be meaningless) and joyfully: 'him all his train / Follow'd in bright procession to behold / Creation and the wonders of his might' (221–3). Even the cold infernal (that is, destined to be used in the construction of the lower regions) dregs are adverse to life only in the sense that other materials are more answerable to God's present purposes. Milton steadfastly refuses to construct a hierarchy which would involve qualitative distinctions between portions of God's created good. Light is the 'Ethereal, first of things, quintessence pure', and it is good: but the angelic choir, hymning, sings the creator '*Both* when first Ev'ning was, and when first Morn'. Later the heavenly lights are instituted to 'divide' the day from the night, and the division is clearly physical, the means of the 'grateful vicissitude' Raphael remarks on at vi. 8. There is no dualism here except that provided by a Manichean reader.[1]

If the reader has been properly attentive in the early parts of the poem, his own perceptions will come back to haunt him here in Book VII. I have already noted the impact of the line 'with Serpent error wand'ring' (302) which can be read properly only by stripping the three words of the meanings they have acquired in the preceding books, that is by acknowledging the irrelevance, in context, of their pejorative associations. A similar manoeuvre is called for when Milton insists on the innocence of icons he has previously used to represent sin. The epic similes of I and II establish habits of mind and patterns of association that are continually useful and relevant. This is especially true of the Leviathan simile which reaches out to embrace Satan and Pharaoh, the serpent and the river-dragon, all the night-foundered wanderers who are misled by false lights or seeming islands, every deceiver and every deception. It is, to say the least, surprising, then, to meet the simile once again in strange surroundings, amidst the joyful numbering of God's created:

> there Leviathan
> Hugest of living Creatures, on the Deep
> Stretcht like a Promontory sleeps or swims,
> And seems a moving Land.
>
> (412–15)

In Book I, Leviathan–Satan lies 'extended long and large . . .

---

[1] Of course, as Jackson Cope points out (*The Metaphoric Structure of Paradise Lost*, p. 126), 'there are limits beyond which liberty in manipulating traditional symbols becomes license'. The traditional associations of good with light and evil with dark operates everywhere in the poem except at moments like this when Milton is reaching back to a time when such symbolism was unnecessary, when darkness was as comforting and holy as light. In general, however, nothing I say here should be taken to contradict Cope's discussion of the manipulation of light imagery as a prime instance of the 'mode of paradox' and the Renaissance tradition of *discordia concors*.

floating many a rood, in bulk . . . huge', waiting until a pilot deems him 'some island'. The verbal echo is undeniable, but it is also irrelevant, at least as a statement about the structure of the universe. It says nothing about the Leviathan whose playfulness (we see him spouting out seas from his trunk) recalls the gambolling of the 'unwieldy Elephant' wreathing 'His Lithe Proboscis'. Both images are deliciously genial and natural, cosmically humorous. But when the Leviathan is viewed through fallen man's distorting lenses he is spoiled, remaining at the same time innocent of his spoiling, just as the language of Paradise remains innocent of the anxieties that are read into it. The creation scene is the most objective presentation in the poem of the cosmic harmony Milton celebrates; it is the reader's misfortune not to be able to imitate the joyous and spontaneous abandon God's other creatures display here. Instead he saddles them with his burden.

The reader's action parallels Adam's. Corruption is not inherent in God's plan or in the matter that flows from him. God wills only good. Evil enters as a consequence of his conditional decree, and the responsibility for it rests with the free agent who defaults on an obligation he has contracted and is capable of meeting. The decree as formulated deals specifically with the contracting parties: 'On the day thou eatest, thou shalt die'. But the effects of sin extend far beyond the person or control of the sinner who is punished, in part, by seeing his sin envelop those innocent of it. In the narrative proper the harmony of nature is not disrupted until after the Fall when God bids his angels 'See with what heat these Dogs of Hell advance / To waste and havoc yonder World, which I / So fair and good created' (x. 616–18). Thus God himself invites the question so many have asked. Why? why is all creation to be given over to Sin and Death? The answer is immediately forthcoming:

and had still
Kept in that state, had not the folly of Man
Let in these wasteful Furies.   (618–20)

Let in. Adam agrees *not* to perform a (negative) action
whose significance (as far as he knows) is as a pledge of faith ;
and the fact that the action has consequences of which he is
not aware does not affect his original obligation or his
capabilities, even though he will be held responsible for
those consequences :

I call'd and drew them thither
My Hell-hounds to lick up the draff and filth
Which man's polluting Sin with taint hath shed
On what was pure.   (629–32)

God does not execute his decree with pleasure, yet he must
allow the forces let loose by man's error to run their course
or deny man the dignity imputed to him by the original
contract. Within fifty lines the landscape that dances before
us in Book VII changes completely :

Beast now with Beast gan war, and Fowl with Fowl,
And Fish with Fish ; to graze the Herb all leaving,
Devour'd each other ; nor stood much in awe
Of man, but fled him or with count'nance grim
Glar'd on him passing : these were from without
The growing miseries, which *Adam* saw.

(710–15)

Which Adam saw, which Adam caused, which we cause
still. In Book x the disruption of nature is effected at a
distance from the reader as a result of events he is involved
in only as an observer. When God cites 'Man' it is a generic
term in a legal indictment ; it might as well be 'party of the
first part'. But in the creation scene it is the reader who
personally 'lets in' sin and there is no one with whom he can
comfortably divide the responsibility.

There is a word for what happens to nature as a result of man's sin: unfair. And John Peter uses it to characterize Milton's treatment of the serpent: 'to condemn the serpent for the deeds which it performs unwittingly, under Satan's control, is grossly unfair. A clear distinction is needed between the reptile and the spirit who has usurped its form.'[1] The distinction is there, made by Satan when after long debate he chooses 'The Serpent subtlest Beast of all the Field . . . / Fit Vessel, fittest Imp of fraud' (ix. 86, 89). This does not mean that the serpent was intended by God to be a vehicle of fraud. Like everything else in the universe, the serpent has his appointed place in the divine order, and the place is good. Satan views the universe from a distorted angle and sees, or more properly creates, properties and uses that are accidental to the essence of the thing. It is evil intent that makes evil instruments.

Peter's objection is interestingly phrased and contains at least one inaccuracy: the serpent is not condemned, but 'accurst' (x. 84). Conviction would belong to the serpent only if he sinned 'wittingly'. But he cannot: although the beasts reason 'Not contemptibly', their reason is necessarily right. Wilful disobedience is not a possibility, because they are willess; for them reason is not choosing, but programmed obedience. The obverse of this is the inability of the serpent or any other unfree agent to resist: nature is, in effect, at the mercy of a consciousness who decides to pervert one of her multiple forms from its natural good, by appropriating it for evil (disobedient) purposes or by setting it up as an idol. (Satan does both in the battle: he perverts the minerals of heaven by fashioning them into weapons to be used against God's angels, and by abstracting matter from its place in the divine order, he makes it his God; Satan is the poem's true materialist.) Once appropriated or idolized, however, the

[1] *A Critique of Paradise Lost*, p. 115.

innocent form becomes part of the sphere of evil which possesses it. Milton emphasizes the passivity of the serpent by having him sleep through his violation :

> Nor nocent yet, but on the grassy Herb
> Fearless unfear'd he slept: in at his Mouth
> The Devil enter'd, and his brutal sense,
> In heart or head, *possessing* soon inspir'd.
>
> (IX. 186–9, emphasis mine)

When evil enters the mind of beast or the substance of matter it *does* leave a spot behind (though no blame) and corruption has occurred. The logic behind Christ's judging of the serpent is carefully explained by the epic voice in a passage Peter finds 'astounding' and 'wholly unacceptable' :[1]

> To Judgement he proceeded on th' accus'd
> Serpent though brute, unable to transfer
> The Guilt on him who *made him instrument*
> Of mischief, and *polluted from the end*
> *Of his Creation;* justly then accurst,
> As vitiated in Nature.
>
> (x. 164–9, emphasis mine)

The language is the same God uses to describe the vitiation of Nature : 'man's *polluting* Sin with taint hath shed / On what *was* pure'. On what is no longer pure. The serpent, and later all of nature, are subject to a kind of infernal transubstantiation. They are literally consumed by evil, and although incorruptible in their essence (when Christ destroys Satan's work in man, 'Heav'n and Earth renew'd shall be made pure') they are impure in their present position and are adjudged so : 'justly then accurst, / As vitiated in Nature'. It is just in that the curse is merely a formal recognition of what has happened ; that which has been corrupted is corrupt. It is of course unjust or unfair if

---

[1] *Critique,* pp. 115–16.

one considers the culpability of the serpent, but that injustice is not God's who merely establishes the laws of his universe and leaves their maintenance to his appointed agents, who are assigned spheres of responsibility. (Peter should be angry at Satan and Adam, not God.) Since these spheres of responsibility are interdependent, a disruption of the order at any one point will affect areas beyond it; in short the innocent will suffer. (Lear threatens the entire structure of his kingdom when he removes his support from a central position.) Adam wrestles with this problem when he cries, 'Ah why should all mankind / For one man's fault thus guiltless be condemn'd, / If guiltless?' The reader knows the answer and so does Adam : 'But from me what can proceed, But all corrupt.' This is the long day's dying Adam laments, the true punishment for his sin :

> if here would end
> The misery, I deserv'd it, and would
> My own deservings; but this will not serve;
> All that I eat or drink, or shall beget
> Is propagated curse.
>
> (x. 725–9)

To Adam's question, 'Why should not Man, / Retaining still Divine similitude / In part, from such deformities be free?' (xi. 511–13), Michael answers, 'Thir Maker's Image ... / Forsook them, when *themselves they vilifi'd*' (515–16), again absolving God of responsibility and returning it to man. The argument that Adam should have known the cosmic implications of his disobedience if he was to be in control of his situation, does not hold because obedience is an affirmation of loyalty despite appearances, and not a decision between visible alternatives. (Actually, Raphael does warn, 'thine and of all thy Sons / The weal or woe in thee is plac't; beware', but Adam cannot know what the angel means.)

Satan's single action — the exploitation of the serpent
— is a model for what man does every day of his sinful life.
He makes things the vehicles of his evil and then puts them
away (judges them accursed) as if *they* were guilty. (Arma-
ments are the extension of the violence in our souls, but we
try to ban *them*.) This is what the reader does in Book VII
when he draws the Leviathan and the serpent into his
polluted consciousness :

> the rest are numberless
> And thou thir Natures know'st, gav'st them Names,
> Needless to thee repeated; nor unknown
> The Serpent subtl'st Beast of all the field;
> Of huge extent sometimes; with brazen Eyes
> And hairy Mane terrific, though to thee
> Not noxious, but obedient at thy call.

(492–8)

This is one of the few times in Raphael's narrative that we
are aware of Adam as narrator ('to thee', 'at thy call'). The
intention is to contrast his naming and understanding with
ours ; to Adam and Raphael (who is ignorant — a very bad
word — of the serpent's role in Adam's fall) the serpent is
merely the last and one of the more interesting of God's
creatures. If there is any significance to his position in the
catalogue, it is a positive one. As the subtlest of all the field
he is closest in intelligence to man, a fact that does not
escape Satan. The irony in the sentence before this one is
double-edged. With every other reader I am condemned to
see in this praise of the serpent an ominousness that is
simply not there. The possibilities are endless : 'Not
noxious? how little you know, Raphael. Obedient at thy
call? would that were so and not the reverse.' But Raphael's
ignorance and Eve's eventual weakness are less reprehensible
(if they do indeed exist) than the reader's overactive and
suspicious intellect. Every commentator who writes on the

creation scene uses the same words, joyous, easy, delightful, happy, fecund, natural, good, innocent. It is no exaggeration I think to say that this is a composite statement of what Book VII is *without us*, and could be for us were we able to lose ourselves in its rhythms. But how can we when every other line demands a readjustment, a purging of what we interpolate? Can we recognize the peacock 'whose gay Train / Adorns him' without recalling his traditional significance? Can we read of insects 'In all the Liveries deckt of Summer's pride' or of swans 'mantling proudly' and know at once, without reflection, that here pride is permissible and good because it is pride in one's nature as God ordained it, and therefore a praise of God? I think not. At best the fit reader will come to see this only after he has been brought up short by the word and reasoned *away from* the meaning it now has for him. Man may have been created in God's image but he has defaced it and now recreates the world in his own. Raphael's narrative ends with a warning 'lest sin / Surprise thee, and her black attendant Death' (546–7). Had he thought of it Adam could have responded with a formula he has used before: 'Whate'er sin is'. We are neither so fortunate nor so ignorantly wise.

4 Standing Only: Christian Heroism

The way of the Lord is strength to the upright.   PROVERBS

INTRODUCTION

When Milton asks of Eve's and Adam's trespass, 'For what sin can be named, which was not included in this one act', he does not mean that in this sin are *potentially* all sins, but that this sin *is* all sins :

> If the circumstances of this crime are duly considered, it will be acknowledged to have been a most heinous offense, and a transgression of the whole law. For what sin can be named, which was not included in this one act? It comprehended at once distrust in the divine veracity, and a proportionate credulity in the assurances of Satan; unbelief; ingratitude; disobedience; gluttony; in the man excessive uxoriousness, in the woman a want of proper regard for her husband, in both an insensibility to the welfare of their offspring, and that offspring the whole human race; patricide, theft, invasion of the rights of others, sacrilege, deceit, presumption in aspiring to divine attributes, fraud in the means employed to attain the object, pride, and arrogance. Whence it is said, Eccles. VII. 29: 'God hath made man upright, but they have sought out many inventions.' James ii. 10: 'whosoever shall keep the whole law, and yet offend in one point, he is guilty of all.'
>
> (*The Works of John Milton*, xv. 181–3)

In effect, the 'whole law' as it is given by Moses and multiplied as situations multiply is no more than a single command : obey God. 'The circumstances of this crime' make it a multiple offence because one's duty to God subsumes all other duties. In Milton's monistic universe, where 'all things are of God' (*de deo*), a sin against the source is a sin against all. A proper sense of one's relationship to God will yield a proper attitude toward everything that flows from him, since all relationships and the values embodied in them depend on his sustaining power. To turn away from God is to turn away from all values and to default on all obligations, whether they be racial, political or familial. Gabriel scorns Satan's characterization of himself as a 'faithful Leader' by pointing out how meaningless the word is divorced from God :

> and couldst thou faithful add ? O name,
> O sacred name of faithfulness profan'd !
> Faithful to whom ? to thy rebellious crew ?
> Army of Fiends, fit body to fit head ;
> Was this your discipline and faith ingag'd,
> Your military obedience to dissolve
> Allegiance to th' acknowledg'd Power supreme ?
>
> (IV. 950–6)

Faith, discipline, obedience — they are one, along with heroism and love ; and none of them can be invoked to sanction a movement away from God.

While the moral structure of the universe — its radical unity — survives the Fall, man's ability to perceive it does not. The impairment of his vision is reflected in the nature of the acts he is required to perform. Adam and Eve need only refrain from doing something to affirm their obedience, for in this one act (not doing something is also an action) they discharge their obligations to all derivative forms, keeping the whole law by keeping one point of it (which *is* the law). But fallen man must keep every point in order to fulfil one. The symbolic force of the single prohibition is transferred to the innumerable instances it originally included ; thus the bondage of the law whose details press in on us always, and the impossibility of fulfilling it. The distinction is one of degree rather than of kind. In both states the decision to obey is made all the time. Adam and Eve obey every second they decline to disobey, even when no one is inviting them to. The tree is always there and eating of it is always a possibility and not eating of it is always virtue. The literal physicality of the law — the fact of the tree — merely makes it easier for them to see what the issue is — obedience to God — for no other reason for not eating exists. (Satan perverts this insight into a reason for eating.) In the Fall, the issue is confused when alternative considerations are created (i.e., Eve's welfare) and as punishment this momentary confusion becomes a permanent part of man's intellectual equipment. That is to say, he is no longer able to see the oneness of God's law and is delivered to the Mosaic law, the perfect reflection of his divided vision. Under the law man is in effect made to commit the original mistake again and again, because the machinery of legalism conspires with his own defective reason to prevent him from seeing that behind every statute is a single command — obey God. (Those who accept Christ live again in prelapsarian freedom because they fulfil the entire law through the single decision to believe that he has redeemed them; this belief is the belief Adam and Eve evidence as long as they do not eat.)

What Milton describes in the *Areopagitica* — the piecing together of the shattered image of truth — is no more than this, the recovery of the unified moral vision of Edenic innocence; and it is the task he sets the reader in the poem. The preceding chapters have been concerned largely with the discovery by the reader of his fallen self; this, however, is but one half of an action requiring for its completion the transformation of the reader's mind into an instrument capable (in Richardson's words) of receiving 'Such Impressions as the Poet intended to give it'. This transformation or education is an extension of the basic pattern we have observed so often — mistake–correction–instruction : first the gross and carnal conception of a virtue or a value is evoked, and subsequently challenged, and finally the reader is asked to infer from the actions or words of personages more reliable than himself the essence that his earthly apprehension had been unable to discern. Invariably the result is the identification of the virtue or value under consideration with the all-inclusive value of obedience. In this way the 'dissevered pieces' of the 'body of truth' are rejoined, 'limb by limb', until, hopefully, the reader is able to perceive the 'perfect shape' whose wholeness had been obscured by his distorting vision. ('The very esssence of Truth is plainnesse, and brightnes, the darknes and crookednesse is our own.')

The degree to which the reader succeeds in reassembling Truth's 'lovely form' will be evidenced in his (considered) response to the act that first violated it. If he has submitted to the discipline of the poem and negotiated the courses of instruction Milton lays out for him, this 'most heinous crime' will be seen in its true light, as 'a transgression of the whole law' and therefore of those values in whose name the original sin is supposedly committed. If, however, he is unwilling to expend the considerable effort necessary to 'repair the ruins' of his first parents, his ability to understand what is happening (as opposed to what appears to be happening or what he might like to believe is happening) is progressively eroded, and he comes to the crucial scene incapable of rebutting the rationalizations put forward by Adam and Eve and by his own unregenerate reason.

What I am proposing is a direct relationship between the (potential) effect the poem has on the reader and his ability to read it ; a curiously circular relationship whose explanation lies in the uniqueness of the poem's subject-matter. In other words, *Paradise Lost* is a primer designed to teach the reader how to interpret it, and especially to interpret it at the point where the characters perform that action which made its writing and reading necessary. The element of risk, in view of Milton's stated intention, to 'justify the ways of God to men', is considerable ; for there is every possibility, and some probability, that many readers will respond inadequately to the poet's challenge, and end by saddling themselves with misconceptions more harmful than any they may have brought with them. The mechanics of the educative process, along with the dangers that attend it, will be examined in this and the two following chapters.

(i) baptiz'd or infidel

One of the more misleading questions that has been asked of *Paradise Lost* is, is Satan really courageous? Misleading because it assumes that an answer, one way or the other, will help to settle a great issue, the identity of the poem's hero ; whereas, in truth, the concept of heroism implied in the question is not the norm Milton would have us accept. In an important way epic heroism, of which Satan is a noteworthy instance, is the antithesis of Christian heroism, and a large part of the poem is devoted to distinguishing between the two and showing the superiority of the latter. Since this involves the debunking of an ideal the reader brings with him from other epics, the reading experience is once again educative and, in a special sense, disillusioning.

Milton's subversion of the ideal of martial valour begins as early as 1. 571, when Satan 'Darts his experienc't eye' through the armed files of his legions :

Thir number last he sums. And now his heart
Distends with pride, and hard'ning in his strength
Glories: For never since created man,
Met such imbodied force, as nam'd with these
Could merit more than that small infantry
Warr'd on by Cranes.

(571–6)

This is rather late in Book 1, and the reader has already been
warned against taking Satanic poses seriously and at face
value. 'Thir number last he sums' alludes to David's prideful
numbering of Israel ('And Satan ... provoked David');
the simile is tainted before it is offered and the reader
fully expects Satan and his host to be damned with faint
praise, as they have been earlier. What he does not expect
is an indirect attack on all the heroes, who, with the best
of intentions, find themselves in Satan's position, leading
armies.

Limited though it may be, James Whaler's method of
classifying similes is helpful because his categories correspond to proportional formulas. This particular simile,
according to Whaler, falls into the fourth category, 'Complex
Pattern with Four Terms in a Ratio' and is diagrammed as
follows:[1]

$$A^1 . S^1(s + s' + s'' \text{ etc.}) = S^1 . S^2$$
$$r$$

A^1 = Satan's host; S^1 = all heroes of history and legend;
S^2 = pygmies ('that small infantry') and r = with respect to
numbers and prowess. Or to transliterate: with respect to
numbers and prowess, Satan's host is to all the heroes of
history or legend as all the heroes of legend and history are
to pygmies. The trouble with this is that it is the result of
an operation made on the text after the fact; it is not a

[1] 'The Miltonic Simile', *PMLA*, xlvi (1931), 1034–74.

description of the relationships as they are perceived in time, and in this case, the statement as formulated is not even accurate.

To the casual reader Whaler's schematization is surprising because of an omission. What has happened to the cranes? One could answer I suppose that the cranes are not a part of the similaic structure; they serve only to identify the 'small infantry' by referring to an exemplum everyone knows. But this ignores the logic of the reading experience in which the cranes are accorded a position before they appear. Like a Ciceronian period, a simile has a rhythm of its own, a rhythm already established when the pivot point is reached, i.e. the equal sign in Whaler's linear presentation. The 'imbodied force' simile is easily mistaken for a 'complex pattern with four terms in a ratio' because it looks like one. In such a ratio, the placing of the first two terms in some kind of proportional relation is sufficient to create an assumption of the third and fourth. In fact, the reader is eager to infer the whole pattern from a part, because it simplifies his task, especially if this simile is hard to keep track of, as this one surely is. The difficulty begins before the simile does: in its position 'created man' could be either an absolute construction or the subject of a verb which has not yet been given. 'Met' only complicates the situation since it seems to be the verb 'created man' is waiting for; 'such imbodied force' would then be the object of 'Met', identified with Satan's host. 'As nam'd with these' shows this to be impossible since 'these' refers to Satan's host which is surely not being compared to itself. (Later, when the 'imbodied force' of legendary heroes is mocked, the mockery attaches itself to Satan's host which, at one point, had seemed to be the body referred to.) The confusion resolves itself finally into 'compared with Satan's host, any force man has marshalled since he was created . . .'. A pattern, apparently proportional, has emerged, and the eye, anticipating its completion, glances forward and fashions, prematurely but understandably, the second half of the simile: 'compared with Satan's host, any force man has marshalled since he was created would be as pygmies are to cranes.' (This misreading, while it seems unlikely in retrospect is the result of the availability of 'small infantry' and 'Cranes' just when two terms are needed.) Of course it doesn't work, and the reading is rejected almost immediately; but for a moment, and a moment is enough, Satan's army is reduced to the status of pygmies or cranes. A second reading will rearrange the four terms into three and yield Whaler's progression of relative magnitudes: Satan's host is to all heroes as all heroes are to pygmies. But this is the reverse of what is meant; the superiority of the heroes to the pygmies is being denied in the simile. (This will be obscured for the reader because 'could merit more' is read without the qualifying 'never', which has been forgotten, and hence seems to imply that the 'imbodied force' *could* merit more than something; whereas the simile is telling us that the 'imbodied force' has no merit at all.) The size of Satan's host is not to be comprehended by reference to an analogous proportion, for in comparison to that army all other forces are reduced to a single level of insignificance. If we retain Whaler's symbols, a new formula (one which emerges from the necessary third reading) can be constructed: A^1 stands in such a relationship to S^1 that S^1 equals S^2 equals S^3 and so on; that is, A^1 is so huge as to make all S's equally unimpressive, no matter what difference may pertain between them on a lesser scale of measurement. This is essentially Newton's reading: 'All the heroes and armies that ever were assembled were no more than pygmies in comparison with these Angels.'[1] 'Small infantry' is merely shorthand for

[1] *Paradise Lost*, 1749.

smallness, i.e. pygmylike; it could as well have been flies
or rabbits. The intention is not in any way to magnify the
strength of human armies, but to denigrate it. The two terms
— pygmies and all imbodied forces — are an equality in
size and merit. The distinction between them, although it is
encouraged for a time by the unfolding of the simile, exists
only in the mind of the reader who expects it because he
identifies military prowess with heroism.

The simile does not wait for the reader to adjust to its
implications, but proceeds to drive home its point with a
vengeance :

> though all the Giant brood
> Of *Phlegra* with th' Heroic Race were join'd
> That fought at *Thebes* and *Ilium*, on each side
> Mixt with auxiliar Gods; and what resounds
> In Fable or *Romance* of *Uther's* Son
> Begirt with *British* and *Armoric* Knights;
> And all who since, Baptiz'd or Infidel
> Jousted in *Aspramont* or *Montalban*,
> *Damasco*, or *Marocco*, or *Trebisond*,
> Or whom *Biserta* sent from *Afric* shore
> When *Charlemain* with all his Peerage fell
> By *Fontarabbia*. Thus far these beyond
> Compare of mortal prowess.   (576–88)

The list of heroes and armies is in apposition to the inadequacy of 'imbodied force'. The sense is, all human forces are
pygmylike even though you were to combine in one force
$S^1 + S^2 + S^3$ etc. ; yet in the space of seven lines, the reader
forgets what he has just learned and tries to make distinctions all over again. There is an obvious and easy progression
in the list from the armies of the oft-discredited giants to
the conspicuously Christian armies of Charlemagne and all
his peerage or, in the typology of the poem, from Satan's
warriors to God's, with sidelong glances at the worlds of
pagan heroes and chivalric knights. The sense of a progres-

sion results in part from the placing of 'brood', 'auxiliar', 'Fable or *Romance*'. These words share a sneering tone that is logically an extension of 'that small infantry / Warr'd on by Cranes'; but within a few lines the roll-call of heroes detaches itself from the simile (it is simply too long a time to keep the simile in mind) and becomes an autonomous unit. In the new framework, 'brood' 'auxiliar' 'Fable' and *'Romance'* seem to exist together on the lower rungs of a ladder that is being climbed in these lines. 'Brood' continues the animal motif of cranes, adding to it the impression of tameness and passivity. (Something we shall see again in the timorous herd of goats cast out of Heaven by the triumphant Son.) The effect of 'auxiliar' is difficult to describe; but it is not unlike the effect of expatiate in 'New rubb'd with Balm, *expatiate* and confer / Thir state affairs' (1. 774–5, emphasis mine). Both 'expatiate' and 'auxiliar' work against the poses assumed by the agents they belong to; 'expatiate' mocks the high seriousness of the bee council, 'auxiliar' unmakes Gods who should, by definition, be necessary rather than auxiliary. 'Fable' and *'Romance'*, of course, bear the taint of fancy and illusion in an age of rationalism (soon Milton will scorn pagan fablers who err). But the reader who is ready and willing to devalue the military exploits of pagans and Saracens is unprepared for the phrase 'Baptiz'd or Infidel'. Again a distinction which had been half-assumed is not allowed; this 'or' is not disjunctive, but inclusive. Crusader or anti-Christ, it doesn't matter according to the ideal put forward by the epic voice, an ideal that is only now beginning to emerge as the result of the negation of other ideals. The equality of baptized and infidel, at least as justifications for the veneration of martial heroism, parallels the earlier equation of all embodied forces and pygmies; and in both cases the reader who perceives the identity must give up a scale of values he probably brings with him. The entire scaffolding of Tasso's *Jerusalem Delivered* falls with 'Baptiz'd or Infidel' and it is never rebuilt in the course of *Paradise Lost*. (It falls again when, through the agency of a parenthesis, the crusading knights are absorbed into the bee simile, and undergo, with the devils, the diminution that follows.)[1]

Milton is not yet done with us. He makes his point for a third time in the short distance between *Aspramont* and *Fontarabbia*. The reader moves easily and almost physically through the *l*'s, *r*'s, *s*'s, and *b*'s of *Aspramont, Montalban, Damasco, Marocco, Trebisond, Biserta* toward the comfortable orthodoxy of Charlemagne whose heroic credentials would have been considered impeccable but a few moments ago, only to be halted at 586 by the syntactical and metrical stress on 'fell'. The verb, with all the associations it calls up, forcibly shatters the spell of names, insisting on the sameness of Charlemagne and all those who have jousted (played) for whatever cause, reminding us that the roll is called only to indicate what devilish might can easily surpass. 'Thus far these beyond / Compare of mortal prowess' How far? so far that the differential cannot be graphed. (One should hear the contempt in 'mortal prowess'.) The simile makes it

---

[1]   '   all access was throng'd, the Gates
And Porches wide, but chief the spacious Hall
(Though like a cover'd field, where Champions bold
Wont ride in arm'd, and at the Soldan's chair
Defi'd the best of *Paynim* chivalry
To mortal combat or career with Lance)
Thick swarm'd, both on the ground and in the air,
Brusht with the hiss of rustling wings. As Bees. . . .'

(1. 761–8)

Because of the parenthesis, it is also the 'Champions bold' (Christian knights) who 'swarm' in the spacious Hall and are 'as Bees'. There is possibly another hit at chivalric heroism in Milton's choosing to suggest that Charlemagne fell at Fontarabbia. In fact, as Newton points out in his note to the line, 'He was at last victorious over his enemies and died in peace'.

impossible to locate heroism in the stance of battle, no matter how noble the standard one follows. Davis Harding emphasizes the ambiguity of Milton's allusions to the heroes of classical epic:

> he builds up a cluster of associations around Satan and his followers which exert a steady pressure upon his readers, inviting them, almost compelling them, time after time to make specific acts of comparison and contrast ... if the implied comparisons with Achilles, Turnus, Odysseus, Aeneas, Prometheus, and other heroes serve to magnify our impression of Satan's heroic grandeur, they also simultaneously provide the grounds for impugning him both as character and symbol.[1]

Thus a similarity between a Satanic speech and one of Sarpedon's is damaging because 'the contrast between the simple, impassioned eloquence of Sarpedon and Satan's artful eloquence calls the latter's sincerity into question.' I would suggest an even more complex and more ambivalent relationship: for if the devils suffer when their actions and motives are contrasted with the actions and motives of epic heroes, these heroes in turn do not escape the taint of Satanism, since their valour is qualified by its availability to devils.[2] The reader who accepts Milton's invitation 'to make specific acts of comparison and contrast' shuttles back and forth between two norms that are finally, and in some sense equally, unsatisfactory. He can only wait on the promise of something more clearly exemplary.

The 'imbodied force' simile has a visual aspect which

[1] *The Club of Hercules*, p. 44.

[2] Newton, in a note to II. 542, comments on the damage done to Hercules in one comparison, although he sees this as a fault on Milton's part: 'But as Mr. Thyer rightly observes, Milton in this simile falls vastly short of his usual sublimity and propriety. How much does the image of Alcides tearing up Thessalian pines ... sink below that of the Angels rending up both rocks and hills.' The point is that Milton is creating a new propriety, in which Alcides' deeds are shown to be lacking in true sublimity.

figures importantly in subsequent restatements of the
insight it offers. We see armies arranged in battle lines, one
against another, Satan and his legions against the collected
strength of all humanity, the pygmies against the cranes, the
giants against Jove, the Trojans against the Greeks, Arthur
and his knights against the uncourteous, Charlemagne
against the Saracens. Time and time again in the poem opposing forces are marshalled in this way; they parade their
might and vaunt their vaunts, and just as the lines are about
to join and resolve an issue, some agency steps in to prevent
the encounter or to imply its futility. While it is not technically
military, the debate in Hell can be viewed as such a scene.
(Forensic wars are not unlike real ones.) Each of the speakers
rises with the intention of ending the battle of words at a
single blow, much as Abdiel and Michael hope to decide
the war in Heaven by the strength of their own right arms;
but Beelzebub's victory (which has been staged by Satan) is
hollow, for there can be no victory, rhetorical or otherwise,
in a contest whose goal is the formulation of a plan to be
used against God. The motions of the debate are so much
shadow-boxing; the conclusion is contrived rather than real
because there can be no conclusion. Like the other exercises
in circularity we see in the poem — Adam's lament, the
recriminations at the end of Book ix, the War in Heaven —
this one finds 'no end, in wand'ring mazes lost'. The council
proceeds on the assumption that the deliberations of created
agents are able to determine the direction of fate; in short it
ignores the reality of God and the absoluteness of his
control. In a world where God is everywhere all councils of
war are futile because all wars are futile; and this judgment
is extended into history in Book xi when we are given other
councils and other wars:

> On each hand slaughter and gigantic deeds.
> In other part the scepter'd Heralds call

> To Council in the City Gates: anon
> Grey-headed men and grave, with Warriors mixt,
> Assemble, and Harangues are heard, but soon
> In factious opposition.
>
> (659–64)

When the devils disperse, some play games of war — all wars are games of the most infantile kind — and they face each other in the now familiar configuration of battle. Here the language of Milton's description indicates the contempt we are supposed to share:

> As when to warn *proud* Cities war appears
> Wag'd in the troubl'd Sky and Armies rush
> To Battle in the *Clouds*, before each Van
> Prick forth the *Aery* knights, and couch their spears,
> Till thickest legions close.
>
> (II. 533–7, emphasis mine)

When thickest legions *do* close — in this image, and in the games the devils play, and in the wars they play at — the result is the meeting of air with air and a loud report that is so much sound and fury, signifying nothing. One might ask what distinguishes these games from the 'Heroic Games' Gabriel's patrol plays to pass the time:

> About him exercis'd Heroic Games
> Th' unarmed Youth of Heav'n, but nigh at hand
> Celestial Armory, Shields, Helms, and Spears
> Hung high with Diamond flaming, and with Gold.
>
> (IV. 551–4)

The answer is, nothing. As actions (apart from intention) the exercises of the good angels and the bad angels have the same value, none at all, and this can be said also of their respective positions in a military hierarchy. If Satan is unable to assault Heaven, Gabriel is unable to bar him from Paradise. To 'Baptiz'd or Infidel' we might add 'Satanic or Angelic'.

Satan is himself a principal in another 'aery' meeting when Death challenges him at the gate of Hell :

> Whence and what are thou, execrable shape,
> That dar'st, though grim and terrible, advance
> Thy miscreated Front athwart my way
> To yonder Gates? through them I mean to pass,
> That be assured, without leave askt of thee:
> Retire, or taste thy folly, and learn by proof,
> Hell-born, not to contend with Spirits of Heav'n.
>
> (II. 681–7)

This is more than conventional vaunting, or perhaps less ; it is bombast, and the overformality of 'athwart' and 'yonder gates' is intended to draw a smile. Death replies in kind ('Back to thy punishment, / False fugitive') and the stage is again set for a clash that is not forthcoming. The reader's expectations are deliberately primed :

> So spake the grisly terror, and in shape,
> So speaking and so threat'ning, grew tenfold
> More dreadful and deform: on th' other side
> Incens't with indignation *Satan* stood
> Unterrifi'd, and like a Comet burn'd,
> That fires the length of *Ophiucus* huge
> In th' Artic Sky, and from his horrid hair
> Shakes Pestilence and War. Each at the Head
> Levell'd his deadly aim; thir fatal hands
> No second stroke intend.   (II. 704–13)

We know before the epic voice tells us that 'each no second stroke intend' for it is always so in single combat. Nor are we surprised by the 'fortuitous' intervention (Summers sees it as comic opera) of the 'Snaky Sorceress', since the cloud image of line 535 returns to extinguish the 'Comet' and deflate the 'tenfold shape' :

> and such a frown
> Each cast at th' other, as when two black Clouds
> With Heav'n's Artillery fraught, come rattling on

> Over the *Caspian*, then stand front to front
> Hov'ring a space, till Winds the signal blow
> To join thir dark Encounter in mid air. (713–18)

The juxtaposition of 'Heav'n's Artillery fraught' with the anticlimactic awkwardness of 'rattling on' is deliberate and effective. The signal blown by winds (perhaps the trumpet of Aeolus, the servant of the Goddess of Fame and other emptinesses) to announce the 'dark encounter' in 'mid air' is inevitable, as is the reconciliation scene when 'horror is transformed to politic compliments, and the promised battle evaporates into mutual congratulations'.[1] Miltonic humour is never side-splitting, but there is more than a smile in the way the poet straightfacedly continues with the epic formulae:

> So frown'd the mighty Combatants . . .
> . . . and now great deeds
> Had been achieved, whereof all *Hell* had rung.
> (719, 722–3, emphasis mine)

As Joseph Summers observes, the entire episode is a parody that serves 'to undercut the "heroism" of Hell'.[2] In the context of all that has gone before it, the parody undercuts *all* heroism, hellish or otherwise, and the laughter of these lines is directed at those who aspire to it.

The drama (or is it farce) is replayed for a third time, and with an intention more obviously didactic, when Zephon and Ithuriel bring Satan to Gabriel. Again the menacing gestures of the mighty combatants:

> While thus he spake, th' Angelic Squadron bright
> Turn'd fiery red, sharp'ning in mooned horns
> Thir Phalanx, and began to hem him round
> With ported Spears, as thick as when a field
> Of *Ceres* ripe for harvest waving bends
> Her bearded Grove of ears, which way the wind

[1] *The Muse's Method*, p. 46.   [2] *The Muse's Method*, p. 54.

> Sways them; the careful Plowman doubting stands
> Lest on the threshing floor his hopeful sheaves
> Prove chaff. On th' other side *Satan* alarm'd
> Collecting all his might dilated stood,
> Like *Teneriff* or *Atlas* unremov'd:
> His stature reacht the Sky, and on his Crest
> Sat horror Plum'd; nor wanted in his grasp
> What seem'd both Spear and Shield.   (IV. 977-90)

The linking phrase that joins this to the encounters noted previously is 'On th' other side', and it is quickly followed by another, the 'now had' or 'might have' formula:

> now dreadful deeds
> Might have ensu'd, nor only Paradise
> In this commotion, but the Starry Cope
> Of Heav'n perhaps, or all the Elements
> At least had gone to rack, disturb'd and torn
> With violence of this conflict.   (990-5)

In the war between the angels this is exactly what happens; Heaven does go to rack, disturbed and torn. In the present instance however, God himself intervenes: 'had not soon / Th' Eternal to prevent such horrid fray / Hung forth in Heav'n his golden Scales' (995-7). These scales have been interpreted as a sign and warning to Satan who is weighed in the balance and found wanting; but the judgment delivered extends to Gabriel in his capacity as a military functionary. The point about the 'doubting Plowman' simile, whether the plowman is Satan or Gabriel, is its indeterminateness. John Peter sees 'a group of heavenly angels whose spears an inappropriately debilitating simile has likened to swaying ears of harvest wheat ... a group of minstrels armed with toy spears — men, as it were, of straw — and when God intervenes ... it is even possible ... to feel that God knows Satan will prevail, and that his method of avoiding a defeat, even a minor defeat, is underhand and

unfair'.[1] Empson interprets the scene differently: 'I do not
see what the incident can mean except that God was determined to make man fall, and had supplied a guard only for
show; as soon as the guards look like succeeding he prevents
them.'[2] Common to both readings is a sense of the futility
of the *situation*. As Broadbent says, 'the need for sentries in
Paradise, their failure to prevent Satan's approach to Eve,
and God's release of Satan after his arrest, are *absurd*.'[3]
What is absurd is what has been absurd before, the efforts of
any agent to cause effects apart from the will of God. Satan
calls Gabriel 'Proud limitary Cherub' and if Gabriel assumes
that because he has been given an assignment (don't let
anything in) he will be able to carry it out, Satan is correct.
Good intentions and a willingness to serve do not assure
success, which comes only if God wills it. If the existence
of Gabriel's patrol is to be justified only in terms of need and
sufficiency, Empson is right; it is for show.

Amidst all these 'ifs' which are, I believe, the reader's
as well as mine, are some certainties: (1) The scales are
tipped against all battles ('all events, / Battles, Realms'), and
against all those who trust in their own strength. (2) Gabriel
knows it:

> *Satan*, I know thy strength, and thou know'st mine,
> Neither our own, but giv'n; what folly then
> To boast what Arms can do, since thine no more
> Than Heav'n permits, nor mine though doubl'd now
> To trample thee as mire.

(1006–10)

Not that Gabriel's strength has actually been redoubled;
but if it were he could take no credit for the results. This is
an open and direct statement of what has previously been

---

[1] *A Critique of Paradise Lost*, pp. 24–25. [2] *Milton's God*, pp. 112–13.
[3] *Some Graver Subject*, p. 200, emphasis mine.

implied: Whatever heroism and virtue are, they do not reside where men have been accustomed to look for them. Later, when the battles and events of Book VI have unfolded, we shall realize that Gabriel is heroic here because he admits that, in the conventional sense, he cannot be.

There are two long-range effects of this series, as it has been constituted here. (1) The reader is sensitized to the emptiness of battlefield rhetoric. (2) The forestalling of so many clashes creates a psychological need for a battle that is fought and concluded. The War in Heaven seems at first to be such a battle. The usual vaunting is followed by Abdiel's swift blow and, at the moment of contact, details from the earlier shadow confrontations are structured into an account of an actual conflict:

> nor stood at gaze
> The adverse Legions, nor less hideous join'd
> The horrid shock: now storming fury rose,
> And clamor such as heard in Heav'n till now
> Was never, Arms on Armor clashing bray'd
> Horrible discord, and the madding Wheels
> Of brazen Chariots rag'd; dire was the noise
> Of conflict; over head the dismal hiss
> Of fiery Darts in flaming volleys flew,
> And flying vaulted either Host with fire.
> So under fiery Cope together rush'd
> Both Battles main, with ruinous assault
> And inextinguishable rage, all Heav'n
> Resounded, and had Earth been then, all Earth
> Had to her Centre shook.
>
> (VI. 205–19)

Behind 'nor stood at gaze / The adverse Legions' are all the times the legions or single foes did nothing else. The rack and violence that had been held in potential by so many 'might haves' are now present in the 'Horrible discord' and 'noise / Of conflict'. In Book IV the epic voice speculates on the effects of a contest between Satan and Gabriel, and wonders if the 'Starry Cope of Heav'n' would be disturbed; in the sixth book, the battle is joined under Heaven's 'fiery cope'. 'Now great deeds / Had been achiev'd' we hear in Book II as Satan faces Death, but in the real war, they *are* achieved:

> deeds of eternal fame
> Were done.
>
> (240–1)

Or are they? There is a qualification attached to the declarative: 'Deeds of eternal fame / Were done, but infinite.' And later we learn that there will be no record of these deeds because the good angels need none and the rebels are granted none. Summers draws the moral: 'In these lines we can recognize the destruction of the old heroic tradition. When "deeds of eternal fame" are "infinite", it is difficult to choose particular ones for heroic celebration ... the rationale for poetry concerned ... with heroic physical action has collapsed.'[1] It has of course collapsed before; this is merely the final collapse, after which no reinflation is possible or even imaginable.

One deed chosen for celebration is Michael's wounding of Satan, the result of the only single combat actually fought in the epic. For the last time, expectation stands in horror (306–7) and cosmic disturbances are predicted:

> from each hand with speed retir'd
> Where erst was thickest fight, th' Angelic throng,
> And left large field, unsafe within the wind
> Of such commotion, such as, to set forth
> Great things by small, if Nature's concord broke,

[1] *The Muse's Method*, p. 129.

> Among the Constellations war were sprung,
> Two Planets rushing from aspect malign
> Of fiercest opposition in mid Sky,
> Should combat, and thir jarring Spheres confound.
>
> (307–15)

This is more impressive than its predecessors because the angels themselves attest to the literalness of the hyperbole by retiring with speed. It is a shock to realize that the *small* thing in the simile is the disruption of Nature's concord and the collision of planets; how infinitesimally small, then, must be the reader's sense of horror compared to the reality of the 'unspeakable fight'. For the last time the adversaries prepare to deliver 'one stroke' whose force will make a second unnecessary ('and not need repeat'); and for once the stroke falls and draws blood, or at least something reddish ('A stream of Nectarous humour issuing flow'd / Sanguine'). Satan is carried away, not, however, to be laid on a funeral pyre or dragged around the field by his conqueror's chariot, but to heal, immediately, without aid, like a puncture-sealing automobile tyre :

> Yet soon he heal'd; for Spirits that live throughout
> Vital in every part, not as frail man
> In Entrails, Heart or Head, Liver or Reins,
> Cannot but by annihilating die;
> Nor in thir liquid texture mortal wound
> Receive, no more than can the fluid Air.
>
> (344–9)

This is informative and educational. It adds to the picture we have of the angel's digestive processes and looks forward to Raphael's description of angelic love or interpenetration. But it is also embarrassing, to Michael who had hoped to end intestine war in Heaven (258–9), to the angels fighting that war, to the reader who has allowed himself to believe that this combat is real in a sense the others were not. There is a hint of what is to come in the introduction to the confrontation: 'for likest Gods they *seem'd*, | Stood they or mov'd, in stature, motion, arms | Fit to decide the Empire of great Heav'n' (301–3). Like Gods, but not Gods, nor are they fit to decide the Empire of Heav'n (the influence of 'seem'd' extends into 303) except with respect to their physical appearances which are irrelevant to the poem's standard of fitness. There is a way in which Michael does emerge victorious (and a hero) from this encounter, but it has nothing to do with the physical trappings of the scene. When the partisan Raphael says, 'Meanwhile in other parts like deeds deserv'd | Memorial' (354–5), he is the victim of a gentle irony, since in context Michael's 'deed' is faintly ridiculous.

What is true of this particular deed is true also of all the deeds that make up the most incredible battle ever fought. The oft-promised contest is one more exercise in futility, all the more absurd because it is played out in full. Armour that confers on its wearer vulnerability, an engagement notable for a run of incredibly bad puns, warriors who literally put themselves back together and rise again to hurl hill-size pies at an invincible enemy — all leading up to what Arnold Stein calls 'the grand finale of physical ridicule',[1] Satan's ignominious exit, pursued by a chariot. (The student of Milton criticism will have observed that I begin by assuming the validity of Stein's interpretation of the book.) The battle decides nothing because battles have no real relationship to the issues one would have them settle. Adam learns this when he mistakenly expects a final struggle between God and Satan:

> say where and when
> Thir fight, what stroke shall bruise the Victor's heel.
>
> (xii. 384–5)

[1] *Answerable Style*, p. 25.

And Michael, who knows from experience how inconclusive any physical contest is, answers :

> Dream not of thir fight,
> As of a Duel, or the local wounds
> Of head or heel . . .
> . . . nor so is overcome
> *Satan*, whose fall from Heav'n, a deadlier bruise,
> Disabl'd not to give thee thy death's wound :
> Which hee, who comes thy Saviour, shall recure,
> Not by destroying *Satan*, but his works
> In thee and in thy Seed.
>
> (xii. 386–8, 390–5)

Perhaps Michael is remembering at this moment that the victor in the struggle against sin (Satan's works) was also the victor in the war he had hoped to end.

(ii) SERVANT OF GOD, WELL DONE

Clearly, the difficulty of regarding the War in Heaven as mock heroic is that the heroics of the good angels are also mocked. Broadbent is uneasy about the language of Book vi because 'it makes no *poetic* distinction between Heavenly and Hellish power'.[1] This is true simply because in terms of power there is no distinction, or to put it another way, the superiority of the loyal angels has nothing to do with power. John Peter doubts Milton's skill; the war is inconclusive and the poet seems 'hesitant'. On one hand, 'we are led to expect that Michael's army will soon prevail', yet 'in the event they can achieve nothing better than a stalemate. The effect is surely to expose them to our disappointment, to make "the excellence, the power Which God hath in his mighty Angels plac'd" (637–8) appear equivocal'[2]. (Peter

---

[1] *Some Graver Subject*, p. 220.   [2] *Critique*, p. 78.

was of course anticipated by Voltaire, who protested in 1727 at 'the visible Contradiction which reigns in that Episode', that is at the failure of the angels to drive out the rebels. 'How does it come to pass, after such a positive Order, that the Battle hangs doubtful?')[1] The disappointment the fit reader feels will be tempered by his understanding of what it means; and if he has learned his lessons well, the disappointment will be minimal, since the arousing of expectations depends on assumptions about the importance and effectiveness of physical action he no longer holds. Raphael's evaluation of the first day of battle — 'For strength from Truth divided and from Just, / Illaudable, naught merits but dispraise' (381–2) — is no surprise to anyone who has seen Satan *v.* Death, Satan *v.* Gabriel, Satan *v.* Abdiel, Satan *v.* Michael, and soon, Satan *v.* Christ. Strength apart from God recoils against the agent who relies on it. Strength in God's service is a gift and not the inevitable reward of virtue. Strength is nothing. Still, as Peter remarks somewhat irritably, this intuition (that the battle is 'pointless') hardly justifies the machinery that accompanies it. He wonders 'what all the fuss has been about, and why the battle should have been reported with such fidelity and at such length'.[2]

Behind Peter's question stands another, more naïve, yet more fundamental, and it is posed forthrightly by H. R. Swardson, who balks at Milton's claim to sing not of wars and of tedious battles feigned, but of 'the better fortitude / Of Patience and Heroic Martyrdom' (ix. 31–32): 'Does Milton really think', Swardson exclaims, 'he is singing "the better fortitude of Patience and Heroic Martyrdom"? Where? What space and prominence does he give to it?'[3]

[1] Quoted in Christopher Ricks's *Milton's Grand Style*, pp. 17–18.
[2] *Critique*, p. 79.
[3] *Poetry and the Fountain of Light* (Columbia, Missouri, 1962), p. 143.

The answer that immediately suggests itself is Abdiel, lauded by Raphael in terms unmistakably Miltonic. Undoubtedly, Abdiel is the exemplar of a better heroism, but he is not a figure whose actions, as they are likely to be interpreted by the reader, can properly serve as a counterpoint to the false heroism Milton is at pains to undercut, at least not in Book v. For, as Broadbent observes, 'the emphasis on Abdiel's faithfulness . . . is obscured by the superficial political motives and military tactics' of the scene.[1] Abdiel's faithfulness is obscured because one can respond to his gesture without being fully aware of the ideal embodied in it. In terms of the distinction between epic heroism and Christian heroism, he is too easy to admire. (The fault of course is the observer's, not his.)

More specifically, there is a discrepancy between the impression Abdiel makes and the language Raphael uses to describe him : '*un*mov'd / *Un*shak'n, *un*seduc'd, *un*terrifi'd / His Loyalty he kept, his Love, his Zeal ; / Nor number, nor example with him wrought / To swerve from truth, or change his constant mind' (898–902, emphasis mine). The words suggest a negative action, a reflex of the mind independent of any physical effort, a decision in fact *not* to do something, but the setting for the action, which determines our response, is theatrical :

> Thus far his bold discourse without control
> Had audience, when among the Seraphim
> *Abdiel*, than whom none with more zeal ador'd
> The Deity, and divine commands obey'd,
> Stood up, and in a flame of zeal severe
> The current of his fury thus oppos'd.
>
> (v. 803–8)

---

[1] *Some Graver Subject*, p. 225. The analysis which follows was first suggested to me by Roger Swearingen, then a student at the University of California, Berkeley.

A lone figure rises — and the eye will imitate the movement of 'Stood up' — to assert himself in the face of overwhelming odds ('The flaming Seraph fearless though alone / Encompass'd round with foes'). This is undoubtedly impressive — Abdiel himself will recall the scene in his later meeting with Satan : 'when I alone / Seem'd in thy World erroneous to dissent / From all' — so impressive as to win approval for any action taken within its sphere. There is no difference between the admiration the reader can feel for Abdiel's refusal to bow to the tyranny of the majority, and the admiration he has felt, if only fleetingly, for Satan's refusal to acknowledge defeat despite the hopelessness of his situation. Ultimately the two actions are not comparable, but as stances or gestures, they appear similar, and in poetry appearances are not only deceiving, they are likely to be conclusive.

In retrospect, Abdiel's heroism can be isolated from the circumstances of its exercise. The essentials are on display in Raphael's first reference to him : 'than whom none with more zeal ador'd / The Deity, and divine commands obey'd.' Love God and obey his commands — this comprehends all. Indeed, the conjunction divides what is really a unity. Loving God implies obedience, obedience flows from a love of God ; both are manifestations of an acceptance of God as the central fact of the universe, and any action rooted in a determination to bear witness to that fact is an heroic action even if it is invisible to the naked eye. Abdiel is a hero because he says 'Shalt thou give Law to God?' (the declarative form would be 'Thy will be done') and he would have been a hero still had he said it to himself in the privacy of his study, as Milton does in the sonnet 'When I consider'. Writing of Mirabeau's resolve to turn highway robber in order to demonstrate his opposition to the laws of society, Thoreau declares

> A Saner man would have found himself often enough 'in formal opposition' to what are deemed 'the most sacred laws of society,' through obedience to yet more sacred laws, and so have tested his resolution without going out of his way. It is not for a man to put himself in such an attitude toward society, but to maintain himself in whatever attitude he finds himself through obedience to the laws of his being.

Virtue does not reside in any one stance, nor does heroism require a particular field of battle. True virtue is a state of mind — loyalty to the best one knows — and true heroism is a psychic (wilful) action — the decision, continually made in a variety of physical situations, to maintain that loyalty. To fix on any one posture, whether it be opposition to the laws of society or standing one's ground in a hostile environment, as *the* heroic posture is to mistake a possible expression of heroism (any posture is potentially that) for the only one; and to seek opportunities to place oneself in that posture is to confuse self-aggrandizement with virtue (this is what Eve does when she decides to test her strength). Abdiel has always been heroic since he has always been free to disavow his allegiance to God, and to date he has declined to do so, at every moment of his life. The reader just happens to be there when Abdiel is being heroic in a conspicuously dramatic context the emotional (rhetorical) force of which obscures the significance of his action.

The problem, then, is to separate the drama from the heroism, an operation which Milton forces on us in Book vi. He presents Abdiel to us fully aware that we are likely to accept him uncritically and uncomprehendingly. Once accepted, the angel is systematically stripped of everything not directly relevant to his heroism, until we are left to recognize (if we are willing) the naked essence itself. In effect, the reader comes to understand heroism by repeatedly adjusting his idea of what makes one hero heroic.

Conventionally, heroes are recognizable because they are successful, not absolutely successful (heroes usually die), but successful in some way that justifies the effort expended. Abdiel leaves the North covered with glory, yet as he approaches friendlier regions, his image begins to lose some of its lustre. In the first place, the warning he had thought to give ('All night the dreadless Angel unpursu'd / Through Heav'n's wide Champaign held his way') is unnecessary :

> War he perceiv'd, war in procinct, and found
> Already known what he for news had thought
> To have reported.
>
> (VI. 19–21)

This is a small disappointment, one felt more by the reader than by the angel who 'gladly' mixes with his allies. A larger disappointment awaits him when the actual fighting begins. When God the Father receives Abdiel amidst joys and acclamations, he gives him congratulations, assurances, and, in concert with his fellows, a new assignment :

> the easier conquest now
> Remains thee, aided by this host of friends,
> Back on thy foes more glorious to return
> Than scorn'd thou didst depart, and to subdue
> By force, who reason for thir Law refuse.
>
> (37–41)

But the easier conquest does not remain, at least not in the conclusive way implied by 'subdue'; although one can hardly blame Abdiel for taking God's pronouncement literally when he challenges Satan :

> wherefore should not strength and might
> There fail where Virtue fails, or weakest prove
> Where boldest; though to sight unconquerable?
> His puissance, trusting in th' Almighty's aid,
> I mean to try, whose Reason I have tri'd
> Unsound and false; nor is it aught but just,

> That he who in debate of Truth hath won,
> Should win in Arms, in both disputes alike
> Victor; though brutish that contest and foul,
> When Reason hath to deal with force, yet so
> Most reason is that Reason overcome.

(116–26)

'The most striking thing about the War in Heaven', according to Summers, 'is that, except for the Father and the Son, everyone is surprised at one moment or another, no one's expectations are perfectly fulfilled.'[1] Reasoning that physical effects should be predictable on the basis of spiritual status, Abdiel defies Satan 'securely' (with confidence), and the reader has every reason to expect, as the angel does, victory and vindication. The beginning is auspicious, even startling,[2] as Satan receives Abdiel's greeting on his impious crest and is displaced :

> ten paces huge
> He back recoil'd; the tenth on bended knee
> His massy Spear upstay'd; as if on Earth
> Winds under ground or waters forcing way
> Sidelong, had pusht a Mountain from his seat
> Half sunk with all his Pines.

(193–8)

Harding discerns an allusion to *The Faerie Queene*, 1. ii, where the serpent falls before the Red Cross Knight's sword : 'So downe he fell, and forth his life did breth, / ... So downe he fell and like an heaped mountain lay.' The parallel, however, is inexact in an important respect : the serpent is slain, while Milton's Satan gets up again and within a short time taunts Michael with this unanswerable question : 'Hast thou turn'd the least of these / To flight, or

[1] *The Muse's Method*, p. 122.
[2] Peter complains, 'The speed of Abdiel's first blow is so emphasized as almost to suggest that he struck unfairly' (*Critique*, p. 76).

if to fall, but that they rise / Unvanquisht?' (284–6); adding a prediction that proves disconcertingly accurate: 'err not that so shall end / The strife'. Of course, the strife does not end as Satan thinks it will, but neither does Michael end intestine war in Heaven, as he hopes to.

The question arises: what advantage does loyalty or being on the right side confer? Hardly any, it seems. True, Raphael thinks otherwise: 'Such high advantages thir innocence / Gave them above thir foes, not to have sinn'd, / Not to have disobey'd; in fight they stood / Unwearied, unobnoxious to be pain'd' (401–4). But if the loyal angels are incapable of pain and cannot be wearied, their ability to stand in fight is hardly remarkable or praiseworthy. Indeed this advantage is a disadvantage if 'difficulty' is one condition of heroism (ultimately, as we shall see, it is not), for it gives Satan and his followers something to put up with, something to rise above: 'Some disadvantage we endur'd and pain, / Till now not known, but known as soon contemn'd' (431–2). This is perverted stoicism, not unlike Belial's argument in Book II, and any attractiveness it might have does not survive the absurdity of inventing gunpowder. Still the picture of Satan gritting his teeth and bearing it does have a certain force, and it is certainly more visibly impressive than anything we see on the other side.

One is not impressed, for instance, by Abdiel. His companions interpret his momentary success as a 'Presage of Victory' (201); this portent, however, is a false one if it is taken to mean *their* victory. He himself had thought to 'overcome', but a much weaker verb would do for this minor skirmish. Sometime later, Satan is said to have 'met in Arms / No equal' (247–8), a silent reflection on Abdiel's military pretensions. (Newton, *Paradise Lost*, 1749, comments: 'the poet did not consider Abdiel as *equal* to Satan, tho' he gain'd that accidental advantage over him. Satan no doubt would have prov'd an over-match for Abdiel only for the general engagement which ensued and broke off the combat between them'.) What remains, then, of the angel's heroism? All of it, if we recall Raphael's encomium, 'His Loyalty he kept', which perhaps is only now properly understood by the reader. Abdiel is a hero because he keeps loyalty even when his objective eludes him and his assumptions fail the test of experience. Believing it only just 'That he who in debate of Truth hath won, / Should win in Arms', he does not abandon his post or question the ways of God when his sense of justice is disappointed; and his steadfastness is all the more remarkable because it is in no sense necessary. God, Abdiel reminds Satan 'with solitary hand / Reaching beyond all limit, at one blow / Unaided could have finisht thee' (139–141). Or as the poet had written in another place, 'God doth not need / Either man's work or his own gifts'.

Milton here touches upon a favourite theme of Herbert's, the temptation inherent in the desire to serve. Herbert contemplates the cross and feels himself undone by the boundless love it symbolizes: 'This deare end, / So much desir'd, is giv'n, to take away / My power to serve . . . / One ague dwelleth in my bones, / Another in my soul (the memorie / What I would do for thee).' What is left to me, he asks, and only when he accepts the answer, 'nothing', and sits down to eat at Love's table can he be said to understand what faith involves and be truly humble. The desire to serve God is a particularly subtle form of pride if it is in fact a desire to feel needed and important. Milton is especially aware of this danger. In 'When I consider' he murmurs against that decree of God's which has rendered him 'useless' and unable to serve, 'though my Soul more bent / To serve therewith my Maker', finally admitting 'They also serve who only stand and wait'. The admission, however, is wrung from him with difficulty, and one wonders how long it will be before the passion to be useful reasserts itself. In contrast, Abdiel's acceptance of his uselessness is impressive precisely because it is unconscious. He is able to regard his own super-fluousness as a matter of praise and feel no personal injury (sense of injured merit) at all. The perfection of his faith, of his willingness to serve God no matter what service may mean, makes it possible for him to meet unanticipated complications without being demoralized by them. No doubt he is surprised when Satan returns unimpaired, but surprise is merely wonder (oh, so that's the way it is), not disillusion-ment; he adjusts to it and goes on. The reader does not see 'Abdiel surprised' or 'Abdiel adjusting' because there is nothing visible or dramatic in his continual accommodation to the circumstances his loyalty thrusts him into. We do see him once more, although it is easy to overlook him in his new role (new to us, that is):

> Nor stood unmindful *Abdiel* to annoy
> The Atheist crew.

> (369–70)

How far this is from the glorious picture of 'The flaming Seraph fearless, though alone / Encompass'd round with foes'. The passivity now exists in the presentation as well as in the language. 'Nor stood unmindful' is trussed in nega-tives and suggests the most limited kind of action, something auxiliary (nor), even inconsequential, and the verb 'to annoy' bears the suggestion out. Flies annoy, minor discomfitures annoy, and mighty angels annoy, if that is what God has in mind for them. The distance between Abdiel as the only righteous in a world perverse and Abdiel as irritant amidst a host of irritants exists only in our eyes, as a consequence of a false conception of heroism. The stylistic contraries, which in I and II reflect the choice between the fleshly and the godly, are represented here by the physical styles of the two heroic ideals, one flamboyant and self-glorifying, the other inward and humble even when it takes a spectacular form. (As before, the reader's response measures *him*.) Abdiel does in Book VI exactly what he did in V; he obeys God. The situations differ, but then situations are incidental to the heroic action which takes place in the mind and the will. Loyalty can be kept with legions as well as 'single'. Abdiel knows this, although he probably doesn't know he knows it, since the distinction is never a problem for him. It is for us, however, as part of the problem posed generally by the entire battle. So that if we regard the angel as our chosen hero, and follow him from episode to episode, we emerge finally with an insight the pure are born to.

What has been said here of Abdiel applies also to his fellow warriors who all fight a battle they know to be pointless, under conditions that can justly be described as humiliating, for a leader who could do very well without them. 'They perceive or come to perceive themselves as agents in an action beyond their anticipations or immediate comprehensions.'[1] Michael's experience parallels Abdiel's exactly, the expectation (to end intestine war), the apparent victory, the final absurdity (Yet soon he healed). Even the small success of drawing blood must be attributed to a piece of special equipment 'from the Armory of God / . . . giv'n him temper'd so, that neither keen / Nor solid could resist that edge' (321–3). This bit of gratuitous detail is a concrete illustration of a point made earlier in the abstract :

> th' Eternal King Omnipotent
> From his stronghold of Heav'n high over-rul'd
> And limited thir might.
>
> (227–9)

God, it seems, will leave his servants nothing but their wills.

[1] Summers, *The Muse's Method*, p. 136.

Empson sees this and finds an explanation in the perversity dwelling in one heavenly breast: 'They know that they failed to defeat the rebels, and that God need never have ordered them to try, indeed must have intended to humiliate them, because as soon as he chose he removed the rebels with contemptuous omnipotence.'[1] Here indeed is a petty tyrant, a cosmic puller of butterfly wings, who exposes his people to ridicule so that he can laugh at them from his prospect high. Empson cites the analogous action of sending Raphael on a fool's errand while the solar system is being created:

> Squar'd in full Legion (such command we had)
> To see that none thence issued forth a spy . . .
> Not that they durst without his leave attempt.
>
> (VIII. 232–3, 237)

'They knew, and they knew that God knew that they knew that this tiresome chore was completely useless . . . Raphael says that . . . he assumes God gave him a job at the time merely to disappoint him.'[2] Not quite. What Raphael says is 'us he sends upon his high behests / For state, as Sovran King, and to enure / Our prompt obedience' (VIII. 238–40). 'To enure', to apply to the use of. The high behest and others like it is an occasion (something to be used) for obedience, supplied by God as a gift to those who would serve him. As a patron, God presents a definite problem. One cannot give him anything, because everything is his in the first place, that is, proceeds from him. It is equally difficult to render him a service, since he is by definition self-sufficient. Praise, in any number of forms, including useless tasks, is the only commodity the suppliant can offer. The angels *need* to sing what Satan calls the servile warblings of Heaven, just as Adam and Eve *need* to work (the work does not need them),

[1] *Milton's God*, p. 110. [2] Ibid.

for otherwise they have no concrete way of showing their loyalty and love. As Christ explains in *Paradise Regained*: 'what could he less expect / . . . From them who could return him nothing else' (III. 126, 129). The battle under these conditions is an occasion for praise and thus for obedience because God makes it impossible to regard it as anything else. That is what the participants learn by fighting it and what we learn by watching it. 'The voice of God . . . called upon them to exert all their individual strength to attempt an action, the final accomplishment of which they discover is beyond their free unaided abilities.'[1] By assigning them a task they cannot accomplish and an enemy whose disloyalty should be a crippling liability but is not, and a physical arena designed to force them into strategic absurdities, God creates a situation in which the conventional motives for heroic fortitude — success, glory, personal fulfilment — do not pertain and perseverance can only be attributed to a faith in the goodness of the Almighty, to obedience. (Even now Raphael participates in a similar action, imparting a warning he knows will go unheeded.) God's insensitivity to the angels' feelings is a compliment to them because it assumes their firmness. It is relatively easy to stand up for something or for someone or with someone, less easy to stand alone, not alone as Abdiel stands alone, against an evil he can see and react to, but simply alone, with nothing but an inner reserve (of faith) to sustain the life of the spirit and stave off despair. The angels might well have looked around them and decided, with Empson, that God was amusing himself at their expense. To their eternal credit (literally) they do not, preferring instead to believe that God has their best interests at heart, no matter how inescapable a contrary conclusion seems to be. (The negative example is available in the council of war where the rebels infer God's intentions and

[1] Summers, *The Muse's Method*, p. 126.

circumscribe his power from their *experience* of one day's battle.) Faith is an existential assurance of God's love.

When the absurdity of the battle is at its height, God intervenes :

> two days are past,
> Two days, as we compute the days of Heav'n,
> Since *Michael* and his Powers went forth to tame
> These disobedient; sore hath been thir fight,
> As likeliest was, when two such Foes met arm'd;
> For to themselves I left them, and thou know'st,
> Equal in thir Creation they were form'd,
> Save what sin hath impair'd, which yet hath wrought
> Insensibly, for I suspend thir doom;
> Whence in perpetual fight they needs must last
> Endless, and no solution will be found :
> War wearied hath perform'd what War can do,
> And to disorder'd rage let loose the reins,
> With Mountains as with Weapons arm'd, which makes
> Wild work in Heav'n, and dangerous to the main.
> Two days are therefore past, the third is thine;
> For thee I have ordain'd it, and thus far
> Have suffer'd, that the Glory may be thine
> Of ending this great War, since none but Thou
> Can end it.
>
> (684–703)

This confirms what we have suspected and what the angels have come to know about the game they have been playing for two days ; and it also gives us a new piece of information, more disconcerting than anything hitherto revealed. All the angels, good and bad, are props in a gigantic stage setting constructed for the sole purpose of providing a moment of glory for God's only begotten son. The epic voice says as much — 'and permitted all . . . / That his great purpose he might so fulfil, / To honor his Anointed Son' (674–6) — and the angels no doubt infer it when they see his chariot : 'far off his coming shone'. Here is provocation

and an incitement to resentment if resentment is to be forthcoming ; but wondrously the angels greet the appearance of
the Messiah and his assumption of their appointed task
with *joy* :

> by his own
> First seen, them unexpected joy surpris'd
> When the great Ensign of *Messiah* blaz'd.

(773–5)

As with Abdiel, the important thing is the distance between
the response the angels give and the response one might
have expected (or given in their place), a distance measured
in understanding, faith, and heroism. Whether or not they
have been successful in an absolute sense, Michael's
warriors have successfully discharged their obligations.
Within the framework permitted to them, they do what they
can, and the intervention of a power greater than theirs in no
way alters the reality of their *personal* achievement. (God
may not need their works, but *they* do.) The angels are
joyful because Christ's coming signals the completion of
their tour of duty and thus gives them legitimate cause for
self-congratulation. They have responded to God's command — drive out the rebels — according to their abilities
('each on himself reli'd / As only in his arm the moment lay /
Of victory') and they know it and they know that God, who
knows all his creatures extensively and intensively, knows it,
even before Christ tells them so :

> Stand still in bright array ye Saints, here stand
> Ye Angels arm'd, this day from Battle rest;
> *Faithful* hath been your Warfare, and of God
> Accepted, fearless in his righteous Cause,
> *And as ye have receiv'd, so have ye done*
> Invincibly : but of this cursed crew
> The punishment to other hand belongs;
> Vengeance is his, or whose he sole appoints;

Number to this day's work is not ordain'd
Nor multitude, *stand only* and behold.

(801–10, emphasis mine)

'Stand only' is the new command, but it has been the old
one as well. Indeed all commands are reducible to this one,
stand firm with God; and the progressive limiting of the
angels' mobility has the advantage of illustrating how non-
spatial is the area heroism operates in. The imposed limitations of the battle serve to make the angels' physical
situation a mirror of their inward state, since the offensive
is taken from them and they are restricted to a holding
action, to standing only. Such an action does fulfil the
requirements of heroism and can be taken anywhere in any
position — immobilized in the enchanter's lair, fettered in
Gaza — and approved, if not needed, by a benevolent God.
One can stand, for example, while rolling :

none of thir feet might stand,
Though standing else as Rocks, but down they fell
By thousands, Angel on Arch-Angel roll'd.

(592–4)

As with an iconographic configuration, the reader moves
from a perception of the inconsistency of detail on the
literal level to the discovery of the kernel meaning : rolling
and falling, ludicrous and undignified in the extreme, the
angels nevertheless remain upright, because they have
assumed their postures in the service of God. Belial's 'game-
some' punning on 'stand' and 'understand' — 'who receives
them right, / Had need from head to foot well understand ;/
Not understood . . . / They show us when our foes walk not
upright' (625–7) — is one more sign of his fatal (and
damning) literalism in a context which has been asserting
that 'The way of the Lord is strength to the upright'.
Looking back, one can apply this insight to Gabriel, *sitting*
on a rock in Paradise, and to the members of his patrol,

playing at some unnamed heavenly game while they stand guard vainly against an invisible enemy. These too are heroes because they are submitting knowingly to a discipline imposed on them by a power they believe in ; in context, their poses, sitting and playing, signify belief. Looking forward, one can see that, for Adam and Eve, life in Paradise, with the forbidden tree always before them, is such a discipline, calling again for a holding action which is physically unimpressive. It has been argued that because Paradise is 'limited to hopelessly inactive virtues' Adam and Eve must fall before they can be truly heroic, but this is to define 'active' much too narrowly, and to reduce heroism to bravado. Obeying God in Paradise *is* an activity, since there is every moment a conscious (active) decision *not* to act in a certain way. Of course it would be *easier* to make that decision in the face of an overt temptation when the lines of battle are clearly drawn ; more immediately satisfactory also, since one could afterwards recall the scene. One part of heroism, however, is an acceptance of the conditions of its exercise. Seeking spectacular occasions for trial and therefore for glory is itself a temptation. So that perhaps the ultimate in heroism, because it bespeaks an unconcern with the false dignity of self, is the willingness to rest easily and happily on days when there are no battles, absurd or otherwise, without yearning to be more than the minstrelsy of Heaven or the gardeners of Paradise; to sit at God's table without feeling constrained to earn a place there.

(iii) OTHER WARFARES AND OTHER HEROES

This, then, to return to Peter's question, is what the fuss is all about ; the battle is 'reported with such fidelity and at such length' in order to allow the reader time to construct from its thrusts and parries a working definition of heroism and to extend it by analogy to the crisis of the Fall. With Abdiel and Michael and the entire host of loyal angels, the reader experiences the disappointments of the war and learns from their response, in so far as it contrasts with his own, to distinguish between the outward form of a self-glorifying exhibitionism and the true (inner) heroism of obedience. (Of course he has the option of persisting in his admiration for the discredited ideal; again the responsive choice.) In addition, he is encouraged to see in the battle an image of the struggle he himself engages in daily. The correspondences between the military situation as it exists in Book VI and the concept of spiritual warfare are easily established:

(1) In both contexts, there is a divine imperative, 'be ye perfect', 'drive out the rebels', which is beyond the individual's unaided capabilities.

(2) As a result, the individual is involved in a series of indeterminate actions whose relationship to the desired end is, from his point of view, oblique. Such actions often *appear* ridiculous and base (i.e. the indignities Christian and Faithful suffer at Vanity Fair).

(3) Heroism consists of accepting (1) and (2), and continuing despite them, or, more properly, because of them; and this continuing is an affirmation of faith in a deity who judges intent and does not ultimately require more than can be performed.

There are some discrepancies. In the angels' case the limitations imposed on them are arbitrary, as arbitrary as the command not to eat the apple. Fallen man's inability to respond fully to the imperative, on the other hand, is a direct consequence of an earlier failure for which he, in the person of Adam, is responsible. And there is some question, both historically and in Milton's own statements, as to whether fallen man is able even to initiate an action of the mind, that is, to believe, without the intervention of grace.[1] In general, however, the analogy holds, especially in terms of the visual image presented, movement simultaneously hesitant and assertive, self-confident and dependent, absurd and glorious, erring and right.

I refer of course to the image of the wayfaring, warfaring Christian, the pilgrim who makes such uneven progress in Bunyan's prose epic and who finds himself again and again in the position Milton reserves for his heroes. Christian fights his version of the War in Heaven when he encounters Apollyon in the Valley of Humiliation. He considers retreat — 'Then did *Christian* begin to be afraid, and to cast in his mind whether to go back or to stand his ground' — but decides to remain for reasons of strategy : 'he had no Armour for his back, and therefore thought that to turn the back to him, might give him greater advantage with ease to pierce him with his Darts; therefore he resolved to venture, and stand his ground.'[2]

Apollyon's weapons are the commonplaces of despair and mistrust which are countered by the more powerful commonplaces of faith. Christ, Apollyon argues, cares not for his servants : 'He never came yet from the place where he is, to deliver any that served him out of our hands.' Christian refuses to believe that God regards not his ways and

[1] See III. 167–304, where God and Christ alternately suggest that (1) man has the option to accept grace but (2) that he is incapable even of seeking it; (3) that by using 'light after light' well he can arrive *safe* but (4) that if he is saved it will be 'not of will in him, but grace in me'. The extent of fallen man's mobility remains unclear. For a contrasting view, see M. Kelley, 'The Theological Dogma of *Paradise Lost*, III. 173–202,' *PMLA*, lii (1937), 75–79.

[2] *The Pilgrim's Progress*, ed. J. B. Wharey, rev. Roger Sharrock (revised edition, Oxford, 1960), p. 56. The following quotations are taken from this edition, pp. 56–60, unless otherwise noted.

interprets his 'forbearing to deliver' as proof of his regard: 'His forbearing at present to deliver them, is on purpose to try their love, whether they will cleave to him to the end; and as for the ill end thou sayest they come to, that is most glorious in their account: For, for present deliverance, they do not much expect it; for they stay for their Glory, and then they shall have it, when their Prince comes in his.' Christian could be speaking for Milton's loyal angels who find their own glory by caring only for Christ's and accept the humiliation of their situation as a trial of constancy 'whether they will cleave to him in the end'. The difference is in the mode of expression. The angels do not verbalize and the reader must infer their theology from their actions. Bunyan's technique is more conventionally didactic, though none the less skilful. The doctrine is given before the battle which can then be read allegorically without the interpretative effort required in Milton's poem.

In the battle Christian conquers again, and with the same weapon — faith. Pressed to the point of despair, he reaches out to find a sword miraculously at hand, 'as God would have it', and thrusts with it, saying, 'Rejoice not against me, O mine enemy: when I fall I shall arise.' The syntax — 'and caught it, saying' — insists on the simultaneity of the two actions; the sword and the word are one and Apollyon is pierced by both and by the evidence of Christian's faith. While quoting from Micah vii. 8, he is bearing witness to Micah vii. 7: 'Therefore I will look unto the Lord; I will wait for the God of my salvation: my God will hear me.' Christian acknowledges his dependence and asserts himself in the same moment; and when he makes no claim to the victory soon to be his, Apollyon is completely routed: 'Christian . . . made at him again, saying, "Nay in all these things we are more than conquerors through him that loved us." And with that Apollyon spread forth his dragon's wings and sped him away, that Christian for a season saw him no more.'[1] The glory is God's and because Christian rejoices in that knowledge, it is also his, for a season. Apollyon will return in many guises and Christian will fall to him, or almost fall to him, and will resist, or be led to resist (the distinction is meaningless), until after long travail and many indignities he arrives safe at the heavenly city, as God would have it.

For Bunyan's Christian and Milton's angels, forward progress is a matter of standing ground at the right time and the shortest distance between two points is an erratic line and self-reliance means trusting in a God who is simultaneously omnipresent and unavailable. These are the conditions of heroism and as paradoxes they flow from a single paradox, the belief in the evidence and promise of things not seen, best exemplified by the description of Abraham in Hebrews xi. 8 : 'By faith Abraham, when he was called to go out into a place which he should after receive for an inheritance, obeyed ; and he went out, not knowing whither he went.' The imperative ('go out') which calls forth an affirmative response ('and he went') expressed in tentative action ('not knowing whither he went') sustained by faith ('These all died in faith, not having received the promises, but having seen them afar off, and were persuaded of them, and embraced them'). In Book xii, Milton rewrites this passage slightly, so as to emphasize the curious blend of definiteness and provisionality he sees as heroic :

> he straight obeys,
> Not knowing to what Land, yet firm believes:
> I see him, but thou canst not, with what Faith
> He leaves his Gods, his Friends, and native Soil
> *Ur* of *Chaldaea*, passing now the Ford

---

[1] The Wharey–Sharrock text omits 'for a season'. Here I follow the text of Louis Martz's edition (New York, 1949), p. 62.

> To *Haran*, after him a cumbrous Train
> Of Herds and Flocks, and numerous servitude;
> Not wand'ring poor, but trusting all his wealth
> With God, who call'd him, in a land unknown.
>
> (126–34)

The conjunctions and negatives (not-yet-but-not-but) help the reader to the necessary distinctions and the verbs tell the story : obeys - not knowing - believes - wandering - trusting. Wandering, but not wandering since he is led by God's call and journeys towards God, who is everywhere. Heroic faith is exercised before an omnipresent deity, who sees all in an eternal present, by created and finite intelligences who see only what is permitted to them. Men and angels who perform God's labours in partial ignorance are blessed by the limitations which make choice necessary and action possible. Time, Donne writes (and we might add space) is a short parenthesis in eternity, but for those who live in it, it is all. There the problems exist ; there the decisions are made ; there we are known and judged.

Each of us is judged in the context of his particular calling ; battles are fought and wildernesses traversed in all walks of life, including the poet's. His battle, his journey, his sphere of proving, is the act of composition itself. By persevering in his task hard and rare, Milton shows himself to be one of the heroes he celebrates. The gift of poetic inspiration carries with it an obligation — prophesy, edify, persuade — and a situation whose difficulties are familiar — finite abilities working in an imperfect medium to effect an impossible goal. In the poem, the problem is articulated not by the poet in his role as narrator, but by Raphael, who serves a similar function for an audience of one :

> and what surmounts the reach
> Of human sense, I shall delineate so,

> By lik'ning spiritual to corporal forms,
> As may express them best.   (v. 571–4)

And later :

> for who, though with the tongue
> Of Angels, can relat e,or to what things
> Liken on Earth conspicuous, that may lift
> Human imagination to such highth.
>
> (VI. 297–300)

The reference is to 1 Corinthians xiii. 1 : 'Though I speak with the tongues of men and of angels and have not charity, I am become as sounding brass or a tinkling cymbal.' Milton's muse, one can assume, does not speak to him in blank verse ; the illumination granted to the seer is intuitive, but if it is to be effective beyond the confines of his mind it must assume a discursive form. What concerns Raphael is the loss suffered in translation : 'For who . . . can relate' is a serious linguistic and philosophical question, which has its antecedents in the 'inexpressibility topos' of the courtly lyric (words fail me when I would describe your beauty).

As a vessel of inspiration, the poet occupies a middle position between the perfect knowledge of God and the clouded intellects of lesser men, and his difficulty extends in both directions : language is inadequate to the reality of his received intuition and to the task of persuasion he would bend it to. A partial solution of the problem is to rely on scripture whenever possible, for scripture is the word of God ; but it is the word of God accommodated to the powers of his creatures and therefore not literal or absolute, as inspiration and grace are absolute :

> When we speak of knowing God, it must be understood with reference to the imperfect comprehension of man; for to know God as he really is, far transcends the power of man's thoughts, much more of his perception.[1]

[1] *The Works of John Milton*, xiv. 31.

Our safest way is to form in our minds such a conception of God as shall correspond with his own delineation and representation of himself in the sacred writings. For . . . both in the literal and figurative descriptions of God, he is exhibited not as he really is, but in such a manner as may be within the scope of our comprehensions.[1]

The safest way, however, may not be sufficient to the occasion, especially when the audience is recalcitrant and unresponsive either to scripture or to the urgings of God's chosen servant. The ministerial office Milton envisions for the poet ends more often than not in disappointment and frustration. In Milton's case the personal disappointment cannot be separated from the national disappointment. 'Methinks', he writes in *Areopagitica*, 'I see in my mind a noble and puissant nation rousing herself like a strong man after sleep, and shaking her invincible locks.' No doubt he also sees himself as the inspired voice who announces this 'rousing', sanctioning it with the seal of prophecy and anticipating the inevitable triumph, for 'who ever knew Truth put to the worse in a free and open encounter?' Michael Fixler discerns the danger in Milton's early optimism: 'By virtue of the fact that as a poet he had undertaken to celebrate the providential justice of God and the glories of his nation, Milton identified his vocation too precariously with the immediate fate of his country.'[2] As early as 1644, in the sonnet 'I did but prompt the age', the poet expresses bafflement and rage at the intractability of his contemporaries.

Classically,[3] there are available two negative responses to this dilemma, (1) despair and inaction (silence) or (2) withdrawal into self-satisfaction ; the latter would be particularly

---

[1] For a discussion of the theory of accommodation, see R. M. Frye's *God, Man, and Satan* (Princeton, 1960), pp. 7–17.

[2] *Milton and the Kingdoms of God* (London, 1964), p. 73.

[3] See my discussions of the burden of prophecy in *John Skelton's Poetry* (New Haven, 1965), pp. 1–35.

attractive in the Puritan context of the elect and the regenerate:

> His dilemma was a reflection and symptom of the whole Puritan position. On the one hand their patriotism, national pride, and belief in national election was inclusive. . . . On the other hand they distrusted and feared all except those who were obvious, self-evident saints . . . at each phase they were to discover that their allies were also unregenerate and no more fit than their former enemies to mould the nation into the shape of God's Kingdom.[1]

If our hearers are defective, if the age will not be prompted, are we not justified in abandoning them? Milton answers this question by continuing to write *Paradise Lost*, and thus accepts, heroically, the confines of the human heart as the battlefield on which he is now permitted to raise God's standard. The divine imperative implicit in the prophetic gift — 'Let all things be done unto edification' — does not cease to be relevant when success seems unlikely or insignificant in political terms. When Saint Paul urges charity, he enjoins communication. For the poet to remain silent or to retreat into the private security of his vision would be an abdication of responsibility in the only sphere of action properly his. Alone, blind, confined to his quarters, dependent on the whims of those who do not understand him, defeated in terms of the programme he had imagined for himself and for his countrymen, Milton nevertheless presses on:

> I Sing with mortal voice, unchang'd
> To hoarse or mute, though fall'n on evil days,
> On evil days though fallen, and evil tongues,
> In darkness, and with dangers compast round,
> And solitude; yet not alone, while thou
> Vist'st my slumbers Nightly, or when Morn

[1] Fixler, op. cit., p. 74.

Purples the East; still govern thou my Song,
Urania, and fit audience find though few.

(VII. 24–31)

The image conjured up recalls Abdiel, alone, encompassed round with foes, yet firm and constant ('unchang'd'). But the poet has even less manoeuvrability than his hero. He can hardly predict an imminent victory ('soon expect to feel / His thunder on thy head') since earlier predictions have proven incorrect and were perhaps presumptuous; truth *has* been temporarily checked, if not put to the worse, in a free and open encounter. These 'evil days' will know no sudden and apocalyptic interruption. Nor can he expect immediate approval for his resolution and firmness. If God does say, face to face, 'Servant of God, well done', it will be in another life in the 'better country' of Hebrews xi when the veil has been removed from his eyes. Meanwhile, he resigns himself to physical immobility and a limited effectiveness and waits patiently for new marching orders and for inspiration.

The inspired elect trust in the promise of another world, but they are still faced with the problem of moving about in this one. Despite their gifts, they share the liabilities and infirmities of the race. Inspiration is fitful, and when it comes it may prove too much for the vessel to bear :

Up led by thee
Into the Heav'n of Heav'ns I have presum'd,
An Earthly Guest, and drawn Empyreal Air,
Thy temp'ring; with like safety guided down
Return me to my Native Element:
Lest from this flying Steed unrein'd, (as once
Bellerophon, though from a lower Clime)
Dismounted, on th' *Aleian* Field I fall
Erroneous there to wander and forlorn.

(VII. 12–20)

Prophets too can fall, wander uncertainly, perhaps errone-
ously, and feel lost in a world in whose making they do have
a share. The 'fit audience' will be sought by the poet only
if the Muse deigns to visit him and it will be found only if
God chooses to make of his work an instrumentality of
divinity. But by holding himself ready ('the readiness is all'),
by standing and waiting, for inspiration or forever, by
believing himself not alone though in apparent solitude, by
being willing to 'annoy' if that is what is asked of him, by
refusing either to revile deity (be 'hoarse') or to default on
his obligations (be 'mute') when cosmic justice seems
inexplicable, by committing himself to expression when the
words are not his own and their effects beyond his control,
Milton does what he can to make himself worthy of God's
service, should he be called to it (as God would have it). He
is, if it can be said of any man, a true and heroic poem.

There is still another hero to be noted in the universe of
Paradise Lost — the reader, who receives his command
from the poet and meets his Apollyon in the poem. The
stylistic intricacies of the verse and the unexpected turns of
the narrative force him into mental operations which correspond to the physical movements of the warring angels. He
begins confidently, almost complacently, is surprised and
disconcerted by unforeseen difficulties, humbled by the
discovery of his inadequacy, revived by a kind word or a
momentary success, thrown back again by a new error ; and
thus he stumbles through the poem, his progress marked by
the many times he is forced to merely stand his ground or
even to retreat. 'He learns', H. R. Swardson remarks with
some irritation, 'that he can't . . . give himself up to Milton's
effect in one place without that meaning and effect being
undermined or destroyed by his response in another place . . .
The trouble is, he wants us to respond to the words in their
full sense in each place, yet he doesn't want to commit him-

self to their full meaning.'¹ More than that, Milton asks us
to respond fully to each of his effects and yet be prepared to
discount one or all of them in the light of better knowledge.
We must commit ourselves and not commit ourselves at the
same time, moving between the immediate experience of
the poetry and the acknowledged authority of a 'hard and
definite outline', remaining open to the first while awaiting
(not demanding) the guidance of the second. In the face of
this, Swardson concludes, 'We finally give up trying to read
him seriously'. But, surely, this is our temptation, not our
duty or our inevitable fate. Admittedly, the poem is a pro-
foundly disturbing experience which produces something
akin to a neurosis; the natural inclination to read on vies
with a fear of repeating old errors and encountering new
frustrations. In this, the poem is a microcosm of the world
and the difficulties of reading are to be equated with the
difficulties of the earthly pilgrimage. The reader's sphere of
action is the poem, and his heroism, like Abraham's, is in
going on (or out), in accepting — on faith — the sup-
position that local failures and discomforts are preludes
to a larger success that awaits him under the ægis of a
controlling and inspired mind. Submitting to the style of
the poem is an act of self-humiliation. Like all heroic acts it
is a decision to subordinate the self to a higher ideal, one
by-product of which is the discovery of the true self. The
imperative is 'read!' and by not giving up, by not closing
the book, by accepting the challenge of self-criticism and
self-knowledge, one learns how to read, and by extension
how to live, and becomes finally the Christian hero who is,
after all, the only fit reader. In the end, the education of
Milton's reader, the identification of his hero, and the
description of his style, that is, of its effects, are one.

¹ Swardson, *Poetry and the Fountain of Light*, pp. 146–7.

5 The Interpretative Choice

Wondering at the 'blind alleys' readers of *Paradise Lost* have been led into, C. S. Lewis moves to 'dismiss that question which has so much agitated some great critics, "What is the Fall?"' by answering, 'The Fall is simply and solely Disobedience — doing what you have been told not to do.' Aligning himself with Addison, for whom 'the great moral which reigns in Milton is ... Obedience to the will of God makes men happy', Lewis poses a question of his own: 'How are we to account for the fact that great modern scholars have missed what is so dazzlingly simple?'[1] This could be profitably rephrased to read, 'How are we to account for the fact that Adam and Eve, when the time comes, miss what is so dazzlingly simple?' For the reader, the poem is a 'life situation', analogous to the situation of the happy couple in Paradise. The 'dazzling simplicity' of the poem's great moral is the counterpart of the dazzlingly simple prohibition, and the obligation of the parties in the two situations is to defend the starkness of the moral choice against sophistications which seem to make disobedience attractive ('Here grows the Cure of all, this Fruit Divine') or necessary ('what seem'd remediless'). The opportunities to yield to such sophistications are provided by God and Milton, respectively, who wish to try the faith and integrity of their charges. Lewis hopes to 'prevent the reader from ever raising certain questions', but Milton insists that the reader raise them, and then that he answer them, either by

[1] *A Preface to Paradise Lost* (Oxford, 1942), pp. 69–70.

recalling the simplicity of the revealed word or by turning inward where there are waiting a ready supply of self-serving rationalizations. These rationalizations become screens behind which the reader may hide from himself facts he finds unpleasant, notably the fact of man's culpability for what happened in Paradise and since. But he is free, on the other hand, to decline the gambit and accept instead the 'desolating clarity' of 'For still they knew, and ought to have still remember'd / The high Injunction not to taste that Fruit' (x. 12–13). Whatever he decides, it is his responsibility, as it was theirs.

Mrs. MacCaffrey observes that in describing the intellectual vanity of the fallen angels, 'Milton is describing *human* preoccupations.' Philosophy may be false, 'but humanity will go on philosophizing'.[1] Certainly the reader will go on philosophizing, and his concerns, as the critical history of the poem proves, are the same as the devils':

> Of Providence, Foreknowledge, Will, and Fate,
> Fixt Fate, Free will, Foreknowledge absolute,
> And found no end, in wand'ring mazes lost.
> Of good and evil much they argu'd then,
> Of happiness and final misery,
> Passion and Apathy, and glory and shame,
> Vain wisdom all, and false Philosophy:
> Yet with a pleasing sorcery could charm
> Pain for a while.
>
> (II. 559–67)

How does one reconcile freedom of will with the absolute foreknowledge of the Creator? How can actions which have been foreseen be free? How can evil proceed from a perfectly good being? The declarative forms of these questions are the staples of anti-Milton criticism:

(1) *Adam and Eve were fated to fall.* 'I do not see what

---

[1] *Paradise Lost as 'Myth'*, p. 183.

the incident can mean except that God was determined to make man fall.' (Empson, *Milton's God*, p. 112.)

(2) *Their disobedience, as we see it, is determined, partly by circumstances, partly by their own natures.* 'Man yields to temptation when he is caught in an archetypal net of circumstance and mixed motivation, from which, being what he is, no amount of faith or foreknowledge can extricate him. . . . The enmeshing of the victims is so beautifully contrived . . . human nature as much as Satan undoes Adam and Eve.' (Watkins, *An Anatomy of Milton's Verse*, p. 141.)

(3) *They were created with a propensity to fall.* 'If they could fall, were they not already in some sense fallen?' (Ricks, *Milton's Grand Style*, p. 99.)[1] Obviously these arguments represent slightly different paths to the same conclusion : God, not Adam and Eve, is guilty of the Fall, and curiously enough, it is God himself who raises them by gratuitously refuting them :

> nor can justly accuse
> Thir maker, or thir making, or thir Fate;
> As if Predestination over-rul'd
> Thir will, dispos'd by absolute Decree
> Or high foreknowledge; they themselves decreed
> Thir own revolt, not I: if I foreknew,
> Foreknowledge had no influence on their fault,
> Which had no less prov'd certain unforeknown.
> So without least impulse or shadow of Fate,
> Or aught by me immutably foreseen,
> They trespass, Authors to themselves in all
> Both what they judge and what they choose; for so
> I form'd them free, and free they must remain,
> Till they enthrall themselves: I else must change

---

[1] Actually the opposite is true: if they could not fall they could not stand; that is, *they* would not be doing the standing, consciously and wilfully. The ability not to fall depends on the ability to fall; free will is a meaningless concept unless the possibility of wrong choice exists.

Thir nature, and revoke the high Decree
Unchangeable, Eternal, which ordain'd
Thir freedom: they themselves ordain'd thir fall.

(III. 112–28)

These assertions are made in the course of a methodical
exposition to which the speaker expects no response; but
the effect on his audience of eavesdroppers is to suggest
'inventions' by means of which the Fall can be circumvented.
As David Daiches points out (not in praise, however), 'the
reader, however much he wishes to read *Paradise Lost* "as a
poem", is forced to read it at this point as logical argument,
and to answer back as he reads.'[1] Whether or not he
'answers back', in the sense of disagreeing, the reader will be
unable to ignore the difficulties involved in the logic of foreknowledge and freedom. These difficulties are acknowledged
(not personally, but as part of a logical proof) by God, and
resolved; but the reader will have been exposed to the
attractiveness of the evasions God disallows — I ordained
their Fall, the shadow of Fate hangs over them, they were
not 'sufficient to have stood' — and thereafter, whenever an
innocent detail is capable of being twisted so that it seems to
forebode the Fall, whenever an isolated incident can be
(illegitimately) structured into a 'net of circumstance', whenever Adam and Eve evidence their ability to fall (the
necessary complement of their ability not to fall), these
evasions, in all their seductiveness, are recalled, and, if we
allow them, they undermine our understanding of the
situation as God and Milton have instituted it.

Undoubtedly, by eliminating some passages and altering
the emphasis of others, Milton could have neutralized the
'pleasing sorcery' of these speculations. That he did not
choose to do so is less an indication of a deficiency in tact
than of a willingness to risk all in order to bring the reader

[1] *Milton* (London, 1957), p. 181.

to self-awareness. One may be proof against the obvious
temptations of the world, the flesh and the devil, but fall to
the promptings of the enemy within, to 'the secret deceit
which we perceive not' but which is working all the while in
the 'many blinde corners, the . . . turnings and windings, the
perplexe labrynths'[1] of the human heart. 'In clearing ourselves when guilty', warns Dyke, 'the heart of man is so
subtle that if it can finde out any other thing or person, that
in the least sort may seem to be but the least peece of an
occasion, that shall be sufficient to free itselfe of all manner
of blame.'[2] (Significantly, one 'tricke' discussed by Dyke is
the imputing of sin to God.[3]) Milton forces to the surface the

---

[1] Daniel Dyke, *The Mystery of Selfe-Deceiving* (1615), pp. 355, 7. See
Miller and Johnson, *The Puritans* (rev. edn., 1963), i. 284: 'A large quantity
of Puritan sermons were devoted . . . to exposing not merely the conscious
duplicity of evil men, but the abysmal tricks which the subconscious can play
upon the best of men.'

[2] *The Mystery of Selfe-Deceiving*, p. 138.

[3] 'Thus did Adam, when he said in defence of his owne eating, the *woman
thou gavest me, she gave me it*, closely taxing God himselfe, as if hee should
have said, unlesse thou hadst given mee this companion, I had not eaten . . .
God that hateth, forbiddeth, threateneth, punisheth sinne, can he possibly
tempt unto sinne? Yea, but thou sayest hee decreed my sinne, for nothing
comes to passe without his will. The *second* causes move not, unlesse they bee
moved by the *first*. I answer the first cause is not the cause of the errour that
is in the motion of the *second*, though it be the cause of the *motion*. As in the
wheeles of a clocke, the principall wheele, with its motion, runnes about the
lower, yet if there be any errour in the motion of the lower, it is no cause at
all thereof. Now, sinne is not properly any motion, but an *errour* in the motion
of thy heart. Gods will being the first cause, is the cause of thy hearts motion
. . . but if there be any sinne, any errour in the motion, thine owne will is the
cause thereof. For all that God hath to doe about it, is his *voluntary permission*
whereby he, withdrawing his grace from thee, leaveth thee to thy selfe, as not
beeing bounde unto thee. He doth not infuse, or instill into thy minde any
wicked motions, as doth *Sathan*. Hee onely setteth the baite, or the net, and
doth not refraine thy concupiscence from carrying thee to it: for he owes thee
no such service: but he doth not take poles, as Sathan doeth, and drive thee
violently into the net. And yet if *Sathans temptation* could not excuse Adam,

deceitful and self-serving thoughts ('the wily suttleties and refluxes . . . from within')[1] employed by the subconscious to avoid uncomfortable truths, and insists that they be submitted to the correction and judgment of the revealed word. Of course, since these thoughts are manifestations of a desire to escape judgment ('Self-love makes one rather excuse what is amiss, than examine it'),[2] the reader may persist in them, even when their subversiveness has been made apparent; but he will at least be conscious of his temerity in affirming against the authority of the poet and scripture.[3]

how much lesse then *Gods desertion'* (152–3). See also Richard Baxter, *The arrogancy of Reason* (1655), p. 65, where the same quibble is considered and rejected: 'Nor is it any deifying of the Creatures will to say it is such a self-determining principle, and so far a first cause, while it had the power of self-determination from God, and so absolutely is no first cause.' Obviously, the various ways of absolving oneself of guilt were much discussed; and this increases the likelihood that Milton would have expected his readers to recognize their objections to the doctrine of free will for what they are, the unlawful urgings of the carnal reason. Another of the 'scapegoats' Dyke disallows is Satan, in a passage that has relevance for *Paradise Lost*: 'The Divell cannot prevaile against us, but by the helpe of our owne corruption. He might strike fire long enough, ere there would be any burning, did not wee finde him tinder' (p. 151).

[1] *Reason of Church Government, Complete Prose Works*, i. 817.
[2] Thomas Watson, *Christian Soldier*, p. 48.
[3] The possibility of being unconsciously subversive is discussed by Milton in the *Christian Doctrine* (*The Works of John Milton*, xiv. 101, 103): 'That the fall of man was not necessary is admitted on all sides; but if such, nevertheless, was the nature of the divine decree, that his fall became really inevitable, *both which opinions, however contradictory, are sometimes held by the same persons,* then the restoration of man, after he had lapsed of necessity, became no longer a matter of grace on the part of God, but of simple justice.' By keeping the two points of belief (the Fall was not necessary, the decree made it inevitable) in separate compartments, the mind entertains blasphemy on a subconscious level, while being outwardly orthodox. Milton makes this manœuvre impossible by forcing an awareness of the contradictions involved in holding these and like opinions, much as the process of dialectic forces awareness (and choice) upon the respondent: 'The respondent now is con-

The result is a reading experience which has been described, disapprovingly, by Waldock: 'our reception of a
given passage can be, and often is, a blend of two things:
what we have really read in the passage, and what we know
Milton is wishing us to read into it' (op. cit., p. 26). I would
say instead that our reception is a blend of what, for various
reasons, we would like to read into the passage, and what we
know, from unimpeachable sources, is really there. So that in
any one scene, including the crucial scenes of Book ix, there
are available two interpretations; one, urged on us by the
epic voice or by our own awareness of the possibilities and
their implications, supports and gives body to the picture of
Edenic reality outlined by God in Book iii, while the other
points, however indirectly, to his villainy and our parents'
(technical) innocence.

As before, the subversive response (interpretation) is first
encouraged and then discredited, leaving the reader to come
to terms with the appeal it has for him. At iii. 127, when God
declares his unwillingness to 'revoke the high Decree / . . .
which ordain'd / Thir freedom', the reader is likely to extend
the influence of the decree to the Fall which is also assumed
to be ordained; but immediately, as if he were anticipating
in advance the 'wily suttleties' of the fallen mind, God

fronted with an alternative and a choice. Either he erred in making the
initial and succeeding agreements leading to this evident, albeit discomfiting,
consequence; or his previous opinions were without foundation. If he decides
that he erred in his initial *doxa* or somewhere along the way, he is obligated
to indicate at what point and why. If he concludes that he was ill-advised in
making concessions to begin with, he is convicted of subordinating truth to
prudential interests. If he determines, willy-nilly, to reaffirm his original
proposition, he must at least concede that he is on record for holding contrary
or contradictory judgments. Eventually he may be led to square himself
with himself. Meanwhile, like Alcibiades in the *Symposium*, the man will be
self-convicted until he is self-convinced (216c).' Robert Cushman, *Therapeia*
(Chapel Hill, 1958), p. 235.

insists, 'they themselves ordain'd thir Fall'.[1] The possibility
of disbelieving him still exists, but disbelief can be maintained only in the face of God's faultless logic which *can* be
understood if the reader is willing to make the effort. There
are then two choices before the reader (1) whether or not to
work through the apparent contradiction between foreknowledge and freedom to an understanding of the distinction between what will happen and what must happen (2)
whether or not to reject completely the alternative reading
which has the advantage (from a 'selfish' point of view) of
excusing the frailty of his first parents,[2] and, by extension,

[1] Cf. III. 128–31: 'they themselves ordain'd thir fall / The first sort by thir
own suggestion fell, / Self-tempted, self deprav'd: Man falls deceiv'd / By th'
other first: Man therefore shall find grace'. The implication in the syntax is
that grace is due man because his error is someone else's responsibility: man
therefore shall find grace. But this is deliberate teasing, if not on God's part,
then on Milton's. The 'therefore' is not logical, but arbitrary; Satan's presence
in the garden is not really an extenuating circumstance; God merely chooses
to make it the basis of an action that proceeds solely from his good will. The
urgings of the Devil may render obedience difficult (or perhaps make it easier)
but never impossible. God points the moral beforehand, 'Sufficient to have
stood, though free to fall' (99), a line that will pursue us into Book IX. Man
does ordain his own fall, and we always know it to be so, but a decoy like
'therefore' is nevertheless able to make us go against our knowledge, for a
moment; we want very much to read 'deserve' instead of 'find' grace, and do
so until the word 'mercy' reminds us that grace is gratuitous, cannot be
earned and certainly not deserved: 'But Mercy first and last shall brightest
shine'. The experience of this passage and others like it can be compared to the
experience of making a typing error. Even as the finger presses the wrong key,
something in the mind flashes a warning signal; but the reflexes are too slow,
a mistake is made, and one simultaneously participates in and analyses a
failure in co-ordination.

[2] As readers of *Paradise Lost*, we are in a curious position, analogous to that
proposed by one critic for the narrator of Chaucer's *Troilus and Criseide*:
'By the beginning of Book IV ... the narrator's love for Criseide has become
such that when he finds himself forced to face the issue of her perfidy he comes
close to denying the truth of his old books.... It is a strange historian who
becomes so emotionally involved with the personages of his history that he is
willing to impugn the reliability of the sources upon which his whole know-

his own frailties. In the middle books (iv–ix) these same choices are structured into a series of scenes which provide a continuing test of the reader's steadfastness and honesty. The technique is again the technique of the 'good temptation' whereby the reader is left to choose, in a controlled situation, which of two roads he will take. That is to say, the interpretative choice — which is to be distinguished from the 'responsive choice' in that it requires a decision concerning the meaning of an action or a scene, and so affects the reader's understanding of the poem itself — is always made consciously and wilfully, and is ultimately a choice between the word of God and the structures reared (self-defensively) by the reader's reason.

(ii) THE CHOICES

In Book iv, when Eve recalls her early life without Adam, the choice is between two readings of the allusion to Narcissus :

> Not distant far from thence a murmuring sound
> Of waters issu'd from a Cave and spread
> Into a liquid Plain, then stood unmov'd

ledge of those personages presumably depends.' (E. T. Donaldson, *Chaucer's Poetry: An Anthology for the Modern Reader*, New York, 1958, p. 967.) This is true to some extent of Milton's narrator, but truer still of his reader who becomes 'emotionally involved' with the originals of himself. Despite certain knowledge of the history and a unique commitment to its source (the sacred text) he finds himself increasingly eager to deny the fact of the Fall and thus avoid the issue of his own perfidy, either by ascribing it to a natural and therefore innocent depravity or by fixing the blame on some other agent. The latter is the more attractive alternative, since it seems to preserve the free will of the victims, at least superficially; actually there is no difference at all between believing that Adam and Eve could not help but fall or believing that their fall was caused by someone else, and in the end this kind of reasoning inevitably returns to God.

Pure as th' expanse of Heav'n; I thither went
With unexperienc't thought, and laid me down
On the green bank, to look into the clear
Smooth Lake, that to me seem'd another Sky.
As I bent down to look, just opposite,
A Shape within the wat'ry gleam appear'd
Bending to look on me, I started back,
It started back, but pleas'd I soon return'd,
Pleas'd it returned as soon with answering looks
Of sympathy and love; there I had fixt
Mine eyes till now, and pin'd with vain desire
Had not a voice thus warn'd me.   (453–67)

One can either conclude with Mrs. Bell that 'we have glimpsed
a dainty vanity in "our general mother" which the serpent
will put to use', or contrive, with Peter and Harding, to
disengage her from the pejorative connotations of the myth:

> The incident is actually one of the most engaging glimpses we
> have of Eve's artless [innocent] simplicity . . . and the childlike
> honesty with which she compares the physical appearances of
> Adam and herself is wholly disarming.

> Eve is saved, as Narcissus is not, by a warning voice, and it
> would be a captious reader indeed who . . . would be inclined to
> read too much into this.[1]

There is much in the text itself to support Peter and
Harding. 'Childlike' (or, better still, infantlike) seems
perfectly true to the reaction Eve displays to her newly
discovered image: the curiosity — 'I thither went / With
unexperienc't thought' — the movement back and forth —
'I started back, / It started back, but pleas'd I soon return'd'
(the patterned repetitions lead the reader to imitate the
motion) — and the (innocent) fascination — 'there I had
fixt / Mine eyes'. And Eve's yielding to Adam would seem
to indicate, as Harding implies and Summers insists, that

[1] *A Critique of Paradise Lost*, p. 102; *The Club of Hercules*, p. 74.

'the point ... is the contrast rather than the comparison with ... Narcissus':

> Narcissus had no 'perfect' partner, no 'other self', and he had no divine guide ... she *has* found fulfillment, ... she had not 'pin'd with vain desire'.[1]

In addition, one should note that, in telling her story, Eve, far from 'unexperienc't', is mature in wisdom; she is now aware, as she may not have been before, of the true significance of her yielding:

> I yielded, and from that time see
> How beauty is excell'd by manly grace
> And wisdom, which alone is truly fair.
>
> (489–91)

This is obviously 'the professed moral of the episode'.[2]

The possibility, however, of *not* reaching for the contrast (an effort is required) and *not* crediting her maturity still remains. Ignoring the evidence to the contrary, evidence Milton is always careful to provide, the reader, whose will is also free, may decide to disbelieve Eve, looking no further than the surface parallel, and thus begin to ease, conscious at some level of the error, into the opinion 'that Adam and Eve must have already contracted ... weaknesses before they can start on the course of conduct that leads to their fall.'[3] (Of course, if the will is free, *no* course of conduct can *lead* to the Fall which is a spontaneous, i.e. free, action.) What the reader cannot possibly do is ignore the problem (the eighteenth-century commentators were already debating it)[4] once the Ovidian allusion is recognized. The presence of

---

[1] *The Muse's Method*, p. 98.   [2] Harding, loc. cit.
[3] Waldock, op. cit., p. 61.
[4] Newton (*Paradise Lost*, 1749) notes that Addison asks 'sarcastically enough [*Spectator*, vol. 5, No. 325.] whether some moral is not couch'd under this place, where the poet lets us know, that the first woman immediately after her creation ran to a looking-glass, and became so enamour'd of her own

Narcissus, even at a remove, is a puzzle, which, like the literal incongruity of some parts of scripture and the appearance during the creation scene of the phrase 'With Serpent error wand'ring', is designed to exercise the reader's mind and to present him with a choice he cannot avoid.

The same pattern is repeated on a larger scale in the episode of Eve's dream, where the suggestion of a tainted consciousness is at odds with the moral drawn by Adam. The suggestion is conveyed to the reader in Book IV, when Satan is seen 'Assaying ... / ... if inspiring venom, he might taint / Th' animal spirits that from pure blood arise / ... thence raise / At least distemper'd, discontented thoughts, / Vain hopes, vain aims, inordinate desires / Blown up with high conceits ingend'ring pride' (IV. 801, 804-9). Presumably, this is the basis of a reading like Northrop Frye's :

> The occasion of her dream was Satan whispering in her ear; but the dream itself, in its manifest content, was a Freudian wish-fulfilment dream.[1]

Notice that Frye assumes Satan's success, while the verse itself leaves the matter in doubt. Satan is *assaying* to reach her Fancy, in the *hope* that he could then 'forge / Illusions as he list;' or, barring that, he will see *if* he can infuse venom into her which *might* then taint her animal spirits. There is more than a hint that his calculations may prove

face, that she had never removed to view any of the other works of nature, had not she been led off to a man.' Newton's defence of Eve sets the pattern for all subsequent defences: 'This account that Eve gives of her coming to a lake, and there falling in love with her own image ... is much more probable and *natural* as well as more delicate and beautiful, than the famous story of Narcissus in Ovid, from which our author manifestly took the hint, and has expertly imitated some passages, but has avoided all his puerilities ... as the reader may observe by comparing them both together' (emphasis mine).

[1] *The Return of Eden*, p. 75.

incorrect. Of course, a careless reader, or one who is eager
to find trouble in Paradise, can easily detach 'Blown up with
high conceits ingend'ring pride' from the syntax of the
paragraph (Milton allows him that latitude) and accept the
line as a statement of fact, applicable to Eve as she sleeps.
He would, however, be guilty of a (wilful) distortion.

A more reliable insight into Eve's state of mind is provided, somewhat indirectly I admit, in the word 'startl'd' :
'Such whispering wak'd her, but with startl'd eye.'
(v. 26) In *Comus*, the Lady, oppressed by 'A thousand
fantasies / . . . Of calling shapes and beck'ning shadows
dire', waking fancies not unlike Eve's, declares forthrightly :
'These thoughts may startle well, but not astound / The
virtuous mind' (210–11). The virtuous mind may be surprised (startled) by an untoward suggestion without
surrendering to it. And even if the body is under evil's spell,
as Eve's is here and will be again when she follows the
serpent to the tree, the virtuous mind is still able to assert
itself :

> Thou canst not touch the freedom of my mind
> . . . although this corporal rind
> Thou hast immanacl'd.

> (*Comus*, 663–5)

This is the point Adam will make when he explains to Eve
the significance of her dream, and it is one we should be
prepared to understand.[1]

---

[1] The distinction between 'startle' and 'astound' is the basis of the definition
of virtue offered in the masque. Milton conceives of virtue as a state of inner
composure, a moral readiness that cannot be shaken, even by something
totally unexpected. The virtuous mind may be surprised (startled) at a
possibility hitherto unknown (as Adam will be surprised to discover that he
can disobey) without losing its balance; it will absorb and assimilate new facts
and situations, not disintegrate before them. On the other hand, a mind that is
astounded has allowed the weight of external pressures to paralyse and rout it;
it has become the plaything of circumstances instead of their master. The
fallen angels are 'astounded' or stupefied by their situation in Hell (1. 281).

The dream is a carefully woven web of echoing and anticipatory detail. Satan's opening 'Why sleep'st thou Eve' is a slightly altered version of his 'earlier' address to Beelzebub, 'Sleep'st thou companion dear?' (673). (The relationship between the two temptations is confused for us since we have not yet been told of the revolt which has already occurred when Satan squats at the ear of Eve.) His first appeal is a parody of Adam's parody of *The Song of Songs*, with a significant difference: Adam invites Eve to enjoy the wonders of God's nature, 'Awake, the morning shines and the fresh field / Calls us' (20–21); Satan invites her to be worshipped, 'Heaven wakes with all his eyes, / Whom to behold but thee?' (44–45). Is this merely another instance, we ask, of the fiend's inability to imagine motives not rooted in self-love, or is it that he knows Eve better than Adam does and can fashion an argument which will sway her? The answer any reader gives will depend to some extent on the meaning he has assigned to the incident at the pool. The angel whose dewy locks distil ambrosia is of course Satan as he was in the meeting with Uriel. Does one deception have any bearing on the probable success of the other? The question will certainly raise itself, and again, the answer will depend on the care the reader is willing to exercise in the drawing of conclusions.

Satan's approach is leisurely, as it will be in Book ix. Flattery ('fair Angelic *Eve*') and Godhead ('be henceforth among the Gods') are the twin prongs of his strategy, merging in a final appeal, 'Ascend to Heav'n, by merit thine' (80). The logic is familiar, as it has been rehearsed for us in Book iv :

> Knowledge forbidd'n?
> Suspicious, reasonless. Why should thir Lord
> Envy them that?
>
> (iv. 515–17)
>
> is Knowledge so despis'd?
> Or envy, or what reserve forbids to taste?   (v. 60–61)

And will be heard again in ix :

> What can your knowledge hurt him, or this Tree
> Impart against his will if all be his?
> Or is it envy?   (ix. 727–9)

The temptation builds slowly, heightening the reader's anticipation of the climax. At the crucial moment, a sensory lure ('Even to my mouth of that same fruit held part / Which he had pluck't') is added to the rhetoric. Eve describes the effect on her physiological processes and on her will :

> the pleasant savory smell
> So quick'n'd appetite, that I, methought,
> Could not but taste. Forthwith . . .
>   (v. 84–86)

Here the interpretative choice is offered in small. 'Methought' and 'Could not but taste' suggest imminent consent, but not consent itself. (I felt as if I had to do it.) One expects 'Forthwith' ('immediately after which' or simply 'then') to be followed by 'I reached' or 'I ate' or even 'I decided to eat.' Instead we read

> Forthwith up to the Clouds
> With him I flew.

We have missed the deed itself and passed to its effects, the literal illusion foreshadowing the metaphorical reality : 'They swim in mirth, and fancy that they feel / Divinity within them breeding wings / Wherewith to scorn the Earth' (ix. 1009–11). How are we to account for this omission? The simplest explanation consonant with the evidence is one which does credit to Eve and to her virtuous mind. Satan is unable to make Eve go through the motions of disobedience, even in her fancy, just as hypnotic suggestion cannot induce actions contrary to one's moral code. The irrevocable gesture is not reported because it does not happen. Thus Adam: 'Which gives me hope / That what in sleep thou didst abhor to dream, / Waking thou never wilt consent to do' (119–21). But some readers, intent on the Fall and on analogies which reflect 'the subconscious desires and longings' of the dreamer,[1] will hear only the irony in Adam's hope, and will assume that Eve has eaten, perhaps in the interval between 'could not but taste' and 'Forthwith', and will assume also, that, because she has, she will again, inevitably.

This interpretation of the dream, implying as it does Satan's success and Eve's involuntary compliance, is challenged at once by her disclaimer: 'but O how glad I wak'd / To find this but a dream' (92–93), which Wayne Shumaker cites as proof of 'the innocence of her will'.[2] Eve's innocence, real and technical, is even more strongly insisted on by Adam, who, with the authority displayed by the epic voice on other occasions, moves to promulgate official doctrine. (Again Milton has allowed us the latitude of speculation, and so induced a train of thought whose wrongness can now be more forcefully exposed.) Evil is present, he acknowledges, but its source can in no way be Eve: 'in thee can harbor none / Created pure' (98–99). And what of an Eve whose subconscious has been violated without her knowing it, against her will? Adam's answer is simply 'impossible!':

> Evil into the mind of God or Man
> May come and go, so unapprov'd, and leave
> No spot or blame behind. (117–19)

Eve could not now be the repository of evil unless her conscious will has wished it so; since her will is otherwise

---

[1] Harding, op. cit., p. 83.
[2] 'The Fallacy of the Fall in *Paradise Lost*', *PMLA*, lxx (1955), 1186.

inclined ('O how glad'), she remains untouched (startled, not astounded) by her experience. Moreover the fact of the assault does not reflect on her firmness ; rather her resistance, like the resistance of the Lady in *Comus*, affirms dramatically a basic tenet of Milton's moral philosophy :

> Virtue may be assail'd but never hurt,
> Surpris'd by unjust force but not enthrall'd,
> Yea, even that which mischief meant most harm
> Shall in the happy trial prove most glory.
> But evil on itself shall back recoil.

(589–93)

(So Satan recoils at the touch of Ithuriel's spear, returning to 'his own shape', when he is discovered in the happy couple's bower.) One critic describes the dream as 'a wedge for separating Eve from Adam by returning her to her mirror state',[1] but if the incident is considered apart from the Fall (as it should be), the opposite seems to be true. The fact of the dream has afforded Adam and Eve an opportunity to exercise their joint responsibilities in the manner God ordained for them. Disturbed by something she does not understand, Eve at once seeks guidance and counsel from Adam, who responds to her need with his superior wisdom.[2] The result is the strengthening of the hierarchical relationship which is the basis of their happiness and the dispelling of the anxiety occasioned by the intrusion of an alien influence. The comment of the epic voice is unequivocal :

> *So all was clear'd*, and to the Field they haste.

(136)

---

[1] Stein, *Answerable Style*, p. 93.

[2] When we first meet Eve she is receiving instruction from Adam's lips; later she is said to prefer his teaching to the angel Raphael's (viii. 50–57). In Book ix, Eve will again seek Adam's approval or counsel, and for the first time he handles the situation badly with what results we know (the separation, not the Fall). Appropriately, the reconciliation scene in Book x is a re-establishment of the old relationship.

Of the two invitations (to worship and to be worshipped) Eve has accepted Adam's.

The alternative reading, in which the dream is a 'portal of temptation', opened by 'some pre-existing sympathy' and leading inexorably to the Fall,[1] rests primarily on the detailed correspondences between the two passages in v and ix. Yet, reasoning from the same details, one can see, with Arthur Barker, how the incident, 'far from foreboding the Fall . . . stands in the sharpest . . . contrast [to] it',[2] just as Narcissus' behaviour, properly viewed, stands in contrast to Eve's. Whereas in Book ix Eve will linger at the tree, allowing Satan's logic a too easy entrance, here, even in sleep, she hears him with horror, escaping gladly to Adam's better guidance. Presumably on some other occasion, when she is not a captive audience, her rejection of the same appeal will be even more emphatic. (One more area has been removed in which virtue can be even surprised.) 'Knowing already the outcome of the story,' asserts Mrs. Bell, 'we cannot believe' Adam when he 'tells her soothingly that "evil into the mind of God or Man / May come and go." '[3] But if we do believe him, as Milton clearly intends us to, our foreknowledge points in quite another direction 'to . . . the fact that the Fall is, as to right action, a parodic obliquity and anomaly.'[4] That is, the response of Adam and Eve to this situation militates against the *inevitability* (not the fact) of their later failure. As always, the pattern the details fall into is determined by the reader, who can either labour to bring the poetic moment into line with the larger perspective, or reverse the priorities by bending the poem's

[1] Millicent Bell, 'The Fallacy of the Fall in *Paradise Lost*', *PMLA*, lxviii (1953), 871; E. M. W. Tillyard, *Studies in Milton* (London, 1951), p. 11.

[2] 'Structural and Doctrinal Patterns in Milton's Later Poems', in *Essays in English Literature From the Renaissance to the Victorian Age presented to A. S. P. Woodhouse*, ed. Maclure and Watt (Toronto, 1964), p. 190.

[3] Loc. cit.   [4] Barker, loc. cit.

moral structure to fit a conclusion drawn too hastily from a local context. Ultimately the choice is between experience, the mould of the perceiving mind, and revelation, a choice mirrored here in the alternatives of believing or disbelieving Adam, and in the further obligation, if we decide to believe him, of understanding what his statement tells us about the Fall.

The episode is meant to show what Adam and Eve are capable of doing, rather than what they must inevitably do. The reader who makes the dream a cause or even a prediction of the Fall compromises prelapsarian freedom, and renders himself incapable of understanding what the loss of that freedom involves. Innocence, Raphael tells Adam and Eve, far from being static, includes large possibilities for growth as well as the possibility of declining to grow. By continuing to obey and by maturing in wisdom, as Eve matures when she recognizes Adam's superior fairness, they may ascend 'in tract of time' from the perfection of Paradise to a higher perfection ;[1] and while they continue to respond to their opportunities as we see them responding here,

---

[1] The term 'perfection' has been the cause of some confusion. Mrs. Bell argues, 'the mind can not accept the fact that perfection was capable of corruption without denying the absoluteness of perfection' (op. cit., p. 863). But if Adam and Eve are perfect, they are perfect with respect to their species, not absolutely perfect. Absolute perfection belongs to God; human perfection demands that man be able (free) to make mistakes. One must distinguish between flaws and limitations; man's limitations (his distance from absolute perfection) are the basis of his dignity and therefore one aspect of his perfection. See Summers, *The Muse's Method*, p. 149: 'We have already noted some of the ways in which the poem presents perfection as moving rather than static, as relative rather than absolute. Adam and Eve are created perfect for their place (although the place may change); they are endowed with the possession or the possibility of perfect fulfilment in time, of perfect happiness and joy and the perfection of all the knowledge of which they are capable in their state; and they are also endowed with the ability to doubt or distrust or forget their happiness and perfection, the ability to deny and to destroy it all.'

affirming the hierarchy they were created in and labouring
to do God's will, the Fall is impossible. The small crises of
the middle books have been defended misleadingly as an
instance of 'necessary faking' in order to avoid too abrupt
a transition from innocence to sin.[1] The abruptness of the
falling away, in relation to the movement of the narrative
before that time, is what Milton wishes to emphasize; and
he leaves us to work out the implications of these domestic
adventures in the hope that we will use them to counterpoint, not circumscribe, the fatal act. The difficulty and the

[1] 'In Book Four of *Paradise Lost* Milton pictured his state of innocence . . . .
But he could not possibly have conducted his account of the Fall with that
picture for sole starting point; the effect would have been sudden and violent
and would have carried no conviction. . . . Instead he resorts to some faking;
perfectly legitimate in a poem, yet faking nevertheless. He anticipates the Fall
by attributing to Eve and Adam feelings which though nominally felt in the
state of innocence are actually not compatible with it.' (Tillyard, *Studies in
Milton*, pp. 10–11.) 'Theologically and symbolically he [Adam] is innocent
until he has to act. But Milton could not construct his fiction entirely from
that perspective; he needed a scope of action sufficient for conflict and he
needed both direct and symbolic action that could borrow meaning, as it were,
by anticipating human experience after the Fall.' (Stein, *Answerable Style*,
p. 99.) 'As a theologian, Milton was compelled to maintain a spotless innocence
in Adam and Eve until that precise moment when Eve actually eats the Fruit.
As a poet, he was compelled to anticipate the Fall by implying in both our
first parents not only a predisposition to sin but the specific frailty out of which
the sin could grow. . . . These two aims are clearly incompatible. . . . To
accomplish by artifice what could not be accomplished in fact, Milton sought
to implant in the minds of his readers a secret, furtive, tentative uneasiness
about Adam and Eve — not so much doubts as the shadow of doubts —
while simultaneously maintaining the illusion of their entire sinlessness.'
(Harding, *The Club of Hercules*, pp. 68–69.) Implied in these statements is a
confusion between the ability to fall and the process of actually falling.
Harding's 'entire sinlessness' is equivalent to Mrs. Bell's 'absolute perfection';
They both assume the staticness of innocence. When Tillyard writes of 'feelings
incompatible with the state of innocence' he is much more purist than Milton
or his God. The only feeling incompatible with innocence is the I-must-eat-
the-apple feeling, and even there the psychic decision to do so and the physical
commission of the deed must follow before innocence is lost.

temptation (for us) reside in our foreknowledge, which is a liability if we ask of every word or gesture, how does this assure the Fall, and an asset if we ask instead, given the freedom of the Fall, what does this mean? Foreknowledge, like innocence, is a gift whose rewards (or hazards) are commensurate with the degree of responsibility exercised towards it. Thus if we read properly and refuse to rest in superficial resemblances, the Fall is continually thrown into brilliant relief as an incomprehensible phenomenon; otherwise we comprehend it, and by comprehending, deny it.

The tension between a responsible reading and one which results from carelessly inferring backwards from the event is particularly noticeable and significant when Adam describes his reaction to Eve :

> here passion first I felt,
> Commotion strange, in all enjoyments else
> Superior and unmov'd, here only weak
> Against the charm of Beauty's powerful glance.
> Or Nature fail'd in mee, and left some part
> Not proof enough such Object to sustain,
> Or from my side subducting, took perhaps
> More than enough; at least on her bestow'd
> Too much of Ornament, in outward show
> Elaborate, of inward less exact.
> For well I understand in the prime end
> Of Nature her th' inferior, in the mind
> And inward Faculties, which most excel,
> In outward also her resembling less
> His Image who made both, and less expressing
> The character of that Dominion giv'n
> O'er other Creatures; yet when I approach
> Her loveliness, so absolute she seems
> And in herself complete, so well to know
> Her own, that what she wills to do or say,
> Seems wisest, virtuousest, discreetest, best;

All higher knowledge in her presence falls
Degraded.

(VIII. 530–52)

Again we see, or should see, the unfallen consciousness
rising to the challenge of its environment. Earlier Adam
had asked in his ignorance, 'What meant that caution
join'd, *if ye be found / Obedient?* Can we want obedience
then / To him or possibly his love desert?' (v. 513–15).
Now, in the light of what Raphael has told him ('That thou
art happy, owe to God; / That thou continu'st such, owe
to thyself'), he is able to pinpoint the area of danger (*here
passion first I felt*') and relate it to his obligations and to his
answering capabilities. He admits 'strange commotions',
as Eve admits her disturbing night phantasms, but, like
her, he keeps his balance (startled not astounded) and
retains his hold on the truth of things as he knows them to be
('For well I understand'). Higher knowledge has *not* fallen
degraded in Eve's presence, and, because the possibility has
been noted, it is less likely to fall in the future. The delicacy
(not frailty) of Adam's understanding is mirrored in the
word 'seems', a verbal extension of his will through which
he controls the illusion of Eve's superiority by insisting on
its status as illusion. ('Seems' is the equivalent of Eve's
'O how glad I wak'd / To find this but a dream'.) The
parallelism of the two experiences extends to the eagerness
in each case to consult with higher intelligences, Eve with
Adam, Adam with Raphael, who, in turn, receives his
information from God. Thus the entire sequence, from the
first words Adam speaks in Book IV ('needs must the
Power / That made us ... / Be infinitely good') to the
sociable angel's departing warning at the close of Book VIII
('stand fast; to stand or fall / Free in thine own Arbitrement
it lies') is an image of the harmonious co-operation possible
between creatures of differing capacities who are united in

their desire to understand and be faithful to the will of God.

The misgivings the captious reader may have are represented by Raphael, who, struggling as we are with the burden of foreknowledge, reacts against a future he cannot hold back and does less than justice to Adam's 'seems'. 'In loving thou dost well, in passion not', he warns. God did not intend you to be 'sunk in carnal pleasure, for which cause / Among the Beasts no Mate for thee was found.' 'Half abash't', largely, I think, because he has failed to make himself clear to someone he is anxious to please, Adam replies with new care, describing in analytical fashion the right working of his faculties :

(1) Eve's beauty, of form ('her outside . . . so fair') and manner ('those graceful acts, / Those thousand decencies that daily flow / From all her words and actions'), is admired as the visible sign of an inner probity; her words and actions 'declare unfeign'd / Union of Mind, or in us both one Soul' (603–4).

(2) Even so, his consciousness of her worth does not make him her captive, because he retains his powers of judgment :

> Yet these subject not; I to thee disclose
> What inward thence I feel, not therefore foil'd,
> Who meet with various objects, from the sense
> Variously representing.   (607–10)

(3) And he concludes by declaring his awareness of the priorities one must follow if reason is to remain right :

> still free
> Approve the best, and follow what I approve.
>   (610–11)

Love (following) waits on the discernment of the best by the reason (approving) and a commitment to this order makes one free. This is the concept of love which is to be applied to the crisis of the poem, and it is delivered crisply and authoritatively here by Adam himself.

Had these words been spoken earlier, they would have been accepted as a true indication of Adam's state of mind. But here in Book VIII, shortly (in poem time) before he is said to be fondly overcome with female charm, the reader may be tempted (literally) to reason as Arnold Stein does :

> That statement, preceding so briefly the events of the following morning and noon, cannot be a satisfactory reflection of unfallen knowledge . . . from the event and our consequent perspective Adam is already undergoing the conflict of temptation.
>
> (*Answerable Style*, p. 99.)

Because we know Adam will soon fall, the argument goes, he could not now be as firm as he seems to be; already corruption has occurred. This is an example of the blind alleys foreknowledge can lead us into if we use it illegitimately to determine the significance of present actions which, with 'bad recompense', then become the cause of what is foreknown. Rushing to meet 'our consequent perspective', Stein slips past the paradox Milton is at pains to impress on us at this conspicuously late stage — Adam is firm, yet Adam falls — and substitutes for it an intelligible sequence of events. Immediately, the uniqueness of the Fall as an action unrelated to its antecedents is obscured, and the focus of temptation is transferred from the will to a temporal process. (The implication that the Fall must have antecedents is a denial of the freedom of the will. Watching Eve leave Adam's side in Book IX Stein comments, 'The eating of the apple is as good as done', thereby assuming, incorrectly, that neither of them can reverse the process their separation has set in motion.)[1] The subversiveness of this reading,

---

[1] *Answerable Style*, p. 102. The decision to separate is unfortunate, but not fatal. Separation no more assures the Fall than staying together would *certainly* have prevented it. Adam explains to Eve that they will be 'most likely'

which can hardly be avoided as a possibility, is apparent
when one sees the ease of reasoning backward from it to
the occasions when Adam feels the weakness he confesses,
and backward still further from those occasions to the
creation of that weakness (the creation of Eve) and finally
to God, who becomes the prime mover in a line of cause
and effect which ends in Adam's yielding. (Stein would
certainly not follow his analysis to this conclusion.) If the
culpability of the sinners is to be maintained as a point of
belief, and understood in the framework of the poem's
legalistic theology, the status of the Fall as an unforced and
wholly free act must be preserved, although the effort
required to isolate it from the circumstances surrounding it
becomes greater as Book ix draws nearer. (The tendency of
the reader to pre-date the corruption of the fallen pair is
seen in another form in his infection of their language; and
there is a corresponding pressure to let in fallen meanings
as the crisis approaches.) The effort must be made, however,
if the reader is to have a meaningful perspective on what does
occur. In the context of the trial the poem represents for
him, the penalty for not making it is failure.

(iii) THE CONSEQUENCES

One can see from this how cumulative are the effects of the
interpretative choices offered by the scenes this chapter
examines. Accept the Narcissus parallel in a superficial way

(ix. 365) to avoid temptation if they do not separate. All actions save one are
lawful in Paradise, although some are inadvisable. No sequence of inadvisable
actions (physical or mental) can overwhelm the unfallen will and determine
its direction, for at any point it can disengage itself from the pressures that
seek to influence it, whether they originate from the outside or from within.
The free will is *absolutely* free.

and Eve's dream is almost certain to receive a Freudian reading. Decide that Adam dismisses the presence of evil too easily in Book v and you are halfway to deciding that he is similarly insensitive to the danger of his feelings for Eve in Book viii. Soon Adam and Eve become the passive victims of Fate, put upon children of destiny, enmeshed, in Watkins' words, 'in an archetypal net of circumstance and mixed motivation'. They need not even be present to be further entangled. When Satan deceives Uriel, 'The sharpest sighted Spirit of all in Heav'n', who is beguiled we are told because 'neither Man nor Angel can discern / Hypocrisy', the reader is invited to ask himself if Eve, in an analogous situation, should be expected to be more discerning than one of God's eyes. The reader who has answered the question (in the negative) before he asks it will have forged another link in the chain which leads Eve to the tree. He may even suppose that Satan's entrance into Paradise, permitted by God in the incompetent persons of Uriel and Gabriel, is decisive. Yet only an instant's reflection serves to discredit the parallel and to illuminate the conditions of Eve's temptation by emphasizing the differences between the two situations. Hypocrisy is not a problem for Eve since she need only recall what God has said in response to any tempter no matter what his appearance. Uriel's failure is excusable, because he is by nature incapable of piercing Satan's disguise; in fact, his virtue works to maximize the probability of his deception. But Eve's failure is a failure of the will, inexcusable because the sufficiency of her will is not affected by the ability of an enemy to appear other than he is. Consequently Satan's presence in the garden does not in any sense assure the outcome. Again the scene is constructed in layers; on the surface one comes upon meanings which challenge the poem's overriding moral; but a slight shift of perspective and the challenge is met by the discovery of deeper and truer meanings which send us back in a new way to the truths God and Milton have proclaimed. The layer any reader reaches depends on the strength of his will and on the quality of his dedication. One may either rest in the deadening implications of the letter or penetrate to the life of the spirit.

'The great events in *Paradise Lost*', Northrop Frye has said, 'should be read . . . as a discontinuous series of crises, in each of which . . . the important factor is not the consequences of previous actions, but the confrontation, across a vast apocalyptic gulf, with the source of deliverance.'[1] The reader must not only see this, he must continually affirm it by refusing at every point to accede to any suggestion which impairs the freedom of such confrontations. The strain is considerable, since the basis of all his inferences is a knowledge of what is to come, and, as we have seen, that knowledge can either be well used or it can be twisted into an indictment of God. The narrator, who is also a reader, feels the strain as well as we do and we occasionally hear him labouring under it. Watching Satan light on Mt. Niphates, he cries 'O for that warning voice, which he who saw / Th' *Apocalypse*, heard cry in Heav'n aloud, / . . . that now, / While time was, our first Parents had been warn'd / The coming of thir secret foe, and scap'd' (IV. 1–2, 5–7). The assumption is of a causal relationship between Satan's presence in Paradise and the Fall, and of a corresponding relationship between the availability of a warning voice and the hope of escape. But the narrator corrects himself by adding a qualification, 'Haply so scap'd', *perhaps* they would have escaped, admitting in effect that warning or no warning, with or without Satan, escape still depends on the exercise of their wills. His 'vain speculation' is an involuntary expression of his concern and sorrow, understandable, but

---

[1] *The Return of Eden*, pp. 102–3.

irrelevant with respect to the point of doctrine (the freedom of the unfallen will) he accepts intellectually, and he draws back from it as we must draw back from it. Later, when Eve, 'like a Wood-Nymph light', moves off into the groves, alone, the narrator's empathy again threatens his self-control, but only for a moment :

> O much deceiv'd, much failing, hapless *Eve*,
> Of thy presum'd return! event perverse!
> Thou never from that hour in Paradise
> Found'st either sweet repast, or sound repose ;
> Such ambush hid among sweet Flow'rs and Shades
> Waited with hellish rancor imminent
> To intercept thy way, or send thee back
> Despoil'd of Innocence, of Faith, of Bliss.
> For now, and since first break of dawn the Fiend,
> Mere Serpent in appearance, forth was come.
>
> (IX. 404–13)

Ricks describes perfectly the effect of the 'hesitating syntax' : 'At first, one takes "deceav'd" and "failing" as absolute in their application to Eve — the poet's imagination is absorbing the full bitterness of the imminent Fall. But then the next line — "Of thy presum'd return !" — declares that she is *deceived in* the one present circumstance : her presumed return.' But his conclusion seems to me to be wrong :

> And the hesitation, as to whether 'deceav'd' and 'failing' are absolute or particular, is resolved here by our realizing that there are not in fact two paths at all, but only one. For Eve to be wrong about anything (even that she would soon be back) is for her to be wrong about everything. Before the Fall, the distinction of absolute or particular failing does not exist.
>
> (*Milton's Grand Style*, p. 97)

But the lines in question are making just that distinction. Eve's failing here is like Uriel's in Book III, innocent, and in relation to the Fall, oblique. The epic voice leaps ahead (with every reader) to what he knows *will* happen, not to what *must* happen. For Eve in the present the 'event perverse' is the event she can still prevent; this event (her leaving) is perverse only for the narrator who, yielding for an instant to the pressures generated by the narrative, imagines a necessary connection between actions which are only contiguous in time. The verse illuminates the path of error, but bars access to it, insisting even now that disaster could be avoided. When the epic voice cries, in anticipation, 'Thou never from that hour in Paradise', the reader involuntarily completes the thought with 'knew innocence' or something equally final. 'Found'st ... sweet repast' is dramatically disappointing, but morally bracing, since it effectively checks a precipitous rush toward an encounter that will come all too soon. 'Despoiled of Innocence, of Faith, of Bliss' seems absolute and present in isolation, but in context, it is controlled by the disjunctive 'or' and thus has the status of one possibility among other possibilities, including perseverance and the non-loss of innocence. The past participle 'despoil'd' is a fact held in potential despite the teasing availability of 'for now' which applies only to the coming forth of Satan. Some two hundred lines later as she contemplates the forbidden tree and considers the serpent's arguments Eve is 'yet sinless' (659), the distance between her and sin measured, as always, by the strength of her will, which is, as always, sufficient; just as the reader's will is sufficient to *his* task, which is to keep in mind, always, her sufficiency.

This pattern, in which the reader is presented with a series of interpretative puzzles whose solution either contributes to or undermines his understanding of the poem's great issues, spans seven books. The boundary lines are God's first speech in iii and Adam's final admonition to Eve in IX. (Significantly, Eve has been urging the half-truths and sophistries with which the reader has been tempted; she is, at this point, the spokesman for his subversive self, and Adam is the voice of his erected wit.)[1] These utterances share a method and a purpose. The method is logical definition, reflected stylistically in the predominance of a schematic rhetoric, and the purpose is to establish, with precision and conciseness, the capabilities and limitations of Edenic virtue (innocence). Addressing himself to the inferior intelligence of Eve and anxious to make his point unmistakable, Adam lingers longer over his argument than God does:

> his creating hand
> Nothing imperfet or deficient left
> Of all that he Created, much less Man,
> Or aught that might his happy State secure,
> Secure from outward force: within himself
> The danger lies, yet lies within his power.
> Against his will he can receive no harm.
> But God left free the Will . . .
> Firm we subsist, yet possible to swerve.
>
> (343–51, 359)

The important distinction is made in the play on the word 'secure'. For a moment 'his happy state secure' is read as a self-contained unit asserting the *absolute* security of man's position in Paradise. (This would be true whether we take 'secure' as an adjective — 'or aught that might his happy

---

[1] Eve confuses heroic virtue with prideful self-assertion when she asks, 'And what is Faith, Love, Virtue unassay'd / Alone, without exterior help sustain'd?' (335–6). She also mistakes the flexibility of the free will for imperfection: 'Let us not then suspect our happy State / Left so imperfet by the Maker wise, / As not secure so single or combin'd. / Frail is our happiness, if this be so, / And *Eden* were no *Eden* thus expos'd.' Her arguments correspond to the speculations entertained by the reader (heroism requires a dramatic situation, if they could fall, they were already in some sense fallen) and he must reject them or agree with Adam's rejection of them. The tension in the scene is a reflection of the tension within him.

state which is secure . . .' — or as a verb — 'or aught that might his happy state keep safe'.) But the repetition of 'secure' with the addition of 'from outward force' qualifies the absoluteness of their security by delimiting it (secure from outward force, but vulnerable to . . .) and the qualification is immediately given body in 'within himself / The danger lies'. The first within ('within himself') points to the location of the danger, and the second within ('yet lies within') refuses to locate it — physically. 'Withinness' becomes an area of spiritual dimension, non-spatial and boundless, defensible even though it is indeterminate. ('Lies' also participates in this concept.) Security for Adam and Eve is a form of anxiety; it is a state *not* without care, and therefore, strictly speaking, insecure. In the confines of the figure ('antanaclasis' or the 'rebound') 'secure' breaks free of its literalness to take on the flexibility of a paradox, 'secure, but not secure, yet secure as long as . . .'. While they do not enjoy the false security of high walls (their walls are high, but not high enough) or effectively deployed sentries, they do enjoy the true security of a virtuous mind. 'Against his will he can receive no harm' is a conclusion that springs proven from the distinctions made in the preceding lines. The flexibility of the will is then emphasized — 'But God left free the Will' — before a reformulation of the original statement is put forward: 'Firm we subsist, yet possible to swerve'.

The speech of thirty-five lines is essentially an expansion of God's 'Sufficient to have stood, though free to fall'. Properly interpreted, the intervening scenes

(1) give body to God's aphorism by dramatizing the delicate balance between the sufficiency to stand and the freedom to fall, and

(2) underline the incomprehensibility of the event. Carelessly (subversively) interpreted, they

(1) contribute to the confusion of the ability to fall with the certainty of falling, and

(2) circumscribe the Fall in a network of circumstance. In one set of readings, the complementary delicacy and strength of innocence are emphasized, and the responsibility of the unfallen pair is insisted upon; in the other, the reader assents to various oversimplifications which support the version of the story he would prefer to believe in. These oversimplifications are reflections of a desire to cheat the poem's morality, and Milton evokes them so that they can (hopefully) be exorcised. This is the most subtle of the forms the poet's 'good temptation' takes and perhaps the most 'to be desired', because by it the reader is forced to acknowledge a tendency of mind of which he may have been (consciously) unaware, and which, undetected and unjudged, could have done him irreparable harm. The temptation is baited with self-love. By the end of Book III, Satan is no longer sufficiently attractive to serve as a recipient of the reader's misguided sympathy, and he is replaced by Adam and Eve, and thus by the reader himself. For, by finding a way to transfer the responsibility for his first parents' sin to a substitute villain (Satan) or a 'natural' process (fate, circumstances), the reader in effect disclaims responsibility for the sins he himself commits; their 'technical' innocence becomes his, as does their subsequent assertion of a guilty God ('thy terms too hard').

The quality of the reader's response to these smaller actions (the deception of Uriel, the incident at the pool, Eve's dream, Adam's confession of weakness, the morning quarrel) affects his response to the Fall itself, which will either be seen in its proper light as a contrast to true virtue and right action, or misinterpreted as a necessary, and perhaps desirable, consequence of the universe's structure. Waldock observes, 'There was no way for Milton of making the transition from sinlessness to sin perfectly intelligible' (*Paradise Lost and its Critics*, p. 61). The unintelligibility, and hence the freedom, of the transition is Milton's thesis. Making it intelligible, and hence excusable, either by compromising the sufficiency of the will or by forging a chain of causality, is the reader's temptation. The seat of temptation is the reason, which, in the service of self-love, begets arguments in accord with the inclination of the affections (reason plays a flatterer's role, not unlike rhetoric's); but temptation can be resisted if the reason is directed to police itself by exposing the speciousness of its own inventions. The path taken is determined, as always, by the will. For the reader too, the danger lies within, 'yet lies within his power. / Against his will he can receive no harm.'

6 What Cause?:
Faith and Reason

> The corrupt nature of man is more prone to
> question the truth of God's word, then to see
> and confess their own ignorance and incapa-
> city. — Richard Baxter *The arrogancy of
> Reason against Divine Revelations repressed:
> or proud Ignorance the cause of Infidelity, and of
> mens quarreling with the word of God.* 1655.

(i) CARNAL REASON

To fall not deceived is to fall because you are not deceived, to
fall to your own analysis of what is involved in a decision to
break union with God. In this study, much has been made
of the danger of rhetoric as an instrument of deception and
as an appeal which panders to the worst in man. But for
those who are able to resist the lure of the rhetorical there
is a greater danger still: the over-valuing of the faculty
one has recourse to when an obvious temptation presents
itself. I refer, of course, to the rational faculty, which
distinguishes man from the animals and testifies to the
residence within him of the image of God. The exercising of reason is its own temptation; its perverse sweetness
ravishes the intellect and diverts one's thoughts from
Heaven 'whose sweetness would make us blessed'. It is
the inquiring and discriminating mind which betrays the
reader in Book II, as he is led to distinguish between
speeches which are united in blasphemy, a blasphemy he
tacitly approves and shares if he judges them on any other
basis (rhetorical effectiveness, strategical soundness).
In terms of the divine imperative — Thou shalt have no

other Gods before me — reason–logic has the same ambi-valent status as passion–rhetoric. 'As long as it was kept subservient to orthodoxy', Miller writes of rhetoric, and by extension of the affections, 'it was admirable, but whenever it became an end in itself, ... whenever through too fre-quent excitation of passion it tended to undermine the empire of reason, then it became "carnal eloquence".'[1] In the same way, reason can become 'carnal' reason if its reach is extended to include the mysteries of divinity and the points of faith. If the light of reason coincides with the word of God, well and good ; if not, reason must retire, and not fall into the presumption of denying or questioning what it cannot explain :

> When God hath put his Seal to it, and proved it to be his own; if after this you will be questioning it, because of the seeming contradictions or improbabilities, you do but question the wisdom and power of the Lord: As if he had no more wisdom then you can reach and fathom: yea then you can censure and reprove? Or, as if he could do no more, then you can see the way and reason of, and are fit to take an account of.
>
> (Baxter, *The arrogancy of Reason*, p. 46)

Reason serves Adam and Eve well in their round of daily tasks. Had they exercised reason on the morning of the fateful day, the imprudence of separation would have been immediately obvious, and an unpleasant situation could have been avoided. But if reason is right, its rightness is irrele-vant to any decision concerning the forbidden fruit. The arbitrariness of God's command, that is to say, its unreason-ableness, is necessary if compliance is to be regarded as an affirmation of loyalty springing from an act of the will :

> It was necessary that something should be forbidden or com-manded as a test of fidelity, and that an act in its own nature

---

[1] *The New England Mind*, p. 307.

indifferent [*quod neque bonum in se esset, neque malum*], in order
that man's obedience might be thereby manifested. For since it
was the disposition of man to do what was right, as a being
naturally good and holy, it was not necessary that he should be
bound by the obligation of a covenant to perform that to which
he was of himself inclined; nor would he have given any proof of
obedience by the performance of works to which he was led by
a natural impulse, independently of the divine command.

(*The Works of John Milton*, xv. 113–15.)

The 'natural' impulse which leads man to good works is
reason. If Adam and Eve agree that it is reasonable and, *as
far as they can see*, attractive to *not* eat the apple, obedience
is not only possible, but easy, and an inadequate test of
faith. They are capable of questioning both the reasonableness (as Satan invites) and the attractiveness (this is the
consideration in Adam's case) and thus of finding all kinds
of *reasons* — intellectual and emotional — to eat. At that
point, obedience to a command beyond reason will not be
easy; but it is still possible, since the nature of the command
makes the assent of reason and emotion unnecessary and
perhaps even suspect. The question of whether or not
Adam and Eve are convinced of the rightness of their
action is beside the point, and should not be asked, though
it surely will be. The more unreasonable seems the command, the more obvious it should be that its rationale lies
in its source. This holds true also for fallen man who must
affirm his faith in the same way, independently of reason.
The explanation is Webster's:

But if man gave his assent unto, or believed the things of Christ,
either because, and as they are taught of and by men, or because
they appear probable ... to his reason, then would his faith be
... upon the rotten basis of humane authority, or else he might
be said to assent unto and believe the things, because of their
appearing probable, and because of the verissimilitude of them,

> but not solely and onely to believe in and upon the author and promise of them, for his faithfulness and truths sake, *and nothing else.*   (*The Examination of Academies*, p. 17, emphasis mine.)

This last is a perfect description of what the loyal angels do in Book vi.

The parallelism between the situation in Paradise and the reader's situation extends to the ambiguous position of reason, at once a source of strength and, in one well-defined circumstance, a portal of temptation. In the context of the reading experience, the bounds of presumption are set by the assertions of the epic voice ('Man, with strength entire, and free will arm'd / ... deserv'd to fall') and by God, and any attempt to reformulate the terms of the narrative situation in order to bring it within the compass of human understanding represents an illegitimate intrusion of the analytical faculty on areas closed to it. The freedom of the Fall (and therefore man's responsibility for it) is a point of doctrine, and the reader must resist the temptation to submit it to the scrutiny of reason, just as Adam and Eve must maintain the irrelevancy of reason to the one easy prohibition. Like them also, the reader is able to discern (or invent) any number of 'seeming contradictions' with which to question divine justice. 'What abundance of seeming contradictions ... do rise up in the eyes of an Ignorant Infidel' cries Baxter (*The arrogancy of Reason*, p. 21); and Thomas Sutton's list of 'curious and unnecessarie questions' includes several that will occur to every reader of the poem :

> Why did God create man apt to fall? why did hee not keepe him from falling? ... Why doth God condemne men for unbeleefe, seeing no man can beleeve, except God conferre faith upon him? ... Is not God unjust and cruell to predestinate men ... before they have done any evil?
> (*Lectures Upon the Eleventh Chapter to the Romans*, London, 1632, p. 460.)

Endowed with 'minds that can wander beyond all limit and satiety' (*Areopagitica*), we come naturally to these questions ; but it is our duty, once they have arisen and shown themselves unanswerable except by blasphemies, to give them over and 'rest satisfied in the bare Word of God' (Baxter, p. 57), accepting on faith what we are unable to understand :

> Let us passe by curious questions, bid adieu to all vaine speculations. Let us exercise our selves in searching the scripture.
> <div align="right">(Sutton, <i>Lectures</i>, p. 461.)</div>

So that, at some point, assenting to the authoritative interpretation of the poem (in contradiction of 'that to which he is himself inclined') is as much an act of faith for the reader as keeping the divine command is for his first parents ; and in both cases reason's best service is to admit its lack of jurisdiction.

In slightly varying situations, but with the same troubled awareness, Eve, Adam, and (possibly) the reader fall when they do not affirm the primacy of revelation against the claims of present circumstances as they are urged by the affections and interpreted by the reason. They fail (unaccountably) to make a leap of faith. Their failure (not its explanation) is the subject of this chapter.

(ii) EVE : 'WITH REASON TO HER SEEMING'

The limits of reason are established in the discussion of astronomy in Book VIII.[1] Adam explains to Raphael how

---

[1] For a full discussion of the subject, see Howard Schultz, *Milton and Forbidden Knowledge* (New York, 1955), esp. chap. iii: 'God's justice was a *datum* to be accepted on faith, even when the Almighty behaved questionably.... "Down reason, then " — William Twisse and the rest of Job's comforters would have gone no further, but Milton's Chorus finished the sentence — "at least vain reasonings down". While reason could still absolve

reason has led him to doubt the wisdom of God's disposing
of the heavens :

> reasoning I oft admire,
> How Nature wise and frugal could commit
> Such disproportions.   (25–27)

Casting his eye about, he has taken the measure of the
universe by confining it within his idea of space and movement. Raphael will allow such speculations ; they are lawful :
'To ask or search I blame thee not.' What is unlawful or
unwise is a conclusion which in effect appoints heavenly
disposition. Apparent disproportions may not be real. Or if
they are real, they merely testify to the distance between
man's sense of what should be and God's limitless power.
Raphael imagines God moved to laughter at the sight of his
creatures' vain attempts to circumscribe him : 'or if they
list to try / Conjecture, he his Fabric of the Heav'ns /
Hath left to thir disputes, perhaps to move, / His laughter
at thir quaint Opinions wide' (75–78). Adam must be
'lowly wise' and reject an anxiety which is a thinly disguised
desire for godhead. As Raphael slyly reminds him, however
the heavens are disposed, their movements 'need not thy
belief' (136). 'He must not be haunted by the fear that the
universe or his own individual world will go to wrack unless
he consciously understands all its details.'[1] Knowledge is not
sinful if it is sought, as it is in Book VII, so that God can be
further praised : 'not to explore the secrets ask / Of his

God from guilt, it had work to do; it was the vain reasoning that doubted
God's ways justifiable to men that must down. Mere human morality had
no case against God for having driven the Nazarite into the arms of the
Timnian bride: "Unchaste was subsequent, her stain not his." If God moved
Samson in mysterious ways, to a Timnian woman or to suicide, reason had a
simple choice: to render a moral verdict in God's favor and support it by logic,
or to render the same verdict and be silent and assenting, confessing its own
feebleness as an advocate' (pp. 132–3).

[1] Summers, *The Muse's Method*, p. 161.

Eternal Empire, but the more / To magnify his works, the
more we know' (95–97); but neither is it necessary to God's
plan or to the keeping of his commandments.[1] The status of
knowledge (knowing facts) is perfectly illustrated by
Raphael's final refusal to answer Adam's proposed 'doubt':

> But this I urge,
> Admitting Motion in the Heav'ns, to show
> Invalid that which thee to doubt it mov'd;
> Not that I so affirm, though so it seem
> To thee who hast thy dwelling here on Earth.
> God to remove his ways from human sense,
> Plac'd Heav'n from Earth so far.   (114–20)

From the earthly perspective, anything can be proven
(affirmed); but proof or affirming here is merely 'seeming'
somewhere else where there is a better vantage point for
viewing (knowing); and God has instituted it thus so that
man will exercise his reason, and, through reason, discover
its inadequacy. As always, the lesson is one of humility, and
it is, as Richardson saw, for us as well as for Adam:

> Thus near 200 Lines are Excellently Employ'd. and are So far
> Useful to Us, that Neither should We presume beyond the
> Means God has been pleas'd to Furnish us with.
> (*Explanatory Notes on Paradise Lost*, p. 351.)

Although Eve is not present when Adam is instructed in
the limitations of 'earthly sight' (reason), her response at
IX. 651 indicates that she has received instruction from him
in the interim:

> But of this Tree we may not taste nor touch;
> God so commanded, and left that Command
> Sole Daughter of his voice; the *rest* we live
> Law to ourselves, our Reason is our Law.
> (651–4, emphasis mine)

[1] In *Paradise Regained*, Christ rejects non-biblical knowledge not because
it is sinful, but because Satan offers it as a substitute for the revealed word of
God.

Yet for all her self-awareness, Eve falls to the reason which is not her law in this one circumstance. I remarked earlier on the significance of the 'though' in 'Into the Heart of *Eve* his words made way, / Though at the voice much marvelling' (550–1). What Eve marvels at are the logistics of the phenomena. How can this beast speak, if the laws of nature — the evidence of everything she has ever seen — declare it an impossibility :

> What may this mean? Language of Man pronounc'd
> By tongue of Brute, and human sense exprest?
> The first at least of these I thought deni'd
> To Beasts.
>
> (553–6)

The question is lawful, but the state of mind is dangerous. Eve speaks 'Not unamazed' (552); the double negative suspends the reader between the two alternatives, amazement and unamazement, as Eve is suspended between them. Being amazed is being 'overwhelmed by wonder' so that nothing but the stimulus to wonder occupies the conscious mind; there is no room for anything else, especially for a reality that is not immediately visible or insistent. On the other hand, there is room for the untruths and half-blasphemies — 'Fairest resemblance of thy Maker fair', 'sole wonder', 'A Goddess among Gods' — that Eve allows to pass unchallenged because her attention is absorbed by the mechanical problem before her. 'Into the heart of *Eve* his words made way.' At the beginning she still has the presence of mind to remember the divine command and thus to protect herself against a surrender to her wonder; but the longer she dwells on this or any other natural phenomena to the exclusion of all else, the easier it is to lose sight of higher considerations, although higher considerations can always be recalled by a simple act of the will (memory). As Eve continues to listen to Satan, she becomes 'yet more

amaz'd' (614), until finally, that is, at some point of time
which follows other points of time, but not necessarily, she
fails to remember what she knows.

Satan's formal temptation builds on the success he has
achieved merely by appearing and attracting Eve's attention.
His entire argument is contained in two phrases:

look on me   (687)

do not believe   (684)

'Look on me'. This is what Eve has been doing all along,
and Satan now urges her openly to infer the truth about God
and his conditional decree from what she *sees*, and not to
believe anything which does not tally with that evidence:
'Thenceforth to Speculations high or deep / I turn'd my
thoughts, and *with capacious mind* / Consider'd *all things
visible*' (602–4, emphasis mine). By all things visible Satan
means all things; all there is in a universe whose limits
correspond to his capacious mind. This is, of course, an
inversion of the proper relationship between the two spheres
of reality, in which experience and the machinery which
gives us experience become the measure of belief, and
therefore of God's power. By offering himself as a model,
Satan invites Eve to taste of his experience, a metaphor
made literal by her subsequent action, and offered in turn to
Adam; 'that what of sweet before / Hath toucht my sense,
flat seems to this, and harsh. / On my experience, *Adam*,
freely taste' (986–8). '*My* experience'. The value Eve finds
in experience (things seen) is the value she assigns to it, and
that will be whatever she wants it to be. Experience is only a
word for what happens to reality when it is filtered through
the medium of time and space — Man's medium not God's.
God accommodates himself to man: 'Immediate are the Acts
of God, more swift / Than time or motion, but to human ears /
Cannot without process of speech be told, / So told as earthly

notion can receive' (vɪɪ. 176–9). And man repays this courtesy by confining him within 'earthly notions', within experience. Satan attempts to mask this solipsism by taking away from man the responsibility for interpreting experience and giving it to something called science :

> O Sacred, Wise, and Wisdom-giving Plant
> Mother of Science, Now I feel thy Power
> Within me clear, not only to discern
> Things in thir Causes, but to trace the ways
> Of highest Agents, deem'd however wise.
> Queen of this Universe, do not believe
> Those rigid threats of death.

(679–85)

With the words 'discern' and 'trace' Satan proceeds to initiate Eve into the mysteries of empirical science. He will determine the truth about higher agents by applying the proper method of 'collecting and concluding upon the senses' to the raw material of experience. Thus: I have eaten ; I have not been visited by death, 'whatever thing Death be' ; therefore if you eat, you will not be visited by death. Do not believe what science does not affirm. As usual Satan is not even reliable within the areas he marks out as his own. Aside from the matter of fact — he lies, he has not eaten — his conclusion is premature, since there are not enough instances to provide data for the formulation of a general rule that could anticipate the effect of an analogous action. Eve herself seems to doubt the sufficiency of the evidence when she says at line 650 'Wondrous indeed, *if* cause of such effects' (emphasis mine). In logic, the effect of an efficient cause depends on the nature of the form receiving it (the material cause). What holds for a serpent, even if it did hold, may not hold for man. Of course in this case, Eve need not look to logical analysis for guidance, since the pattern of cause and effect is known to her from an infallible source: 'for know, / The day thou eat'st thereof, my sole command / Transgrest, inevitably thou shalt die' (VIII. 328–30). The true objection to Satan's method is the presumption, which the word 'science' is meant to conceal, of assuming that God cannot work effects contrary to those his creatures are able to discern in nature, 'As if they would confine th' interminable' (*Samson Agonistes*, 307). Eve is told, 'these and many more / Causes import your need of this fair Fruit' (730–1), but a thousand causes seen operating in nature would count as nothing against the certainty of the divine command.[1] (By making Satan an empiricist, Milton dramatizes for the seventeenth-century projectors the traditional warning against intellectual pride.)

The causes Satan pretends to discern and to trace in things are second causes, if they are causes at all and not accidents of conjunction taken for causes by an observer who sees only part of the picture. The first cause remains forever a mystery, not discoverable by the reason and therefore not to be confined within the limitations of the reason, that is within its own effects. 'No philosopher', David Hume will write in the next century, 'who is rational and modest, has ever pretended to assign the ultimate cause of any natural operation . . . It is confessed, that the utmost effort of human reason is to reduce the principles, productive of natural phenomena, to a greater simplicity, and to resolve the many particular effects into a few general [second] causes, by means of reasonings from analogy, experience, and observation. But as to the causes of these general

---

[1] See Baxter, *The arrogancy of Reason*, p. 18: 'Moreover this corruption doth often discover itself in that men will not believe the *truth* of the thing revealed, because they cannot reach to understand the *causes* of it'; also, p. 22: 'These self-conceited ignorant Souls do imagine all to be impossible which exceedeth their knowledge.' For Milton on the relationship between natural law and God's prerogative, see *Samson Agonistes*, 300–25 where the chorus explains that the operation of natural causes does not bind God.

causes, we should in vain attempt their discovery ; nor shall we ever be able to satisfy ourselves.'[1] Satan eliminates first (unchartable) causes by refusing to admit the existence of anything he cannot see : 'that all from them proceeds, / I question it for this fair Earth I see, / Warm'd by the Sun, producing every kind, / Them nothing' (719–22). Throughout the scene the metaphor which controls his temptation is sight : 'Your Eyes that seem so clear, / Yet are but dim, shall perfetly be then / Op'n'd and clear'd' (706–8). The purview of mortal sight, whose deficiencies have been emphasized in the ambiguous praises of Galileo and his glass, 'less assured', is here extended by Satan to take in all reality, and self-worship is introduced in another guise. Believing in experience, in reason, in things seen, in the patterns (causes) the mind discerns (or creates) in nature, is believing in oneself, and urging that belief is the ultimate in flattery. 'Queen of the Universe' is a form of flattery easily resisted because it is so obvious, but as soon as Eve begins even to consider the prohibition as a subject for rational discourse, she accepts the same title with a slight variation : 'Judge of the Universe.'

Even as Satan speaks, the counter-argument to his blasphemies emerges in the double sense of his words, as in a medieval punctuation poem. 'Wonder not, sovran Mistress' (532) could be read as a command and should be received as one by Eve. If 'Queen of this Universe, do not believe' is separated from 'Those rigid threats' (685), and we allow for a characteristically Miltonic inversion, Satan is saying to Eve, under God's direction, 'do not believe me when I call you Queen of this Universe.' A few seconds later, he promises her godhead on the basis of a proportional analogy : 'That ye should be as Gods, since I as Man, / . . . is but

[1] *An Enquiry Concerning Human Understanding*, section iv, part 1, in *The English Philosophers from Bacon to Mill*, ed. E. A. Burtt (New York, 1939), p. 601.

proportion meet, / I of brute human, yee of human Gods'
(710–12). All too true in a sense Satan does not intend : if he
is human, he is brutishly human, sub-human, less than
human, and as is meet, they will become human Gods,
humans posing as Gods, not Gods at all. Satan is unaware of
these meanings, but they are available to any attentive
reader, and to Eve, if she is willing to reach for them. (She
too is faced with an interpretative choice.) Unfortunately,
Eve takes Satan at face value in more ways than one, and
when she stands before Adam, her speech is a tissue of
Satanic echoes :

> But strange
> Hath been the *cause.*
>
> (861–2)
>
> This tree is...
> of Divine *effect*
> To *open Eyes*, and make them Gods who *taste.*
>
> (863, 865–6)
>
> the Serpent wise...
> *Reasoning* to *admiration*, and with mee
> Persuasively hath so prevail'd, that I
> Have also tasted, and have also *found*
> Th' *effects* to correspond, *opener mine eyes.*
>
> (867, 872–5)
>
> On my *experience*, Adam, freely taste.
>
> (988)

Satan shows himself to Eve and bids successfully for her
undivided attention ; and Eve in turn approaches Adam
with only one argument :

> Look on me.
> Do not believe.

The last question she asks herself before deciding to eat is
'How dies the Serpent?', an indication of how thoroughly

she is committed to the empiricism Satan preaches. She does not reproduce any of his questionable syllogisms in her appeal to Adam, because they are less important than her willingness to listen to them. The moral Raphael draws from the battle in Heaven is, 'listen not to his Temptations'. Listening is not sinning, but it does signify a tacit acceptance of the situation and of the relevance of logical or experimental inquiry to a commandment of God's. Eve need not be won by reasons, merely won to reason. The proper response to the tempter's sophistries and to her own doubts is not a counter-argument, but Abdiel's simple declaration, 'Shalt thou give Law to God?'

(iii) THE READER : WHAT CAUSE?

The error of substituting the law of reason and the evidence of things seen for the law of God is repeated by the reader if he regards Eve's failure as a failure of reason and declines to judge her in accordance with the terms of God's decree. Eve loses herself in reason's wandering mazes, forgetting that, in this instance alone, reason is not her law; and by following her in an attempt to 'trace the ways' of her defection, the reader exposes himself to the temptation of the process whose danger he is charting. His responsibility parallels hers : she must remember that the reasonableness of eating does not alter the status of the divine prohibition ; he must remember that she is required to perform an act of the will, signifying faith, not understanding, and that lapses in logic do not affect her sufficiency ('the seat of faith is not in the understanding, but in the will')[1] ; she has merely to pull back at any point from the invitation to reason, and assert, 'God said not to'; he has merely to recall at every

---

[1] *The Works of John Milton*, xv. 407.

point that the dialogue he is reading is a tactical diversion, intended, like the marvellous speaking of the serpent, to obscure the real issue (obedience to an absolute command). The difficulties are considerable. First of all, he must hold in abeyance the analytical powers whose use the poem has encouraged elsewhere. Specifically, he must distance himself from the rhythm of the exchange, and not fall into the mistake of considering Satan's propositions on his terms, that is as if they were relevant either to the question of eating or to the intelligibility of Eve's action.

The temptation to argue with Satan is real enough, especially since so much of the poem has been devoted to exposing the fallacies he urges. To the phrase 'dauntless virtue' (694) one can oppose the example of the faithful angels who equate virtue with obedience; to the question 'what is evil?' (698) the knowledgeable reader can reply 'breaking union' and the bondage of purposeless freedom; the syllogism 'God therefore cannot hurt ye, and be just; / Not just, not God' (700–1) is false, as we learn in Book III; for by punishing man, God accords him the respect due a free agent, and is therefore just; and the proper response to Satan's 'What can your knowledge hurt him?' (727) is Raphael's:

> Knowledge is as food, and needs no less
> Her Temperance over Appetite, to know
> In measure what the mind may well contain,
> Oppresses else with Surfeit, and soon turns
> Wisdom to Folly, as Nourishment to Wind.
>
> (VII. 126–30)

At this point, the ambivalent status of reason is mirrored in the reader's situation. Wholly intent on detecting Eve's errors of omission, he himself may slip into the error of believing that she might not have fallen, had she been a better logician. While she is busily inquiring into the ways of higher agents, he is in danger of imitating her action by presuming to anatomize (understand) it ; for both, empiricism is the vehicle of temptation. Once the events antecedent to her decision are allowed any real (determining) importance, the pressure is removed from her and transferred surreptitiously to the situation as a whole. The reality of the Fall as a failure of will, free and spontaneous, gives way gradually to the appearance of a succession of smaller and understandable failures which divide between them the blame that belongs properly to Eve ; and it is this appearance, or the possibility of creating it, which holds out a temptation in the reader.

The reader's dilemma has been recognized by John Peter : 'to brand her [Eve] as infamous requires an effort, and one which the reader is encouraged to neglect.' Merely to analyse the process by which she arrives at her decision, he continues, 'is to go part of the way toward excusing her ... *tout comprendre, c'est tout pardonner*'.[1] Here Peter touches inadvertently on the place of this scene in the poem's most rarefied temptation, the temptation to inquire into the causes of matters which are specifically exempted from such inquiries. The Fall is no more an object of understanding than the prohibition it violates. Both are to be accepted as articles of faith in their respective contexts (the poem and Paradise), primary points of reference from which other points may be examined, but themselves not subject to examination. If the command of God is submitted to rational analysis, the meaning God has stipulated for it ('the Tree ... / ... which I have set / The Pledge of thy Obedience and thy Faith') is rejected in favour of the meaning reason may discover ; the reason gives law to God. ('When ye received the word of God ... ye received it not as the word of men, but as it is in truth, the word of God.')[2] If the Fall is

[1] *A Critique of Paradise Lost*, pp. 128–9.
[2] *The Works of John Milton*, xv. 399.

explained or 'understood' it is no longer free, but the result of some analysable 'process' which attracts to itself a part of the guilt. Thus freedom of will is denied, the obloquy of the action returns to God (who set the process in motion), and again reason — the reader's reason — has given law to God. Old errors return in a new guise as the reader's analytical powers betray him into a position those same powers had previously rejected. Eve keeps faith if she upholds God's word against the urgings of her reason ; the reader keeps faith if he continues to affirm the spontaneousness of the Fall (and her culpability) in the face of the alternatives his reason presents to him. And the crisis for both occurs simultaneously, at the moment of eating, for 'if the circumstances of this crime are *duly* [*attentius*] considered' by the reader, he will acknowledge it 'to have been a most heinous offense', and, making the effort required, he will 'brand her as infamous'.[1]

The reader who loses sight of Eve's crime in a maze of reasons will have been prompted in part by the poet's declaration of purpose :

> That to the highth of this great Argument
> I may assert Eternal Providence,
> And justify the ways of God to men.

This is usually interpreted as a promise to defend God in terms men will find comprehensible and logically satisfactory, but a more accurate reading is provided by L. A. Cormican :

> . . . by justification Milton did not mean a merely logical demonstration which would prove an intellectual conclusion and bring God within the framework of the rational universe. He uses the word with the overtones it acquired from New Testament usage, where it implies a divine, not a human or

[1] *Christian Doctrine, The Works of John Milton,* xv. 181.

logical understanding, a supernal illumination from the Holy
Spirit. . . . If the ways of God can be justified, it must be
through a purification of the heart rather than by the reasonings
of the intellect.[1]

Undoubtedly, this is the meaning Milton intends us to
attach to justification, but only after 'to show the reasonableness of' has been tried and found wanting. In conjunction
with the lines 'Say first . . . / . . . what cause / Mov'd our
Grand Parents . . . / . . . to fall off', justify the ways of God
to men is a deliberate invitation to 'give the reins to wand'-
ring thought'[2] by prying into areas where speculation is
fruitless, an invitation accepted by most readers. 'When
Milton's Adam ate the forbidden fruit', Paul Turner wrote
in 1948, 'he created a number of problems for posterity ; and
not the least of these was the task of discovering what,
exactly, caused his Fall.'[3] To the list of 'causes' Turner
reviews we can now add six or seven additional, no one of
which is finally more satisfactory than those offered in the
poem :

> not deceiv'd
> But fondly overcome with Female charm.   (ix. 998–9)

> For still they knew, and ought to have still remember'd.

> (x. 12)

The first, as has often been remarked, is lamentably weak ;
the second, simply uninformative (they forgot). Together
they assert what every reader should have by now realized :
there is no cause of the Fall as it has been sought, merely
an ever-expanding description of what is *comprehended* in the
act, a description Milton anticipated when he answered his

---

[1] 'Milton's Religious Verse', in *The Pelican Guide to English Literature,
Volume III, From Donne to Marvell*, ed. Boris Ford (Penguin Books, revised
edition, 1960), p. 175.

[2] *Samson Agonistes*, 302.

[3] 'Woman and the Fall of Man', *English Studies*, xxix (1948), 1.

own question, 'For what sin can be named, which was not included in this one act?' Each of the sins he enumerates — gluttony, uxoriousness, sacrilege, pride, arrogance — has been taken up at some time, but the result is always a deeper insight into what the Fall *means*, and not the discovery of 'what exactly caused the Fall'. The answer to the question, 'what cause?' is given in the first line, 'Of Man's First Disobedience'. Mrs. Bell objects, 'it is no explanation that our Grandparents disobeyed because they were disobedient'.[1] Exactly! It *is* no explanation, and because no one could take it for one, it has the advantage of preserving the autonomy of the Fall as an expression of free will, unlike other 'explanations' which transfer the onus from Adam and Eve to an abstraction. The reader who finds a cause for the Fall denies it by denying its freedom, and succumbs to still another form of Milton's 'good temptation'.[2]

For if the search for cause goes on, and, along with it, the attempt at a rational justification, it is because Milton promotes them. Just as God mocks the presumption of man by placing the heavens far from human sense, so the poet dangles before us the bait of justifying God's ways and the

---

[1] 'The Fallacy of the Fall in *Paradise Lost*', *PMLA*, lxviii (1953), 864.

[2] Properly seen, these more sophisticated analyses of cause are merely amplifications of the word 'disobedience', indicating, variously, what disobedience involves (presumption, ingratitude), what Adam and Eve commit themselves to by disobeying (lust, anxiety), which parts of their personalities are dominant when disobedience occurs (the affections), the extent to which disobedience implies a distortion of perspective or a misunderstanding of the structure of the universe, and so on. To any one of these we can still demand, why? (what cause) and receive no satisfactory reply. It is the habit of criticism to use one description of the Fall to explain another. Thus Adam disobeys because he makes Eve his God; he makes Eve his God because he undervalues himself; he undervalues himself because he does not exercise his reason properly; he does not exercise his reason properly because he allows his passion for Eve to dictate his choice; he allows his passion for Eve to dictate his choice because he has made her his God.

ignis fatuus of cause, designedly perplexing the reason with
riddles it cannot possibly solve. Those who 'trouble their
braines' in curious and vain speculations, warns Sutton,
'shall be oppressed by the brightnesse of Gods Majestie
and confounded in [their] owne imaginations'; they find
themselves 'plunged . . . into such inextricable labrynths and
mazes, that they have never been able to come out of them'[1]
except by returning in humility to the revealed word. This is
the motion Milton hopes to induce in the reader by allowing
the reason scope to discover its own insufficiency. The
technique may be unorthodox, but the *moralitas* is not:
'How unsearchable are his judgements and his ways past
finding out' (Romans xi. 33). The reader proves the truth
of this commonplace himself by trying for nine books to
find a formula 'which would . . . bring God within the
framework of the rational universe' and at all times he has
the option of preferring the formulas his reason manu-
factures, transparently circular though they may be, to the
conclusion Milton wishes him to reach : man disobeys by
exercising, without constraint, the free will God gave him,
and to describe the Fall in any other way, to find a *cause* for it,
is to imply that God can only institute conditions which we,
as fallen men, can imagine or participate in. As we have seen,
the easy rationalizations with which the reader is tempted in
the middle books — circumstances (fate) undo Adam and
Eve ; an inherent weakness debilitates them ; they comport
themselves heroically by breaking free of a dependent
passivity — correspond to the 'causes' he seeks in an effort
to soften the fact of the Fall ; and, as we have seen, these are
continually made available to those who wish to embrace
(discover) them ; but at every point the authoritative
counter-assertion (they have sinned inexcusably and must
be judged) is also available, in the reminders of the narrative

[1] *Lectures Upon the Eleventh Chapter to the Romans*, pp. 459–60.

voice, in the symbolism of the action, and, above all, in the memory (will) of the reader, who is repeatedly asked to choose between the interpretation which comforts him and the interpretation which is true. The choice is made difficult by the persuasiveness of local contexts, and it is particularly difficult in Book IX where the lure of Satan's scientism is joined to the appeal Eve has as a fellow creature who is, in effect, falling toward her judges. So that, provided with reasons of his own invention, as Eve is provided with Satan's reasons, the reader may decline to look beyond them for guidance, and, by excusing her, resolve to fall with her, not deceived. Concerning his obligations, the epic voice is silent, leaving him, in Arthur Barker's words, 'to decide, in terms of his response to the controlled mimetic movement, what is happening and is meant'.[1] He may possibly decide to look on her and not believe.

(iv) ADAM: WHAT SEEM'D REMEDILESS

The third figure in this triptych of wilful self-deception (the reader may escape this category) is, of course, Adam. The manœuvre by which he too chooses to close his eyes to the true significance of what he sees is on display in the interior soliloquy of lines 896–917 :

> O fairest of Creation, last and best
> Of all God's Works, Creature in whom excell'd
> Whatever can to sight or thought be form'd,
> Holy, divine, good, amiable, or sweet!
> How art thou lost, how on a sudden lost,

---

[1] 'Structural and Doctrinal Pattern in Milton's Later Poems', in *Essays in English Literature from the Renaissance to the Victorian Age Presented to A. S. P. Woodhouse*, ed. Millar Maclure and F. W. Watt (Toronto, 1964), p. 178.

Defac't, deflow'r'd, and now to Death devote?
Rather how hast thou yielded to transgress
The strict forbiddance, how to violate
The sacred Fruit forbidd'n! some cursed fraud
Of enemy hath beguil'd thee, yet unknown
And mee with thee hath ruin'd, for with thee
Certain my resolution is to Die;
How can I live without thee, how forgo
Thy sweet Converse and Love so dearly join'd,
To live again in these wild Woods forlorn?
Should God create another *Eve,* and I
Another Rib afford, yet loss of thee
Would never from my heart; no no, I feel
The Link of Nature draw me: Flesh of Flesh,
Bone of my Bone thou art, and from thy State
Mine never shall be parted, bliss or woe.

At first his participles ('Defac't, deflow'r'd') make Eve the
victim of an evil external to her; but Adam, who knows very
well what must have happened, immediately corrects the
distortion in his language with the word 'rather', and returns
the responsibility to her: 'how hast *thou* yielded'. Yet,
within three lines, Eve is again the object of the action
('beguil'd'), which ruins her and with her Adam, who enters
into a conspiracy with himself by pretending to believe in
his own linguistic sleight of hand. To protect himself from
pain he has conferred on the fact of disobedience a meaning
he will feel comfortable with: Eve does not sin, she is undone by 'some cursed fraud'. Presented with a fact too unpleasant to contemplate directly, but too large and insistent
to suppress, Adam finds a way to think about it without
truly confronting it, just as the reader does if he turns away
from the Fall to concentrate on its anticipations and finds
its cause in some past action or in Eve's flawed nature. In
both cases the mind confers on disobedience a meaning it
feels comfortable with — Eve, Adam decides, does not sin,

she is undone by 'some cursed fraud' — ignoring the meaning stipulated by God and so exalting itself above His Word. Once Adam has excused Eve by foisting her sin on the yet undiscovered Satan, he is free to educe additional 'reasons' for following her, all of them equally specious. The question, 'How can I live without thee?', is answered by Adam himself. He can live without her as he has before ('to live *again*'). As a serious query this cry has no more force than Eve's obviously rhetorical address to her flowers: 'from thee / How shall I part?' (xi. 281–2). His appropriation of Genesis is similarly irrelevant, an instance of the devil, or someone about to enter his service, quoting scripture. Nor is his action an expression of love, as Eve believes it to be when she cries 'O glorious trial of exceeding Love'. Eve is the victim of Adam's passion, for by choosing her he implicates her in his idolatry, absorbing her into a love that is self-love. 'To lose thee were to lose myself.' Even this is a distortion or an equivocation, for the self as a stable entity is lost as soon as it breaks union with God :

> The human integer . . . can maintain wholeness only by maintaining a common allegiance to the source of all integrity. In the fall men rebel as parts against unity and, in consequence, become isolated and antagonistic fragments.
>
> (R. M. Frye, *God, Man and Satan*, p. 56.)

What we see here is the construction by Adam of the 'Cycles' and 'Epicycles' of his 'frame' (viii. 83), the means by which he contrives to 'save the appearances' (viii. 82) of the lie he decides to believe in.

The epic voice's comment on Adam's resolution is muted but telling. Adam, he informs us, submitted 'to what seem'd remediless'. Submitting to what seems remediless is a blend of resignation and wilfulness, the colloquial equivalent of which is, 'as far as I can see, there is no way out'. Usually, however, 'as far as I can see' is an equivocation for 'I would rather not see further'. Adam looks on Eve, fills his mind with her and fashions a dilemma to accommodate his disinclination to take into account anything but the need he feels at the moment : Eve or God. In a God-centred universe this is obviously a false dilemma, since it divides a link of nature from the source and support of nature. When all values proceed from and are defined in terms of God, the assumption of a clash between any two of them (love and obedience) is possible only if the situation is considered from a point of view that excludes God, and a point of view delimiting alternatives to what is seen does exactly that. This is what 'submitting to what *seem'd* remediless' means : acquiescing in the appearance of remedilessness without questioning it or turning to someone who might see beyond it to remedies not yet discovered. Adam, no less than Eve, arrogates Godhead when he accepts the horizon of his own perspective as final. He, too, is an empiricist. The important word in the epic voice's summary phrase is 'seem'd', because it insists on the modesty of the claim being made. Like as far as *I* can see, 'what *seem'd* remediless' is a statement about the observer and not necessarily an accurate description of the situation ; one should not stake too much on it. The disposition of the heavens may correspond either to Copernican or Ptolemaic principles, or, more probably, Raphael implies, to neither. Earthly sight presumes by limiting possibilities to those immediately visible. What is required is a willingness to infer (illogically) the probable existence of a frame of reference other than that assumed in the formulation of the problem. If Adam is unable to conceive of an alternative to opposing courses of action which seem equally disastrous he should seek counsel from higher intelligences before committing himself to either of them. He does not because the insolubility of the dilemma, as his reason poses it to him, is attractive and useful.[1]

The circumstances of Adam's crisis establish a pattern which is repeated in *Samson Agonistes* and *Paradise Regained*. For seven hundred lines Samson 'labors his mind' (1298) in order to extricate himself from his slough of despond : 'Nor am I in the list of them that hope ; / Hopeless are all my evils, all *remediless*' (647–8, emphasis mine). His progress is at first slow and uneven and then dramatically swift when Harapha's taunt of 'Heav'n's desertion' draws a reaffirmation of faith :

> these evils I deserve and more,
> Acknowledge them from God inflicted on me
> Justly, yet despair not of his final pardon
> Whose ear is ever open ; and his eye
> Gracious to re-admit the suppliant ;
> In confidence whereof I once again
> Defy thee to the trial of mortal fight.   (1169–75)

As it is formulated here, Samson's new faith is part of a reflex response to the physical challenge Harapha represents. Will it survive the test of a more difficult situation, one Samson cannot meet with a boast or a threat? The answer comes with the Philistine messenger who presents the revived hero with a problem for which there is no ready solution, and, in the terms he first conceives of it, no solution at all. Matters are now, as the chorus points out, 'strain'd / Up to the height' (1348–9). Refusing the Philistine command may result in new orders and further humiliations ; going to the temple will involve him in a violation of Hebraic law, 'By prostituting holy things to idols ; / A *Nazarite* in place abominable' (1358–9). Samson's first instinct is to answer this challenge with the same peremptoriness he

---

[1] Cf. Mrs. Ferry, *Milton's Epic Voice*, p. 61.

has shown to Dalilah and Harapha : 'Can they think me so broken, so debas'd / With corporal servitude, that my mind ever / Will condescend to such absurd commands? / . . . I will not come' (1335–7, 1342). Here the matter might have rested had not the Chorus interposed itself to dispute with Samson the interpretation of the law :

> *Sams.* 'Vaunting my strength in honor to thir *Dagon*? . . .'
>
> *Chor.* 'Yet with this strength thou serv'st the *Philistines* . . .'
>
> *Sams.* 'Not in thir Idol-Worship, but by labor Honest . . .'
>
> *Chor.* 'Where the heart joins not, outward acts defile not . . .'
>
> *Sams.* 'Where outward force constrains, the sentence holds,
> But who constrains me to the Temple of Dagon?'

One feels the dialogue could go on forever and still be inconclusive, defining first outward acts, and then constraint, and then the conditions necessary to establish the existence of a state of constraint, and so on. As it is, the exercise leads Samson in a circle to his original position : 'If I obey them, / I do it freely ; venturing to displease / God for the fear of Man, and Man prefer / . . . which in his jealousy / Shall never, unrepented, find forgiveness' (1372–6). Apparently Samson remains locked in the rigidity of mind which has already borne fruit in the excessive over-justness and self-critical rigour of his despairing speeches (it is not for Samson to say what God will allow or when he will forgive). The discussion of the alternatives seemingly open to him has served only to sharpen the sense of dilemma.

And then, without preparation or logic, suddenly, Samson breaks free of the restrictions imposed by his own view of the matter to assert

> *Yet* that he *may* dispense with me or thee
> Present in Temples at Idolatrous Rites
> For some important cause, *thou needst not doubt.*
>
> (1377–9, emphasis mine)

This resolution does not follow or spring from the distinctions made in the preceding lines. It comes despite them, completely outside the limits of choice set by Samson and the Chorus and the law. 'Yet' means putting aside all we have said, and, along with 'may' it admits the existence of possibilities not presently available or even discoverable to the intellect. In short it admits the existence and omnipotence of God, complementing the intuition of the Chorus at line 309:

> Who made our Laws to bind us, not himself,
> And hath full right to exempt
> Whom so it pleases him by choice.

At this moment Samson joins the worthies of Hebrews xi, who take provisional actions (going out not knowing whither they go) in the name of a certain faith. Samson still does not know what will follow when he goes to the temple; what need not be doubted, however, is the power of God to do anything, through anyone, in any circumstance. And it is trust in that power rather than in the calculation of probabilities or knowledge of the law which is the motive force behind Samson's 'I with this Messenger will go along' (1384). This is the truly heroic moment in the play, as it could have been for Adam in *Paradise Lost*, when the spirit declares its independence of the terrestrial mould and of the *visibilia* which press in on it, looking homeward and moving forward, impelled by its own assurance of the goodness and graciousness of God.

In the second book of *Paradise Regained* Satan prepares a banquet for Christ and sets up a choice which is itself a trap. The meats, Satan explains, are not 'by the Law unclean' (327), therefore Jesus may eat of them. But in fact they are unclean. Michael Fixler explains the dilemma:

> ... the banquet which Satan offers was intended to lure Jesus into knowingly violating the Jewish dietary laws or into confessing

that he who came as the Messiah to abrogate the Mosaic
law could not eat because the same laws bound him to the
scrupulous observance of ritual purity.

(Milton and the Kingdoms of God, p. 256)

Christ eludes Satan by neither accepting nor rejecting the
food; instead he declares his independence of it and of the
problem Satan invents. 'With my hunger what hast thou to
do?' (389) Christ asks pointedly. He has already declared
his intention to put himself into the hands of the Father, to
trust in him for sustenance, physical and spiritual; and since
his hunger is not yet a source of real distress ('Without this
body's wasting, I content me, / And from the sting of Famine
fear no harm'), he need not risk even the appearance of
depending on someone else ('Mee hung'ring more to do my
Father's will'). Nor is he obliged to answer the riddle posed
by its status under the law. The action taken is, as Fixler
remarks, evasive, denying the claim of the situation as it
seems to be; it is an affirmation of faith and trust, and does
not reflect at all on the issues Satan tries to attach to it.

Later, Satan places Christ on the pinnacle of the temple,
hoping in this way to force Christ to reveal himself: either
he will fall and prove himself mere man ('for Honors,
Riches, Kingdoms, Glory / Have been before contemn'd,
and may again') or he will cast himself down in anticipation
of heavenly intervention and seem to claim his divinity
before the time God has appointed for its revelation. There
is a third possibility, one, however, which Satan does not
take seriously; 'to stand upright / Will ask thee skill'
(iv. 551–2). But Christ does stand, or as Barbara Lewalski
brilliantly says, he quietly maintains 'the position into which
he has been thrust by violence',[1] and *waits* for a sign of
God's will. Thus his standing is a perfect expression of

[1] 'Theme and Structure in *Paradise Regained*', *Studies in Philology*, lvii
(1960), 218.

resignation, of his willingness to forgo action until God calls him to action, of his faith, which dissolves the Gordian knot of Satan's riddle. As he continues to 'await the fulfilling' (II. 108) he does not know, any more than Samson knows, how the situation will resolve itself. But he knows that God knows, and this knowledge which is not knowledge through reason, but through faith, is his stay against the illusion, however compelling, of remedilessness.

What, then, ought Adam to have done? Any number of things, all of which, admittedly, would seem forced and 'unnatural' in comparison to what he does do. He might have said to Eve, 'what you say is persuasive (impregn'd with reason to my seeming), but I would rather not make such a momentous decision without further reflection.' Or, as Lewis suggested, he might have 'chastised Eve and then interceded with God on her behalf'.[1] The second course of action recommends itself particularly because it would accord with everything Adam knows about God. 'Whatever was to be risked', Irene Samuel explains, 'demanded only Adam's faith that the benevolence he had always known would remain benevolent . . . Eve was not irredeemably lost, as Adam at once concluded in his immediate assumption of a hostile universe.'[2] (Nor does this necessarily involve believing that God has lied when he promulgated his absolute decree, for it is not inconceivable that the Almighty should find a way both to fulfil justice and to show mercy.) Christ, continues Miss Samuel, offers himself as a sacrifice confidently, declaring 'I shall rise Victorious', not because he foreknows his resurrection, but because he trusts in 'the

[1] *A Preface to Paradise Lost*, p. 123.
[2] 'The Dialogue in Heaven: A Reconsideration of *Paradise Lost*, III, 1–417', *PMLA*, lxxii (1957), 601–11, reprinted in *Milton: Modern Essays in Criticism*, ed. Arthur E. Barker (New York, 1965), p. 243.

omnipotence and perfect benevolence of the Father'. 'Adam
... might, like the Son, have risked himself to redeem Eve.'[1]
Of course Adam does not know anything of Christ, but as an
analogue which argues for the 'possibility ... for every
being' of 'the trust that confronts and by confronting
changes',[2] the example of Christ is pertinent, as is the more
available example of the good angels, who stand their ground
although circumstances and appearances would seem to
dictate otherwise. This is surely the moral Adam draws
from Raphael's narrative : obedience founded on a base of
boundless trust which is proof against the evidence of sense
or reason. It is a moral he could have remembered and
acted on, and on that basis we must judge him.

To this Empson would reply, 'The poem somehow does
not encourage us to think of an alternative plan',[3] and Milton
would say in return : true, the poem does not encourage you
to think of an alternative plan, just as the situation (as it
seems to be) does not encourage Adam to think of an
alternative plan ; but I require you to think of one yourself,
drawing encouragement from an inner resource which pre-
vails against the claims of a dramatically persuasive moment,
even if the moment is one I have provided ; and God requires
the same of Adam. The inner resource is, of course, faith,
which is what remains to Adam and the reader (and to Eve)
when circumstances and their own intelligences misinform
them. Faith supplies the strength of will that enables us to
recall the simplicity and inclusiveness of the moral issue —
God or not God — in the face of the more immediate claims
of subordinate and, in some sense, illusory, issues. (A leap of
faith is always a refusal to accede to what, at the moment,
seems remediless.) Here is the ultimate 'responsive choice',
where the spiritual ideal, to which the reader's faculties
should be answerable, is absent, and must be supplied by his

[1] Ibid., p. 242.   [2] Ibid., p. 243.   [3] *Milton's God*, p. 189.

own sense of what is real and truly beautiful. Again the poet is silent, except for the mild and muted disapproval of 'fondly overcome with Female charm', leaving us 'to decide, in terms of [our] response to the controlled mimetic movement, what is happening and is meant'. With Adam we may decide to believe in the appearances which flatter our desires (choosing Adam, we choose ourselves, or at least our baser selves) or we may insist that he cling with us to the dazzling clarity of the divine word and see things truly. The relevance of our decision to Milton's great purpose can be seen in the fact that, while in the analogues (*Jerusalem Delivered* and *The Aeneid*) and in his other poems, we are asked to measure our response against that of the hero, in *Paradise Lost* we are asked to condemn the hero's response, and, moreover, to condemn it because, at the moment of crisis, he is too much like ourselves. John Peter says as much : 'only by inverting our own natures and values can we even begin to reproach him.'[1] But the inversion of our natures is exactly what the poem hopes to achieve by bringing us to put off the Old Adam — the body of sin, the conformity to the world, the inborn tendency to evil — and to put on the New. Here, in Book ix, looking in fact on the Old Adam and having to judge him, we are given that (interpretative) choice, and, as before, our response measures us.

This is the terminal point of the reader's education, the trial to which he will be adequate only if he has succeeded in recovering the vision Adam now proceeds to shatter. The specific act he is asked to perform is literary, simply the determination of meaning ; but by deciding, as he has had to decide before, exactly what the poem means, he decides between the philosophical and moral alternatives mirrored in the interpretative possibilities (Adam is right, Adam is wrong), and in this instance these possibilities embrace the

[1] *A Critique of Paradise Lost*, p. 131.

full range of contraries whose differentiation has been his concern in the body of the poem — true and false heroism, true love and love of self, freedom and licence, in sum, union with divinity and therefore with everything of value, or thraldom to the false values created by a distorting perspective. In short, if the reader has applied himself assiduously to the lessons the poem would teach him, and so effected the purging of his intellectual ray, the superficial appeal of Adam's gesture will be neutralized by his understanding of what it means — a transgression of the whole law and therefore of those obligations in whose name the sin is committed ; but if, on the other hand, he has been slack and inattentive, and so failed to penetrate 'far below the surface' to the truth Milton encloses in his knotty riddle, the Fall will appear to him in one or all of the guises discoverable to a still-unregenerate reason. Not that the poem is finally ambiguous, at least as a moral statement ; rather, its readers are ambiguous, and their ambiguities (crookednesses) are reflected in the interpretations they arrive at. There is, however, only one true interpretation of *Paradise Lost*, and it is the reward of those readers who have entered into the spirit of Milton's 'good temptation' and so 'become wiser by experience' : others 'sport in the shade' with half-truths and self-serving equivocations and end by accusing God or by writing volumes to expose the illogic of His ways.

(v) DEXT'ROUSLY THOU AIM'ST

While Adam and Eve fail us as models in Book ix, accepting the promptings of carnal reason before the law of God, after the Fall they do perform truly heroic actions. Left to his own devices when Christ re-ascends to join the Father,

Adam quickly falls into a variation of his original error and
laments a new remedilessness. Haunted by the anticipated
reproaches of his progeny ('Ill fare our Ancestor impure, /
For this we may thank *Adam*'), he implores God to blame
him only 'as the source and spring / Of all corruption'
(x. 832–3), but in the same moment realizes how 'fond' his
wish is : 'couldst thou support / That burden heavier than
the Earth to bear?' Once again he thinks himself trapped by
an insoluble problem :

> Thus what thou desir'st,
> And what thou fear'st, alike destroys all hope
> Of refuge, and *concludes* thee miserable . . .
> O Conscience, into what Abyss of fears
> And horrors hast thou driv'n me; *out of which*
> *I find no way*, from deep to deeper plung'd!
>
> (837–9, 842–4, emphasis mine)

The conclusion of misery, arrived at through a logical
analysis of his plight, is inescapable only if Adam ignores
the possibility, and on the basis of what he knows of God,
probability, of mercy. There is a way out, though it will not
be found in the abyss of despair or in the mazes of his
reason. It is finally Eve who points Adam in the right
direction (and by Eve we are to understand the Holy Spirit
working through her) by suing for *his* forgiveness when
there is no reason to believe he will grant it :

> Forsake me not thus, *Adam*, witness Heav'n
> What love sincere, and reverence in my heart
> I bear thee, and unweeting have offended,
> Unhappily deceiv'd; thy suppliant
> I beg, and clasp thy knees; bereave me not
> Whereon I live, thy gentle looks, thy aid.
>
> (x. 914–19)

The parallel to his own case with respect to God is too
obvious to go unnoticed. Eve has heard Adam's lament and

now hears his impassioned rejection of her: 'Out of my sight, thou Serpent . . . / . . . But for thee / I had persisted happy, had not thy pride / And wand'ring vanity, when least was safe, / Rejected my forewarning' (867, 873–6). This is no more than a continuation of the quarrel Adam and Eve initiate when they awaken from the drugged sleep of sin, a 'vain contest' of which it is said there 'appear'd no end'. But Eve breaks the cycle by gesturing beyond the contest to a reconciliation rooted not in justice or in adjudication, but merely in love. She asks for pardon even though she deserves none (does one ever deserve a pardon) and more importantly expects none. She denies nothing ('unweeting have offended') and appeals in the name of the dependency she had earlier rejected: 'forlorn of thee, / Whither shall I betake me?' (921–2). As a tactic this would seem calculated to draw a hostile response (i.e. you might have thought of that before); indeed the entire speech is strategically unsound, delivered to the wrong person at the worst possible time, when the desired end is least likely to be effected. In a similar situation, Dalilah makes essentially the same appeal ('Let weakness then with weakness come to parle') with disastrous results.

But this is not reasoned strategy, no more than a cry for help or a prayer is strategy. Eve's speech is occasioned by a genuine need and informed 'by a love sincere' (this distinguishes her from Dalilah) whose expression takes precedence over the reckoning of probable effects. As an action, Eve's speech is foolish, absurd, and technically in error (she cannot take the punishment on herself and is wrong to want to, 'too desirous, as before . . . who desir'st / The punishment all on thyself'), but its inappropriateness is one measure of its value. That is, what Eve does is important because she does it, 'not so repulsed' by Adam's professed enmity. Like the faithful, Eve 'against hope believed in hope' (Romans

iv. 18) and moves forward, blindly, haltingly and finally, as God would have it, effectively.[1] The merit of this speech and the one that follows it does not reside in their literal content; in rapid succession Eve counsels abstinence and suicide as means of avoiding the consequences of her sin; yet even in 'vehement despair' her words are acceptable, because mistaken as they are, they are the product of remorse and contrition. (Eve's despair is not so reprehensible as Adam's which proceeds from a conviction of eternal misery and is thus a mortal sin: 'Despair is a mortal sin when it arises from distrust of God's goodness and fidelity; venial when due to melancholy or to fear of one's own weakness.' The latter is clearly Eve's case.) It would be too much to expect Eve to be *right*; she herself assumes quite the opposite: '*Adam*, by sad experiment I know / How little weight my words with thee can find, / Found so erroneous.' '*Nevertheless*', '*hopeful*' (the words are hers), she hides not her thoughts, but offers them tentatively, trusting in a reality larger than her mind, one which can accommodate her probable errors and make of them something good. Eve is looking outside herself beyond what her reason tells her is possible and soon Adam is doing the same, also tentatively, certain only of the power and benevolence of a deity who can find remedies where there appear to be none: 'As the feasibility of Eve's attempt at Adam's redemption did not matter, so now the actual speech of Adam and Eve does not matter: only the position, the attitude, the state of the heart are important.'[2] Thus Adam abandons his own negativity and begins to search for a way out of the abyss that had become his living tomb. Eve's remedies are rejected because they would eliminate occasions for grace: 'No more be mention'd then of violence / Against ourselves, and wilful

---

[1] That is, the effectiveness is God's. See Chapter 1, p. 18.
[2] Summers, *The Muse's Method*, pp. 183–4.

barrenness, / That cuts us off from *hope*' (1041–3, emphasis mine). With no more information than he had earlier, Adam now 'conjectures' as to the true identity of the serpent ('our grand Foe / *Satan*, who in the Serpent') and with Eve begins to seek 'Some safer resolution'. What has changed is his orientation and with this change old facts and impossible dilemmas rearrange themselves into new patterns of hope. Adam sees with the eyes of faith and at once the visible world is transfigured; the 'assumption of a hostile universe' is replaced by its exact opposite and all things (situations are also things) are interpreted as opportunities for the granting of grace, instances of God's benevolence at work in the world. Adam's regeneration, the creation afresh, 'as it were' of 'the inward man', of 'a new creature'[1] is complete when he declares of God: 'Undoubtedly he will relent' (1093) and comes full circle from the conviction of remedilessness. Relenting is God's prerogative and his inclination, not man's desert; yet Adam's 'undoubtedly' is not presumption or even prophecy, but an expression of his faith in God's infinite mercy (like Samson's 'I with this Messenger will go along' and Christ's standing). ' "Faith is the substance of things hoped for," ' writes Milton in the *Christian Doctrine*, 'where by "substance" is understood as certain a persuasion of things hoped for, as if they were not only existing, but actually present.'[2] True faith sees the objects of hope and believes them ours; true faith places Lycidas in Heaven on the sole authority of God's promise, 'that whosoever believeth in him should not perish, but have eternal life'; true faith would have entrusted Eve willingly and confidently to God; true faith hopes against hope and affirms against reason and leads one to say 'undoubtedly'.

In the first part of Book xi Adam grows in faith: he recognizes the literal improbability of God's concern (what

---

[1] *The Works of John Milton*, xv. 367.   [2] Ibid., pp. 395, 397.

is man that thou art mindful of him?) but is *persuaded*, nevertheless, that his prayers have been heard favourably :

> that from us aught should ascend to Heav'n
> So prevalent as to concern the mind
> Of God high-blest, or to incline his will,
> *Hard to belief may seem; yet* this will prayer . . .
>
> (143–6, emphasis mine)

A sequence like 'hard to belief may seem, yet' contains all the linguistic signs of faith, the independence of belief from what seems logical and from appearances ('may seem'), and the willingness to break out of the visibly relevant to another level of discourse ('yet'). Again Adam operates largely on a conviction of God's placability and mildness and this certainty allows him to conjecture concerning matters less certain : '*persuasion* in me grew / That I was heard . . . / . . . *Assures* me that the bitterness of death / Is past, and we shall live' (152–3, 157–8, emphasis mine).

Adam continues to interpret the 'mute signs in Nature' correctly, concluding from the flight of beasts and fowl and from the sudden eclipse that 'some furder change awaits us nigh' (193). The epic voice comments approvingly, 'He err'd not', a statement which is increasingly ironic in retrospect since from this moment on Adam errs in every respect possible, slipping by degrees, as fallen man always does, into his old ways. First, he laments his exile from the presence of God and is reminded, benignly, by Michael, not to confine the deity in the spatial limitations which apply to man : '*Adam*, thou know'st Heav'n his, and all the Earth, / Not this Rock only . . . / . . . surmise not then / His presence to these narrow bounds confin'd' (335–6, 340–1). 'Surmise not then' is equivalent to 'appoint not heavenly disposition' ; the bounds Adam would set on God correspond to the area his own consciousness is aware of. In the course of his conversations with Michael, Adam will repeatedly appoint heavenly disposition until he has once again fallen into an 'Abyss of fears' out of which he can find no way. Repeatedly he draws the wrong conclusions from what he sees because he relies too much on what he sees. Thus the sight of Cain slaying Abel draws this question : 'have I now *seen* Death?' (462, emphasis mine). Many shapes has death, replies Michael, who might have added that incorporeal beings are only imperfectly known through their physical manifestations. The point is a small one, but the same way of thinking can be dangerous if it is extended into the sphere of moral decision. When Adam is shown some of the miseries life holds for his children, he turns stoic with alacrity : 'Henceforth I fly not Death, nor would prolong / Life much, bent rather how I may be quit / Fairest and easiest of this cumbrous charge' (547–9). Adam conceives of his options too narrowly ('Nor love thy Life, nor hate') because he conceives of his obligations as merely terrestrial. Mortality is not a self-contained (rhetorical, rational) experience to be met with an easy formula or a morality whose end is comfort ('fairest and easiest') ; it is, rather, the medium within which man attests to his commitment to God, and every action taken must be taken in the name of that commitment. By limiting his choice to a short and quiet life or a long and uncomfortable one, Adam ignores the possibility of living for God, which is what Michael counsels when he advises 'what thou liv'st / Live well' (553–4).

The same turn of mind characterizes Adam's attitude towards history which becomes a series of isolated events, existing independently of each other and emptied of all significance beyond the physically immediate. Inevitably, his emotional state varies with each new appearance, since no single vision unites them for him ; and his response to these appearances is consistently unfortunate. In the begetting of the race of giants he finds joy and hope : 'True opener of mine eyes, prime Angel blest, / Much better seems this Vision, and more hope / . . . Here Nature seems fulfill'd in all her ends' (598–9, 602). Not so, corrects Michael; the ends of nature have nothing to do with what you see here, since nature begins and ends in the divine : *Judge not* what is best / By pleasure, *though* to Nature *seeming* meet, / Created, as thou art, to nobler end / Holy and pure, conformity divine' (603–6). The eyes Adam thinks open are the eyes of the flesh ; he has lost the interior illumination which had brought him to 'humiliation meek' at the close of Book x. From hope and joy his tendency to overreaction brings him full cycle to despair and a new complaint. The evidence of visions seen leads him to assume the end of mankind. How could there *possibly* be a future for the race when so few have survived the flood ? The 'undoubtedly' of faith now becomes the assurance of disaster and the universe is once again hostile : 'Man is not whom to warn ; those few escap't / Famine and anguish will at last consume / Wand'ring that wat'ry Desert' (777–9). Adam is now not to be distinguished from Sarah, who as 'the type of carnal reason, laughed at the promise, conceiving it impossible in reason that she should have a child'.[1] He goes so far as to place himself in the list of those who no longer hope : 'I had hope / . . . peace would have crown'd / With length of happy days the race of man ; / But I was far deceiv'd' (779, 781–3). If Adam is deceived it is not by hope, but by the deductive (carnal) reasoning he substitutes for hope. 'Hard to belief' may seem the salvation of the few against such odds ; but to true belief, which asserts independently of the probable and even of the possible, nothing is too hard, since nothing is too hard for the Lord.[2]

---

[1] John Webster, *The Examination of Academies*, p. 17.

[2] In the opening lines of Book xi, Adam and Eve are compared to Deucalion and Pyrrha, who against reason obey an apparently absurd command and thereby effect the restoration of mankind. For a discussion of another use of

Once again Adam is in danger of losing sight of this truth because of the illusion of remedilessness. Noah and his sons do, of course, reach dry land, and Adam sees them, and above them a rainbow, and for the first time his response is true to the situation as it is *sub specie aeternitatis* :

> over his head beholds
> A dewy Cloud, and in the Cloud a Bow
> Conspicuous with three listed colors gay,
> Betok'ning peace from God, and Cov'nant new.
> Whereat the heart of *Adam* erst so sad
> Greatly rejoic'd, and thus his joy broke forth.
>   O thou who future things canst represent
> As present, Heav'nly instructor, I revive
> At this *last sight*, *assur'd* that Man shall live.
>
>   (864–72)

Adam's breaking forth of joy can hardly be the result only of the 'sight' before him. Noah may be saved, but what of those who have perished amidst the destruction of an entire world, and those who may perish if new floods pour down? Louis Martz, for one, 'finds it hard to share in Adam's joy at the ending of the Flood', for 'in the circumstances the cry may well strike the reader as the unfatherly utterance of a rigorous doctrinaire.'[1] The point is that Adam now reads the world and everything in it as an expression of God's goodness, that is figuratively; and the reader must now measure his own response against that of his first parent's, the reverse of his obligation in Book ix. Adam's joy, like the joy of the good angels who welcome the appearance of Christ in Book vi, is inexplicable only to those who are still in bondage to the evidence of things seen. Life as fallen man knows it is filled with facts — disease, war, pain, death —

this mythological parallel as an illustration of faith operating in the world see my *John Skelton's Poetry* (Yale, 1965), pp. 161–2.
   [1] *The Paradise Within* (New Haven, 1964), p. 154.

which on their face are irreconcilable with the idea of a God who is love. The problem is directly analogous to the problem of interpreting scripture in those places where the literal meaning appears to be blasphemous or conducive to cupidity. Such locutions, counsels Augustine 'should be subjected to diligent scrutiny until an interpretation contributing to the reign of charity is produced'. The words of scripture are the signs of God, invested with his meaning which is available to those who are willing to search for it; the phenomena of experience are his signs also, the words of the book that is his universe and they too must be diligently scrutinized before their true meaning emerges, lest the observer become 'subjected to the flesh in pursuit of the letter', taking 'figurative expressions as though they were literal . . . a miserable servitude of the spirit . . . so that one is not able to raise the eye of the mind above things that are corporal and created to drink in eternal light.'[1] To Adam, who knows nothing yet of covenants ('Whereat' in line 868 refers to the dewy cloud, not to 'Cov'nant new' in 867; another trap for the careless reader), the rainbow might have signified any number of things, if he had sought its meaning on the surface or made it the reflection of his own small faith. (The binding of the watery cloud could be a silent threat.) Instead, he *chooses* — there is no other word for it — to see in it the signification a merciful God must have intended :

> But say, what mean those color'd streaks in Heav'n,
> Distended as the Brow of God appeas'd,
> Or serve they as a flow'ry verge to bind
> The fluid skirts of that same wat'ry Cloud,
> Lest it again dissolve and show'r the Earth?

(879–83)

---

[1] *On Christian Doctrine*, trans. and ed. D. W. Robertson, Jr. (New York, 1958), p. 84.

Adam hazards a guess, but it is an informed guess, informed
by a conviction of a fortunate universe benevolently ruled,
a conviction which springs quite illogically (it is literally
a leap of faith) from a context of violence and punishment:
'I revive / At this last sight, assur'd that Man shall live.'
It is the sight transfigured by his faith, affirming against
reason, which assures him. And Michael approves his new
way of seeing, as one approves an archer who, suddenly, after
long trial and many misses, finds the mark : Dext'rously thou
aim'st. (884). Later, when the angel reports on the progress
of Abraham's journey from Ur, he says, 'I see him, but thou
canst not, with what Faith', and in context, 'with what Faith'
refers simultaneously to Abraham who moves with faith
(not knowing whither he went) and to Adam who sees with
faith (not seeing).

The final word on reason and rationalizations as they are
related to the 'contemplation of eternal things' is quite
properly Adam's in the lament of x. 720–844. Here all the
will-o'-the-wisps the mind has pursued through ten books
are collected and judged. Adam poses directly the questions
we may have only half formulated. Does he deserve his
punishment? Can God be justified? What is the cause of
the Fall? And the answers are familiar because they have
at times been ours :

> Did I request thee, Maker, from my Clay
> To mould me Man, did I solicit thee
> From darkness to promote me, or here place
> In this delicious Garden? as my Will
> Concurr'd not to my being, it were but right
> And equal to reduce me to my dust,
> Desirous to resign, and render back
> All I receiv'd, unable to perform
> Thy terms too hard by which I was to hold

> The good I sought not. To the loss of that,
> Sufficient penalty, why hast thou added
> The sense of endless woes? inexplicable
> Thy Justice seems.
>
> (743-55)

In other words, why was I born, a cry each of us has echoed when the burden of living seems too heavy. The accompanying accusations, half angry, half defensive — it isn't fair ('Thy terms too hard'), I couldn't help it ('unable to perform') — are Adam's version of the argument from necessity, to which every reader has at least partially assented despite its manifest absurdity. And the conclusion (in the formal sense) — 'inexplicable / Thy justice seems' — mocks the promise of that early statement of intention : 'and justify the ways of God to men'. Have we come this far only to hear a confirmation of our darkest suspicions?

Adam, however, is still not deceived or self-deceiving; he easily disposes of his own arguments : 'yet to say truth' the terms were understood and accepted : 'too late / I thus contest' ; besides, the creature can hardly be a party to his own creation : 'God made thee of choice his own, and of his own / To serve him, thy reward was of his grace, / Thy punishment then justly is at his Will. / Be it so, for I submit, his doom is fair' (766-9). Thus far has his reason brought him, to a conviction of his own guilt which can no longer be in doubt when the defendant himself admits it. The search for cause ends here, discredited by Adam's terse and unequivocal 'his doom is fair', a conclusion he reaches in only twenty-five lines although most readers conscientiously avoid it for nine and one half books. That problem solved, however, merely raises another : 'Ah, why should all mankind / For one man's fault thus guiltless be condemn'd / If Guiltless?' (822-4). There is a tendency to place the question-mark after 'condemn'd' with the end of the line, but Adam's 'If guilt-

less' questions his question and shows that he is already
preparing an answer to it : 'But from me what can proceed, /
But all corrupt, both Mind and Will deprav'd / . . . how can
they then acquitted stand / In sight of God? Him after all
Disputes / Forc't I absolve' (824–5, 827–9). Again reason
is triumphant, but in the ambiguity of 'Forc't' — have his
reasonings forced him to absolve God or were his doubts the
results of forced (strained) reasoning — one hears Adam's
awareness of how meaningless his success is :

> all my evasions vain
> And reasonings, though through Mazes, lead me still
> But to my own conviction.
>
>   (829–31)

Reasonings and evasions are carefully distinguished : the
fancy (wishful thinking) begets evasions on itself which are
then scrutinized and rejected by the reason (the sequence is
one the reader knows well from his experience of the poem).
One cannot fault the workings of the mind — the Mazes
have been negotiated — but the process is hopelessly
circular, and it leaves Adam where he began, 'To sorrow
abandon'd' :

> O Conscience, into what Abyss of fears
> And horrors hast thou driv'n me; out of which
> I find no way.
>
>   (842–4)

The way out is there, but not through reason, which conspires, like rhetoric, to prevent the mind from looking beyond
the artificial coherence of a limited system. What is required
is 'the faith of *Abraham*', not the reasonings of Sarah, 'a
simple and naked believing and relying upon the bare and
sole word of the Lord, though reason & mans wisdom can

see no way how possibly it can come to pass . . . for reason is a monster, and the very root and ground of all infidelity ; *for the carnal mind is enmity against God, and is not subject to the law of God.*[1] Imprisoned in the mazes of his rational intellect, Adam can only await the redeeming inappositeness of Eve's unthinking gesture.

[1] Webster, op. cit., p. 17.

7 So God with Man Unites

The works of Milton cannot be comprehended
or enjoyed unless the mind of the reader co-
operate with that of the writer. . . . He strikes
the Keynote, and expects his hearers to make
out the melody.

MACAULAY

(i) NOT SO MUCH AN INTANGLING AS A TEACHING

With Adam's lament the reader enters into the last phase of his relationship with the poem. No longer a participant, he is here returned to the more conventional role of spectator, concerned, but detached. It is Adam who must now adjust to circumstances of which he has had no prior knowledge, and his struggles with difficulties (physical and intellectual) the reader has already encountered, in life and in the poem, are interesting and significant, but not unexpected. One can almost feel comfortable with his distress because it is familiar as innocence never was. In some ways the poem demands less of the reader here than it has before, and this continues to be true in the final books where he is asked to provide traditional interpretations for a succession of biblio-historical tableaux. Few new revelations await him in these books ; instead, the series of *exempla* offers a restatement, in a manner frankly didactic, of the lessons he has proven on his pulse in the body of the poem. So that, paradoxically, the narrative is felt less personally and immediately as it expands to include the events of fallen human history. At the same time, however, a different kind of vigilance must be exercised, less *self*-conscious, but conscious nevertheless : with

the addition of the historical perspective, which also includes
or is absorbed into the eschatological perspective, new levels
of reference are created to which everything must now be
referred. Thus Adam's education, the nominal subject of xi
and xii, is to be read simultaneously as an extension of his
personal story, as an image of the racial experience, and as a
conveniently concise summary of what the poem has taught
diffusely. His failures parallel our own at every point and his
successes recreate the process by which we as readers have
attained the unity of vision he must now regain; at the end
of Book xii, as Richardson saw, he is brought 'into the
Condition in Which We Are, on *Even Ground* with Us'.[1]
The chronicle of human backslidings, relieved only by the
sporadic appearance of a single Nazarite, is on its surface a
linear progression of events which occur in time; but it is
also decidedly cyclical, a depressing testimony to the persistence of sin and corruption ('sinful man') even in the face
of a benevolent deity ('supernal grace') and thus a corrobora-
tion in history of the doctrine of natural depravity; the
reader sees the weaknesses he has acknowledged in himself
writ large in the calendar of nations. In addition, the
chronicle is an extended argument for the necessity of the
intervention of Christ, the last of the only righteous in a
world perverse, the substance of whom the others are but a
shadowy promise. At each point in the narrative, the reader
must keep separate these multiple significances and yet look
forward to their ultimate unity in the person of Christ (this
has always been his duty). Obviously this involves considerable effort of intellect and will, but the effort is well rewarded
when Michael's relentlessly low-keyed presentation takes
on the resonance and power of its anticipations. Then the
personal drama of Adam's regeneration, the national drama
of God's chosen people, and the final drama of the unfolding

[1] *Explanatory Notes on Paradise Lost*, p. 535.

gospel, merge for the reader in a poetic intuition of oneness which is beyond poetry and outside time.

   Much of what is usually thought to be unsatisfactory in Books xi and xii results from the substitution of Adam for the reader in the dialectic of trial and error which is the basis of Milton's method. There is still to be sure a drama of the mind, but it is Adam's, and the reader stands in relation to him as an advanced pupil to a novice. The pedagogical aspect of the situation is formalized and objectified to a degree we have not seen before. Michael assumes the duties of the epic voice, but with a difference. He is given a physical classroom which is its own image, a hill of learning from whose summit the instructor can literally point to the material to be studied. More important, his function as a teacher (Adam gives him that title at xi, line 450) both defines and limits him. Unlike the epic voice, that great amphibian whose personal involvement complicates and enriches the discharging of his public obligation, the angel's individual presence is hardly felt. His performance is controlled by the divine command : 'Dismiss them not disconsolate; reveal / To *Adam* what shall come in future days, / As I shall thee enlighten, intermix / My Cov'nant in the woman's seed renew'd ; / So send them forth, though sorrowing, yet in peace' (xi. 113–17); and his tone ranges from mild reproof to still milder approval. His methods are more forthright than those of Milton's *persona*; in place of the indirect rebuke, the delayed verb or adverb appearing diffidently, almost impersonally, to correct an impression too easily acquiesced in, Michael delivers formal admonitions sententiously : 'Nor love thy Life, nor hate', 'From Man's effeminate slackness it begins', and in another vein, but with the same patiently detached condescension, 'Dext'rously thou aim'st'. And instead of disappointing the expectations

he has aroused, the angel remains faithful to his announced
syllabus :

> that thou may'st believe, and be confirm'd,
> Ere thou from hence depart, know I am sent
> To show thee what shall come in future days
> To thee and to thy Offspring; good with bad
> Expect to hear, supernal Grace contending
> With sinfulness of Men; thereby to learn
> True patience, and to temper joy with fear
> And pious sorrow, equally inur'd
> By moderation either state to bear,
> Prosperous or adverse.
>
> (XI. 355–64)

This is the straightforward declaration of purpose and
method ('thereby' is Michael's shorthand for 'as a result of
your reacting to and reflecting on') Milton might have
offered earlier were it not for the advantage he discerned in
equivocation and surprise. 'That thou may'st believe and be
confirm'd' would have been a more honest — literal is the
better word — *propositio* than 'justify the ways of God to
men', just as 'supernal Grace contending / With sinfulness
of Men' is more truly descriptive of what the reader should
expect to hear than 'Of Man's First Disobedience'. Of man's
first disobedience we learn, finally, very little, except for the
fact itself, undeniably there, but inexplicable ; of the sinfulness of men as a consequence of that disobedience we learn
a great deal, especially when the sinful men are ourselves,
contending with or at least resisting the guidance and
counsel of supernal grace in the person of the inspired epic
voice. The true patience Adam will acquire, the quiet,
unemotional (because it is beyond emotion) confidence which
is sustained by nothing visible but by a promise, is exactly
the patience we as readers have become inured to, as first
one and then another of the supports held out to us in the

world of 'things which do appear' is taken away. And the moderation Adam will be taught to practise is the Christian virtue of fortitude as it has been exemplified for us in the loyal angels' indifference to all ('Prosperous or adverse') but the will of God.[1]

There is again a difference. Adam is not erratic and unreliable as we tend to be. His mistakes, once corrected, are not repeated whenever slightly altered circumstances make their repetition possible. His progress is regular and measurable, marked by the experiencing of insights which do not desert him under pressure. Once he has guessed at the significance of the rainbow, he ceases to be the captive of the appearances which temporarily dominate his field of vision. Henceforth he abhors 'justly' (xii. 79), discerns 'with . . . joy' (xii. 372), and understands clearly (xii. 376).[2] A great deal has been made of Michael's decision to alter the manner of his narration : 'Much thou hast yet to see, but I perceive / Thy mortal sight to fail . . . / Henceforth what is to come I will relate' (xii. 8–9, 11). The explanation is simply that it is no longer necessary to expose Adam to the misleading evidence of things seen. If his mortal sight now fails, it has been replaced, in the course of the conditioning process he undergoes in Book xi, by the interior illumination the epic voice prays for in the invocation to Book iii. Significantly, Michael retains the verb : 'Much thou hast yet to *see*', although you are unable to see. A favourite Miltonic metaphor is made physical as it will be again in *Samson Agonistes*. The present circumstances do not allow

---

[1] For a discussion of fortitude as the virtue which 'strengthens one against both prosperity and adversity', see William O. Harris, *Skelton's Magnyfycence and the Cardinal Virtue Tradition* (Chapel Hill, 1965), pp. 71–126.

[2] Not that Adam's performance is letter perfect in Book xii. As H. R. Mac-Callum points out, he still tends 'to overleap the mark' (*Milton and Sacred History*, p. 164). But the problem is simply to extend the insight he has achieved at the end of xi into all levels of action and thought.

the explicitness of the gloss provided by the Semi-chorus in its comment on Samson's triumph — 'he though blind of sight, / ... With inward eyes illuminated' — but the situations are spiritually analogous. (Later Adam himself will proclaim, 'now first I find / Mine eyes true op'ning'.)[1] The division of the original tenth book into the eleventh and twelfth is meant to call the reader's attention to this turning point in Adam's education (renovation) which proceeds so much more rapidly than his own. Within thirteen hundred lines of Michael's benign reproof — 'surmise not then / His presence to these narrow bounds confin'd' — Adam has advanced sufficiently to be able to deliver a speech praised by the angel as 'the sum of wisdom':

> Henceforth I learn, that to obey is best
> And love with fear the only God, to walk
> As in his presence, ever to observe
> His providence, and on him sole depend.
>
> (XII. 561–4)

'To obey is best'. 'And on him sole depend'. The reader will have remarked on the unity of the universe as Milton sees it and as he tries to make his readers see it: each attempt to locate a virtue ends in the person of God, the source of all virtue; any action which seems worthy is shown to have been initiated by God or for the sake of his glory; all truly meritorious actions are merely expressions of obedience to God; all poetic styles strain toward a wordless (styleless) genuflection to God. It is, in a sense, *easy* to say with Herbert and with others who have understood this, 'Thy will be done'; but the gesture is one many readers find impossible to make, even after twelve books written to convince them of its wisdom. Adam is truly wise.

[1] See Barbara Lewalski, 'Structure and Symbolism in Michael's Prophecy', *Philological Quarterly*, xlii (1963), 30–31.

In essence, then, this extended scene gives us the poem again, but without the irregular movement and exquisite shading which make reading it so much like living it. In stylistic terms it is the difference between the representation of experience as it rushes upon the perceiving mind and the subsequent arrangement of it into easily graspable patterns. Adam's education is not only formal, it is schematic, following closely the process of regeneration as Milton outlines it in *The Christian Doctrine* : renewed in spirit (as Adam and Eve are renewed when Prevenient Grace removes the stony from their hearts), sinful man repents of the sins he now detests and turns humbly to God (as Adam submits himself humbly to Michael's instruction), believing on the promise of salvation and eternal life (as Adam will believe when he descends from the mount of speculation). The reader is expected to recognize the stages of his growth and to relate them to his own spiritual history :

> ... 'tis Delightful to see how Finely *Milton* observes all the Growth of the New Man. Creation was all at Once, Regeneration is like the Natural Progression, we are Babes, and come by Degrees to be Strong Men in *Christ*.[1]

Negatively viewed, this stylized formality has been seen as evidence of a 'decline in poetic power', but one should understand that the regularity and predictability of the pattern allow the reader to use it as a framework within which he gathers together and orders the disparate intuitions he has brought with him from the earlier books.

Let us examine, by way of illustration, one of the episodes in Book xi, keeping in mind the two audiences (Adam and the reader) who are continually responding to its stimuli. Adam is shown the courtship and marriage rites of the sons

---

[1] Richardson, *Explanatory Notes*, p. 484. See also the note to xii. 270: 'Regeneration goes On, the New Man is Strengthened More and more' (516).

of Seth and the daughters of Cain, a union which results in the race of giants who perish in the flood. In his enthusiasm, he confuses sensual delight with true happiness, and hears Michael reply swiftly, 'Judge not what is best / By pleasure' (603–4). The sequence is familiar — the untutored response to a fair-appearing good which is immediately corrected by an authoritative voice. But here the reader is allowed to stand outside the centre of the temptation where he is able to predict its development and draw the moral long before Michael speaks ; in this way he is protected from errors he would have surely fallen into earlier. As before, some lines are delicately balanced between the innocence isolation lends them and the taint they acquire retroactively when the context is fuller :

> Such happy interview and fair event
> Of love and youth not lost, Songs, Garlands, Flow'rs,
> And charming Symphonies attach'd the heart
> Of Adam, soon inclin'd to admit delight
> The bent of Nature.
>
> (593–7)

Until the ambiguity of 'charming' (either attractive or spellbinding) this could surely be a catalogue of 'unreproved pleasures free'. Even 'The bent of Nature' is a sinister phrase only if the adjective 'fallen' is silently added to it. There is no danger, however, for the reader because the scene is disarmed of its surface allure before these innocent seeming lines can exercise their potentially seductive effect :

> They on the Plain
> Long had not walkt, when from the Tents behold
> A Bevy of fair Women, richly gay
> In Gems and wanton dress; to the Harp they sung
> Soft amorous Ditties, and in dance came on:
> The Men though grave, ey'd them, and let thir eyes
> Rove without rein, till in the amorous Net

> Fast caught, they lik'd, and each his liking chose;
> And now of love they treat till th' Ev'ning Star
> Love's Harbinger appear'd; then all in heat
> They light the Nuptial Torch, and bid invoke
> *Hymen*, then first to marriage Rites invok't.
>
> (580–91)

The women approach 'richly gay'; alone either modifier would be disturbing; together they are accusing, especially in connection with the following half line, 'In Gems and *wanton* dress'. The men greet them with glances rather than words: 'The men though grave, ey'd them, and let thir eyes / Rove without rein'. The eye is traditionally the entry place for the arrow of lust: 'For all that is in the world, the lust of the flesh and the lust of the eyes, and the pride of life is not of the Father' (1 John ii. 16). By giving themselves to their own cupidity, they weave a net and fall victims to it: 'till in the amorous Net / Fast caught' ('Let the wicked fall into their own Nets'. Psalm 141) as Adam does when he applauds their actions. Of course Adam sees the vision directly, without the intervening (and corrective) screen of Milton's weighted vocabulary. One can only guess at what he would substitute for 'richly gay' or 'wanton'. Certainly he would not use the words 'in heat' to describe the joys of the nuptial ceremonies. Adam's heart here is attached by the sense of touch whose pleasures Raphael had reminded him are 'the same voutsaf't / To Cattle and . . . beast' and are also the same he has succumbed to, in heat, only yesterday: 'Carnal desire *inflaming* hee on *Eve* / Began to cast lascivious eyes, she him / As wantonly repaid; in *Lust* they *burn*.' These allusions to the scriptures and to previous moments in the poem are not recondite; every reader will be aware of most of them and come to Adam's 'True opener of mine eyes' in full control of the irony Milton intends.

Any superiority we enjoy in respect to Adam is, of course,

accidental, the result of having been granted information deliberately withheld from him. This too is deliberate, less a reward or a privilege than a way of assuring that our attention is not distracted by considerations which are now secondary. The direct involvement of the reader in the experience of a problem is no longer the function of the verse. Truths apprehended in the excitement and insularity of self-discovery are now to be extended in application to include larger units of being until the entire universe becomes a receptacle for them, as it is from the vantage point of eternity. To this end, the reader must have both the time and the leisure to make the kind of connections I describe in the preceding paragraphs. To keep him in suspense would be beside the point, much like reading the *Book of Job* without the introductory scene and thus without the advantage of knowing whether or not Job is, after all, righteous; one would simply worry about the wrong things. The impact of the scene depends on our being distanced from it, and the stylistic virtues of another book would be liabilities here.

The reverse also is true: taken by itself, Michael's *moralitas* is 'bad poetry', dull, overlong, and unnecessary since it has been anticipated and discounted even before Adam speaks.

> Those Tents thou saw'st so pleasant, were the Tents
> Of wickedness, wherein shall dwell his Race
> Who slew his Brother; studious they appear
> Of Arts that polish Life, Inventors rare,
> Unmindful of thir Maker, . . .
> . . . that fair female Troop thou saw'st, that seem'd
> Of Goddesses, so blithe, so smooth, so gay, . . .
> Bred only and completed to the taste
> Of lustful appetence, to sing, to dance,
> To dress, and troll the Tongue, and roll the Eye.
> To these that sober Race of Men, whose lives

> Religious titl'd them the Sons of God,
> Shall yield up all thir virtue.
>
> (607–11, 614–15, 618–23)

Yet these 'faults' are positive assets because we are freed by them from our obligation to the immediate context and allowed instead to concentrate on the associations it recalls for us, associations which take their place in a pattern that has already begun to emerge. Adam is no doubt surprised to learn that the 'Inventors rare' whose art he has admired, are, in truth, atheists, 'Unmindful of thir Maker' (611); but for the reader, this information merely confirms an identification he makes tentatively when the scene is introduced :

> He look'd and saw a spacious Plain . . .
> . . .   whence the sound
> Of Instruments that made melodious chime
> Was heard, of Harp and Organ; and who mov'd
> Thir stops and chords was seen; his volant touch
> Instinct through all proportions low and high
> Fled and pursu'd transverse the resonant fugue.
> In other part stood one who at the Forge
> Laboring, two massy clods of Iron and Brass
> Had melted (whether found where casual fire
> Had wasted woods on Mountain or in Vale,
> Down to the veins of Earth, thence gliding hot
> To some Cave's mouth, or whether washt by stream
> From underground); the liquid Ore he drain'd
> Into fit moulds prepar'd; from which he form'd
> First his own Tools; then what might else be wrought
> Fusile or grav'n in metal.
>
> (556, 558–73)

These lines reproduce almost all of the details found in the description of the building of Pandemonium:

> Nigh on the Plain in many cells prepar'd
> That underneath had veins of liquid fire
> Sluic'd from the Lake, a second multitude

With wondrous Art founded the massy Ore,
Severing each kind, and scumm'd the Bullion dross:
A third as soon had form'd within the ground
A various mould, and from the boiling cells
By strange conveyance fill'd each hollow nook;
As in an Organ from one blast of wind
To many a row of Pipes the sound board breathes.
Anon out of the earth a Fabric huge
Rose like an Exhalation, with the sound
Of Dulcet Symphonies and voices sweet,
Built like a Temple.

(1. 700–13)

The correspondences are not exact. The organ metaphor of
the earlier passage is made literal in Book xi where fugues
are built instead of temples, but with the same impiety. The
accompanying symphonies in Book i are the charming
symphonies which attach Adam's heart. Generally, the
impression is of a slightly blurred echo in which phrases are
disjointed and then reassembled in new but related groupings. Thus the 'massy ore' founded from 'liquid fire' is
poured by Mulciber's workers into 'A various mould' while
the sons of Lamech drain 'liquid ore' which is 'gliding hot'
into 'fit moulds prepar'd'; both processes begin in the earth,
proceed through water and end in fire; the setting for both
is a plain. Pandemonium rises after 'veins of liquid fire' are
'Sluic'd from the Lake' (if it be lake); the materials brought
to Tubal's forge are 'massy clods' which have been conveyed
by 'veins of earth' and then, perhaps, 'washt by stream'.
The pattern of recombinations is not static; single words
move back and forth between the two contexts — 'massy
ore', 'massy clods'; 'massy ore', 'liquid ore'; 'liquid fire',
'gliding hot'; 'veins of liquid fire', 'liquid ore'; 'veins of
liquid fire', 'veins of earth'; 'Anon out of the earth', 'veins
of earth' — until the scenes merge in the reader's consciousness to form a single and continuing comment on the

activities they separately describe. The building of temples
and the practising of the 'arts that polish life' are alike
meretricious if they are undertaken for their own sake and not
for the glory of God. 'Unmindful of their maker' is a judgment applying equally to the artisans Adam sees and to the
infernal host which finds its spokesman in Mammon's
'And what can Heav'n show more?' There is finally no
distinction to be made between them, despite their apparent
separation in time, especially when one remembers, with
William Massey, that Mulciber and Tubal-Cain are one
and the same :

> Mulciber is another Latin Name for *Vulcan*. His Name amongst
> the *Greeks* was *Hepaistus* and in *Hebrew* (as some suppose)
> *Tubal-Cain*; from which some learned Men are of Opinion that
> the Name *Vulcan* had its Origin.
>
> *Remarks Upon Milton's Paradise Lost* (1761), p. 46

Since Hebrew is what remains of the original language, this
is a truer version of the story from which pagan fablers
depart to err.[1]

Another link between the race of Cain and the fallen
angels is provided in the designation 'Inventors rare', a
reference, no doubt, to Satan, who becomes the father of
invention when he 'concocts' gunpowder :

> Th' invention all admir'd, and each, how hee
> To be th' inventor miss'd, so easy it seem'd
> Once found, which yet unfound most would have thought
> Impossible : yet haply of thy Race
> In future days, if Malice should abound,
> Some one intent on mischief, or inspir'd
> With dev'lish machination might devise
> Like instrument to plague the Sons of men.
>
> (VI. 498–505)

---

[1] See I. 740–51. Samuel Mather also alludes to the identification of Mulciber
and Tubal-Cain in *The Figures or Types of the Old Testament*, 1683.

This is chronologically the first triumph of technology or 'subtle Art' (513) and like the others in the poem, it proceeds in two stages (1) a movement downward ('deep underground') in search of 'materials dark and crude' and (2) the application of fire :[1]

> up they turn'd
> Wide the Celestial soil ...
> ... Sulphurous and Nitrous Foam
> They found, they mingl'd ...
> Part hidd'n veins digg'd up (nor hath this Earth
> Entrails unlike) of Mineral and Stone ...
> ... part incentive reed
> Provide, pernicious with one touch to fire.
>
> (VI. 509–10, 512–13, 516–17, 519–20)

The pattern reappears in the building of Babel : 'The Plain, wherein a black bituminous gurge / Boils out from under ground, the mouth of Hell ; / Of Brick, and of that stuff they cast to build / A City and Tow'r, whose top may reach to Heav'n' (XII. 41–44). In the background of all these passages is the panorama of Hell with its subterranean closeness ('a Dungeon horrible') and livid flames ; also Spenser's Cave of Mammon, similarly endowed with a 'hundred fournaces burning bright' and 'golden metall, ready to be tryde'.

Once these associations suggest themselves, the way is open to read the vision allegorically : Cain–Satan begets Daughters–Sin (Eve is another possibility here, one which occurs readily to Adam)[2] who then seduce(s) sons of Seth–Adam–Mankind. The sober race of religious men surrender

---

[1] See Mrs. MacCaffrey, *Paradise Lost as 'Myth'*, p. 165: 'Whenever ... Milton prepares to explore the underground regions in *Paradise Lost*, we become aware of a sense of danger.'

[2] 'But still I see the tenor of Man's woe / Holds on the same, from Woman to begin' (XI. 632–3). Michael replies sharply: 'From Man's effeminate slackness it begins.'

their virtue in imitation of Adam who now compounds his original sin by condoning theirs. More abstractly, the marriage represents an unholy union of complementary idolatries, the worship of sensual pleasure ('lustful appetance') and the worship of art; both are symbolized in the scene by the element of fire (the forge and the torch of nuptial passion) and their union releases evil energies which are destroyed finally by a deluge from Heaven:

> for which
> The world erelong a world of tears must weep.
>
> (XI. 626–7)

With this prophecy, which alerts the reader to the next vision, Michael concludes his sermon to take up again the thread of the narrative proper. He leaves both his audiences in his debt, albeit in different ways: Adam is chastened and instructed; the reader, if he has been attentive, brings together within a single framework incidents he has not connected previously, thereby gaining an insight into the sameness of all spiritual experience. Despite its predictability then, the sequence is illuminating and even moving.

(ii) ALTERED STYLE

A number of critics have addressed themselves in recent years to the rehabilitation of Books XI and XII. Mrs. Lewalski and Messrs. Prince, Sasek, Summers, and MacCallum have succeeded in establishing the coherence of Milton's design and in doing so have countered Lewis's criticism that the historical survey is an 'untransmuted lump of futurity'.[1] Another of Lewis's contentions, 'that the actual

---

[1] *A Preface to Paradise Lost*, p. 125.

writing in this passage is curiously bad' still finds its ad-
herents. As recently as 1964, Louis Martz, after conceding
that Milton's plan is clear and theologically sound, concludes
reluctantly, 'poetically it is a disaster'.[1] Without question
the verse exhibits few of the characteristics usually thought
of as Miltonic — the sonorous richness of sound, the
intricate but precise syntax, the wealth of pointedly relevant
ambiguities; in their place, in the words of a critic who comes
to praise, there is substituted 'a rhetoric that consistently
avoids all deeper imaginative surprise; the surface of things
dominates, clear, cold, hard.'[2] Also, I might add, *bare*, not in
the sense exactly of 'unadorned' (the watchword of Puritan
pulpit rhetoric) but more nearly as a synonym for 'toneless'.
There is, once or twice, an echo of the earlier manner, but
exaggerated to the extent almost of self-parody, as if Milton
were telling us that while spectacular effects are still within
his scope, they are no longer necessary or desirable. An
example is the studied virtuosity of the roll-call of cities and
empires to whose organ tones Michael and Adam ascend.
The excess, as Martz observes, is obvious, indeed Asiatic, so
much so that the reader is able to see the falseness beneath
the glitter long before it is exposed formally by the deliberate
anti-climax of 'but to nobler sights':

> Rich *Mexico* the seat of *Montezume*,
> And *Cusco* in *Peru*, the richer seat
> Of *Atabalipa*, and yet unspoil'd
> *Guiana*, whose great City *Geryon's* Sons
> Call *El Dorado*: but to nobler sights...
>
> (XI. 407–11)[3]

[1] *The Paradise Within*, p. 150.

[2] Arnold Stein in a review of Martz' *The Paradise Within*, *Modern Language Quarterly* (December, 1965), p. 599.

[3] See the excellent study by Robert A. Bryan of this passage in relation to the *translatio imperii* and *translatio studii* traditions ('Adam's Tragic Vision in '*Paradise Lost*', *Studies in Philology*, xi, 1965, 197–214). Bryan argues

'But to nobler sights' flicks out contemptuously (like the verb 'fell' at 1. 586) to mock the pomp and decadence of false earthly paradises, and to dismiss along with them the 'swelling epithets' of literary styles. For the reader, however, there is no surprise at this dismissal; he has long ago put away these childish things. The entire sequence is ornamental, though instructively so, and even as ornament it is the exception rather than the rule. For the most part there is merely the straightforward narration of the course of man's woe and misery, 'not unlike a bad dream remembered with relentless accuracy'.[1]

The justification of a style characterized by its controlled anonymity must come from the context. In this case, the bareness, the avoidance of 'all deeper imaginative surprise', make it the perfect conductor for the reserves of emotion stored up in the reader in the course of a long poem, and also a perfect (i.e., unobtrusive) medium for the conveyance of doctrine. Lewis observes of Milton's Paradise: 'We are his organ: when he appears to be describing Paradise he is in fact drawing out the Paradisial stop in us.'[2] Presumably the paradisial stop is one we all have because it is rooted in an archetypal myth; there are also local 'stops', tied to patterns of association that do not antedate the artifact, but are established within its confines; and these are particularly numerous in *Paradise Lost* where so much is involved in

that in these lines the 'honorific design' of these concepts is inverted to show 'that sin and corruption, rather than art, learning, and empire have moved from east to west' (201). Surveying the contemporary associations of the place-names Milton marshals, he concludes: 'the places Adam sees in the vision bring to mind the one clearly discernible common denominator of the travellers' accounts from which they are taken: in their painful record of the failure of man's frail reason to control his animal passion, these accounts are reinactments of that first great failure — and fall — in the Garden of Eden (214).

[1] Stein, loc. cit.   [2] *A Preface to Paradise Lost*, p. 47.

pattern. In order to draw forth a response rooted in any one pattern, that is, in order to pull out a particular stop, the poet need only provide a link between the text at hand and the sources of energy existing in his reader's mind. The impact of the verbal texture resides not in the arrangement of the words on the page or in the moral commonplaces the words present, but in the reader who responds to them as he responds to old melodies which have become a part of him by having been a part of his experience. Of course the reader in whom the melody finds no answering strain will not be moved by the verse at all. The force generated by the 'altered style' of Books XI and XII will vary in proportion to the effort the reader has expended in reaching them. If they fail now, it is because he has failed before.

Thus the account of the war of the Giants (XI. 638 ff.) alludes to at least four earlier scenes whose juxtaposition (if they are recalled) points to a single moral. The games the devils play in Hell are fought out in earnest now, and in the same images :

> Part wield thir Arms, part curb the foaming Steed.
>
> (XI. 643)

> Part on the plain, or in the Air sublime . . .
> Part curb thir fiery Steeds.
>
> (II. 528, 531)

Soon the decorum of military manoeuvres ('the civil game' or 'cruel Tournament') turns to confusion and carnage, just as it does in Book VI :

> which makes a bloody Fray;
> With cruel Tournament the Squadrons join;
> Where Cattle pastur'd late now scatter'd lies
> With Carcasses and Arms th' ensanguin'd Field
> Deserted.
>
> (XI. 651–5)

the battle swerv'd
With many an inroad gor'd; deformed rout
Enter'd and foul disorder; all the ground
With shiver'd armor strown, and on a heap
Chariot and Charioteer lay overturn'd
And fiery foaming Steeds.

(vi. 386–91)

The 'flock of timorous Goats' pursued by Christ's chariot over the plain of Heaven in vi are in xi actual 'bleating Lambs', herded 'over the Plain' by marauding bands who also attack the shepherds (648–50), 'scarce with Life the Shepherds fly' (later this image will take its place in the traditional ecclesiastical allegorization of pastoral life: 'Wolves shall succeed for teachers, grievous Wolves'). With the echoes of individual words and phrases goes a familiar attitude toward wars and warriors :

On each hand slaughter and gigantic deeds,
In other part the scepter'd Heralds call
To Council in the City Gates: anon
Grey-headed men and grave, with Warriors mixt,
Assemble, and Harangues are heard, but soon
In factious opposition.

(659–64)

'On each hand slaughter and gigantic deeds' is reminiscent of 'deeds of eternal fame / Were done, but infinite' (vi. 240–241); the difference is that 'slaughter' mocks 'gigantic' beforehand while 'but infinite' is read after 'deeds of eternal fame' has been accepted literally ; in the later instance the reader is the master of the irony, not its victim. Ironic statements are like this in xi and xii, obvious and unsubtle, without the elaborate machinery which makes their detection a part of the reader's education. The council of war whose ceremonial (if specious) dignity is preserved through some five hundred lines in Book ii is here exposed immediately in the short distance between 'Grey headed men and grave . . . Assemble' and 'Harangues are heard . . . / In factious opposition'. Within this network of associations, Enoch serves a unifying function :

> till at last
> Of middle Age one rising, eminent
> In wise deport, spake much of Right and Wrong,
> Of Justice, of Religion, Truth and Peace,
> And Judgment from above : him old and young
> Exploded, and had seiz'd with violent hands,
> Had not a Cloud descending snatch'd him thence
> Unseen amid the throng.
>
> (XI. 664–71)

The manner of his rising recalls both Beelzebub and Abdiel, and as his words ('much of Right and Wrong, / Of Justice, of Religion, Truth and Peace') prove him to be an Abdiel figure, the analogy to Christ, who also intervenes 'at last' when war threatens to destroy the world, asserts itself. Within this analogy further complexities are suggested : in his reliance on 'Judgment from above' he prefigures Christ's reliance on the Father in the face of Satan's temptations ; he is then an example of Christ's example, imitating (prefiguring) his actions in the wilderness and on the cross. In the account of his rescue, as MacCallum notes, there are details from the description of Elijah's translation. Enoch is a type of Christ's ascension before the law, Elijah a type under the law. Christ's actual (that is historical) ascension marks the success of his attempt to free man from the bondage of the law. Enoch, because he appears when he does, contains all these aspects of Christ within himself and prepares the reader for the coming of the actual Christ whose entrance into history is the climax of Michael's narrative. In this way the reader comes to the end of the passage fully attuned to the reverberations of its allusiveness and yet at the same time in step with the surface movement of the poem as it proceeds more or less in sequence towards a conventional denouement. The impact, it seems to me, is tremendous, and it is so because the style as style makes so few demands.

Broadbent objects that 'the precepts that Michael and Adam draw from all this seem naïve : "now I see Peace to corrupt no less than war to waste" (xi. 783), for example.'[1] This is true only because we have apprehended these precepts earlier as a result of a process more complex and attenuated than the one recorded here. Yet the reactions of Michael and Adam do have an interest for us, insomuch as they are comments on our own performances in a similar situation. The ready scorn of Michael's 'For in those days Might only shall be admir'd / And Valor and Heroic Virtue call'd' (689–90) is a reproach to our own slowness in abandoning a position the angel does not even bother to refute; whatever true virtue is (a definition will be forthcoming at the conclusion of the visions), it is certainly not to be located in the obvious absurdity of might. Adam, too, unhesitatingly condemns a course of action (the waging of war) which is to him incomprehensible in its pointlessness and perversity : 'O what are these, / Death's Ministers not Men, who thus deal Death / Inhumanly to men?' (675–77). As one vision succeeds another the technical advantage the reader enjoys over Adam is of less and less significance, and at this point something of the old relationship is reasserted along with a renewed awareness of Adam's superiority ; even with his portion of our common disability, he understands things more quickly than we do and his naïvety is merely a negative indication of the sophisticated intellectual contortions he can dispense with and we are bound to. The reader who sees this infuses that much more meaning into the

[1] *Some Graver Subject*, p. 275.

passage and finds his reward in the increased relevance it has for him ; and he will have been helped to that relevance by the schematic simplicity of the passage, the unobtrusiveness of its style.

Philosophically, the bareness of these books returns us to the expository rhetoric of God's speeches and to the flinty clarity of his illusionless vision ; and once again our reaction is an indication of the distance we have (hopefully) travelled since our original infatuation with the Satanic grand style. One should note (for future reference) the careful neutrality of this style, the remarkable diffidence with which it treats the phenomena it records ; as if to say, here are not points of view, here is only what is. Even the epic voice's 'point of view' is absorbed into the relentless drone. When Michael emphasizes God's omnipresence by referring to Paradise as 'this Rock' (xi. 336), the reader will be disturbed to find the object of longing whose loss is the occasion of the poem so described. Milton uses this 'stylistic shock' to prepare us for the transformation of Eden into 'an Island salt and bare, / The haunt of Seals and Orcs, and Sea-mews' clang' (834-5), and for the moral God intends :

> To teach thee that God attributes to place
> No sanctity.
>
> (836-7)

The hard literalism of 'Rock' warns us against 'attributing overmuch' to a 'fair outside'. By seeing the *essential* unimpressiveness of physical objects on a purely physical level we are moved to seek the spirit whose presence gives them value, in this case the 'true Rock' upon whose foundation man can build his inner (non-corporeal) life. This has been the purpose of the poem — to induce in us this motion — and the reader who is able to greet the 'bodiless' style of xi and xii as Adam does, with joy, attests to Milton's success.

(iii) TILL TIME STAND FIXT

The form of Michael's presentation is linear and represents, or so it would seem at first, a return to a way of perceiving the reader abandons when he enters imaginatively into the poem's mythic structure. Things proceed in an orderly fashion, without confusion, and on a scale the mind is capable of contemplating (there are miracles, but they are presented as miracles, exceptions to rules that apply most of the time); objects remain objects even when they are examined through a glass, spears wound permanently, distances are travelled slowly and arduously, cultures develop and decay, time passes. But the difference between historical experience and the atemporal vision of the last things is only apparent, and Milton allows us to assume it so that we can be brought by degrees to its contrary and encouraged to continue in a habit of mind adopted in response to a literary situation. This is a dramatic reversal of the adjustment the reader must make in Books I and II, when he is introduced to the concept of the eternal present and asked to abandon his conventional modes of perception ; here the action seems to be again taking place in the familiar world of time and space, but within that framework Milton returns us inexorably to the simultaneity he had insisted upon earlier. For whenever the text recalls us to some earlier passage, the distinction, between the dimensionless infinity the poem's divine personages inhabit and the more familiar outlines of the actuality we are accustomed to think of as real, is invariably blurred, and finally disappears.

An example is the reappearance in Book XI of Death's menacing figure :

> The other shape,
> If shape it might be call'd that shape had none
> Distinguishable in member, joint, or limb,
> Or substance might be call'd that shadow seem'd,
> For each seem'd either; black it stood as Night,
> Fierce as ten Furies, terrible as Hell,
> And shook a dreadful Dart.   (II. 666–72)

The promise of specificity in the word 'shape' is disappointed
immediately by the following line, although the illusion of
observable physical characteristics is preserved by the
momentary isolation of 'Distinguishable in member, joint,
or limb'. The reader is teased by the beginning of a description that soon shades into the obfuscating parading of
paradoxes: 'Or substance might be call'd that shadow
seem'd, / For each [which?] seem'd either [what?].' The
'it' which stands black as Night (another abstraction,
perhaps Spenser's) in line 670 is still the antecedent of
'shape' (Satan styles it 'execrable shape') but that word has
been emptied of all its significance and refers to nothing
visible or describable. Only the dreadful dart is real in the
ordinary sense, the single detail attributable to Death's
presence, and we carry away from the passage the impression
of a projectile coming at us out of some impalpable obscure.
In Book XI, it all seems quite different: there is a profusion
of detail, so much that one critic protests against the 'vivid
and relentless horror'.[1] Abel dies before our eyes, in slow
motion: 'he fell, and deadly pale / Groan'd out his Soul with
gushing blood effus'd' (446–7); others linger in the grip of
merciless diseases enumerated with medical precision. And
yet Adam's question — 'But have I now seen Death?' — is
the question the description of the bodiless apparition raises
and refuses to answer. Nor is it answered here, except by
referring back to that earlier passage: 'Death thou hast

[1] Martz, op. cit., p. 150.

seen / In his first shape on man ; but many shapes / Of Death,
and many are the ways that lead / To his grim cave, all
dismal' (466–9). All we see of Death is dying, the visible
effects of an invisible presence, a shadow. The substance
has a reality apart from the bodily forms expressing it,
although the bodily forms are what we as finite creatures see
and must reflect on. The non-shape of Book ɪɪ is no less
'real' than the 'many shapes' of xɪ.

When Broadbent observes that through such 'linkages'
between the first and last books, 'the poem's image of Hell
is revealed as the actuality of the fallen world', he refers to
the story of the rebellion and Fall as if it were a poetic fiction
entertained for a time because it provided a convenient way
of talking about what happens in 'real life'. But Milton, I
think, wishes the reader to reach quite a different conclusion :
life is real only when it is lived with an awareness that
through it one participates in the image of eternity the poem
gestures towards. *Paradise Lost* is not a microcosm of the
human condition, but an instrument for seeing through it to
something more substantial ; and these last books not only
present a vision of history, they imply a *theory* of history, a
theory which is the sum of all the correspondences noted by
the reader as he prepares to exit from Eden into everyday
life. Gradually, history comes to be seen as one term in a
Milton pseudo-simile, with eternity the other ; and as we
move through its spaces, the unity of the two terms is more
and more apparent and the superficial differences less and
less striking. By 'pseudo-simile' I refer to the characteristic
manoeuvre by which what is offered as an analogy is perceived finally as an identity. That is, the simile ostensibly
compares *A* with *B* (Satan with Leviathan, Satan's host with
Pharaoh's legions), but ends by discovering that *B* is a
manifestation, in another form, of *A* or, alternatively that
both are embodiments of a complex entity *C*. 'Milton's

worlds', Mrs. MacCaffrey observes, 'all fit exactly inside
each other; in noting their points of similarity, he is not so
much joining different objects as observing the same thing
on a smaller or larger scale.'[1] Other poets' similes join two
universes of discourse in such a way as to imply and *confirm*
their more usual separation; the similarities they uncover
are occasional and one assumes that when the rhythm of the
figure has spent itself, the objects compared return to their
respective worlds and are no longer thought of in conjunction. Milton's similes are unique in suggesting that only in
their one-dimensional plane are things displayed as they
really are with a clarity their natural settings only obscure.
His analogies are expressions of cosmological unity articulated, for the most part, within the system of correspondences we know as typology. The connections his readers
finally make are the connections 'they were accustomed to
make when they read the Bible or heard it expounded from
the pulpit',[2] or, for that matter, when they read the classics
of pagan and Christian literature — connections between
the life and works of Christ, the life of nations, real or
imagined, and the spiritual life of the individual. It follows
then, that the informed reader would recognize Christ in
Moses, or even in Hercules, without having to see them
isolated together in the artificial confines of a rhetorical
figure. The superfluousness of the simile as an instrument of
perception is, I believe, part of Milton's point. That is, one
aspect of the experience of a Milton simile for the reader is
the realization that he has passed beyond the discursive
way of thinking of which similes are one form. By dividing
and analysing, a simile, like any other logical mode of
thought, helps man to 'unite those dissevered pieces which

[1] *Paradise Lost as 'Myth'*, p. 142. The following discussion owes much to
her analysis of the Miltonic simile. See esp. pp. 119–78.
[2] James H. Sims, *The Bible in Milton's Epics* (Gainesville, 1962), p. 11.

are yet wanting to the body of truth'; but those who walk with faith and see Christ in everything and everything in Christ (with the aid of an official network of interchangeable equivalencies) in effect neutralize the crookedness of their natural vision and are able, *immediately*, to discern the unity in diversity. This does not involve a distortion or violation of the literal configurations of objects, but an apprehension of the true significance of those configurations and hence of those objects. When things are seen with the incorporeal eye, they are not transformed, but revealed; a veil is removed, not put on.

All this is reflected in the collapse of the simile's structure. In place of the confining rhythm of two answering clauses — just as, ... so ... — similar in movement to an anti-thetical period, Milton's simile exhibits an imbalance in its members: just as B, B^1, B^2, B^3, etc. . . . , so A. As a result, the sense of argument, of analysis in progress, fades away. Usually, the rhythm of a simile, if it is followed through, organizes thought, provides places for point and contrast, and satisfies the limited expectations the first clause arouses; without it, the simile becomes open ended and additive or paratactic (the 'so' clause does appear, but when 'just as' has been forgotten, and it has very little *logical force*) an example of what Aristotle calls the ' "free-running" style ... the kind that has no natural stopping place' (*Rhetoric*: 1409a). The inference is that any number of B's could be adduced that stand in the same relation to A. Rather than concentrating on a single point of contact, the simile expands, opening up on a vista of innumerable connections. The pleasure a patterned utterance usually gives is tied to its limiting definiteness: 'the hearer always feels that he is grasping something and has reached some definite conclusion' (1409b). For this Milton substitutes the greater pleasure of coming upon an analogy one knows to be truer and more valuable than any a completed simile could have revealed. Of course the scaffolding of the complete simile remains, but only as a means of marking out an area for the eye to move in. It is an artificial space, with no reference to the physical world of either the observer or of the characters in the plot, and it is unconnected with the determination of meaning. To the educated (fit) eye, the icons Milton marshals wear their meanings on their faces, and there is no need for a syntax to give them a context or a pattern to lend them force. They are imbedded in a structured artifact, but are themselves unstructured except for the relationships the unifying reality of Christ implicates them in. Because each simile finds a kind of form within a system and not in its own internal coherence (although many of them have that too), they reach out to one another and join finally in an endless chain of interchangeable significances : Leviathan to Pharaoh to River Dragon to Serpent to Giant to Locusts to bees to pygmies and cranes to imbodied force to sedge to fallen leaves to barbarian hordes and pagan Gods on the one side ; Moses, David, Orpheus, Josiah, etc. on the other.

A mind that 'sees ... all things as incarnations of the values which inform them'[1] will see those values in those things whenever and wherever they appear. Thus when the components of the similes are exhibited again in Books xi and xii, but secured now to their historical moorings, the reader responds to them just as he did before. The account of the persecution and Exodus from Egypt (xii. 159–216) reverberates with echoes of the description of Satan's rallying of his defeated legions (i. 282–355), a passage noteworthy for the cluster of similes it contains. Again the locusts swarm in Egypt's evil day; the Leviathan-river dragon-Pharaoh, his heart the residing place of the barbarian hordes poured from the frozen North ('his stubborn heart, . . . still

[1] R. Tuve, *A Reading of George Herbert* (London, 1952), p. 105.

as Ice / More hard'n'd after thaw') pursues the sojourners of Goshen who again 'Safe towards *Canaan* from the shore advance' (xii. 215); once more the broken chariot wheels bestrew the flood; and if the earlier scene ends in a vision of the devilish multitude spreading 'Beneath *Gibraltar* to the *Lybian* sands' (i. 355) this one sees the children of Israel advancing not directly into the land of milk and honey, but 'Through the wild Desert' (xii. 216). The similes, one is tempted to say have come true; they are really happening; what was before a vehicle for the idea of 'devilishness' is now tenor and has a substance in its own right. But the reverse is true; history is still the vehicle for the drama of Hell and Heaven. Even though the characters interact within the narrative and engage in actions which have immediate and visible consequences, both characters and actions are invested immediately with the meanings we have responded to in the similes. These locusts, if they were placed under a microscope, would be seen to have 'shapes . . . like unto horses', and 'hair as the hair of women' and 'breastplates of iron' and 'tails like unto scorpions' (Revelation ix. 7–10). And in direct contradiction to the literal sense of the text the reader will know that they do 'not hurt the grass of the earth, neither any green things, neither any tree; but only those men which have not the seal of God in their foreheads' (Revelation ix. 4). In Book i, Satan unwittingly calls up his legion-locusts against himself, not knowing that they are God's scourge and that he commands them in God's service, as he does in Revelation: 'And they had a king over them, which is the angel of the bottomless pit, whose name in the Hebrew tongue is Abaddon, but in the Greek tongue hath his name Apollyon' (Revelation ix. 11). The locusts of Book xii do not have an identity apart from their predecessor's (in poem time) or their antitypes (in God's time), especially since the plague that follows them is a type of the pit they erupt from and of the death Christ rises from, victorious :

Darkness must overshadow all his bounds,
Palpable darkness [palpable obscure] and blot out three days.

(xii. 187–8)

The reader does not progress through this passage or any other passage in Book xii in a linear fashion ; before moving from one image or figure or single action to the next he has referred the first upward to the significance it shadows ; this is true even though the structural links that are absent or aborted in the similes — a sustained syntax, a straightforward order of events, a clear line of surface development — are present and operative here. Two forces tug at the reader, one horizontal, generated by the verbal units as they succeed one another on the page, the other vertical, pushing upward toward the myth everything belongs to (thus the proliferation in these books of ascension imagery, Enoch ascending, Christ ascending, always the promise of the soul ascending). The latter predominates, forcing the structural members into the background (just as the outline of a simile's structure fades away as tenor and vehicle merge) and imposing a static pattern on the fluidity of the reading experience. Time is consumed, but motion is frozen and in addition to a chronicle depicting human agents acting humanly, we have a series of stylized abstractions alive from the *inside* with the life of a true and great myth.

On a larger scale this applies to the sweep of the narrative as a whole. It is sometimes objected that Milton's presentation of history is poorly articulated, with weak transitions and a pronounced lack of proportion. The description is accurate, but the intention is, I think, to blunt the sense of continuity one usually associates with a running narrative, and to minimize the importance of the position events happen to occupy on the *continuum* of the story line. (Although, as we shall see, sequence *is* important in another sense.) Large tracts of time are hidden in a parenthesis, others expanded into one hundred lines. As a result certain images are thrown up in relief on a flat dimensionless plane (like the area of a simile) and the reader is directed to the relationships that pertain between them *always*, not merely in sequence. Thus Cain is like Tubal is like Nimrod is like Pharaoh who are all to some extent like the reader who may, if he chooses, be like Abel or Enoch or Noah or Abraham or Moses or David or, finally, in a limited way, like Christ. The technique is reminiscent of *The Faerie Queene* where phrases like 'many a day' or 'meanwhile' or 'it fortuned then' are there only to separate one part of the allegory's total statement from another. (The reader walks around the object because he is unable to view it in a single glance.) Very soon Michael's transitions take on this character: 'Now prepare thee for another scene' does not mean 'let us see what happens next', but, rather, 'here is another aspect of the reality we have been looking at all along.'

In respect to all three structural units — the simile, the episode, the book (or books) — Milton's point is the same: *Correctly interpreted, the icons the visible world presents to us will always have the same meaning no matter what formal configurations surround them* (the ethical analogue of this is the self-sufficiency of virtue: 'He that has light within his own clear breast / May sit i' th' centre, and enjoy bright day.' *Comus*, 381–2). Meanings may, as Mrs. MacCaffrey puts it, deepen,[1] or more properly, our apprehension of them may deepen as we find them again and again in a variety of contexts, but they will not change. The difficulty is to find them amidst the distracting camouflage a limited vision creates for us. The word of God is inscribed whole on the

---

[1] *Paradise Lost as 'Myth'*, p. 45.

length of history, but individual man, from the vantage point he is restricted to, sees only a portion of the whole ; his proportion is disproportion, and must be violated if a truly comprehensive view is to be approximated. Milton's similes violate proportion in just this way ; they are true, and the linear presentation of history becomes a viable mode when within it can be seen the similaic form, that is, when we come to regard the time–space mould of experience as an unfortunate consequence of our finitude and mortality, a refraction of reality rather than reality itself. And this is what happens when our attention is again and again taken away from the *progress* of the narrative and returned to earlier portions of the poem. This response to history is a learned response (Milton is teaching it to us in Books xi and xii at the same time that Michael is teaching it to Adam), but not because it is 'unnatural' or distorting. Our present (fallen) perspective is unnatural and distorting, and, hopefully, temporary. Reading (or living) history figuratively is not a repudiation of literalism, but the way to literalism, to the literalism we enjoyed before the Fall.

Of course history is more than a veil ; it is the unfolding of God's redemptive plan, the fulfilment of the promise made to Adam in the Garden :

> The Lord having convinced them of their Sin gave them that famous Promise, *that the Seed of the Woman should break the Serpents Head*, Gen. iii. 15.
> This was the first Beam of Gospel Light that ever broke unto lost and fallen Man: A comprehensive Promise, which includes the whole Gospel.
> Samuel Mather, *The Figures or Types of the Old Testament*
> (London, 1683), p. 28.

The whole gospel is revealed gradually, in stages, and with each new illumination of 'Gospel Light' man increases in understanding, both of his situation and of the remedy that

Christ has procured for him. The oracular prophecy is a
riddle set by God so that by thinking on it man will participate in the discovery of his own salvation : 'As a Child by
learning his A.B.C. and his Primer' is fitted to progress
'into a higher, harder Book' (p. 57). ('Light after light well
us'd they shall attain, / And to the end persisting, safe
arrive.') One stage in this sequence of programmed learning
is the giving of the Law whose manifest imperfection (or
incompleteness) Michael tells us, is intended as a stimulus to
inductive reasoning :

> that when they see
> Law can discover sin, but not remove,
> Save by those shadowy expiations weak
> The blood of Bulls and Goats, they may *conclude*
> Some blood more precious must be paid for Man.
>
> (xii. 289–93, emphasis mine)

From this conclusion man proceeds 'From shadowy Types to
Truth, From Flesh to Spirit' until the discipline of time
resigns him 'Up to a better Cov'nant'. (God's method in
drawing men forward is the method by which Milton leads
his reader from a conviction of his own weakness to the
righteousness of Christ.) At this point the victory foretold
obscurely to Adam in the garden will be achieved by one
greater man. Man is thus at once the means God chooses to
employ for the victory, the agent for whose sake the victory
is won, and the decipherer of the oracle that predicts the
victory ; and time, whose self-consummation will mark the
victory, is meanwhile the vehicle of fulfilment and the crucible
of faith. For while history derives its ultimate meaning from
the drama of redemption, the meaning at any moment for
the individual who lives in history is determined by his
willingness, expressed in response to actual situations, to
wait on the promise.

The racial experience is adumbrated by Adam, who is not

lectured to, but led gradually 'by a series of graded steps' to a 'full and spiritual understanding of the Son's prophecy concerning the war between the seed of the woman and the serpent.'[1] The progress of his understanding, notes John Parish, coincides with the 'triumphant ascent' of his spirit from abject despair to joyous faith;[2] and when at last Adam raises his eyes from the visible world to the promise he is now able to discover in the Rainbow, Michael rewards him with the first explicit revelation of the 'good news' awaiting 'long wander'd man' at the end of his journey through time. In the covenant God now makes with Noah ('I establish my covenant with you and with your seed after you') are included all the covenants; the promulgation of the first to Adam not only signifies the others, but makes them certain.[3] The rainbow whose 'flow'ry verge' protects the world from destruction by water will preside over its destruction by fire:

> Over the Earth a Cloud...
> His triple-color'd Bow, whereon to look
> And call to mind his Cov'nant: Day and Night,
> Seed time and Harvest, Heat and hoary Frost
> Shall hold thir course, till fire purge all things new,
> Both Heav'n and Earth, wherein the just shall dwell.
>
> (XI. 896–901)

With this revelation, the active phase of Adam's education comes to an end, as the reader's has earlier. He need no longer labour his mind in an effort to discover order and meaning in the world, for the realization that God is working

[1] MacCallum, 'Milton and Sacred History', p. 160.
[2] 'Milton and God's Curse on the Serpent', *Journal of English and Germanic Philology*, lviii (1959), 241.
[3] See Mather, *The Figures or Types of the Old Testament*, p. 70: 'The Types were not only Signs but Seals; not only Signs to represent Gospel Mysteries unto them, but also Seals to assure them of the certain and infallible exhibition thereof in Gods appointed time.'

through history towards a definite end provides both, and
gives direction to his subsequent questions and conjectures.
Further revelations will extend the implications of this insight without superseding it. At the same time, the reader
feels the toll the poem is taking of his intellectual energies
lessen, largely because the several strains of the narrative
coalesce, making possible a less diffuse response to the
surface action. Before there had been at least three focuses to
the reading experience :
    (1) the maturing of Adam's faith.
    (2) the linkages forged by the echoes of earlier books.
    (3) the typological significance of literal and historical
         actions.
For much of Book xi the reader divides his attention between
(1) and (2), keeping track of Adam's progress and recalling
his own in counterpoint, while (3) remains in the background, impinging on the consciousness, but never occupy-
ing it wholly. (Abel and Enoch are types of Christ's passion
and ascension, respectively, but here they impress more as
heroic examples of fortitude in the tradition of Abdiel.)[1]
In the account of the Flood, every detail of which bears a
typological significance,[2] (1) and (2) dovetail into (3).

[1] Within the system of typology, there are degrees of congruency ('some
things or persons were only Types of Christ in some one particular thing,
others in many things', — Mather, p. 73) corresponding roughly to the
order of their appearance in time. Thus Abel and Enoch are only 'partial
types' in contrast to Noah, Moses and David who are 'total types', with the
reservation implied by the term itself: 'there never was any that did or could
possibly resemble him perfectly in all things.' The more total the type,
the more likely the response to him as type rather than as individual.
And the reverse holds also: one can read about Abel without thinking of him
as a type of the crucifixion, especially if there are other focuses to the reading
experience, as there surely are early in Book xi; but the pressure to read figuratively is irresistible when Michael elaborates the story of Noah.
[2] 'Noah was a Type of Christ in regard of his saving those that did believe
his Preaching.' 'The deluge was a shadow of the day of Judgement.' 'Noahs

Adam's great success occurs when he infers the spiritual sense of the rainbow without Michael's prompting (one might say he *invents* figurative reading here); hereafter, with the angel's guidance, he moves unimpeded from one shadowy type to another, until 'with . . . joy surcharged' he greets the appearance in time of the antitype. The reader too now finds that the connections he had been struggling to make (between his own experience and Adam's, between individual lessons learned and the great lesson to be learned from the example of Christ) are now made for him, as everything gravitates naturally, and with a minimum of effort to an appointed place in an increasingly insistent pattern. From their different vantage points, one discovering, the other anticipating, Adam and the reader have been working to extract the rhythm of eternity from the irregular fluctuations of the visible world, and when the mainspring of that rhythm is manifested in the rainbow, their consciousnesses are taken over by it, and they rush together with increasing speed toward the intersection of divine purpose and human destiny. Everything converges on the centre which is the reader's consciousness; and that in turn is impelled forward towards a new centre (Christ) of whose existence he has always been aware. The pressure exerted by the previous books coincides with the pull exerted by the waiting conclusion. The movement is that of a suspended period, the slow ascent while the mind is made aware of individual parallelisms which point forward to a single unifying parallel ('the syntax remains incomplete . . . with phrases and clauses tending to mass themselves on both sides of the turning point'), and then a turn followed by the falling away to a conclusion that is implicit in the arrangement of the smaller units in the intro-

Sacrifice when he came out of the Ark, was a manifest Type of the Sacrifice of Jesus Christ.' (Mather, 91, 97.) The different parts of the ark were also allegorized.

ductory clause ('ascending construction secured by forward dependence').[1] The psychological bases of the rhetoric are expectation and resolution; and when the expectations are answered and the resolution can be anticipated with certainty, the reflective intellect relaxes and in effect abdicates to the onward sweep of an utterance hurrying to complete itself. If this seems to contradict my earlier description of the visions as static, let me hasten to add that it is the observer (Adam, the reader) who moves, with accelerating speed, through the *spaces* of history towards a point at which time stands fixed and all can be seen at a single (intuitive) glance. Here time, as Mrs. MacCaffrey explains, 'is a series of horizons, not a process lived through — the living will come soon enough.'[2]

Coinciding with this acceleration, and to some extent a consequence of it, is a growing impersonality of tone. Michael and Adam are no longer dramatic characters, reacting to each other with a measure of psychological realism, but voices in a ritual dialogue, one proclaiming set speeches oracularly, the other responding with the proper antiphon. The skeleton structure of the pedagogical situation is retained, but Adam is less a pupil than a prompter, stepping in, when Michael pauses, to ask the obvious question ('why ... So many and so various Laws,' 'what will betide the few'), then fading back as the answer grows into a monologue. (When Adam 'interposes' at Book XII. 270, it is the first we have heard of him in nearly two hundred lines.) Both speakers, to be sure, refer from time to time to the dramatic basis of the scene — 'I see him, but thou canst not', 'Since thy original lapse', 'Favor unmerited by me' — and we are

---

[1] Jonas A. Barish, *Ben Jonson and the Language of Prose Comedy* (Cambridge, Mass., 1960), p. 48; George Williamson, *The Senecan Amble* (London, 1951), p. 50.

[2] *Paradise Lost as 'Myth'*, p. 61.

continually reminded of the distance Adam has travelled since his despairing soliloquy in Book x — 'my heart much eas'd, / Erewhile perplext with thoughts', 'now clear I understand / What oft my steadiest thoughts have searched in vain'; but the lessons of true patience and moderation have been learned and the emotional excesses which marked Adam's spiritual immaturity give way to the stability and equanimity of faith. As a result, personality (or the expression of a merely personal vision) recedes, and along with it the sense of a personal style, to be replaced by two levels of anonymity, the flat, prosy, almost clinical drone of the angel and the breathless frenzy of Adam's exclamations of joy. The distance between the two, which has occasioned some critical grumbling, underlines the extent to which Adam is responding to a vision rather than to a direct emotional stimulus. (He is our model here.) Before, Adam had projected the implications of specific sights into a reading of heavenly disposition; now the meaning of what he sees or hears is determined by his conviction that Heaven is disposed to mercy. The apparent bleakness of man's race through time is transformed for him by his deepening comprehension of what is to come at the end of it. 'Yes, yes, now I see,' is the import of everything he says, and we can, perhaps, eliminate the personal pronoun and emend this to 'yes, yes, seeing'. As he becomes more and more attuned to the spirit that informs all things, his individuality and sense of self are abandoned to that spirit. What is happening to Adam, through the agency of Michael's revelations, is described in the early poem 'On Time':

> For when as each thing bad thou hast entomb'd,
> And, last of all, thy greedy self consum'd,
> Then long Eternity shall greet our bliss
> With an individual kiss;
> And Joy shall overtake us as a flood, . . .

When once our heav'nly-guided soul shall climb,
Then all this Earthy grossness quit,
Attir'd with Stars, we shall for ever sit,
    Triumphing over Death, and Chance, and thee
    O Time.

(9–13, 19–23)

At some point, joy, the emotional complement of the intuition he is climbing to ('heav'nly-guided'), *overtakes* Adam
(Heaven is stooping to him) and lifts him out of himself
and out of time into union with the divine; the harmony
between creature and Creator, which was broken at the Fall,
is momentarily restored, and Adam is once more able to
hear the music of the spheres, to which he adds his own
voice: 'O goodness infinite, goodness immense!' (XII. 469).
The moment of supreme recognition, available to every
Christian who ascends through meditation to a glimpse of
the Truth, occurs for Adam when the full meaning of the
prophecy of the seed is revealed to him in the image of the
incarnation and the crucifixion.[1] His responses, 'with such
joy / Surcharg'd' and 'Replete with joy', are an involuntary
(non-intellectual) testimony to the completeness of his
understanding, to a sense of well-being (of which words are
but the 'vent') so complete that it is not to be distinguished
from the Good of whose apprehension it is the product.
(This is not the 'short joy' Adam experiences at the vision
of the unholy marriage, but a joy entered into rather than
felt, a disinterested, *impersonal* joy, the joy of belonging to a
fortunate universe.)[2] He has dissolved in ecstasy because

---

[1] See Martz, *The Paradise Within*, pp. 3–102 for a discussion of meditative
techniques. See esp. p. 50: 'Thus the mind, having caught the flash of truth,
lives a life that mixes memory and desire, striving always to renew the
glimpse.'

[2] The paradox of the Fortunate Fall does not affect the 'great moral' of the
poem at all. It merely asserts that any failure on the part of his creatures can
not impair or harm God; on *his* level of being, all is turned to good. But evil

'through his ear' all Heaven has been brought before his
eyes :

> There let the pealing Organ blow
> To the full voic'd Choir below,
> In Service high and Anthems clear,
> As may with sweetness, through mine ear,
> Dissolve me into ecstasies,
> And bring all Heav'n before mine eyes.
>
> (*Il Penseroso*, 161–6)

The reader too is caught up into the rhythms of eternity
and teased out of thought by the iterative schemes which
overwhelm Michael's syntax in the description of the
crucifixion :

> For this he shall live hated, be blasphem'd,
> Seiz'd on by force, judg'd, and to death condemn'd
> A shameful and accurst, nail'd to the Cross
> By his own Nation, slain for bringing Life;
> But to the Cross he nails thy Enemies,
> The Law that is against thee, and the sins
> Of all mankind, with him there crucifi'd,
> Never to hurt them more who rightly trust
> In this his satisfaction; so he dies,
> But soon revives, Death over him no power
> Shall long usurp; ere the third dawning light
> Return, the Stars of Morn shall see him rise
> Out of his grave, fresh as the dawning light,
> Thy ransom paid, which Man from death redeems,
> His death for Man, as many as offer'd Life

does exist within the frame of reference the evil-doer inhabits, and it would
have been better for him not to have sinned at all, no matter what resolution
God may finally effect. 'Happier, had it suffic'd him to have known / Good
by itself, and Evil not at all.' God is able to bring good out of evil, and so
assure a 'happy ending'; but while in the ultimate sense evil cannot 'matter' to
God, it does matter for his creatures whose state of being is defined by their
relationship to it (and thus to God). In the same way, God does not need
man's works, but man needs them so that he can have a sphere of action within
which to prove himself.

> Neglect not, and the benefit embrace
> By Faith not void of works: this God-like act
> Annuls thy doom, the death thou shouldst have di'd,
> In sin for ever lost from life; this act
> Shall bruise the head of *Satan*, crush his strength
> Defeating Sin and Death, his two main arms,
> And fix far deeper in his head thir stings
> Than temporal death shall bruise the Victor's heel,
> Or theirs whom he redeems, a death like sleep
> A gentle wafting to immortal Life.
>
> (411–35)

Each of the participles — 'hated', 'blasphem'd', 'seiz'd',
'judg'd', 'condemn'd', and the climactic 'nail'd' — strikes,
like so many hammer blows, at the body, which is even now
being nailed to the cross. The contemporaneity of the event,
its continuing occurrence, is emphasized too by the pro-
longing of the long 'a' sound in 'shameful', 'nail'd', 'Nation',
'slain', 'nails', and by the shift from future perfect to present
tense. But the most significant, because most un-Miltonic,
detail, is the reversibility of 'nails' and 'slain', an almost
occult bit of word-play heralding the transition in the
passage from referential language to something approxima-
ting ritual incantation. Dies, revives, Death, light, rise,
grace, light, death, redeems, death, man, life, Faith, God-
like, doom, death, died, sin, life; the words push up against
each other, closely packed theological counters, all receiving
heavy stresses, making it difficult for the conscious mind to
get in between them. The submergence of the syntactical
structure is another manifestation of the imposition of an
eternal present on the linear form, and the effect is exactly
that ascribed by Broadbent to God's schematic formulations
of dogma in Book III:

> Milton has got the better of language ... he leads us into a
> corridor of verbal mirrors in which unbodied concepts are

defined by their antitheses so all we can do is mark time with our lips.[1]

There is also some affinity to the repetitive technique Cope associates with Quaker style and Martz with Augustinian meditation, 'sound waves of . . . exhortation', on which one can be 'drawn . . . into the vortex of . . . divine mystery, until through the word itself', there is discerned 'the light at its centre'. Through the 'hypnotic utterance of the divine names', the audience is able to participate in a 'time conquering *stasis* of Christian perfection'.[2] The key phrase is 'So God with man unites', but the meaning, for man, of that union lies in a realm beyond discursive thought. The reader is not responding to the single idea conveyed by death, or life, or sin, or redeems, but to the literally inconceivable idea ('That God, this Lord, the Lord of life, could die, is a strange contemplation')[3] which is suggested by the conglomeration of these conceptual antitheses as they circle around the figure on the cross. The surrender of the reflective intellect, the opening of the mind to a flood of undifferentiated associations, is the opposite of what has been asked of the reader previously ; yet the painful working-out of precise and logical distinctions — between true and false beauty, true and false heroism, true and false freedom, true and false love — has been a preparation for this moment of realized (felt) fusion, which succeeds only if the components of a total (supra-intellectual) response lie ready in the mind. Milton's poetry, said Macaulay, works 'not so much by what it expresses, as by what it suggests ; not so much by the ideas which it directly conveys, as by other

[1] *Some Graver Subject. An Essay on Paradise Lost*, p. 147.

[2] *The Paradise Within*, pp. 43–54; *The Metaphoric Structure of Paradise Lost*, pp. 40–41.

[3] John Donne, 'Death's Duel', in *Devotions Upon Emergent Occasions Together With Death's Duel* (Ann Arbor, 1959), p. 182.

ideas which are connected with them. He electrifies the mind through conductors.'¹ Here the generator is the image of Christ, but the circuit will be complete only if the connecting links, fashioned through the efforts of the reader, are there to be energized. The reader labours consciously to recover a lost unity of vision, which, when found, absorbs and nullifies the consciousness. The effect Milton hopes to achieve corresponds to the height he thinks poetry capable of :

> For surely divine poetry has the heaven-given power to lift the soul with its crust of earthly filth aloft and enshrine it in the skies, to breathe the perfume of nectar upon it, to bathe it with ambrosia, to fill it with heavenly bliss and whisper to it of immortal joy.

(Prolusion III)

If he has done his part, the reader is raised to an imaginative, almost mystical apprehension of what the poem has continually asserted from a thousand varying perspectives — salvation is through Christ — and he is left in the position Donne commends to his auditors :

> There we leave you in that blessed dependency, to hang upon him that hangs upon the cross, there bathe in his tears, there suck at his wounds, and lie down in peace in his grave, till he vouchsafe you a resurrection, and an ascension into that kingdom which He hath prepared for you with the inestimable price of his incorruptible blood.²

The emotional release provided by the appearance of Christ is a reflection, in the reader's response, of his unifying function in the poem and in the structure of reality. Christ is the word by which all things were made ; he is the embodiment of all values ; he is involved in all actions and is the

---

¹ Quoted by Helen Gardner, *A Reading of Paradise Lost* (Oxford, 1965), p. 46.
² 'Death's Duel', p. 189.

model for all actions ; everything points to him and all things and times meet in him. This is a theory of history and being which is not only expounded to the reader but experienced by him when each of the strands he has been following in Books xi and xii and indeed in the entire poem returns to its source and end in the figure on the cross. Adam's education, tied to his discovery of what is comprehended in the prophecy of the seed, and tracing out the pattern of history, ends here. The nobler sights promised by Michael, the line of single men asserting their faith in the midst of corruption, end here in the noblest sight of all. And the cycles of history to which men are bound by their sinfulness are broken here by the victory over sin and death. Here too the definition of heroism, which begins when the heroism of Satan is challenged in Book i, and continues into the war of Book vi, is complete. Here language whose intransigence the poet has attempted to master is replaced by the true eloquence of perfect submission. Here finally is the reader's reward for having submitted to the arduous task of negotiating the poem. Here is the reality to whose memory he has had to be faithful in so many interpretative crises. Here are beauty, love and virtue in their ideal shapes. Here is the world redeemed.

Christ's godlike act not only dispels the jarring chimes of disproportioned sin in the universe ('At a Solemn Music'), it also dispels the jarring disproportions that have been occasions of strain in the reading experience. Throughout the poem meaning is conveyed to the reader when his responses to a situation or a speech or an action have been contrasted (sometimes unfavourably) to the responses of one or more of the characters or to the assertions of the epic voice ; thus the 'harassed reader'. Here in Book xii, the various perspectives whose juxtaposition has so often been the source of discomfort (and instruction) merge into a single perspective, that of fallen humanity. Where the reader might have resisted the preaching of the pure word in Book III, and felt some difficulty in sharing the joy of the angelic choir, here resistance disappears along with self-consciousness, and joy (of an impersonal kind) is induced by the verbal techniques I have been describing. The aloofness of the epic voice has long since given way to something more recognizable; like us he 'is human, corrupted and disinherited because he is fallen'.[1] Satan, to whose glozing lies the reader too often listened has been hissed off the stage (for a season) and does not influence our response to the incarnation and crucifixion. The innocence of Adam and Eve, in relation to which the reader has been made to feel guilt and shame, is no more; they, like the epic voice, have joined us. And God, too, has stepped down from his prospect high to unite with man, to share his pain, his trials, and his temptations.

At this point, when Adam cries 'O goodness infinite, goodness immense', Milton (some readers note wistfully) might have ended the poem, or proceeded directly to the 'inimitable close', and spared us Michael's anticlimactic 'so shall the World go on, / To good malignant, to bad ... benign'. But the anticlimax is necessary and right, simply because the world does go on. And as Adam must descend from the mount of speculation to take up his new life on the subjected plain, so must we descend from this imaginative height, from this total and self-annihilating union with the Divine, to re-enter the race of time where 'wolves, grievous wolves' flourish and to knowledge deeds must be added answerable. The shattered visage of truth has been put back together in the experience of the poem, indeed *by* the experience of the poem, which, with our co-operation, has slowly (and sometimes deviously) purged our intellectual ray

[1] Anne Ferry, *Milton's Epic Voice*, p. 24.

so that it is once more proportionable to truth the object of it. But the moment of direct apprehension cannot be prolonged, nor should it be, since meditation is only a preparation for action, and everlasting bliss can only be ours in God's good time (as God would have it). The memory of this moment, however, and of the experience of the entire poem, will be a source of energy to which the spirit can repair for sustenance as it labours in the world. Meanwhile, like the sojourners of Goshen who 'advance', not into the land of milk and honey (another expectation disappointed) but into the 'wild Desert', we are left to live on and for the promise.

Appendix 1: Notes on the Moral Unity of *Paradise Lost*

(i)

When Christ is commanded to end the chaos of the heavenly battle, he wonders aloud at the revolt against God 'Whom to obey is happiness entire.' This is only one in a series of equivalences asserted in the poem, all with obedience as the second term. Happiness is obedience. Virtue is obedience, as Satan acknowledges when he sees virtue visible in Zephon's loyalty ('Virtue in her shape how lovely, saw, and pin'd / His loss'). Heroism is obedience: an entire book is devoted to that equation. If innocence is not obedience it is a state whose duration is co-extensive with obedience. Raphael answers Adam's astronomical questions by not answering them, advising instead 'Solicit not thy thoughts with matters hid, / Leave them to God above, him serve and fear.' Knowledge is obedience. When Adam declares 'Henceforth I learn, that to obey is best', Michael applauds his resolution: 'This having learnt, thou hast attain'd the sum / Of wisdom.' Wisdom is obedience. Paradoxically, freedom (liberty) is obedience because true freedom is the freedom to follow the best, while freedom from God is servitude. Abdiel both illustrates and expatiates on this distinction:

> Unjustly thou deprav'st it with the name
> Of *Servitude* to serve whom God ordains,
> Or Nature; God and Nature bid the same,
> When he who rules is worthiest, and excels
> Them whom he governs. This is servitude,
> To serve th' unwise, or him who hath rebell'd
> Against his worthier, as thine now serve thee,
> Thyself not free, but to thyself enthrall'd.

(VI.174–81)

These equivalences follow logically in a universe where 'all things are of God' (*de deo*) : since value is always defined in terms of the highest good, at some level of generality all values are one, and in any situation the 'value decision' or 'value action' is at base a decision to remain allied with the source of all values, that is with God. 'All values' is a misleading phrase. There is only one value — maintaining alliance, not 'breaking union' — and the distinctions we customarily make represent different (linguistic) perspectives on the same thing. Virtue is being allied to the source of goodness ; happiness is the psychological peace of being allied to the source of goodness (this will serve for innocence also) ; heroism is choosing to remain allied to the source of goodness ; knowledge and wisdom are the recognition of the source of goodness. And we can move backwards : the identification (knowledge) of the highest good necessarily involves choosing it and choosing it is being allied to it since alliance is a state of mind. Socrates' pursuit of the *summum bonum* in the dialogues proceeds exactly in this manner, from one temporarily isolated value to another until all are united in the apprehension of their oneness.

(ii)

If all values are one, the clash of any two is impossible (or the creation of a distorting vision) and the basis of Waldock's reading of Adam's Fall is removed :

> The matter then may be summed up quite bluntly by saying that Adam falls through love ... through love as human beings know it at its best, through true love, through the kind of love that Raphael has told Adam 'is the scale / By which to heav'nly Love thou maist ascend' ...

It is by no means enough to set over against this powerful human value the mere doctrine that God must be obeyed.

(*Paradise Lost and its Critics*, 51–52, 55)

This is, of course, another equivalence and the most important — love and obedience. It is explained by Raphael in Book v :

> freely we serve
> Because we freely love, as in our will
> To love or not; in this we stand or fall.
>
> (538-40)

And again in Book viii :

> Be strong, live happy, and love, but first of all
> Him whom to love is to obey, and keep
> His great command.
>
> (633-5)

For a being whose faculties are unclouded love is a function of reason : 'Love refines / The thoughts, and heart enlarges, hath his seat / In Reason, and is judicious, is the scale / By which to heav'nly Love thou may'st ascend' (viii. 589-92). The scale is the scale Diotima describes in the *Symposium* : the lover begins by loving a single form and 'soon he will of himself perceive that the beauty of one form is akin to the beauty of another'. This perception initiates a search which ends finally in the discernment of the essence of beauty and a recognition of that essence as the highest object of love :

And when he perceives this he will abate his violent love of the one . . . and will become a lover of all beautiful forms; in the next stage he will consider . . . the beauty of the mind . . . until he is compelled to contemplate and see the beauty of institutions and laws . . . and after laws and institutions he will go on to the sciences . . . and at last the vision is revealed to him of a single science.

(210)

And the true order of going, or being led by another, to the
things of love, is to begin from the beauties of earth and mount
upwards for the sake of that other beauty.

(211)

In short what one loves is the godliness inherent in individual
forms, even before Godliness itself is known in its essence,
because whatever is good in a thing proceeds from God.
(For Adam the process is reversed : he knows the reality of
God — he will later lament his alienation 'from the face /
Of God, whom to behold was then my highth / Of happiness'
— and he seeks expressions of that reality in the visible
world ; he operates deductively as opposed to the inductive
method proposed in the dialogue). This is what Paul means
when he says 'unto the pure all things are pure' because the
pure value things as the manifestation of their creator ; and
what Augustine means by his distinction between the use and
the abuse of beauty : the things of this world merit a full
response if the response is a response to the spirit that
informs them : such a response is indeed praiseworthy, since
it indicates a motion toward that spirit : 'And the Artificer,
so to speak, gestures to the spectator of His work concerning
the beauty of that work, not that he should cling to it completely, but so that his eyes should scan the corporal beauty
of things that are made in such a way that the affection
returns to Him who made them.'[1]

Love, then, is a desire to possess or be united to the highest
good and the desire extends to the multiple forms in which
the highest good resides. For the agent who loves, love is the
affective complement of what the intellect discerns. Once
this concept of love is firmly grasped, Waldock's opposition
of a 'powerful human value' and 'the . . . doctrine that God
must be obeyed' is untenable. If love for an object signifies
a recognition of its share in godliness, love cannot possibly

[1] Quoted in Robertson, *A Preface to Chaucer*, p. 66.

involve a falling away from obedience, since obedience is a recognition of godliness itself. To disobey God 'for the sake of' someone or something is to do a disservice to that someone or something by making it an idol and separating it from God ; the object becomes an extension of the idolator's ego and it is absorbed or destroyed by a love that is self-love. By dislodging an object from its position in God's order, the lover robs it of value, and indicates his inability to regard the object for what it is, and thus his inability to love it. When Eve cries 'O glorious trial of exceeding Love', she is unconsciously ironic and the joke is on her. She is the victim of Adam's passion, for by choosing her he chooses against her. The selflessness some see in Adam's choice would be there if his action was determined by a consideration of what was best for Eve. That is true love. What is best for Eve is the preservation of her relationship to God and if Adam would prove his love for her ('O glorious trial') he should attempt to maintain her in that relationship or if the worst happens intercede for its restoration.

(iii)

In the context of the theocentric universe *Paradise Lost* presupposes, another of Waldock's contentions, that Satan is 'degraded', is less damaging than he thinks :

> A character in a piece of imaginative literature degenerates when we are in a position to check his progress by what we know of him: when we are made to feel that this or that change, once we are shown it, does follow ... The changes [in Satan] do not generate themselves from within: they are imposed from without. Satan, in short, does not degenerate: *he is degraded*.
>
> (*Paradise Lost and its Critics*, p. 83)

Satan's changes *do* generate themselves from within because change is his essence. Since all agents maintain their positions and their identities by virtue of their relation to God, selfhood, too, is preserved through obedience. When an agent 'breaks union' (v. 612) he voluntarily cuts himself off from a fixed point of reference and moves from a dependence that preserves his dignity to an independence that destroys it. The responsibility of keeping union belongs to the agent and continuity of character is merely persevering in this holding action. Apart from God there can be no stability and no true, that is internally consistent, self. 'Men are free when they belong to a living, organic, believing community, active in fulfilling some unfulfilled, perhaps unrealized, purpose.... Men are not free when they are doing just what they like. The moment you can do just what you like, there is nothing you care about doing. Men are only free when they are doing what the deepest self likes' (D. H. Lawrence). Satan's independence is an illusion because he is in bondage to the freedom to do as he likes and he becomes the captive of momentary purposes and the plaything of master strategists (God, Milton) who make of him what they will ; *his* will does not exist (he has no 'deepest self'), except in a Satanic never-never-Land where evil could be someone's good. This reversal is impossible in a universe where God is God and when Satan admits 'myself am Hell' he, in effect, says 'myself am not', since hell is the state of disunion from God's sustaining power and hence a state of nonbeing : 'Having abandoned his true being, he becomes the continuous *poseur*, forever striking attitudes and pretentious postures.'[1] Even Satan's poses are not struck on his own initiative, but as involuntary responses to external

---

[1] R. M. Frye, *God, Man, and Satan* (Princeton, 1960), p. 36. See also the recent rejoinder to Waldock in Thomas Kranidas's *The Fierce Equation* (The Hague, 1965), pp. 119–29.

stimuli (one sees this most clearly in Book x when he takes the form of a 'monstrous Serpent', reluctantly); he does not adapt himself (the pronoun is meaningless) to situations; situations appropriate him, or, to be more accurate, create the 'him' of the moment. Perhaps the most ironic of his boasts is this one: 'What matter where, if I be still the same' (1. 256). The sameness of evil is the sameness of chaos, a stability of instability where the identity and form of any atom or cluster of atoms is a matter of chance unless an ordering power is imposed; Satan is condemned to restless wandering until God or some deputy of God finds a use for him and endows him with motives and opinions and powers to fit the role 'imposed from without'. He is a convenience, available for any and all duties, and to treat him as such does not violate his character, since, as we usually understand the word, he has none. It suits Milton's purpose to grant him a temporary consistency in Books 1 and 11; if the reader is to locate himself in the poem by analysing and coming to terms with his vulnerability to the Satanic appeal, that appeal must appear to have at least the illusion of integrity or wholeness; but the illusion is dispelled as early as the comic opera vaunting scene at 11. 681 ff. Satan as ruined archangel has performed the function Milton set for him, and since his continued presence in a single role might make him seem more important than he really is (even as a temptation he is less dangerous than other temptations), he is replaced by another Satan, or by a variety of Satans, who cannot command even a disinterested and detached admiration.

Satan's status (or non-status) as an entity is illustrated at iv. 819, when, at the touch of Ithuriel's spear, he starts up 'in his own shape', but finds that the angels do not know him:

> Know ye not then said *Satan*, fill'd with scorn
> Know ye not mee?   (827–8)

By delaying the pronoun 'mee', Milton emphasizes the 'selfness' of Satan's concern. It is for this that he has rebelled and in the context of his egocentric vision 'non-recognition' is more than a social slight. Zephon answers:

> Think not, revolted Spirit, thy shape the same . . .
> . . . thou resembl'st now
> Thy sin and place of doom.
>
> (835, 839–40)

Satan's 'shape' like his mind, is now an extension of his place, which usurps the selfhood in whose name he had declared himself injured. The final proof of this of course is his involuntary metamorphosis (at x. 511) into a shape that is not his own, or more properly into the shape that has overtaken and become him.

Appendix 2: Discovery as Form in *Paradise Lost*

(i)

Recently I have argued that the true center of *Paradise Lost*[1] is the reader's consciousness of the poem's *personal* relevance, and that the arc of the poem describes, in addition to the careers of the characters, the education of its readers.[2] This education proceeds in two stages: in the first, the reader is brought face to face with the corruption within him, as he is made aware of the confusion reigning in his scale of values and of the inadequacy of his perceptions; in the second, he is invited to cooperate with the poem's effort to effect his regeneration, invited, in Milton's words, to purge his intellectual ray' until it is once more 'fit and proportionable to Truth the object, and end of it, as the eye to the thing visible.'[3] These stages correspond to the stages of Plato's dialectic, the inducing in the respondent of a 'healthy perplexity' followed by the refinement of his inner eye to the point where it recognizes and embraces the Supreme Good;[4] and the poem's operation is analogous to that of the Mosaic Law which, we are told in *The Christian Doctrine*, calls forth 'our natural depravity, that by this means it might...bring us to the righteousness of Christ.'[5] In its potential effect, then, *Paradise Lost* may claim the status of what Bunyan

---

[1] A shorter version of this paper was read before the Milton section of the Modern Language Association meeting, 1967. (The paper was later published in *New Essays on Paradise Lost*, ed. Thomas Kranidas (Berkeley, 1969).

[2] *Surprised by Sin: The Reader in Paradise Lost.*

[3] Milton, *Complete Prose Works*, Vol. I, ed. D. M. Wolfe (New Haven, 1953), p. 566.

[4] See Robert Cushman, *Therapeia* (Chapel Hill, N.C., 1958), p. 89.

[5] *The Works of John Milton*, ed. F. A. Patterson *et al.* (New York, 1933), XVI, 131.

calls a 'work of grace' in the soul; for it gives the sinner 'conviction of sin, especially of the defilement of his nature, and the sin of unbelief.'[1]

This description of *Paradise Lost*, as a poem concerned with the self-education of its readers, if it is accepted, throws a new light on some old questions. Specifically, it dictates a reorientation of the debate concerning the structure or form of the poem; for if the meaning of the poem is to be located in the reader's experience of it, the form of the poem is the form of that experience; and the outer or physical form, so obtrusive, and, in one sense, so undeniably there, is, in another sense, incidental and even irrelevant. This is a deliberately provocative thesis, the defense of which will be the concern of the following pages; and I would like to begin by explaining more fully what is meant by the phrase 'the form of the reader's experience.'

The stages of this experience mark advances in the reader's understanding, in the refining of his vision rather than in the organization of material. In *Paradise Lost*, *things* are not being clarified or ordered; rather, *eyes* are being made capable of seeing things as they truly are already in the clarity of God's order. The process, and its relationship to a truth that is evident to those who have eyes to see it, is adumbrated in this passage from *Of Reformation*:

> The very essence of Truth is plainnesse, and brightnes; the darknes and crookednesse is our own.... If our *understanding* have a film of *ignorance* over it, or be blear with gazing on other false glisterings, what is that to Truth? If we will but purge with sovrain eyesalve that intellectual ray which *God* hath planted in us, then we would beleeve the Scriptures protesting their own plainnes.[2]

[1] *The Pilgrim's Progress*, ed. J. B. Wharey, rev. R. Sharrock (Oxford, 1960), pp. 82–83.
[2] Milton, *Complete Prose Works*, I, 566.

In Augustine's *On Christian Doctrine* the Scriptures themselves are the instrument by which the understanding can be
made proportional to their plainness; and Augustine's description of what happens to the attentive reader of God's
word is not unlike my description of the reader's experience
in *Paradise Lost*:

> The student first will discover in the Scriptures that he has been
> enmeshed in the love of this world.... Then... that fear which
> arises from the thought of God's judgment... will force him to
> lament his own situation.... And by means of this affection of
> the spirit he will extract himself from all mortal joy in transitory
> things... and turn toward the love of eternal things... he purges
> his mind, which is rising up and protesting in the appetite for
> inferior things, of its contaminations.[1]

Augustine then describes five steps or stages leading to a
sixth where the aspirant 'cleanses that eye through which
God may be seen, in so far as He can be seen by those who
die to the world as much as they are able.' 'From fear to
wisdom,' he concludes, 'the way extends through these
steps.'

To some extent Augustine's 'steps' suggest a regular and
predictable, that is, linear, progression to wisdom; but, of
course, the movement from one step to the next cannot be
predicted or charted since the operative factor is the 'purging of the mind' or 'the cleansing of the eye'; and the extent
to which the mind is distracted by the appeal of transitory
things, and, consequently, the period of time which must
elapse before the eyes are made clear, will vary with the
individual, who dies to the world as much as *he* is able. Nor
will progress be regular (linear) within the discrete stages
enumerated by Augustine. In how many differing contexts

[1] *On Christian Doctrine*, trans. D. W. Robertson (New York, 1958),
pp. 39–40.

must the eye be challenged to distinguish true beauty from the 'false glisterings' of 'fair outsides' before it is able to see what is and is not truly beautiful *immediately*? No one answer will serve for all eyes. In Plato's dialectic, A. E. Taylor explains, the apprehension of Reality 'comes as a sudden "revelation" though it is not to be had without the long preliminary process of travail of thought.'[1] Taylor's point is that the relationship between the 'travail of thought' and the 'revelation' is indeterminate, partly because the thing to be known cannot be known by 'discursive knowledge about it,' and partly because, as Robert Cushman observes, the effort that must be expended 'to disengage the mind from preoccupation with sensibles' will be in proportion to the strength of the 'fetters' binding the individual mind to earthly perception.[2]

Consider the case of Samson, whose experience in Milton's verse drama parallels that of the reader in *Paradise Lost*. When Manoa quarrels with God's dispensing of justice— 'methinks whom God hath chosen once / . . . He should not so o'erwhelm' (ll. 368–370)—Samson answers firmly 'Appoint not heavenly disposition' (l. 373). But within a few lines he too begins to appoint heavenly disposition when he declares himself ineligible for service to God in his present condition—'to what can I be useful?'—for, in effect, he is putting limits on God's ability to use him. No straight line can describe Samson's spiritual journey. At times, as in this instance, he seems to make an advance toward understanding, only in the next minute to embrace in another guise the error he has just rejected. When clarity of vision does come to Samson, we can look back and see a series of starts (gestures) toward it—intimations, partial illuminations—

[1] *Plato: The Man and his Work* (Meridian Books, New York, 1957), p. 231.
[2] Cushman, *op. cit.*, pp. 163, 166.

344 Discovery as Form in Paradise Lost

but no chartable and visible progression. Let me here anticipate a later argument by pointing out that since the concern
of the play is Samson's regeneration, Dalila, Harapha, the
messenger, the Chorus, and Manoa are important, not for
themselves, but for the opportunities they bring to Samson's
laboring mind.

In *Paradise Lost*, the reader is repeatedly forced to acknowledge the unworthiness of values and ideals he had previously
admired, yet, like Samson, he will often fall into the same admiration when the context changes slightly. To take as an
example something I have treated at length elsewhere: in
the early books, Satan's false heroism draws from the reader
a response that is immediately challenged by the epic voice,
who at the same time challenges the concept of heroism in
which the response is rooted. Subsequently, Satan's apparent
heroism is discredited by covert allusions to other heroes in
other epics, by his ignoble accommodation to the 'family'
he meets at the gates of Hell, by his later discoveries squat-
ting at the ear of Eve in the form of a toad, and, most
tellingly, by his own self-revelations in the extended soliloquy that opens Book IV. At *some point* during this sequence
of actions, the reader becomes immune to the Satanic appeal
because he has learned what it is, or to be more precise, what
it is not. 'Some point,' however, will be a different point for
each reader, depending on the extent to which he is committed to the false ideal Satan exemplifies. Nor will the
progress of any reader—of whatever capacity—be regular,
since the learning of an individual lesson is not a guarantee
against falling into a generic error. The reader who in Book I
is led to resist the sophistries of the Satanic line when they
are offered directly, may not recognize them in Book II
when they are put forward in the Grand Council, especially
if he has surrendered too much of his attention to the thrust
and parry of the debate, that is, to the strategy rather than to

the morality of the scene. And this same reader, when he is presented with a true hero in the person of Abdiel, is likely to admire him for the wrong reasons. That is to say, his response to Abdiel's action at the close of Book V will be a response to the melodramatic aspect of the situation—a lone figure rising to assert himself against innumerable foes—and therefore a response not enough differentiated from that originally given to the now discredited Satan. In Book VI, during the War in Heaven, the reader is given the opportunity to distinguish Abdiel's heroism from the *incidental* circumstances of its exercise. So that, at *some point* in the course of his struggles with the interpretative problems raised by the battle, the reader discovers the naked essence of heroism itself. It is important to realize that the poem does not move to this revelation; it has been there from the first, plainly visible to the eye capable of seeing it. It is the reader who moves, or advances, until his cleansed eye can see what has always been there. At least the reader is given the *opportunity* to advance. He may not take it, and so remain a captive of his clouded vision. It follows, then, that between Books I and VI Satan does not change at all. His degradation is a critical myth. The reader's capacity to see him clearly changes, although that change is gradual and fitful, uneven, unchartable, to some extent invisible, not easily separated from parallel changes in the reader's capacity to see other things clearly—virtue, heroism, love, beauty. (I am thinking, for example, of the contrast between the good and bad poetry of Satan's and God's speeches. I leave you to apply the labels.)

If Satan has not moved or altered, the only alteration being the reader's, it follows that the episodes in which Satan appears are not important for any light they throw on *him*, or for the challenges they present to *him*, but for the function they serve as a whetstone to the reader's laboring mind. Moreover the action of the poem is taking place in that mind, not in the narrative, whose world is static. For, strictly speaking, the plot of *Paradise Lost*, in the sense of a linear movement toward a dramatic and moral climax—the Fall—does not exist; simply because the concept of free will, as Milton defines it, precludes the usual process of decision—the interplay between circumstance, motivation, and choice—which in other works fills up a plot. The decision of an absolutely free will cannot be determined by forces outside it, and, in a causal sense, such a decision has no antecedents. I would suggest that the point of the scenes in Paradise from Book IV to Book IX is their irrelevance, as determining factors, to the moment of crisis experienced by the characters; and the action taking place in these scenes is the reader's discovery or comprehension of that irrelevance. In the middle books, and especially at those points where Milton has been accused of 'necessary faking'—the phrase is Tillyard's—the reader is presented with a series of 'interpretative choices.' On the surface, the account of Eve's infatuation with her reflected image, and the fact of her dream, and of Adam's admission to Raphael of his weakness, seem to deny the freedom of the unfallen will by circumscribing our first parents in what Watkins has termed a 'network of circumstance.' Yet in each instance Milton provides evidence that makes it possible for the reader to disengage these incidents from the Fall—I am thinking for example of Adam's statement, 'Evil into the mind of God or Man / May come and go . . . and leave / No spot . . . behind'—and finally to see them as moving away from, rather than toward, that crisis. This is the poet's solution to the problem of building a poem around an event that has no antecedents. He gives us a plot without a middle —Adam and Eve fall spontaneously—but he allows for a *psychological* middle, a middle to the reading experience, by leaving it to us to discover that the narrative middle does not, indeed could not, exist.

(ii)

Now, for the obvious question: if the poem does not move, but the reader moves, if there is no plot except for the plot of the reader's education, and if the true form of the poem is the form of the individual reader's experience rather than the visible form represented by the division into twelve books; if, in sum, the action is interior, taking place inside the reader's mind, what is the function of the exterior form? Why is it there? What do we say, for instance, about the intricate patterning of words and phrases continually being uncovered by modern criticism? There are several answers to this question. The divisions in the narrative, in the physical artifact called *Paradise Lost*, mark out areas within which the process of regeneration can go forward, while the instances of parallelism provide 'stations' at which the progress of the process can be checked. When the reader comes across a word or a phrase that recalls him to an earlier point in the poem, he is not being asked to compare the contents of two scenes now juxtaposed in his mind, but to apply whatever insights he has gained in the *psychological* interim to the single content these two scenes share. That is to say, the meaning of the parallel is determined not by its existence but by the success the reader has had in purging his intellectual ray. Anyone, even a computer, can point out echoes. Only a reader who has learned, only a reader with a cleansed eye, can create their meaning. *He* does it, not the poem. Echoes and cross-references are not saying, 'Look at this.' They are saying, 'Do you know what to make of this *now*?'[1] The important time in the poem is psychological time. In

[1] Again we find an analogue in the dialectic of Plato, where apparent progressions and/or digressions unexpectedly return to the point of origin, and the hapless respondent is asked to reassess his original position in the light of the truth he has ascended to, or, as is the case in most of the dialogues, in the light of the truth Socrates has drawn out of him.

the time consumed while reading, the poem is not developing, the reader is (or he isn't). And any significance one can attach to the sequence of events is to be found not in their relationship to the narrative situation—whose temporal structure, as many have observed, is confused—but to the reader's situation. Milton in effect tells us this when God sends Raphael down to warn Adam in Book V. In this way, the epic voice explains, 'God fulfills all justice.' But God here fulfills more than justice if Adam is meant, because Adam is sufficient to his test without Raphael's warning. Justice is being done to the reader, who is being given the opportunity Adam does not need, although what Adam will do in Book IX created the imperfection that makes it necessary for the reader to *now* have the opportunity. When at the end of Book VI the phrase 'nine days they fell' returns us to the opening lines of Book I, our attention is not being called to what has happened to Satan since he was first expelled (of course nothing has happened to Satan), but to what has happened to ourselves. Satan is in the same place; we, one hopes, are not. Thus, this halfway point in *Paradise Lost* (in its outer form, that is) *is* there for a reason; it does mark the end of something, not, however, of something going on in the world of the characters (in that context we are right back where we started), but of something going on in the world of the reader. This, in fact, is the end of the poet's attempt to refine the reader's sense of what true heroism is. And later in Book IX the superficial nobility of Adam's gesture will pose once again the same question, 'Do you understand now?' And in his response the reader will give his answer.

What I have said here with reference to the single problem of heroism applies to other problems and to other patternings. In Book III, God delivers a speech whose arguments, if they are understood, assure a correct reading of the crucial scene in Book IX. At irregular intervals, phrases from this 'ur speech' are repeated (I am thinking especially of 'sufficient to have stood, though free to fall'), and each repetition asks a silent question, 'Do you understand *now*?' In the intervals between repetitions, the same question is posed indirectly by the events of the narrative. When Eve questions the perfection of her situation ('frail is our happiness if this be so'), she betrays a complete misunderstanding of the concepts God has been at pains to define, and thus her speech becomes a negative test of the reader. That is, the reader's ability to perceive the fallacies· in her argument measures the extent to which he *now* understands God's logic. And once again we return to a point made earlier: since the misconceptions Eve entertains here cannot affect her performance at the moment of temptation ('the seat of temptation is in the will, not in the understanding'), her speech is more important for the reader's state of mind than for her own; in relationship to the Fall, her state of mind does not matter. It is the reader who has the most at stake in the scenes preceding the crisis; and the patterns, the repetitions, the time passing—they are all for him.

In addition to providing the reader with stations at which he may check his progress, and with cases or problems whose consideration is the vehicle of that progress, the poem's Aristotelian superstructure—beginning, middle, end—has a negative value as one form of a way of knowing Milton believes to be inferior or secondary. Plato makes a distinction between knowledge 'by way of division,' that is, knowledge whose end is the clarification of objects in the material world (*dianoia*), and knowledge by illumination, knowledge whose end is the recognition of a suprasensible reality (*episteme*); and this distinction corresponds to that made by Augustine and other theologians between *scientia* and *sapientia*. In one sphere, the mind, with the help of certain aids —deductive logic, enumeration, denotation—performs a refining operation on the data of experience; in the other, the mind itself is led to transcend the flux of experience and to reinterpret it in the light of the reality to which it has ascended. True knowledge, then, is not reached by following a chain of inferences or by accurately labeling *things* (although inference and labeling may have some part in the attainment of it), but is the possession of the mind that has been made congruent with it; true knowledge cannot be brought to the mind (it is not transmissible), the mind must be brought to it; to the point where there is no longer any need for the aid logical inference can offer. One must take care not to extend illegitimately the province of *scientia* and so fail to distinguish between that which can be seen and measured by the physical eye and that which reveals itself only to the inner eye of the aspiring soul. It is this danger to which Milton deliberately exposes his reader when he suggests in the opening lines that the purpose of his poem is to provide a verifiable answer to the question 'What cause?'; in its position, this question holds out a promise that proves in the course of the poem to be false, the promise that if the reader follows Milton's argument, from its beginning to its middle to its end, he will find the answer and along with it a rational justification of God's ways, awaiting him, as it were, at the end of a syllogism. But this is not the case. The promise is given so that its falseness can be more forcefully exposed and so that the reader can learn not to rely on the way of knowing it assumes, but to rely instead on illumination and revelation. Just as the search for cause and for a rational justification is an attempt to confine God within the limits of formal reasoning, and is thus a temptation, so is the temporal-spatial structure of the poem, by means of which that search is supposedly to be conducted, a temptation, since the reader may fall into the error of looking to *it* as a revealer of meaning: that is, to the limited and distorting, though organized, picture of reality it presents, rather than to the inner light developing within him. (The more the inner light develops, of course, the less a temptation the outer formal structure will offer, since the reader's need of it, or of anything else, will progressively lessen.) The reader's situation parallels Adam's and Eve's, who are also tempted to look to the organization of experience, and to the meaning conferred on things by accidents of time and space, for guidance, rather than to revelation. So that, in summary, what we can call the outer form of the poem—twelve books, a regular plot line, the illusion of cause and effect—is (1) unnecessary (finally) to correct perception, and (2) a temptation, since dependence on it is enslavement to it and to the earthly (rational) perspective of which it is one manifestation. In other words, part of the poem's lesson is the superfluousness of the mold of experience—of space and time—to the perception of what is true; and thus the epic's outer form, inasmuch as it is the area within which the inner eye is purified, is the vehicle of its own abandonment. Like the hierarchical structure of the early Church as it is described in *The Reason of Church-government*, the outer form of the poem is a 'scaffolding' which 'so soon as the building is finished' is but a 'troublesome disfigurement' that is to be cast aside.[1] And this casting aside is imitated in the *conceptual* movement of *Paradise Lost* by the rejection of the external trappings of a public heroism in favor of a better heroism whose successes are not visible to the physical eye.

(iii)

And what does the reader who has reached this point discover at the end of his labors? The truth, of course, or

[1] Milton, *Complete Prose Works*, I, 791.

Truth, as it awaits those who have climbed the Platonic ladder: the Supreme Good concerning which nothing can be predicated, since it is the basis of all predication; 'a principle that requires justification and explanation by reference to nothing besides itself,'[1] because it is the basis of justification and that in the light of which all else is to be explained; a good whose value cannot be measured because it is the measure (or norm) of value. In Milton's poem, the position occupied by Plato's Supreme Good is occupied by Christ, whose action in Book XII—taking place not there but everywhere, not at one point in time, but at all points—is the measure of all other actions and the embodiment of everything that is truly valuable.

I began this paper by suggesting that the physical form of *Paradise Lost* has only an oblique relationship to its true form, which I identified with the form of the reader's experience. That experience, however, does not lend itself to the kind of description one usually associates with the word 'formal'; here are no readily discernible beginning, middle, and end, no clearly marked transitions, no moments of crisis at which issues are preeminently resolved; instead, the form, if it can be called that, follows the convolutions of the reader's education, now describing an advance, now a backsliding, at one moment pointing upward, at another, downward, at a third, in both directions at once. Still, there is a pattern into which the experiences of all successful readers fall (although there are as many variations within it as there are readers) and we are now in a position to trace out that pattern:

(1) During the poem, the reader is being forced by the verse to sharpen his moral and spiritual perceptions to the point where they are answerable to those essences of which

---

[1] Cushman, *op. cit.*, p. 177. See *Symposium*, 211*b*.

he has hitherto had only an imperfect and partial knowledge. This refining process is desultory and wandering, concerned randomly with the entire range of moral abstractions.

(2) At regular intervals, the reader is asked to assess his progress, asked if he is able to recognize the true form of one of these abstractions.

(3) There are in the poem two places where the answerability of the reader's vision to the *unity* of the conceptions he has been considering singly is tested: first in Book IX when Adam violates all of the values with whose identification the poem has been concerned—significantly he sins in their name and this 'misnaming' becomes the legacy he leaves his sons—and again in Book XII when Christ restores to these much abused terms their true, that is spiritual, meaning.

The experience of the entire poem, then, moves toward this moment when the arc of the narrative action and the end of the reader's education coincide. (It is no accident that Adam's understanding is made perfect at the point where Christ is brought before his eyes at the end of a process very much like the education of the reader.) Knowledge of Christ is the end of all the smaller investigations and searches that go on in the body of the poem, investigations of the nature of heroism, love, beauty, innocence, happiness. He is the measure of them all and His essence *informs* them all. He gives form to the universe and to everything in it, including the things in this poem, including the poem itself. In an ultimate sense, *He* is the poem's true form,[1] and His

---

[1] William Madsen makes a similar point in a review of Frye's *The Return of Eden*: 'If it is formal symmetry we are looking for in *Paradise Lost*, the nearest approach to it is provided by the image of Christ which radiates from the exact center of the poem' (*Criticism* [Fall, 1966], p. 393). See also C. A. Patrides, *Milton and the Christian Tradition* (Oxford, 1966), p. 260: 'I am persuaded that the God-man in *Paradise Lost*...renders coherence to the entire epic.'

relationship to the temporal-spatial structure of the poem is a reflection of His relationship to the temporal-spatial structure of post-Edenic experience. He enters both structures at once to fulfill them and to supersede them as conveyors of meaning by making good on the promises they could not keep. The promise to justify God's ways to men, for instance, cannot, we discover, be fulfilled within the rational and linear framework of the physical *Paradise Lost*; but it *is* fulfilled when the reader, who has been led to an intuitive understanding of Christ's significance, understands, at that moment, how much the mercy of God exceeds the requirements of reason. (Mercy, the word taking flesh and sacrificing itself, is unreasonable.)

For the reader who has been so led, the poem no longer has any parts; rather, like the universe God sees from his prospect high, it constitutes a unity, infused at every point with a single stable meaning. This meaning is apprehended through what become its parts when one is limited to anything but an all-inclusive glance. As the reader moves (irregularly) toward this illuminative height, the divisions into books and episodes, and all other markers indicating subordination and emphasis, recede into the background and reveal themselves finally as artificial heighteners of what is self-evident to the purged eye.[1] The units of the poem are

---

[1] In this overview the argument concerning the poem's crisis is resolved, or, to be more precise, dismissed. Since every moment at which there is the possibility of seeing or not seeing truly (that is, every moment) is a crisis—this statement applies also to Adam and Eve—the concept becomes meaningless. Some 'crises' are merely (and accidentally) made spectacular. See Jackson Cope's description of the poem as having no 'center from which one might measure the distances relating beginning, middle, end, or "crisis"' (*The Metaphoric Structure of Paradise Lost* [Baltimore, 1962], p. 77). See also G. A. Wilkes, *The Thesis of Paradise Lost* (Melbourne, 1961), p. 42: 'The weight of Milton's conception is not poised on one episode...its weight is distributed through the whole structure.'

now interchangeable, one with another, receptacles all of the good and merciful news Christ proclaims in Book XII. The illusion of a multiplicity of parts, or even of a clash of values (i.e., love vs. obedience), is now seen to have been the creation of the distorting perspective of local contexts, a perspective that no longer delimits the horizons of the reader's vision. In short, the reader who finally knows Christ will experience none of the difficulties associated with Milton's poem; although, paradoxically, it is these difficulties (tests, trials, temptations) as they have been encountered in those (illusory) parts which have led him to that knowledge.[1]

This leads me naturally to the question some of my readers will have been asking. If knowledge of Christ is sufficient to all our needs, including the needs *Paradise Lost* speaks to, what claim does the poem have on us beyond a successful first reading? The answer is bound up in the inability of the fallen mind to prolong the moment of vision to which dialectical self-examination can occasionally bring it. Augustine's spiritual history is a case in point:

> And now came I to have a sight of those invisible things of thee, which are understood by those things which are made. But I was not able to fix mine eye long upon them: but my infirmity being beaten back again, I was turned to my wonted fancies; carrying along with me no more but a liking of those new thoughts in my memory, and an appetite, as it were, to the meat I had smelt.[2]

The perishability of the insight that awaits us at the end of *Paradise Lost* assures the poem's continuing relevance. We

---

[1] Wilkes argues that these local difficulties are finally 'submerged' in the wholeness of the 'great argument.' What he does not see is that they do exist for the reader while he is *inside* the poem, and that they *lead* him to comprehend the 'great argument.'

[2] Quoted by Louis Martz, *The Paradise Within* (New Haven, 1964), p. 50.

may have succeeded to some degree in purging our intellectual ray, but the 'film of ignorance' is not so easily removed, and a 'sovrain eye-salve' may be needed again. And in that (certain) event, the first reading holds out the promise of another success. In the meantime, the abandoned outer form —which has been the vehicle for the apprehension of meaning, although meaning is not imbedded *in* it—remains as an area within which the interior journey can be renegotiated. With Adam, we exit from the poem into experience; but we can return to it, as he returns to the memory of Paradise, for strength and sustenance.

Index of Authors and Titles

Index of Subjects

(References are to chapters and chapter sections)